ART IN EARLY MODERN LAW

sidestonepress

ART IN EARLY MODERN LAW

EVOLVING PROCEDURES FOR HERITAGE PROTECTION IN 15TH- TO 18TH-CENTURY EUROPE

CHIARA MANNONI

TEXTS TRANSLATED BY AMEDEO CERESA GENET AND CHIARA MANNONI

Published by Sidestone Press, Leiden
www.sidestone.com

Lay-out & cover design: Sidestone Press
Photograph cover: Foreground: Heinrich Bünting, *Europa Prima Pars Terrae in Forma Virginis*, print, 1582. Background: Carel Allard, *Chart of Europe*, copperplate print, late 1600.

ISBN 978-94-6426-131-8 (softcover)
ISBN 978-94-6426-132-5 (hardcover)
ISBN 978-94-6426-133-2 (PDF e-book)

This project has received funding from the European Union's Horizon 2020 research and innovation programme under the Marie Skłodowska-Curie grant agreement No. 837857 – "LawLove. The origins of the legal protection of heritage. Legislation on the safeguard of monuments and artworks issued in 15th- to 18th-century Europe".

European Commission

Contents

1

Introduction

In 2018, when I submitted my proposal "LawLove" to the annual Marie Skłodowska-Curie – Horizon 2020 call, the research questions and the subjects I planned to delve into were broad and, to some extent, audacious.[1] The outcomes which I proposed for the project included uncovering whether there had been long-standing "proto-European" principles and attitudes on heritage protection in early modern Europe: and, if that was the case, what authority and models could these offer to current European society, culture, and policymaking?

In the present day, the strategies to preserve and supervise historical, archaeological, and artistic heritage in Europe are essentially delegated to the member states in which the artefacts are located.[2] The solutions available at an international level to protect tangible heritage in times of peace arise basically from the broader Unesco *Convention concerning the Protection of the World Cultural and Natural Heritage* of 1972;[3] the return of stolen and illicitly exported artefacts, on the other hand, is governed by the Unesco *Convention on the Means of Prohibiting and Preventing the Illicit Import, Export, and Transfer of Ownership of Cultural Property* of 1970,[4] together with the – much-contested and generally unaccepted – principles defined by the Unidroit *Convention on Stolen or Illegally Exported Cultural Objects* in 1995.[5] At a specific European level, instructions for the safeguarding of archaeological heritage are offered within the so-called *Valletta Treaty*, drafted in 1969, and updated in 1992.[6] To these few instruments, informal charters can be added – such as the *European Charter of Architectural Heritage*,[7] and the charters for the restoration of historic monuments of Athens and Venice – which, for their part, offer simple non-

1 The project full title is: "LawLove. The origins of the legal protection of heritage. Legislation on the safeguard of monuments and artworks issued in 15th- to 18th-century Europe" (grant agreement no. 837857). It has been hosted and administered by the University Ca' Foscari Venice, Department of Philosophy and Cultural Heritage. Project website: https://pric.unive.it/projects/law-love/home.

2 The specific concepts of heritage with which this project deals are outlined in Part One.

3 For the text of the 1972 convention, see the Unesco webpage: https://whc.unesco.org/en/conventiontext/.

4 For the text of the 1970 convention, see the Unesco webpage: https://en.unesco.org/fighttrafficking/1970.

5 For the text of the 1995 convention, see the Unidroit webpage: https://www.unidroit.org/instruments/cultural-property/1995-convention/.

6 For the text of the 1992 *Convention for the Protection of the Archaeological Heritage of Europe*, see the European Council webpage: https://www.coe.int/en/web/culture-and-heritage/valletta-convention.

7 For the text of the 1995 charter, see the Icomos webpage: https://www.icomos.org/en/resources/charters-and-texts/179-articles-en-francais/ressources/charters-and-standards/170-european-charter-of-the-architectural-heritage.

mandatory guidelines.[8] It is clear that common policies to catalogue, administer, and defend heritage in Europe are altogether scarce and inadequate.

I founded my project proposal on the assumption that a cohesive European Union should recognise the functions and peculiarities of each member state before fostering common history and culture; but I thought this would be possible by encouraging a shared system to protect, or at least control, the different local heritages within the broader European heritage. To me, the fact that the supervision of the local artefacts was still subjected to the different visions, interests, and policies of the acquiring countries against the supplier countries seemed rather controversial and divisive. In addition, I perceived that there were several drawbacks in procedures for ratifying transnational conventions within each national system which would have to be resolved, or at least minimised, before these could have effects on the global safeguarding of heritage. These issues, I asserted, would have negative effects not only on heritage protection, but also on the construction of a solid European awareness.[9] Based on these assumptions – and acknowledging that the establishment of a protocol to oversee heritage across the Union was long-overdue – I proposed to analyse the laws issued to protect "precious artefacts" in European countries between the early 1400s and the end of the 1700s, to discover aspects and models that could be useful to construct new common policies in this field in the present day.

After three years of research, and approaching the end of the project, I would no longer support the idea of introducing shared regulations to protect heritage in Europe with the same enthusiasm I had at the beginning. Indeed, the two-year-long pandemic reinforced the inclination of each country to undertake actions and decisions independently, shaping also new political scenarios. Furthermore, the diverse responses of the various governments to the emergency reflected differences of comprehension and assessment, which should be acknowledged when protecting artefacts, as well as people. I believe that we will need more time and critical detachment to reconnect to major collective perspectives beyond specific interests after this phase: the new tendencies that have arisen go past the assumptions and directions originally proposed for this project. Nevertheless, even within this framework, my intention to examine the laws that were launched to protect what was perceived as "heritage" in the early modern European countries is still compelling and, all the more so, since such a study could envision new courses and forms of collaboration within the Union and among its member states. The questions that drove my thoughts at the outset, however, needed to be put into a revised perspective for the purposes of this book, and reshaped to follow a simple, straightforward historical angle. Were there frequent concepts and instruments to protect "heritage" in European countries between the 1400s and the 1700s? If so, how were these related one to another in a broader, collective perspective?

In Part One of this volume, legislation will be explored from a legal and art-historical perspective in order to understand how cultural, political, and social factors influenced

8 For the text of the 1931 Athens charter of restoration, see the Icomos webpage: https://www.icomos.org/en/167-the-athens-charter-for-the-restoration-of-historic-monuments. For the text of the 1964 Venice charter of restoration, see the related project webpage: https://www.charta-von-venedig.de/790.html.

9 The project incipit was quite assertive in this regard: "The process of construction of a strong European identity should include shared practices to protect the historical, archaeological, and artistic heritage which is spread throughout the European countries".

the introduction of the first systems for safeguarding heritage in early modern Europe. The origins of the idea of protecting specific categories of artefacts by law will be examined, comparing both concepts and practices developed in different states; attention will be essentially on the development of new definitions of "antiquity", "artwork", and "monument" in the edicts issued in these areas. A number of legal instruments will be considered from a cultural perspective as well: both systems of punishment and supervision procedures – such as the first inventories and catalogues – will be compared to one another, and explained within their relevant backgrounds. It should be emphasised that not every kingdom or county in Europe issued regulations to protect heritage at this early stage. According to data currently available, such sets of rules were introduced in only the Papal States, the Grand Duchy of Tuscany, the Kingdom of Denmark, the Kingdom of Sweden, the Kingdom of Naples, the Republic of Venice, the Duchy of Milan, the Kingdom of Portugal, the Prussian States, the Margraviate of Ansbach-Bayreuth and the Landgraviate of Hesse-Kassel in the German-speaking area, the Kingdom of Spain, and the Province of Drenthe in the Dutch Republic. The objective of this section is to offer a broad account of how these regions conceived and implemented pioneering systems to care for their important artefacts between the 1400s and the 1700s, pursuing a comparative analysis of the most valuable instruments and concepts they established.

In Part Two, the transcriptions of the laws discussed in the first section are presented together with their English translations: the original texts of these regulations were in early modern Italian, Spanish, Swedish, Portuguese, Danish, Dutch, German, and even Latin. A few of them were reissued after some time in the relevant state without major variations: for this reason, both documents and records have been rigorously selected in order to avoid repetition. The sequence of regulations is arranged according to the criteria of geography and issuing date. Such a collection should be understood as a research instrument, or an apparatus, that can be expanded with new texts and sources whenever new archival records are discovered in Europe.

The progression of this research, as well as the publication of this volume, has been achieved thanks to the support of several academics, friends, and institutes in Europe. I am grateful to Chiara Piva, Giovanni Maria Fara, Elizabeth Rankin, the librarians of the University of Erlangen, Wijnand van der Sanden, Jan Albert Bakker, Madalena Costa Lima, Sebastian Keimel, and of course my colleague Amedeo Ceresa Genet, who has carried out the largest part of the extremely challenging work of translating the old documents and regulations.

2

Translators' Notes

Amedeo Ceresa Genet and Chiara Mannoni

Based on the quantity of the sources available, as well as their linguistic features and varieties, we divided the work of translation into two main portions. The first one included the Old Italian States – that is the Papal States, the Grand Duchy of Tuscany, the Kingdom of Naples, the Republic of Venice, and the Duchy of Milan – where legislation was generally issued in early modern Italian. Mostly following the legal traditions derived from both Roman law and Canon law, these countries published extensive numbers of edicts, regulations, and sanctions throughout the early modern centuries.[10] These documents have been translated together, since they present the same linguistic, lexical, and morphological issues, as well as similar legal and conceptual characteristics.

The second group of translations embraced the other countries in Europe – that is the Kingdom of Portugal, the Kingdom of Spain, the Prussian States, the Margraviate of Ansbach-Bayreuth and the Landgraviate of Hesse-Kassel in the German-speaking area, the Province of Drenthe in the Netherlands, the Kingdom of Denmark, and the Kingdom of Sweden. The protocols and guidelines issued in these places were significantly fewer than the Old Italian States, but their importance and meaning were no less substantial. Even though these documents have been translated together for practical reasons, their linguistic, syntactical, and conceptual attributes are extremely diverse, and vary according to the epoch and place they were issued.

While these linguistic and morphological aspects shaped the work of translation, in Part Two the sequence of laws, regulations, and edicts is arranged according to the criteria of geography and issuing date, grouping together the documents published in each region from the oldest to the most recent one. The succession of states and counties is organised as follows:

- The Papal States
- The Grand Duchy of Tuscany

10 As will be explained in Part One, the Republic of Venice was the only exception, as it followed a system of common law. The Papal States, on the other hand, were the most devoted to the models of Roman law and Canon law.

- The Kingdom of Denmark
- The Kingdom of Sweden
- The Kingdom of Portugal
- The Province of Drenthe
- The Duchy of Milan
- The Kingdom of Spain
- The Kingdom of Naples
- The Republic of Venice
- The Margraviate of Ansbach-Bayreuth
- The Landgraviate of Hesse-Kassel
- The Prussian States

The Old Italian States

Translations and revision: Amedeo Ceresa Genet

One thing I would not have expected before translating this corpus of laws is how straightforward it would be to comprehend the language and vocabulary of my country's ancestors. Or, to be more accurate, to understand the ruling classes that ran the states in which the country was divided in the early modern period. In retrospect, it is prevalent for the average Italian to regard their peninsula as a land that was not linguistically unified until the mid-1900s. Moreover, some even doubt that cultural coherence has ever been achieved at all.

Second only to China in its ratio of idioms to speakers, contemporary Italy now stands out in the world for the numerous dialects spoken from North to South. In many regions, it is still common to encounter people who prefer expressing themselves in their vernacular rather than in the common language crafted by Dante in the early 1300s, and perfected by Manzoni in the 1800s.[11] Also, for the unsuspecting visitor, it might be surprising to find just how skilled the country's natives are at tracking a speaker's provenance down to within tens of kilometres of their precise town or village of origin.

On the contrary, the lexicon found in the corpora of laws issued by the Old Italian States presents itself as surprisingly homogeneous and similar to contemporary Italian. Therefore, from a practical point of view, the difficulties of this translation did not regard the text's vocabulary as much as the layout, sentencing, and logical sequencing of the concepts expressed.

The Papal States' earliest attempts at legislative intervention date back to the first half of the 1400s.[12] In this period, the lexical and syntactical constructions and the use of Latin reflected the legislator's will to provide broad and generic declarations of intent. Subsequently, the 1600s witnessed the beginning of a gradual yet steady shift towards a more standardised and accurate terminology together with the use of early modern Italian.[13] Accordingly, my reproduction of the jargon employed by modern-day Anglo-

---

11 For a history of Italian language, see Maiden 1995.

12 The original texts of the edicts issued in the Papal States in the 1400s and 1500s are in Tomassetti 1857-1872, vol. 4, 716-718; Fea 1802, 82-103. The translations of the edicts issued in 1556 and 1562 could not be achieved for the purposes of this volume, as their use of early modern Latin is extremely convoluted and misleading, while sentence construction appears too long and complex to be translated, even for linguists.

13 The original texts of the edicts issued in the Papal States in the 1600s and 1700s (until 1803) are collected in Emiliani 1978, 67-126.

Saxon legislative bodies is intended to convey the gradual push towards an established, unified codification. As in most sections of these translations, the content has been digested into shorter paragraphs.

In keeping with the developing papal legislative experience, the articulation of the edicts issued by the Grand Duchy of Tuscany includes highly detailed lists of items, situations, and painters.[14] In this instance, the original layout has been maintained to render the fastidiousness with which the spirit of these laws is pervaded.

Interestingly, the laws and forms published in the Duchy of Milan and the Republic of Venice appear to be closer to the contemporary reader's mentality in that they effectively combine lexical conciseness and syntactic formality.[15]

One final aspect to consider is that the Old Italian States were not always governed by officials educated to write the language spoken by their subjects, as is apparent in the phrasing utilised in the Kingdom of Naples, which was ruled by the Spanish Bourbons from the 1730s onwards.[16] Not until the reader reaches the Neapolitan sanctions written in both Italian and Spanish is it realised how some of the decrees were conceived and formulated by civil servants who were not necessarily educated in law, and mixed these two languages to be understood by their king. Finally, the formal features of what can be defined as "legislative extravagance" contribute to the text's asperity in that the paragraphing, punctuation, and number of subordinate clauses make the content somewhat hard to follow for the eye of the untrained. Herein lies the main difficulty in translating edicts that consist of twenty-line-long paragraphs into English, a *lingua franca* famous for being the "language of brevity".

The Other States and Counties in Europe

Translations: Chiara Mannoni. Revision: Amedeo Ceresa Genet

Compared to the laws produced in the Old Italian States, the regulations and protocols published in the other early modern European regions appear rather limited in their quantity and length, even though they present substantial issues related to the variety of their linguistic, morphological, and conceptual features. The specific epoch in which each directive was released, together with the different administrative and social systems enforced in the relevant place of production, contributed to the lexical and syntactical complexity of these texts. In regard to their quantity, the fact that some of these areas issued only a few regulations did not necessarily mean that the rulers were not concerned about local heritage. Rather, it might imply that the prescriptions they issued were fully effective and successful, so that there was no need to reinforce them, or that they followed different agendas to fulfil their scope.

The translations of the laws issued in the Province of Drenthe in the Netherlands and the Kingdom of Sweden have been achieved working on the interpretations offered in

14 The original texts of the laws issued in the Grand Duchy of Tuscany are collected in Emiliani 1978, 25-56.

15 The original text of the regulation issued in the Duchy of Milan are collected in Emiliani 1978, 153-159. The original texts of the protocols issued in the Republic of Venice are collected in Emiliani 1978, 159-170.

16 The original texts of the sanctions issued in the Kingdom of Naples are collected in Emiliani 1978, 227-241.

published literature.[17] The older English versions of these complex, long-sentenced texts have been fully reshaped based on new specific analysis carried out for this project, and revised following the updated principles of sentence brevity and clarity.

Interestingly, the announcement issued by the Kingdom of Denmark presented major questions concerning its interpretation and translation, as not only was the original text quite convoluted and archaic, but it also mixed Latin and early modern Danish.[18] In updating its language and layout into English, therefore, a few additions have been included in brackets in order to ensure both readability and fluency.

On the other hand, the law published in the Prussian States, together with the regulations issued in the Margraviate of Ansbach-Bayreuth and the Landgraviate of Hesse-Kassel in the German-speaking area, seem to be more understandable for current readers.[19] As these texts were based on a practical approach that mixed morphological conciseness with specific legal aspects, it has been possible to condense their essence in short, straightforward enunciations.

Similarly, the permission released in the Kingdom of Portugal was constructed on a logical layout that moved from the general concepts and definitions to the particular prescriptions.[20] Its translation, therefore, remains quite faithful to the original text in terms of syntax and sentencing.

As regards the Kingdom of Spain, on the other hand, the available documents concerned, for the most part, informal instructions and communications between academics and the state representatives,[21] as no official decree was issued about heritage protection before the early 1800s.[22] These sources and their related translations largely reflect the timeliness and style of state missives, in which, for the most part, no legal dictates and formalities were followed.

Editorial Addendum

The names of internationally renowned kings, dukes, princes, popes, as well as recognised artists and scholars have been translated following their standard English forms. Where it was necessary, further clarifications on these names and their variations in the original languages have been added in the footnotes or in brackets.

The names of local administrators, inspectors, council members, and academics, as well as priests and ecclesiastic ministers, have been transcribed as they were in the

---

17 The original text and the English translation of the law issued in the Province of Drenthe are in Bakker 2011, 166-167. The original text of the law issued in the Kingdom of Sweden is in Schück 1932, 264-267; its English translation is in Adlercreutz 2017, 14-15. Regarding Sweden, only the law issued in 1666 is included in this volume. The translations of the subsequent 1666 protocol and the 1686 law could not be achieved at this stage, as their lexicon and syntax are extremely convoluted and archaic, while sentences appear too long and complex to be deciphered, even for linguists.

18 The original text of the announcement issued in the Kingdom of Denmark is in Tuneld 1934, IX-X.

19 The original texts of the laws issued in the Prussian States, the Margraviate of Ansbach-Bayreuth, and the Landgraviate of Hesse-Kassel are in Huse 1984, 26-29.

20 The original text of the law issued in the Kingdom of Portugal is in *Collecção* 1819, 415-418.

21 Copies of the original documents concerning heritage protection in the Kingdom of Spain are available in the online library Miguel de Cervantes: https://www.cervantesvirtual.com/.

22 The original text of the edict issued in the Kingdom of Spain in 1803 is in *Real Cédula de S. M.* 1803.

original documents. Where it was possible, they have been updated according to the spelling they have in their respective current languages.

Where research has produced suitable solutions, the abbreviated names have been resolved. On the other hand, when this could not be achieved, these names have been transcribed in the abbreviated forms as per the original document.

The names of renowned churches and basilicas, as well the designations of saints, have been translated following their standard English forms. Where it was possible, the names of countries, regions, cities, and towns have been translated following their standard English forms.

The original capitalisation of names, titles, artistic terms, and so on, has been retained in transcribing and translating the documents into English in Part Two. Some grammatical embellishments have been made for readability and clarity; these additions are inserted in square brackets. As mentioned, a number of excessively-long and convoluted paragraphs with no punctuation have been condensed into shorter, concise sentences.

In part, the definitions and terminologies used to explain historical occurrences in Part One derive from current scholarship, and are applied retrospectively to the early modern centuries. Explanations about these conceptual aspects will emerge throughout the narrative.

Part One

Art and Law. The Origins of Concepts and Procedures

3

A Comparative History of Concepts and Procedures

The concepts of heritage and the related meanings of protection are not the same in different societies and contexts. Moreover, their interconnected definitions have evolved significantly throughout the centuries, forming a narrative that is elusive and difficult to sketch in a sequential way. In broad terms, the idea of heritage is determined by a collective understanding of what it is that needs to be kept for the benefit of the entire community. Accordingly, preservation can be considered the practical consequence of shared awareness on the cultural and historical importance of an artefact or any other expression of human creativity.[23] To be constructed, a history of heritage protection requires evaluation of specific artistic perceptions, aesthetic taste, and social paradigms, as well as an analysis of the religious, economic, and political issues that characterised each society and epoch.

While scholars have generally understood heritage as a recent concept formed from the late 1700s, and especially in the 1800s, pre-modern societies had already developed systems to care for objects that were believed to have cultural value – if we can use this contemporary term. From this perspective, early modern legislation offers a solid instrument to grasp both what was recognised as heritage in different places between the 1400s and 1700s, and the principles followed to attribute importance to the artefacts that were thought of as worthy of protection. This evaluation process, at least initially, did not imply any particular acknowledgment of the objects' artistic and aesthetic qualities. As will emerge in the following pages, the focus was rather on the functions and possible uses of specific old items according to rulers' political and economic agendas for their kingdoms. In this regard, it should be acknowledged that the vast sector of so-called intangible heritage was not accepted in early modern legislation,[24] and of course neither were more recent cultural and creative expressions, such as photography and the cinema. Indeed, the typologies of heritage included in these pioneering regulations corresponded, in broad terms, to the current idea of historic material artefacts – that is to say, monuments, utensils, sculptures, drawings, paintings, buildings, books, and other objects which

23 For the relationship between collective awareness on the cultural and historical importance of an artefact and its practical preservation, see Emiliani 1974.

24 See, for instance, the definition of intangible heritage on the Unesco webpage: https://ich.unesco.org/en/what-is-intangible-heritage-00003.

have both historical depth and unchanging physical components.[25] As opposed to other categories of heritage, since the early modern centuries tangible artworks have generally required twofold practices of protection, entailing practical interventions of restoration and maintenance alongside programmatic systems of control and management – such as those imparted within the legal prescriptions described here.

Regarding this founding legislation, it should be observed that not every country in Europe dealt with the supervision of its local relics in the early modern centuries. It is significant that major places that might be expected to be concerned about the safekeeping of their artefacts, such as France or England, did not issue any rules on this topic at this stage. Evidently, their interests in the arts responded to paradigms that were different from the questions about the physical and legal safety of worthy old relics that arose in other regions. Indeed, between the 1400s and 1700s very few European states and counties launched sets of rules for administering their local heritage; as already mentioned in the Introduction, these were the Papal States, the Grand Duchy of Tuscany, the Kingdom of Denmark, the Kingdom of Sweden, the Kingdom of Naples, the Republic of Venice, the Duchy of Milan, the Kingdom of Portugal, the Prussian States, the Margraviate of Ansbach-Bayreuth and the Landgraviate of Hesse-Kassel in the German-speaking area, the Kingdom of Spain, and the Province of Drenthe in the Dutch Republic.[26] These regions issued regulations which largely reflected the visions of "heritage" and "protection" accepted by their rulers and the greater part of their societies, incorporating also specific characterisations of both objects and procedures intended for preservation – corresponding to what in current legislation would be known as the "object of law". Comparative evaluations of these directives provide a clear outline of the early measures established to care for local relics in each area, together with the gradual development of new concepts and practices for their management throughout the centuries. Legislation, in this perspective, can be seen as the most reliable instrument to construct a short chronicle on the protection of heritage in early modern Europe.

Defining "Heritage" in Early Modern Law

Within this short history of heritage legislation, the first significant set of concepts and formulas to take into consideration is contained in the royal decree *Placat*, issued in the Kingdom of Sweden in 1666 [fig. 1]. Although this was not the earliest regulation published in Europe, its prescriptions allow us to reconstruct one of the most distinctive ideas of heritage expounded in the Baroque period. Following the initiative of the state Board of Regents, this ordinance established that the materials to be preserved for the benefit of the country were "antiquities, remains, and monuments of time immemorial".[27] These "antiquities" were specifically identified as "castles, houses, fortresses, strongholds or cairns, [...] standing stones or stones with runic inscriptions, [...] mounds of earth and

25 See, for instance, the definition of tangible heritage on the Paese Cultura webpage: http://www.paesecultura.it/beni-culturali-materiali/.

26 This data is based on investigations carried out for this specific project. I hope that this list will expand in the future with different forms of legislation and evidence, possibly thanks to new research. The list provided here follows a random order.

27 A major analysis on this legislation is in Adlercreutz 2017, 6-13; see also Mannoni 2021a. For this quote and the following ones, see Schück 1932, 264-267.

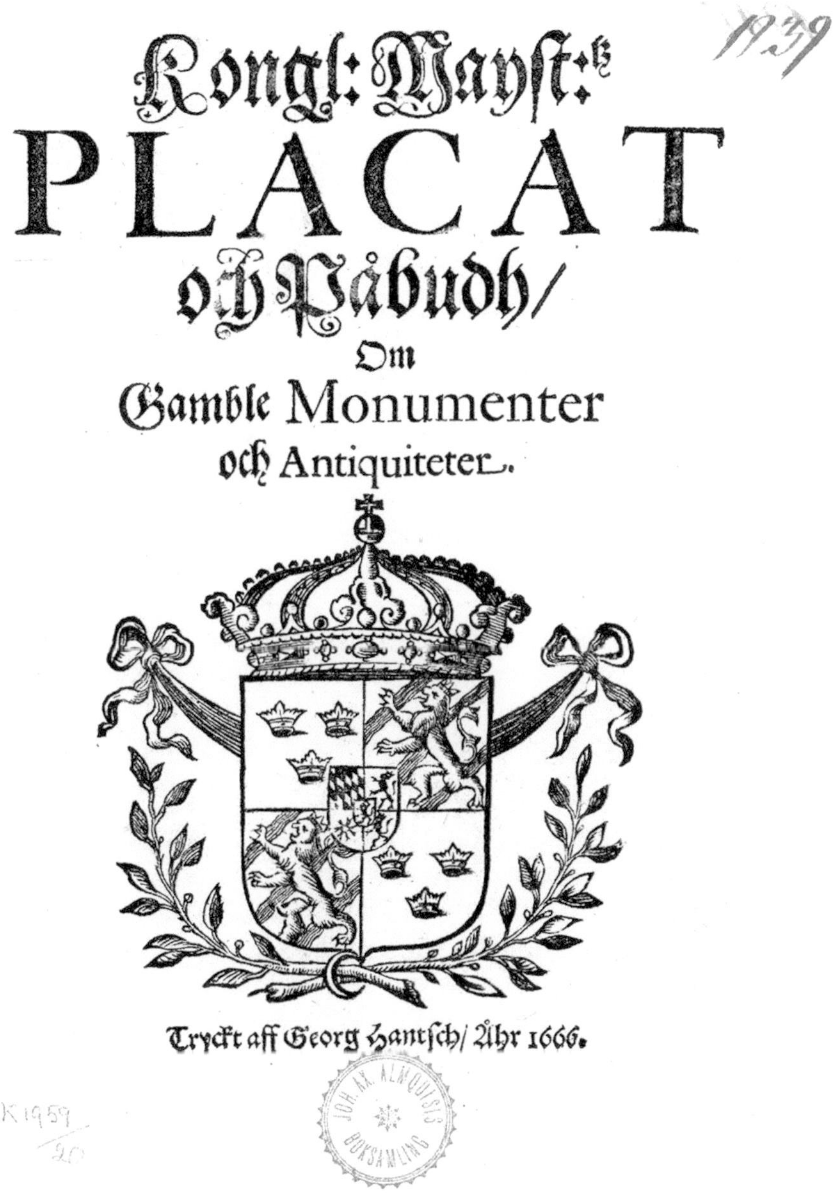
Kongl: Mayst:tz
PLACAT
och Påbudh/
Om
Gamble Monumenter
och Antiquiteter.
Tryckt aff Georg Hantsch/ Åhr 1666.

Figure 1. Kingdom of Sweden, *Placat*, front page, 1666.

burial sites [of] kings and other worthy people, [...] churches and monasteries with all their supplies, accoutrements, decorations on walls and windows", which were scattered across the realm. As emerges from this description, the first legal definition of heritage introduced in Sweden comprised for the most part monuments evoking noble heroes and the ancestors of the country, as well as antiquities bearing symbolic value for the construction of local historical narratives, such as dolmens and runic inscriptions. Indeed, at this stage the accounts of the Swedish past were formed essentially on epic genealogical dimensions, involving legends and mythological components alongside real historical evidence. Within the growing fashion of Gothicism in the late 1500s,[28] the royal family had started being associated with the ancient valiant Goths, who were not only recognised as the forefathers of the latest Swedish monarchs, but also as "the oldest tribe [that] ever existed in Europe".[29] Ensuing the attestations that Swedish people "were the first" based on mythical interpretations,[30] subsequent local chronographers would misconstrue also the *Placat*, improperly greeting it as "the first law published on the protection of monuments and antiquities in the world" until recent years.[31] Such a solid construction of traditional tales and juridical formulations sought to legitimise royal dynastic power, by proving its age and historical authority; it also involved the support of antiquarianism, and particularly the new evidence and findings that the Swedish scholars could uncover about local monuments. In this regard, it is undeniable that the remains "of time immemorial" quoted in the *Placat* methodically intertwined antiquarian discoveries, sagas, and legislation to endorse Sweden as a long-standing hegemonic country in Northern Europe. Since these relics were acknowledged as the traces of a glorious – legendary – national past, they were to be identified, analysed, and preserved, in order to increase the state's power and prestige at the time.

In respect of its legal prescriptions, the *Placat* forbad any "ruination, destruction, [...] abuse, disorder, or damage" of the abovementioned categories of materials; plundering and robbing of royal tombs and churches was prohibited too.[32] Each transgression was assessed in terms of the amount of harm caused to the artefacts, following for the most part a restrictive system of law. The decree, moreover, was particularly clear regarding the purpose of the new protective procedures: all the local "antiquities, remains, and monuments", as well as the churches and monasteries, were considered the kingdom's property. Any of these goods, placed either in the public domain or any other "land pertaining to the crown, [...] taxable property, regardless of whether it is now our property or was it so in the past", was safeguarded for the state's benefit. As can be observed, the differences between public and private property were quite blurred at this stage. Even so, the earliest rules on heritage protection issued in Sweden seemed to govern all of these assets equally, considering primarily the interest of the state rather than the private owner in the value of local monuments.

Within the same timeframe, the definition of antiquities introduced in Denmark was constructed on the basis of rather different prerequisites and intentions. It is possible to ascertain the nature of such a concept by investigating the proclamation that King Christian IV made known in this kingdom in 1622, some years before the *Placat* was issued in Sweden. With his announcement, the monarch launched a vast campaign of "[identification] and recording of all kinds of antiquities and documents" scattered

28 Cucina 2005; Johannesson 1991.

29 Jensen 2006, 14.

30 Adlercreuz 2017, 12. Adlercreuz reassessed the old misinterpretations of the *Placat*, asserting that the idea that this was "the oldest antiquities' legislation in the world" was strictly connected to Gothicism and the mythological tales of the 1600s.

31 Klindt-Jensen 1975, 27; Jensen 2006, 14.

32 For this quote and the following ones, see Schück 1932, 264-267.

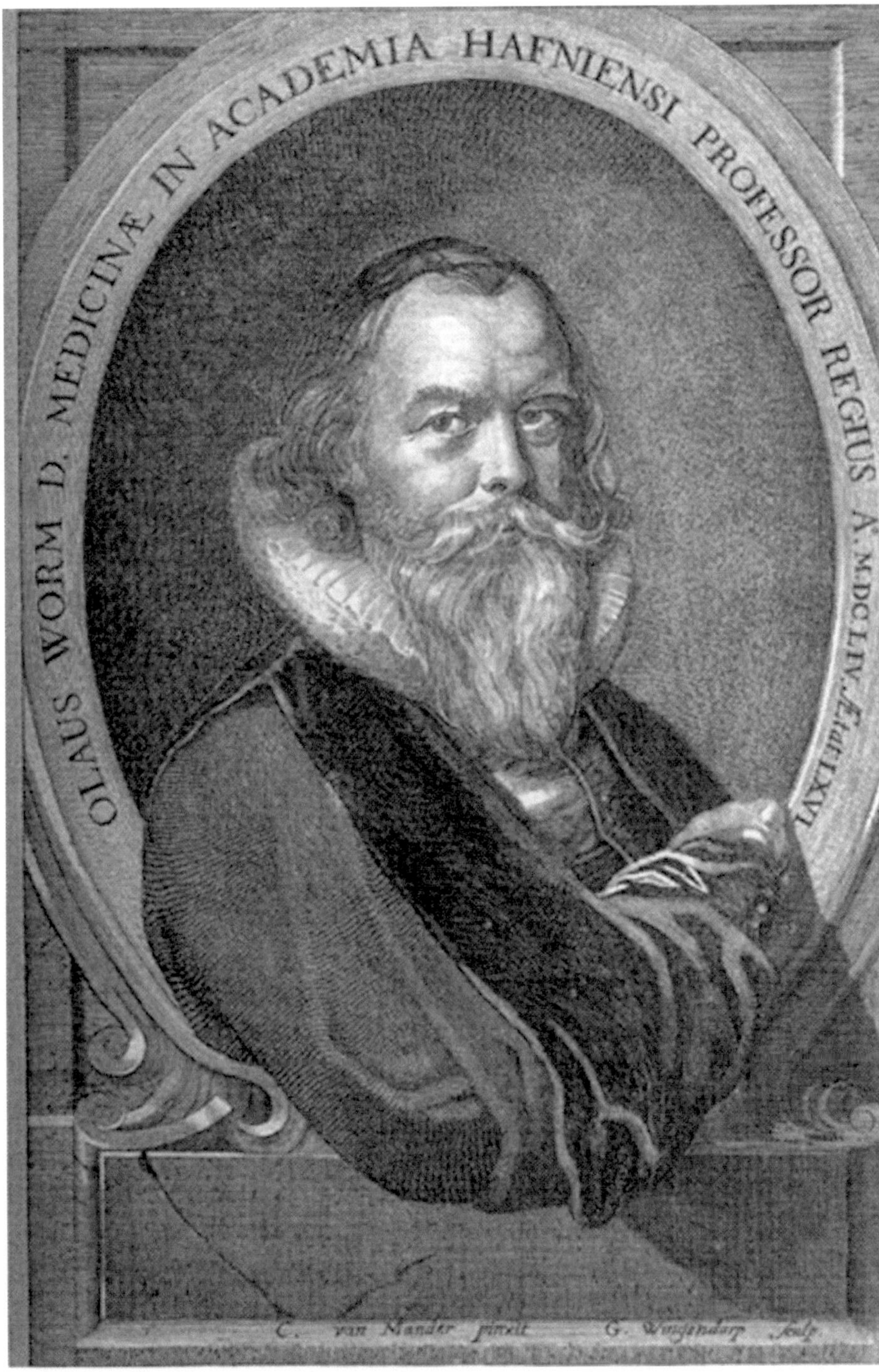

Figure 2. Unknown artist, *Ole Worm*, engraving, 1654.

across the Danish provinces;[33] Protestant priests and clergymen were required to compile "transcripts and notes" of all the materials which were located in their respective parishes, to "submit to the [kingdom's offices of] Chancellery [...] before Easter". Enclosed in this proclamation, a detailed record enumerated "handwritten historical documents, [...] runic inscriptions, [...] stone houses, [...] coins, weights, measurement [systems]", together with several other *antiquitatibus*, among the items to register.[34] The king's declared purpose was *antiquitates gentis nostrae at deducere*, "to discover about the country's ancientness". Most probably this extensive project stemmed from the prolific discoveries of antiquities that local explorers were carrying out in Northern Europe, and was further constructed on the systems that the Danish scholar Ole Worm elaborated to classify both natural and ancient worlds in the same years [fig. 2].[35] As a personal scientist and advisor of Christian IV, Worm not only devoted his life to the study and categorisation of ancient relics and runic inscriptions scattered across Denmark, publishing several volumes on his findings, but was also directly involved in the issuing of the 1622 despatch.[36] The classification systems proposed to register Danish antiquities were indeed structured on the distinctive criteria of comprehensiveness and functionality that Worm applied to his studies: for instance, he employed them to identify "sanctuaries, altars, sepulchres, epitaphs, circuses, milestones, and sacred precincts" according to their characteristics and purposes.[37] Worm's cabinet of curiosities – the so-called *Museum Wormianum* – was also structured in representative categories, including plants, animals, fossils, and minerals alongside carved stones, antiquities, and prehistoric items [fig. 3].[38]

In this scenario, what it is fundamental to note is that, in launching this vast initiative in 1622, Christian IV was probably unaware of the fact that he was introducing in Denmark the first-ever model of a general catalogue of heritage. The king's intention was to detect old artefacts and determine the age of the country, to legitimise his authority in the Scandinavian regions by using historical evidence and antiquities. As would occur in Sweden later on, in Denmark too regal authority was shaped and reinforced by interconnecting knowledge of the past, the control of local relics, and the issuing of related legal prescriptions. Nevertheless, at this stage these innovations appeared not to be fully understood by the local clergymen: in fact, quite a few of them failed to submit the descriptions of the antiquities that were kept in their parishes, as the royal announcement had required.[39] It should be observed that the definition of heritage proposed within the despatch was quite controversial too. The wide-ranging characterisation of *antiquitatibus*

---

33 Arvidsson 2018, 14. For this quote and the following ones, see Tuneld 1934, IX-X. I am grateful to the librarians of the University of Erlangen for allowing me to consult Tuneld's extremely rare volume.

34 This and the following quote are purposefully transcribed in their original language, that is Latin.

35 For a history of antiquarian research in Denmark, see Schnapp 1993, 141-157.

36 Ole Worm (1588-1654) was also a doctor, biologist, collector, and early ethnologist. On runic language and inscriptions, he published his *Fasti Danici* in 1626, his *Runir seu Danica literatura antiquissima* in 1636, and his renowned *Danicorum Monumentorum* in 1643. Regarding his interests in collecting, see Grice 2015; Hafstein 2003.

37 Schnapp 1993, 144.

38 The *Museum Wormianum* is currently kept in the Statens Naturhistoriske Museum of Copenhagen.

39 In 1934, Tuneld reported that only a few descriptions were kept in the diocese of Lund; in Blekinge and Halland, on the other hand, he found no reports. It is possible that a number of them have been lost. Tuneld 1934, IX-XV.

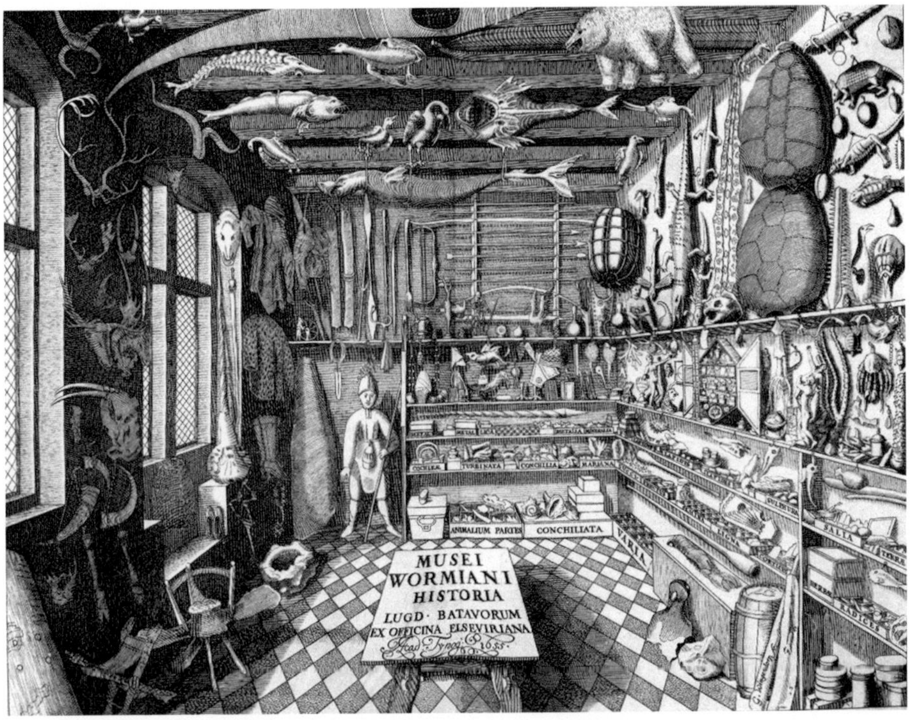

Figure 3. *Museum Wormianum*, engraving, 1655. In: Willum Worm, *Musei Wormiani Historia*, front page.

intended for the state's registers rested largely on the classical erudition of the Southern regions of Europe, as the use of Latin also evidenced; furthermore, alongside dolmens and runic inscriptions, the record referred to items that were not directly a part of Danish history and culture. By contrast, for instance, the subsequent 1666 *Placa*t focused exclusively on remains that had been produced in Sweden, identifying their distinctive qualities in comparison to other forms of heritage. In this respect, it can be thought that Ole Worm's classifications of nature and antiquities were too general, or perhaps too "international", to meet the operative requirements of the Danish catalogue, which was intended to cover strictly local artefacts. This is the reason why, most probably, the initial royal announcement was subsequently suspended, and replaced with a second document requiring different data for the state survey, strictly related to a census on the population, mills, and streets.[40]

Comparative evaluations of the directives issued in Denmark and Sweden shed light also on the role that early heritage protection played within broader European politics in these years. Scandinavian antiquities had acquired growing significance since the late 1500s,

40 Based on his analysis of the records kept in different Danish dioceses, Tuneld concluded that a second royal announcement (with no date) was introduced to replace the first one. Even though its aim was still to form a state catalogue, the second document required specific data related to the population, mills, and streets. Tuneld 1934, XI.

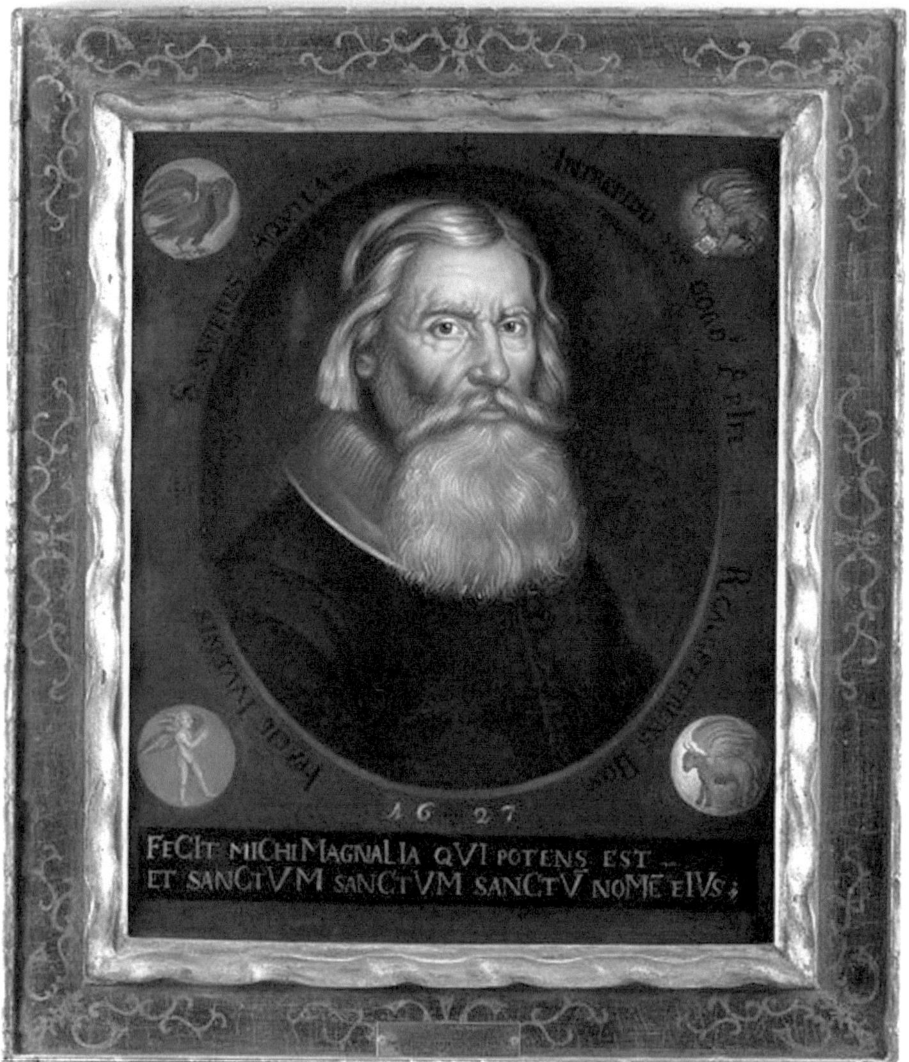

Figure 4. Unknown artist, *Johan Bure*, oil on canvas, 1627.

particularly in the context of the disputes between Danes and Swedes in the Baltic Sea, as well as between Catholics and Protestants in Europe at large. Before the Peace of Westphalia in 1648, the two Scandinavian crowns competed for the symbolic use and control of local remains. Their cultural disputes, in this case, involved specifically the rediscovery and study of the most representative evidence of antiquities in Northern Europe – that is to say, runic inscriptions. The appreciation of these items derived essentially from a philological interest in the runic alphabet and language, which scholars of both countries accepted as the "most ancient idiom in the world".[41] Deciphering these inscriptions, therefore, would

41 Schnapp 1993, 138-141.

have provided authoritative support for their respective claims in the Baltic Sea. On the other hand, the recognition of specific Scandinavian heritage and history was also crucial to define the otherness of Protestants as opposed to Catholics. It can be surmised that Denmark and Sweden, while contending for the control in the Baltic area, finally succeeded in disengaging from the Catholic domain because they gradually identified their distinctive Scandinavian history and culture.[42] In line with these events – and possibly challenging the Danish catalogue – in 1630 King Gustav II Adolfs of Sweden requested the scholar and linguist Johan Bure to classify and interpret the runic inscriptions that were scattered across his realm [fig. 4]. By appointing him as State Antiquarian, the king not only introduced one of the earliest chairs devoted to the supervision of public heritage in Europe,[43] but also acknowledged the significance that these local artefacts had in his national and international affairs. It is evident that the sovereigns of Denmark and Sweden, in spite of their mutual dislike, both understood the importance of affirming their central authority in connection to state history and identity at this stage. The awareness of the prestige that antiquity could grant drove them to inaugurate the first legal and administrative procedures dedicated to heritage protection in their respective realms.

The first ordinance issued to protect the antiquities in the Netherlands can be considered in comparison with the regulations launched in Denmark and Sweden. In 1734, the small province of Drenthe in the north-eastern part of the Dutch Republic promulgated a declaration to save the local hunebeds – that is, prehistoric dolmens – from destruction and illicit sale [fig. 5.1 and 5.2].[44] Even though Drenthe and Scandinavia had different milieus and historical backgrounds, as well as diverse geographic locations and administrative powers, the so-called *Resolutie van Drenthe* (*Resolution of Drenthe*) fostered awareness that the local megalithic structures were "venerable monuments and longstanding memorials" of the district's history,[45] and embraced the same responsibility for their preservation that had motivated the broader Swedish and Danish state initiatives a century earlier. Most likely the protection of the hunebeds was prompted by the re-issue of Johan Picardt's *Brief Description of some Forgotten and Hidden Antiquities* [...] in 1731, which described the exceptional value and rarity of Drenthe's "enormous stone-heaps" as being the "antiquities of antiquities" of central Europe.[46] Although Picard believed that these structures were originally giants' beds –

42 For a history of antiquarian research in Scandinavia, see Klindt-Jensen 1975.

43 Johan Bure (1568-1652) was also a genealogist, mystic, and antiquarian; he is acknowledged as "father of runology". At this date Ole Worm was already working for Christian IV of Denmark. However, I detect a fundamental difference between a personal advisor (devoted to the king's interests) and a state antiquarian (dedicated to the public benefit). Adlercreutz 2017; Mannoni 2021a; Schnapp 1993, 138-141.

44 For major analysis on the early protection of the hunebeds, see Bakker 2010 and 2011. I am grateful to Dr. Wijnand van der Sanden, former Curator of Archaeology at Drents Museum, for providing me with the original text and the pictures of this law. I am also grateful to Dr. Jan Albert Bakker for gifting me his important monograph of 2010.

45 Bakker 2011, 167.

46 Johan Picardt (1600-1670) was a doctor, Calvinist pastor, and theologian; he believed in witches, ghosts, and the devil, and offered an early explanation on the dolmens as being ancient giants' beds (the name hunebeds derives from his interpretations). His volume *Korte Beschryvinge van eenige Vergetene en Verborgene Antiquiteten der Provintien en Landen gelegen tusschen de Noord-Zee, de Yssel, Emse en Lippe* on the antiquities of Drenthe was published in Amsterdam in 1660. Here I support the analysis of Bakker, who connected the reissuing of this volume to the publication of the *Resolutie*. For this quote and the following ones, see Bakker 1979, 143-147.

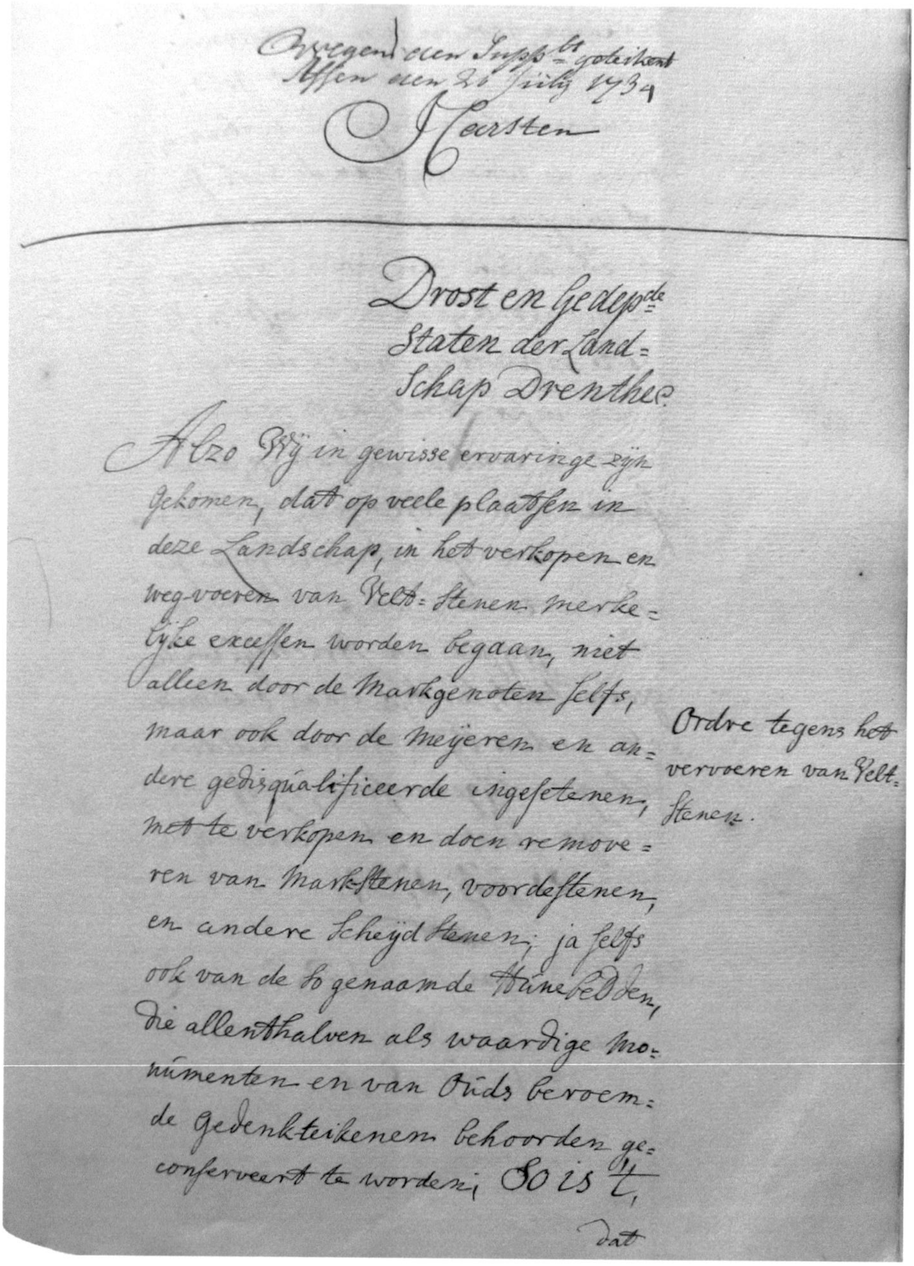

Overgegeven den Suppl[ian]ten = geteikent
Assen den 20 Julij 1734
O. J. Haersten

Drost en Gedep[uteer]de
Staten der Land=
Schap Drenthe.

Alzo Wij in gewisse ervaringe zijn
gekomen, dat op veele plaatsen in
deze Landschap, in het verkopen en
weg-voeren van Velt=Stenen merke=
lijke excessen worden begaan, niet
alleen door de Markgenoten selfs,
maar ook door de Meijeren en an=
dere gedisqualificeerde ingesetenen,
met te verkopen en doen remove=
ren van Markstenen, voordestenen,
en andere Scheijd Stenen; ja selfs
ook van de so genaamde Hunebedden,
die allenthalven als waardige Mo=
numenten en van Ouds beroem=
de gedenkteikenen behoorden ge=
conserveert te worden; So is 't,
dat

Ordre tegens het
vervoeren van Velt=
Stenen.

Figures 5.1 and 5.2. Province of Drenthe, *Resolutie van Drenthe*, full text, 1734.

following a mythological interpretation of the past which was similar to the one produced in Sweden – his account reported how they had been carelessly “razed to the ground, [...] removed, [...] sawn-off to be used in the masonry of churches and towers, and [placed] below the foundations of houses” since 1660. Interestingly, recent Dutch scholars have also acknowledged the Drenthe *Resolutie* as the “third law” issued on the protection of antiquities in

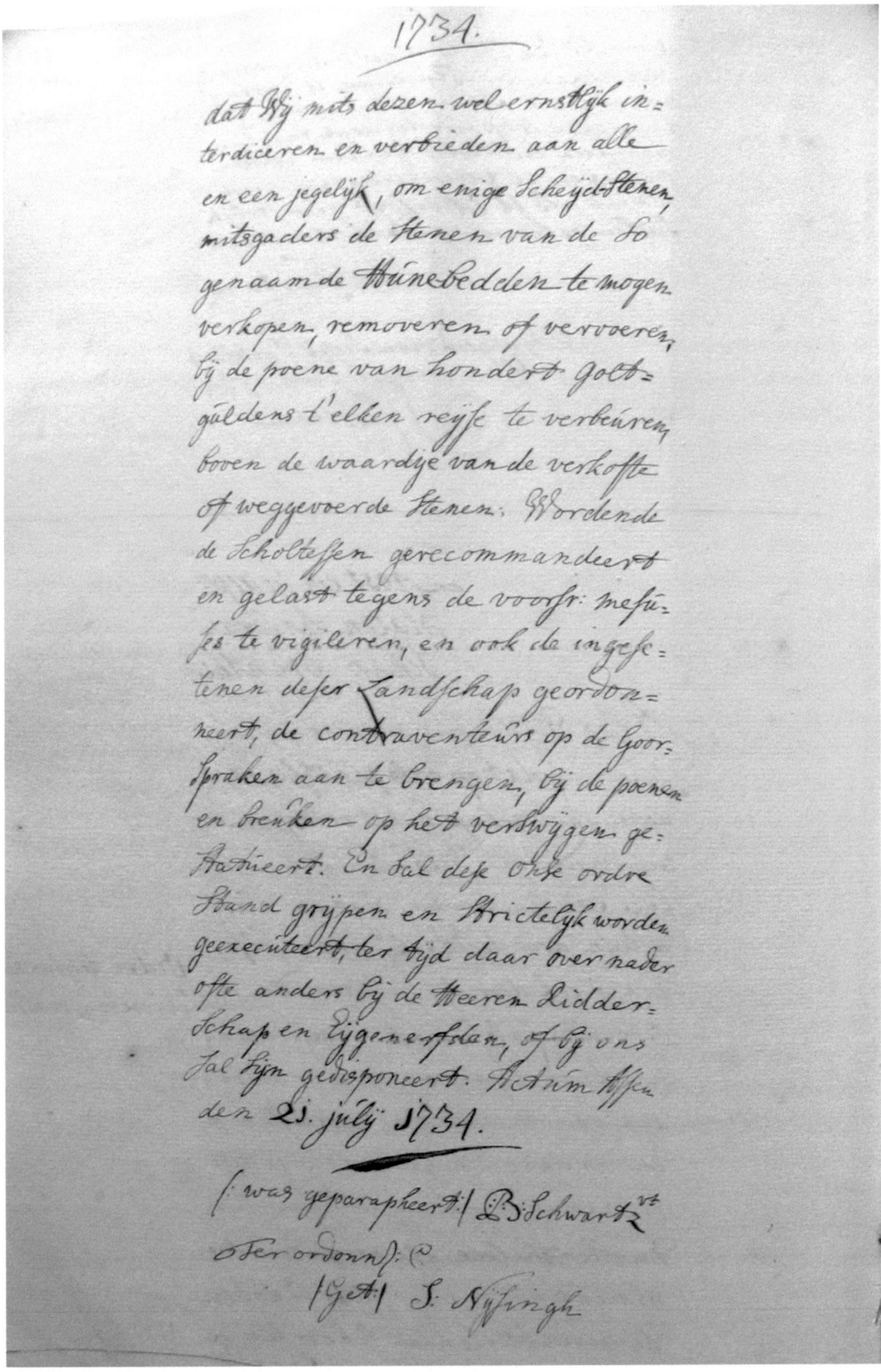
1734.

dat Wij mits dezen wel ernstlijk in=
terdiceeren en verbieden aan alle
en een jegelijk, om enige Scheijdtstenen,
mitsgaders de Stenen van de so
genaamde Hunebedden te mogen
verkopen, removeren of vervoeren,
bij de poene van hondert Golt=
guldens t'elken reijse te verbeuren,
boven de waardije van de verkofte
of weggevoerde Stenen: Wordende
de Scholtessen gerecommandeert
en gelast tegens de voorsr: mesu=
ses te vigileren, en ook de ingese=
tenen deser Landschap geordon=
neert, de contraventeurs op de voor=
spraken aan te brengen, bij de poenen
en breuken op het verswijgen ge=
statueert. En sal dese Onse ordre
Stand grijpen en strictelijk worden
geexecuteert, ter tijd daar over nader
ofte anders bij de Heeren Ridder=
schap en Eijgenerfden, of bij ons
sal zijn gedisponeert. Actum Assen
den 25. julij 1734.

(: was geparapheert:) B: Schwartz vt
Ter ordonn: &
(Get:) S. Nijsingh

Figures 5.1 and 5.2. Province of Drenthe, *Resolutie van Drenthe*, full text, 1734.

the world, possibly following the perception that the Danish catalogue and the Swedish *Placat* were respectively "the first and the second one" to be launched.[47] Even though these accounts reveal evident historical mistakes and incongruities – as these regulations were not the first, the second, and the third in line – it is noteworthy that they all linked the establishment of early domestic practices for heritage protection to a greater "international" history. In regard to the *Resolutie*, the new prescriptions were intended specifically to prevent the demolition of dolmens and hunebeds in the region of Drenthe, and to limit the usage of ancient stones as building materials by native farmers. Prohibiting anyone to "sell, remove, or transport" any of these boulders, the district representatives were conscious of the need to promote both the safety of the local monuments and the expansion of knowledge on Drenthe's history. From this perspective, it can be affirmed that the policies introduced to preserve ancient remains in the aforesaid places had all accepted a twofold implication right from the beginning: as the Dutch and Scandinavian laws seemed to suggest, these relics were considered part of both local history and the collective history of Europe.

In order to fully understand the development of early awareness about how heritage functioned in Europe, the laws issued to care for the artefacts in a Catholic country should be evaluated as well. The Papal States offer an excellent example for comparison as not only did the Catholic Church oppose the Northern countries as regards religious matters, but it also introduced different concepts of "heritage" and "protection" within its legislation. However, evaluating all the definitions of heritage included in the edicts issued in Rome over four centuries would undermine this essay's broad focus, since the popes undersigned more than 30 regulations on the defence of antiquities and artworks between the 1400s and 1700s. Moreover, the policies that the Papacy implemented to defend its local ancient remains are well known to scholars, and have been analysed in terms of both their legal and cultural repercussions in contemporary legislation in Italy, as well as their influence on the regulations issued to protect artefacts in the Old Italian States.[48] For these reasons, readers might approach the collection of texts included in Part Two of this volume directly to appreciate the gradual expansion of these concepts in papal legislation, while here I will limit myself to a few significant examples. The 1425 edict *Etsi in Cunctarum orbis Provinciarum* ([...] *In all the Provinces*) of Pope Martin V itemised "buildings made of stone and wood, walls made of beams, [...] roofs, floors, [...] storages, and staircases, gates, passages, watercourses, canals, and pipe drains", placed both in "public and private places", in the list of the items to care for.[49] This was the first bill issued to look after community assets in the Papal States, and by extension can be considered the

47 Bakker 2010, 60-63 and 2011, 293-296. Bakker has observed that "as far as we know" the *Resolutie van Drenthe* was the "third law issued to protect historic monuments in the world". He positioned it after the issuing of a regulation in Denmark in the 1620s, and a law in Sweden in 1630. Nevertheless, no regulation was published in Sweden at that stage; this variation of data can depend on the use of different calendars in the 1600s.

48 See, for instance, the Italian studies of Condemi 1987; Curzi 2004; Emiliani 1978; Speroni 1988, 11-48. In English see Levi 2008; Mannoni 2021b; Mannoni 2022a.

49 Tomassetti 1857-1872, vol. 4, 716-718. In recent years, Italian legal historians have interpreted this edict as a set of prescriptions dedicated to the general maintenance of public city spaces, and not as an early regulation on heritage protection. While their explanation is extremely strong and convincing, here I follow the older interpretations of Italian art historians, who have generally included the *Etsi in Cunctarum orbis Provinciarum* in the construction of early systems of heritage protection in the Papal States. Condemi 1987; Curzi 2004; Valsecchi & Carcereri De' Prati 2009; Valsecchi 2022.

earliest regulation to safeguard "heritage" in early modern Europe. Although its effects on social life and attitudes are difficult to ascertain, as it seems that its prescriptions were not fully enforced at this stage, this pioneering decree fostered awareness that supervising public properties would bring manifest benefits to the entire society – a vision that the later Swedish *Placat* would also embrace. In 1562, the *Motu Proprio* of Pope Pius IV further expanded the enumerations of objects, including "ancient marbles, both raw and worked, statues, busts, metals, precious stones, coins, vases, and cups made of bronze, silver, and gold, as well as slabs and inscriptions" under the protective umbrella of law.[50] The definition of heritage gained yet further extended meanings in 1646, in the *Editto Sforza* issued under Pope Innocent X:

> Statues, figures, bas-reliefs, columns, vases, alabasters, agates, jaspers, amethysts, and other marbles, precious stones, wrought stones, uncut stones, busts, heads, fragments, pillars, pedestals, inscriptions, [as well as] other ornaments, friezes, medallions, cameos, or carvings made on any sort of stone, metal, gold, silver, both ancient and modern, [and also] figures, ancient paintings, or other works sculpted in any material, painted, carved, assembled, or crafted.[51]

At the outset, the popes focused on the safeguarding of the bulky antiquities which were scattered – or discovered – across the city of Rome. Legislation, therefore, was constructed on quite a limited appreciation of specific ancient monuments, although from the first half of the 1600s onwards small cameos and medals made of new materials started being included too, as the *Editto Sforza* specified. In this regard, it is noteworthy that, after focusing on "immovable" structures and buildings in the earliest edicts, the popes gradually embraced statues, busts, vases, and other "movable" antiquities in legislation issued from the 1500s onwards. By assigning value to transportable items, they not only aimed to increase the varieties of protected heritage, but also provided supervision for the artefacts that were particularly easy to export and smuggle because of their small dimensions. To fully achieve this goal, in 1534 Paul III appointed the scholar and poet Latino Giovenale Manetti as the first-ever papal Commissary of Antiquities,[52] entrusting him to oversee both excavations and the sales of ancient items throughout Rome. Considering the date of establishment of this office, it can be affirmed that the Catholic Church preceded even the resourceful Scandinavian monarchies in setting up legal procedures to administer and control local remains.

As regards the meanings of heritage and its protection, a broad scrutiny of papal legislation shows that between the 1400s and 1700s the Catholic Church pursued the custody and rediscovery of antiquities of Roman origin above all – that is to say, the

50 Fea 1802, 99-102. As mentioned in the Introduction, the translation of the 1562 *Motu Proprio* could not be achieved for the purposes of this volume.

51 Emiliani 1978, 69-75. From the beginning of the 1600s, papal laws were named after the surname of the Cardinal Camerlengo (the papal Chamberlain) who wrote them. For instance, the *Editto Sforza* was issued by the Cardinal Federico Sforza.

52 Latino Giovenale Manetti (1486-1553) was also a papal diplomat and poet, and has been recognised as "father of modern Rome" since the late 1500s. In 1515 Pope Leo X had appointed Raffaello *Praefectus marmorum et lapidum* of Rome; however, following Settis 2020, his duties concerned the reuse of ancient materials, rather than their conservation. See also Ridley 1992.

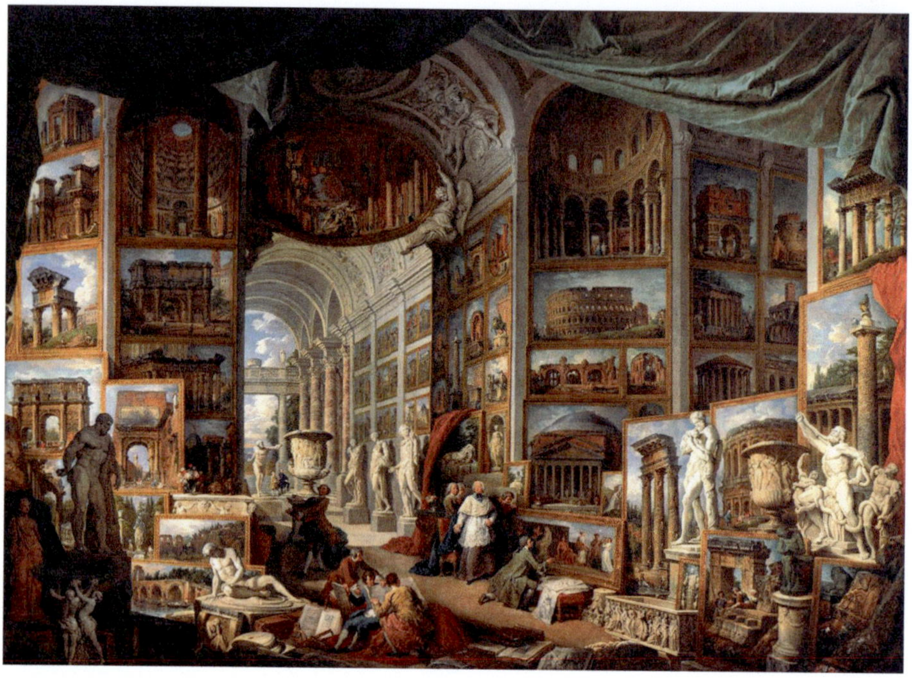

Figure 6. Giovanni Paolo Pannini, *Gallery of views of ancient Rome*, oil on canvas, 1758.

numerous pagan remains from the Roman Empire which were to be found in Rome and its surroundings. As with the Scandinavian rulers, the pontiffs too understood that the custody of local ancient relics would be of advantage to their reputation and influence in Europe. Nevertheless, in the Papal States such a political program implied a different cultural assumption: it involved assimilating profane Roman works into Catholic ethics, by means of programs purposefully launched to protect, adapt, and restore them. Indeed, right from the beginning in Rome, the legal protection of antiquities developed alongside practical activities for their preservation and restoration, reaching their peak towards the mid-1700s.[53] Within the timeframe of four centuries, the progressive refinement of both theoretical definitions and concrete procedures for safeguarding heritage – achieved by the papal chamberlains and officers – gave form to major collections and museums in Rome, as well as a substantial *corpus* of edicts composed of more than 30 regulations, as mentioned above [fig. 6]. Such a vast legislation evolved within broader Canonical law, and possibly derived paradigms from ancient Roman law too.[54] As already stated, the papal *corpus* of laws constituted the basis for the formation of current strategies to protect heritage in Italy; taking a broader perspective, it can be affirmed that it also offered

53 The analysis of the practices developed to restore antiquities in the Papal States between the 1400s and 1700s goes beyond the focus of this research. For a good introduction on these aspects, see Piva 2007; Rossi Pinelli 1986; Price, Talley & Melucco Vaccaro 1996.

54 For an introduction to these two prominent legal traditions, see Le Bras 1976; Padoa Schioppa 2016; Stein 1999.

an inspirational model for issuing directives to preserve artefacts in other European countries.[55]

The regulations examined in the previous pages demonstrate that the earlier concepts of heritage incorporated mostly antiquities – whether movable or immovable, Roman or prehistoric, in Northern or Southern Europe. Nevertheless, what these laws were missing were specific provisions to protect the other, generally most accepted subdivision of tangible heritage. I am referring to easel paintings – that is to say, movable pictures executed on canvas or wood panel especially from the 1400s onwards, as opposed to those, most often murals, that were of greater antiquity.

Between the 1500s and 1600s, movable paintings gained increasing significance for scholars and art collectors all over Europe, circulating more and more within the international markets. To find early mention of "paintings" in a regulatory framework, therefore, we should turn our attention to one of the most active hubs in the production of these works at that time: the Grand Duchy of Tuscany. In 1602, revealing an attitude of strong protectionism, Ferdinand I de' Medici established severe prohibitions and limitations on the exports of the "good paintings [...] by the departed painters" that were located in Florence [fig. 7]. These "dead" artists were identified for the most part as the masters of the Florentine Renaissance, who had been universally acknowledged as outstanding after the publication of Giorgio Vasari's *Lives of the most Excellent Italian Painters, Sculptors, and Architects* in the mid-1500s.[56] According to the ducal order, any painting sold in Florence was to be examined by one of the professors of the local Academy of Drawing prior its exportation; in cases where a piece was valued "good" on the basis of its quality, subject, and style, its transferral abroad was blocked. Ferdinand I imposed in particular a list of eighteen great painters whose works must not be sold under any circumstance. These, quite obviously, were the foremost celebrities of the Renaissance and Mannerist arts, who attracted the interest of the duke as well as that of the international collectors: Michelangelo, Raphael, Andrea del Sarto, Domenico Beccafumi, Rosso Fiorentino, Leonardo, Francesco Francia, Perin del Vaga, Jacopo da Pontormo, Titian, Francesco Salviati, Agnolo Bronzino, Daniele da Volterra, Fra' Bartolomeo (Baccio della Porta), Sebastiano del Piombo, Filippino Lippi, Antonio da Correggio, and Parmigianino, with Pietro Perugino added as a nineteenth name in a subsequent postscript.[57] On the other hand, the ordinance explicitly encouraged the sales of the works of living artists, including "portraits, landscapes [...] and [paintings] that often are hung at the bed's head"; its purpose, evidently, was to incentivise the expansion of both the local fine art industry and the market for pieces considered of minor value.

The introduction of procedures to protect early modern paintings in the Grand Duchy of Tuscany responded to political and economic concerns connected to international power, reputation, and status, combined with domestic cultural and social questions. Most importantly, it satisfied the grand duke's confidence that Florentine Renaissance art

55 The influence of the papal laws on the edict issued in 1834 Greece is evaluated in Mannoni 2022a. See also Galanakis 2022. The impact of the papal laws on the Swedish *Placat* of 1666 is discussed in Mannoni 2021a.

56 Giorgio Vasari (1511-1574), painter and art historian, published his second version of *Vite de' più eccellenti Pittori, Scultori e Architetti*, which I mention here, in 1568. Rossi Pinelli 2014, 3-11.

57 For this list of names and the following quote, see Emiliani 1978, 30-34.

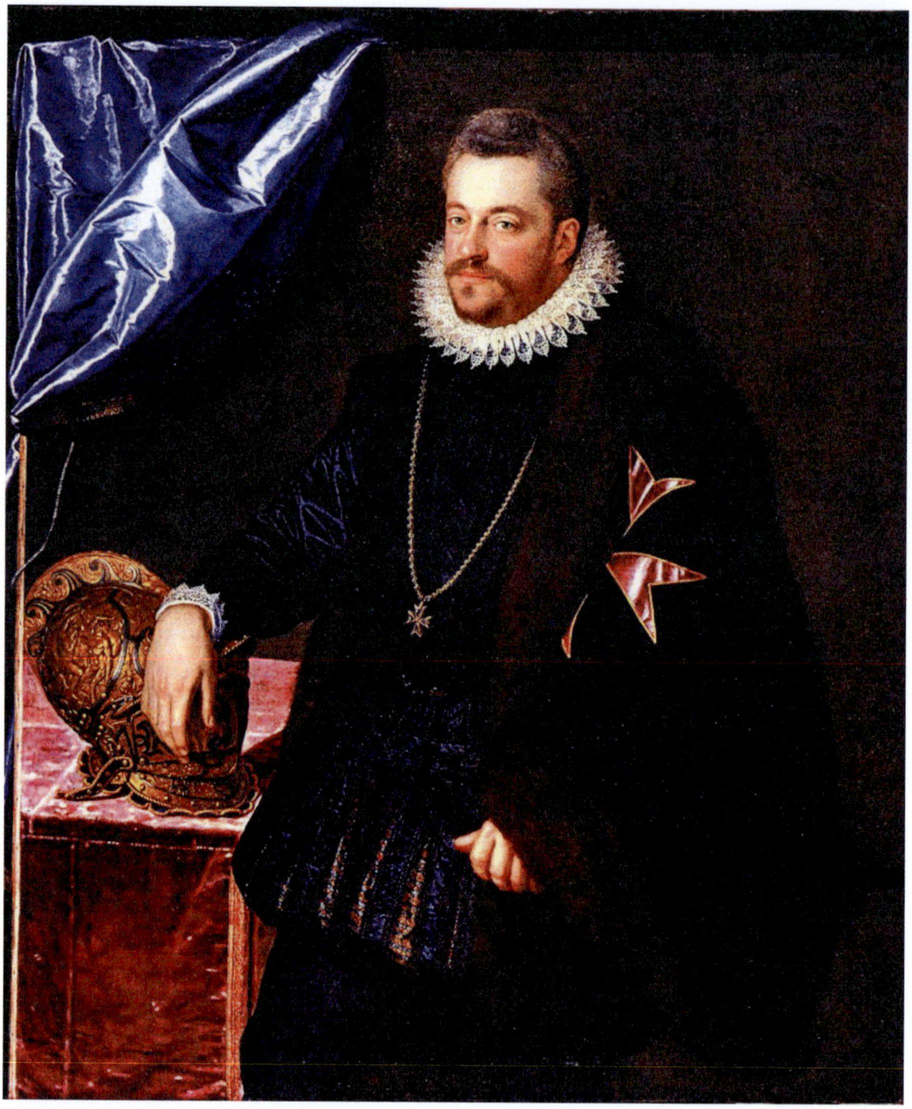

Figure 7. Scipione Pulzone, *Ferdinand I de' Medici*, oil on canvas, 1590.

surpassed the authority of Roman antiquity both locally and internationally. In this respect, the Medici ordinance can be interpreted as the first legal construct that acknowledged the specific artistic and aesthetic qualities of the artefacts it governed, going beyond the functions that they could have in a ruler's agenda. In the following years, the Florentine regulation was extended also to other provinces in the Grand Duchy: first to Siena in 1602, where a list of three artists, Beccafumi, Raphael, and Sodoma (Giovanni Antonio Bazzi), was defined; then to Pisa, Pistoia, and Arezzo in 1603.[58]

58 While Siena defined a specific list of painters, the other centres adopted the list from Florence. Emiliani 1978, 30-34.

In contrast, in the Papal States, although an early form of safeguard for selected artefacts made of "modern materials" was prescribed in the first half of the 1600s, no easel paintings or canvases were mentioned in papal legislation before the second quarter of the 1700s. Indeed, only the *Editto Albani* of 1733 incorporated the protection of "pictures, mosaics, and paintings [...] [both] ancient and modern", finally challenging – although not ending – the primacy of antiquities in Rome.[59]

Besides the conceptual formulas, an interesting aspect to take into account in early modern legislation concerns the methods that were stipulated to discipline transgressions. The Florentine ordinance of 1602, for instance, did not specify any punishment for misdemeanours regarding the protected paintings: its clauses simply alluded to the general customs procedures to regulate cases of smuggling, possibly because inspections were quite effective in that sector. The Swedish *Placat* of 1666, as already observed, required specific assessments of damage to an artefact; nevertheless, the related violations were generally prosecuted with sentences that appear quite abstract to us, such as royal disgrace. The Dutch *Resolutie van Drenthe* of 1734, on the other hand, imposed a fine of "one hundred gold guilders [...] on top of the value of the sold or removed stones" to those who were caught breaking the law, with the final sentence handed down by the local judiciary. For its part, the papal *Editto Valenti-Gonzaga* of 1750 assessed the transgressions based on the damage caused to the goods, the offenders' standing within society, and their individual role in the misdemeanour. Following this system, different charges were prescribed for "porters, carters, sailors, boatmen, [...] diggers, vintners, labourers, stonemasons, [...] innkeepers, tavern keepers, servants", as well as officers, patrol executors, and ministers of the customhouses.[60] The top ecclesiastics, on the other hand, were asked to comply with the instructions in a rather vague, unclear way: most probably this ambiguousness was intentional, allowing a number of loopholes for high-ranking clerics to assemble their rich art collections. The overall aim of this edict was to improve the system of supervision for exports and excavations of artefacts in Rome, by establishing a body of three assessors to assist the main commissary. The new officials were expected to take care "respectively, of painting; sculpture; cameos, medallions, engravings, and any other antiquity", including all procedures related to the inspection and management of these works.

An interesting model of administration for both heritage and related transgressions can be found in the two injunctions introduced in 1780 in the Margraviate of Ansbach-Bayreuth and the Landgraviate of Hesse-Kassel in the German-speaking area. The contents of these documents are so closely related that it is possible to affirm that the latter – published in December – was an improved transcription of the former – published in April.[61] According to both texts, the local guilds of "woodworkers, locksmiths, bricklayers, and carpenters" were to conform to the prescriptions in order to avoid "severe punishments".[62] These, however, were not specified. On the other hand, the categories of possible offences

---

59 Emiliani 1978, 90-95. The *Editto Albani* was issued by the Cardinal Annibale Albani under Pope Clement XII.

60 For this quote and the following ones, see Emiliani 1978, 96-108. The *Editto Valenti-Gonzaga* was issued by the Cardinal Silvio Valenti-Gonzaga under Pope Benedict XIV.

61 Huse dates the ordinance of Hesse-Kassel to 1779, and the ordinance of Ansbach-Bayreuth to 1780. Nevertheless, I favour the information of Kroll, who date the former to 1780 as well. Huse 1984, 26-29; Kroll 2006, 39.

62 For this quote and the following ones, see Huse 1984, 26-29.

relating to heritage attributes and features were accurately defined, and in some detail. To give but a few examples, the artefacts located in churches were described as items exposed to the impairments of introducing new pews; the works located outside, as well as the buildings themselves, as subjected to the negative effects derived from "humid[ity] and damp, or [...] the weather conditions"; then again, "monuments made of metal, stone, or wood, and consisting of gravestones or other stones, as well as wooden tablets on which coats of arms or inscriptions are dug, carved or painted" could be harmed by wilful misconduct, such as smashing, cutting, perforating, and whitewashing.[63] As can be observed, the itemisation of objects introduced in these two ordinances followed the models of the papal and Scandinavian laws; at the same time, however, different solutions were proposed for specific groups of artefacts which were jeopardised by destruction. This was particularly evident in the regulation issued in the Margraviate of Ansbach-Bayreuth. After recommending the regular monitoring of the conservation of local castles and fortresses, this document required the preparation of detailed reports on the "location and nature" of the most unstable of them, which were to be collected in the archives of Plassenburg "before [these precarious structures] became utterly unavailable to posterity due to their total destruction". Based on this information, it can be surmised that this was the first regulation to endorse local archives as repositories of data related to heritage: connecting to the up-to-date attitudes of the Enlightenment, antiquities increasingly emerged as historical evidence, which were not only documents of the past, but also needed to be documented and recorded in turn.

The *Allgemeine Landrechts* (*General Land Law*) issued in the Prussian States in 1794 followed similar criteria of precision and conciseness as the two injunctions of Ansbach-Bayreuth and Hesse-Kassel. Included in a frame of broader prescriptions comparable to an early model of civil code, the Prussian rules on heritage supervision supported the "perpetuation and the promotion of the common benefit" according to a restrictive system of law.[64] Indeed, the punishments imposed for damaging, annihilating, and destroying artefacts were quite firm and resolute: the government was entitled to order and "penalise the failure to [care for heritage] by penal law". In the Prussian States, therefore, the prosecutions for breaking the directives on the protection of "statues, monuments, [...] and buildings" were not prescribed by means of financial penalties as in the other places, but in penal and criminal terms.

We next turn our attention to the Iberian Peninsula, namely the Kingdom of Portugal. In 1721, King John V (João V) issued the so-called *Alvarà de Lei* (*Law Permit*) introducing the first system of protection for "buildings, [...] statues, blocks of marble, milestones, metal sheets, medals, coins, and other artefacts", both in good condition and in states of disrepair, which were scattered across his realm [fig. 8].[65] Among these materials, he

63 These categories of objects and impairments are quoted with no significant variations in the ordinances issued in both the regions of Hesse-Kassel and Ansbach-Bayreuth.

64 For this quote and the following ones, see Huse 1984, 29.

65 For this quote and the following ones, see *Collecção* 1819, 415-418. I am grateful to Dr. Madalena Costa Lima from the University of Lisbon for providing me with a copy of this text, which I could use when research institutes in Europe were closed due to the pandemic.

EU EL-REY Faço ſaber aos que eſte Alvará de Ley virem, que por me repreſentarem o Director, e Cenſores da Academia Real da Hiſtoria Portugueza, Eccleſiaſtica, e Secular, que procurando examinar por ſi, e pelos Academicos os Monumentos antigos, que havia, e ſe podiaõ deſcobrir no Reyno, dos tempos, em que nelle domináraõ os Phenîces, Gregos, Perſos, Romanos, Godos, e Arabios, ſe achava que muitos, que pudéraõ exiſtir nos edificios, eſtatuas, marmores, cippos, laminas, chapas, medalhas, moédas, e outros artefactos, por incuria, e ignorancia do vulgo ſe tinhaõ conſumido, perdendo-ſe por eſte modo hum meyo muy proprio, e adequado, para verificar muitas noticias da veneravel antiguidade, aſſi Sagrada, como Politica; e que ſerîa muy conveniente á luz da verdade, e conhecimento dos Seculos paſſados, que, no que reſtava de ſimelhantes memorias, e nas que o tempo deſcobriſſe, ſe evitaſſe eſte damno, em que póde ſer muito intereſſada a gloria da Naçaõ Portugueza, naõ ſó nas materias concernentes á Hiſtoria Secular, mas ainda á Sagrada, que ſaõ o inſtituto a que ſe dirige a dita Academia. E deſejando eu contribuir com o meu Real poder, para impedir hum prejuizo taõ ſenſivel, e taõ damnoſo á reputaçaõ, e gloria da antiga Luſitania, cujo Dominio, e Soberanîa foi Deos ſervido dar-me; Hey por bem, que daqui em diante nenhuma peſſoa, de qualquer eſtado, qualidade, e condiçaõ que ſeja, desfaça, ou deſtrúa em todo, nem em parte, qualquer edificio, que moſtre ſer daquelles tempos, ainda que em parte eſteja arruinado; e da meſma ſorte as eſtatuas, marmores, e cippos, em que eſtiverem eſculpidas algumas figuras, ou tiverem letreiros Phenîces, Gregos, Romanos, Goticos, e Arabicos; ou laminas, ou chapas de qualquer metal, que contiverem os ditos letreiros, ou caracteres; como outro-ſi medalhas, ou moédas, que moſtrarem ſer daquelles tempos, nem dos infe-

rio-

Figure 8. Kingdom of Portugal, *Alvarà de Lei*, front page, 1721.

required in particular the identification of those "from the times in which Phoenicians, Greeks, Carthaginians, Romans, Goths, and Arabs" dominated ancient Lusitania. The earliest legal definition of heritage in Portugal embraced a great variety of antiquities, even those that were created when the country had been subjected to other peoples: these were believed to provide invaluable evidence to authenticate "the reputation and glory" of the state in the past as well as the present day. John V instituted the first domestic systems of heritage defence within his broader political strategy to promote and relaunch Portugal, considering that the kings before him had been more concerned with their overseas colonies than with furthering their cultural and political prestige in Europe. While particularly loyal to the Catholic pope, he was eager to gain international diplomatic recognition.[66]

Known as "the Sun King", John was exceptionally enlightened and ingenious in terms of his patronage of the arts. He attracted several artists from all over Europe, particularly Italy, to contribute to his new palaces and art collections in his kingdom, and funded the Royal Academy of History with the explicit aim of saving and studying Portuguese antiquities. Within his diplomatic policy, knowledge and the protection of antiquities served to re-establish international relationships, which had been overlooked for a long time, and reaffirm the role of Portugal in the fast-growing European networks. The sanctioning procedures stipulated in the *Alvarà de Lei*, for their part, were particularly interesting and shrewd. Violations of heritage were associated with counterfeiting money; the punishments dispensed for the respective misdemeanours were thus the same. Nevertheless, in the case of the *Alvarà*, the penalties applied only to "the persons of inferior status". All the other high-class people could in fact rely on the decisions of the Royal Academy of History – and perhaps the king in person – following a system of privileges that was very similar to the one established within the papal hierarchies at the same time.

Located also in the Iberian Peninsula, the Kingdom of Spain offered different definitions of "heritage" and "protection", and they were elaborated as a result of non-governmental endeavours. As had already occurred in the Papal States throughout the early modern centuries, in Spain the construction of a consistent concept of heritage progressed step by step during the 1700s, even though at this stage the ruling house of Bourbon issued no formal regulations on this subject. The earliest initiatives to identify monuments and antiquities, both movable and immovable, encouraged by King Ferdinand VI (Fernando VI) in 1753 in his *Real Decreto* (*Royal Decree*), were extended to include also the "renowned paintings and sculptures of dead artists" in the deliberations of King Carlos III in 1761.[67] Nevertheless, apart from these proposals, the announced intention to "follow the model of the most cultured states" of Europe did not evolve into an effective administrative system for supervising excavations, sales, and exports of artefacts in Spain.[68] The Bourbons'

66 For a historical and cultural contextualisation of King John V, see Nizza da Silva 2009. See also Levenson 1993.

67 Ferdinand VI approved the former projects in his *Real Decreto* of 1753, as described in the next paragraph. Carlos III, for his part, approved in principle the deliberations "on paintings and sculptures" proposed by the Academy of History in 1761, but he undertook no action to implement them afterwards. For a history of heritage protection in Spain, see López-Trujillo 2006; see also Maier Allende 2012. For deeper analysis on the initiatives of Carlos III in this field, see Gabardón de la Banda 2017.

68 Navarrete Martínez 1999, 429.

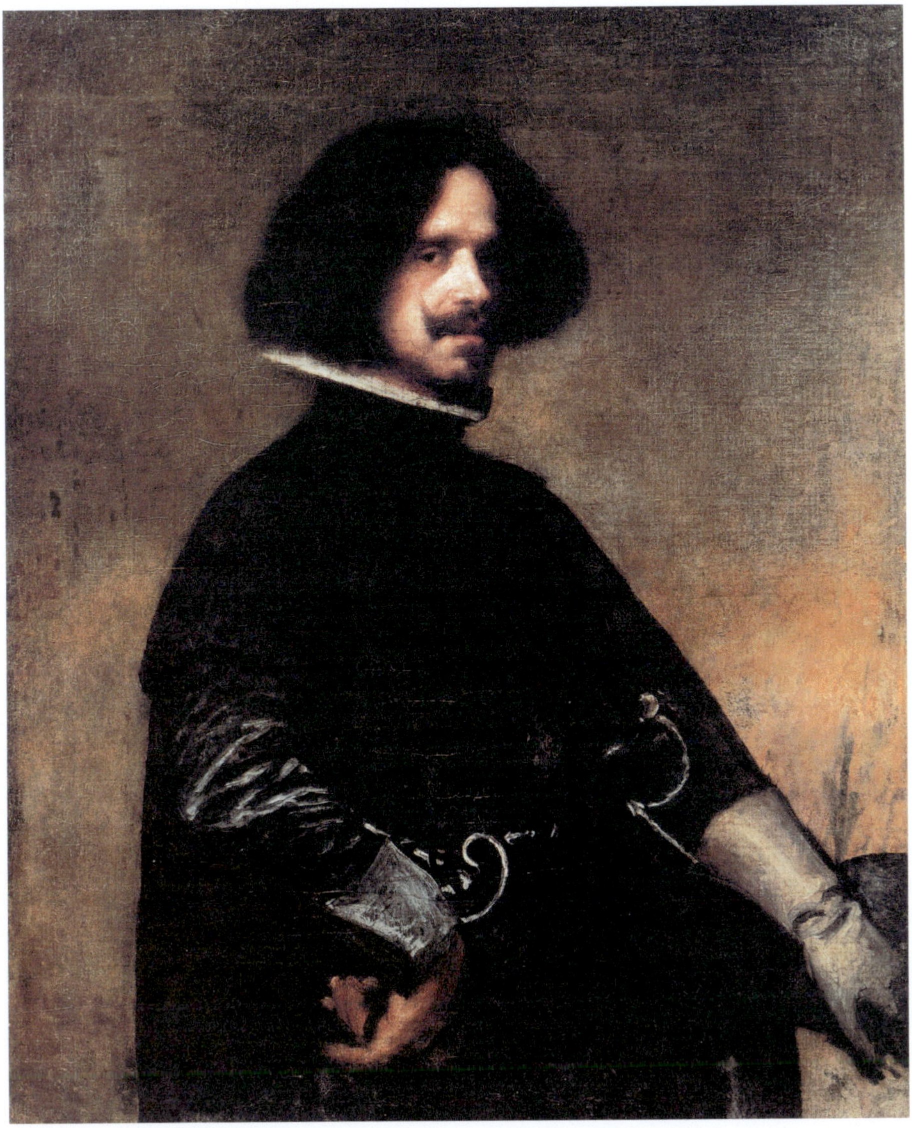

Figure 9. Diego Velázquez, *Self-portrait*, oil on canvas, 1645.

involvement on state heritage was, in fact, restricted to supporting the investigations and explorations undertaken by the two royal academies, the Academy of History and the Academy of San Fernando.[69] On the other hand, the royal family proved to be quite active in taking care of and expanding its private art possessions: for instance, as early as 1640, King Philip IV (Felipe IV) of Hapsburg appointed the artist Diego Velázquez as

69 For the history of the Royal Academy of San Fernando, see Bédat & Lafuente Ferrari 1989; García Sánchez 2008. For the Royal Academy of History, see Almagro Gorbea & Maier Allende 2003; Maier Allende 2002.

first Conservator of the Royal Paintings in Madrid, with the duty to monitor the state of preservation of each piece and increase the dynastic collections [fig. 9].[70]

Scholars have demonstrated that fundamental principles on the protection of monuments and antiquities in Spain were defined in the campaign of cataloguing launched by the Royal Academy of History in 1752, although it was endorsed, as already mentioned, by Ferdinand VI the following year. The initiation of this project has generally been attributed to the mighty Marquis de la Ensenada, Secretary of the State and personal advisor to the royal family [fig. 10],[71] who persuaded the king to appoint his protégé, the antiquarian and academic Luis José Velázquez,[72] to "discover and recognise all the antiquities" which would be useful to "illustrate and discover [the history] of Spain".[73] While the background of this mission, as well as the different stages of its conception and implementation, are thoroughly expounded in Spanish literature,[74] here it is relevant to consider some of the definitions that were included in the so-called *Instrucción de Viaje* (*Travel Instruction*), the criteria that the Academy of History designed to complete the catalogue. According to this document, Luis José Velázquez was asked to travel across the provinces and the minor towns of the state in order to collect information on the places "where battles [...] or other memorable events occurred"; he was also required to identify the "most magnificent buildings, such as theatres, amphitheatres, circuses, naumachias, aqueducts, bridges, trophies, arches, temples, thermal baths, and tombs" which were placed in "the famous ancient villages" throughout Spain. As can be observed, the Spanish academics constructed the survey on the basis of antiquarian knowledge, and in particular on the centuries-old Greek and Roman erudition of Southern Europe. On the other hand, they framed the data collection on the most advanced standards of classification derived from the Enlightenment: in fact, they expected their appointee not only to "measure, draw up, and explain" each of the items listed in the *Instrucción*, but also to carry out accurate excavations *in situ* and inspections in the local archives in order to obtain further solid information on them; this included also recording data on the state of preservation of each item. From this perspective, the project was based on a strong research methodology that went beyond antiquarianism. However, this broad mission involved also a secondary intention: to acquire "statues, bas-reliefs, cameos, engraved stones, medals, as well as other verified relics from antiquity" to expand the royal collections.

---

70 Diego Rodríguez de Silva y Velázquez (1599-1660) was the most acknowledged Spanish artist at the court of King Felipe IV, and one of the most renowned Baroque painters in Europe. For his role as Conservator of the Royal Paintings, see López-Trujillo 2006, 94-98.

71 Zenón de Somodevilla y Bengoechea (1702-1781), first Marquis de la Ensenada, was one of the most powerful statesmen in Spain in the 1700s. He supervised the Treasury, the Departments of Finances, Justice, War, and the Navy, as well as the office in charge of administering the Spanish colonies; he was Secretary and Notary of the State, Lieutenant, and personal advisor to several Spanish kings. Rodriguez Villa 1878.

72 Luis José Velázquez de Velasco y Cruzado (1722-1772), known as Marquis de Valdeflores, was an historian, writer, and tenured member of the Academy of History. He studied law and philosophy, and obtained a Doctorate in theology in Rome. Salas Álvarez 2010.

73 Copies of the original documents related to this broad initiative are kept in the online library Miguel de Cervantes: https://www.cervantesvirtual.com/. For this quote and the following ones, see the relevant texts in Part Two.

74 There are several studies on this extensive survey across Spain; for the purposes of this essay, I recommend Almagro Gorbea & Maier Allende 2003; Salas Álvarez 2010; Maier Allende 2002 and 2012.

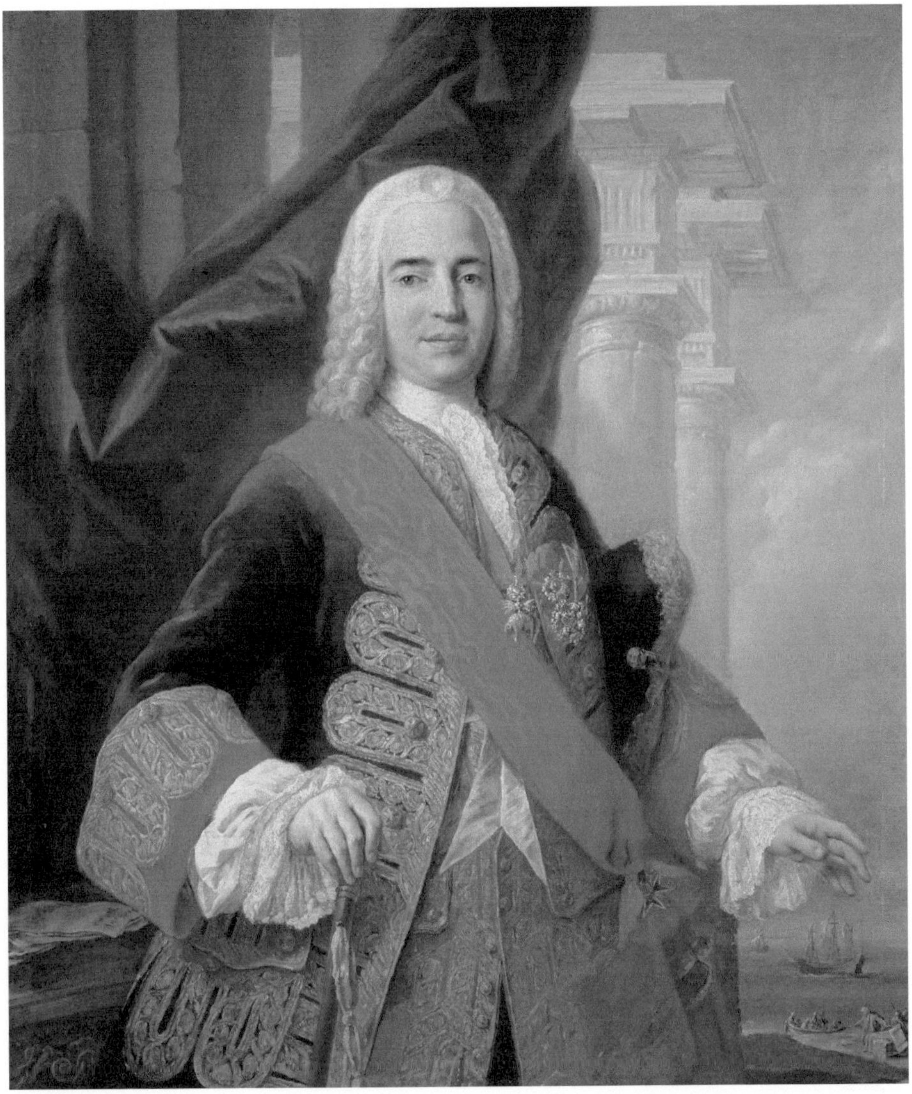

Figure 10. Jacopo Amigoni, *Zenón de Somodevilla y Bengoechea, first Marquis de la Ensenada*, oil on canvas, 1750.

In spite of the advanced criteria that the academy fostered in its *Instrucción*, this extensive campaign of cataloguing was never achieved, as Ferdinand VI stopped financing it in 1754.[75] As already mentioned, the Spanish Bourbons appeared quite reluctant to deal with state heritage in these years, and generally disengaged from any activity of protection and study that did not primarily involve their private assets. It is difficult to affirm whether the monarchs' approach was to neglect heritage preservation in general: it

75 Luis José Velázquez self-financed his mission across Spain for a few more years, publishing his *Noticia del Viaje de España* in 1765. The outcomes of his work are thoroughly explained in Salas Álvarez 2010.

seems likely that they rather understood dynastic heritage and state heritage as completely separate typologies of resources, and hesitated to define clear guidelines to preserve the latter throughout the 1700s. In any event, the peak of early modern definitions of heritage in Spain was reached in 1803, when King Carlos IV finally approved the so-called *Real Cédula* (*Royal Charter*) "on the methods to collect and conserve ancient monuments" [fig. 11].[76] This document established a long-overdue central system of protection based on refined typological classifications derived from the Enlightenment, supporting extended awareness on the importance of antiquities for the "knowledge of history and the arts":

> Ancient monuments are intended as statues, busts, bas-reliefs of any material, temples, sepulchers, theatres, amphitheaters, circuses, naumachiae, arenas, thermal baths, avenues, roads, aqueducts, gravestones or inscriptions, mosaics, coins of any class, cameos; pieces of architecture, milestones; musical instruments, such as sistrums, liras, castanets; sacred objects such as praefericulum, sìmpulum, lituus, knives for sacrifices, axes, aspersoriums, vases, tripods; weapons of any species, such as bows, arrows, lead bullets, shells, shields; civil [objects], such as weighing scales and their weights, roman scales, sundials or mechanical clocks, bracelets, collars, crowns, rings, seals; any kind of utensil, instrument of both liberal and mechanical arts; and finally any other thing, that is also still unknown, considered ancient, also Punic, Roman, Christian, and even Goths, Arabic, or Medieval [items].

This definition demonstrates an advanced appreciation of both local relics and the tools and artefacts introduced to Spain by other civilisations, such as *praefericulum, simpulum,* and *lituus,* which were respectively bronze vases, ladles, and rods used for rituals and sacrifices in ancient Roman society. At the same time, as well as providing a broad "catch-all" clause at the end of the list – "anything that is still unknown" – the chronologies were extended to artefacts of the Middle Ages, most probably for the first time in a legal construct in Europe. The value of musical instruments, weapons, and mechanical tools, such as clocks and sundials, was also recognised. With regard to protection, state heritage was entrusted to the Academy of History, which had to provide "the proper solution" for its optimal maintenance in agreement with the "authorities of the district" where each object was found. Scholars agree that the *Real Cédula* marked the beginning of legislation on the protection of antiquities in Spain.[77] In the context of our discourse, it can be added that it also inaugurated the involvement of the Spanish crown in broader state heritage.

For most of the 1700s, the state affairs of the Kingdom of Spain were closely intertwined with those of the Kingdom of Naples, as the house of Bourbon controlled both countries from 1734 onwards. Interestingly, Carlos III of Spain – the Bourbon king that we have already mentioned in the previous pages – had been monarch of Naples before moving to the Iberian Peninsula as the Spanish king in 1759 [fig. 12]. As sovereign of Naples, Carlos experienced the impressive discovery of Herculaneum in 1738, as well as the even

---

76 For this quote and the following ones, see *Real Cédula de S. M.* 1803. A copy of this text is also available online: https://books.google.it/books?id=4DCRrE36tQkC&printsec=frontcover&hl=it&source=ggbs_ge_summary_r&cad=0#v=onepage&q&f=false.

77 See the fundamental essay of Maier Allende 2003.

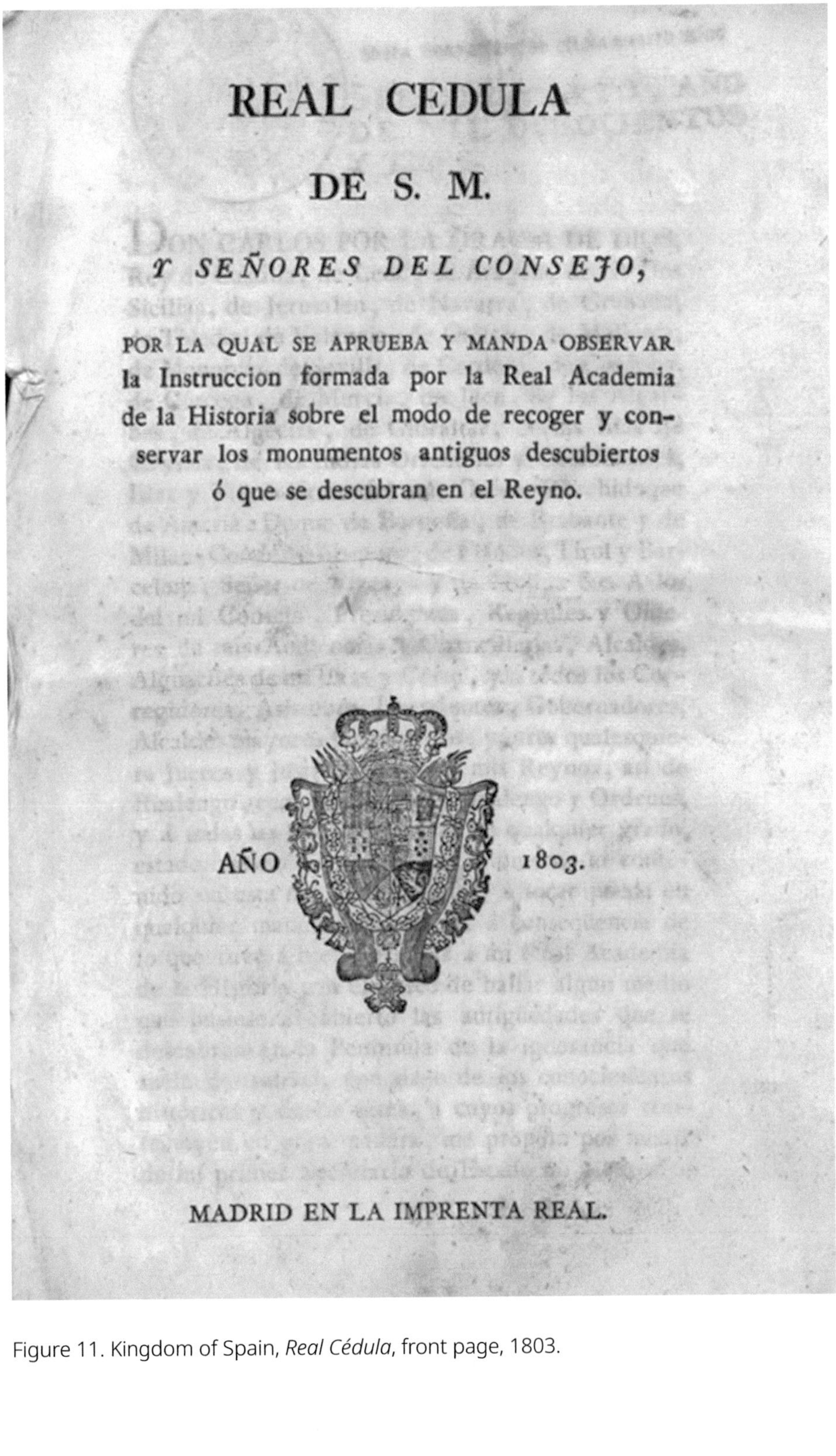

REAL CEDULA

DE S. M.

Y SEÑORES DEL CONSEJO,

POR LA QUAL SE APRUEBA Y MANDA OBSERVAR la Instruccion formada por la Real Academia de la Historia sobre el modo de recoger y conservar los monumentos antiguos descubiertos ó que se descubran en el Reyno.

AÑO 1803.

MADRID EN LA IMPRENTA REAL.

Figure 11. Kingdom of Spain, *Real Cédula*, front page, 1803.

more extraordinary unearthing of Pompeii ten years later. He encouraged excavations and collections of massive quantities of findings from the two sites, also organising initiatives for their restoration and conservation in a dedicated museum in his villa in Portici. In 1755, Carlos issued the so-called *Prammatica LVII* and the *Prammatica LVIII* (*Pragmatic Sanctions*) to protect Neapolitan heritage, explicitly quoting the model of "the most cultured States of Europe" for the measures he set up to control excavations and the export of artefacts.[78] In this, he was likely referring to the procedures that had long been adopted in the neighbouring Papal States. The two *Prammaticae* were intended to encompass any kind of antiquity under supervision, including "statues, both small and big, tablets bearing inscriptions, medallions, vases", as well as "ancient paintings, canvases, panels in wood, copper, and silver".[79] However, not all such items were automatically banned from export, but only those that for their "rarity, inventiveness, and excellence [...] deserve the highest esteem", that is, items considered top-quality according to Neapolitan artistic taste. Significantly, safeguards for ancient paintings "cut from walls" were also recommended, in response to the practice of removing frescoes from buildings, which was pioneered as a technique after the unearthing of Herculaneum and Pompeii. The laws also introduced one of the earliest forms of protection for domestic and common instruments found during digs. Clearly, the discovery of these two sites was also revealing new ranges of materials, and introducing innovative studies, classifications, and models related to the idea of antiquity. Together with these conceptual innovations, the *Prammaticae* also touched on the practical implications of heritage protection by establishing a body of three assessors. These were responsible for statues and monuments, paintings, and quarries and marbles respectively, carrying out all attendant supervision and inspection procedures.

It seems curious that Carlos of Bourbon, who was so active in decreeing instructions for the supervision of the Neapolitan artefacts in 1755, was so hesitant in doing the same for the safeguarding of Spanish heritage after he became king of Spain in 1759.[80] This circumstance makes it possible to maintain that it was actually the administrative establishment of the Neapolitan court – rather than the king himself – that worked so actively to issue the two *Prammaticae*, and urged Carlos to ratify them. In this regard, scholars have confirmed the crucial role of Giuseppe Canart, royal sculptor and restorer in Herculaneum and Pompeii, in taking care of the antiquities found in and around Naples; in 1751 he exhorted the king to release a regulation to control them, ultimately resulting in the *Prammaticae LVII* and *LVIII*.[81] Considering their legal constructs, these regulations can be regarded as one of the most complete systems conceived to protect state heritage in the mid-1700s; they embraced vast varieties of antiquities and new artefacts, providing for their concrete management thanks to specific programmes of inspection, collection, and restoration. On the other hand, it should be noted that – as opposed to the Spanish

---

78 For this quote, see Speroni 1988, 81. For a broad history of heritage protection in Naples, see D'Alconzo 1999.

79 For this quote and the following ones, see Emiliani 1978, 227-235.

80 For a detailed comparative analysis on the heritage protection in Naples and Spain in these years, see D'Alconzo 2011 and 2022. The indifference of Carlos III towards the Spanish antiquities is also underlined in Mora 1998.

81 Giuseppe Canart (1738-1790) was also one of the top experts in removing frescos from walls in Herculaneum and Pompeii; he was to be appointed Assessor for Statues and Monuments in 1755. For the role of Canart on the heritage protection in Naples, see D'Alconzo 2022; Toscano 2007.

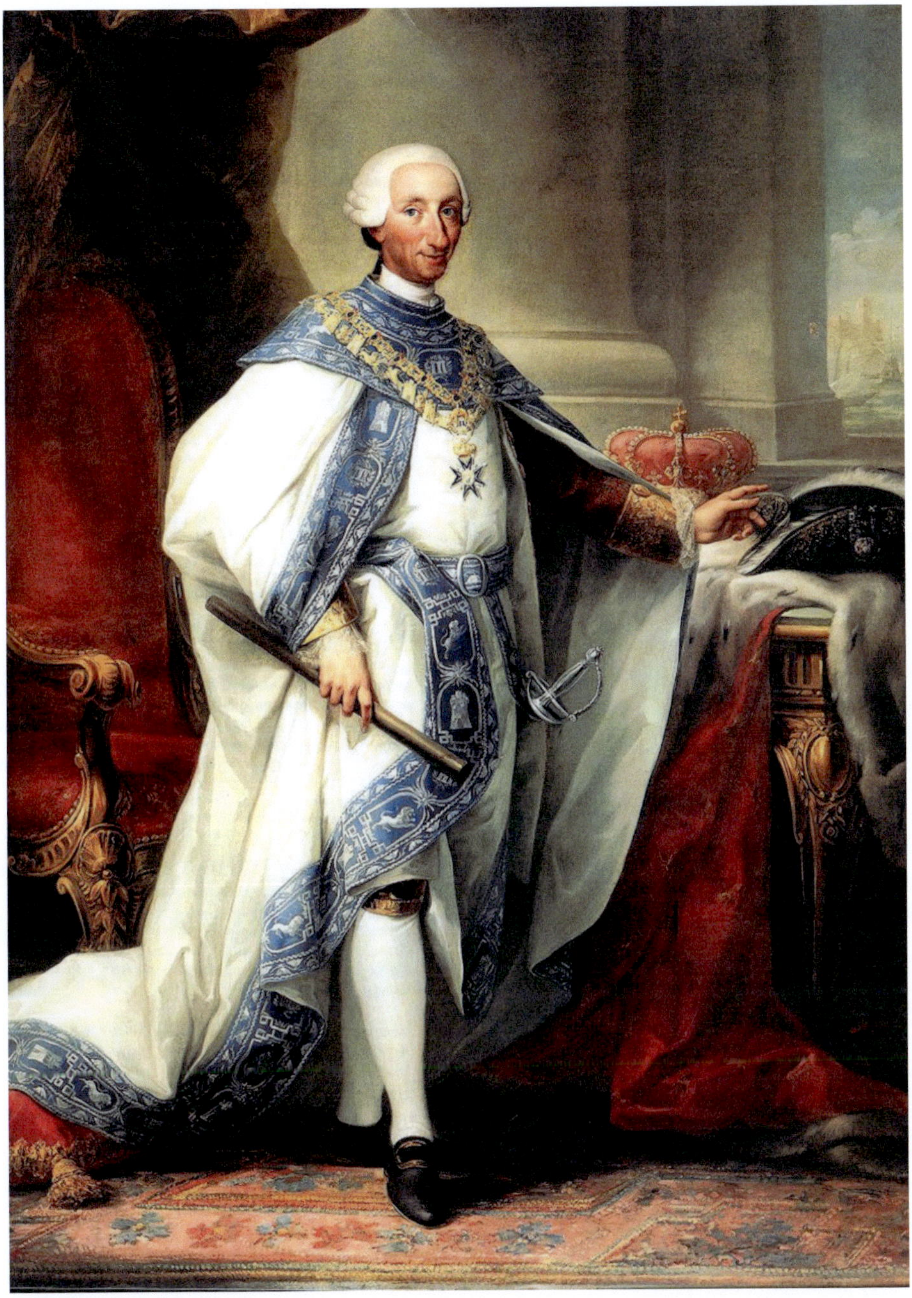

Figure 12. Mariano Salvador Maella, *Carlos III of Bourbon*, oil on painting, 1783-1784.

Instrucción of 1753 – the Neapolitan directives did not cover artefacts and excavations in the remote districts of the state, focusing only on the richest and most popular sites in the central areas. Furthermore, the control of both private excavations and the exports of findings from these sites remained inadequate even after 1755 – although, from a broader perspective, at this stage it was a flaw in all legislation issued in Europe to protect heritage. In spite of these few weaknesses, however, the *Prammaticae* were reconfirmed in 1766 and 1769. Indeed, the Bourbons' different attitude towards the protection of heritage in the Kingdom of Naples as opposed to the Kingdom of Spain was protracted for many years, until the beginning of the 1800s.

Before turning our attention to specific organisational practices devised for heritage protection in the early modern centuries, the regulation issued in the Duchy of Milan in 1745 should be briefly evaluated. Signed by the Empress Maria Theresa of Austria, this document was probably presented to Georg of Lobkowitz, the governor of Milan appointed for the house of Hapsburg, by the members of the local Academy of Arts.[82] Quite interestingly, the system of protection they solicited for Milanese "paintings, sculptures, and architecture" did not draw inspiration from the updated practices that other European regions had trialled since the early 1600s, but rather followed the older model of the artistic corporations and guilds.[83] The decree reaffirmed the severe instructions on the making of artefacts imposed after the Council of Trent, and redefined also educational practices in the local art workshops. The Academy took control over the activities of artists and retailers, and was entitled to carry out inspections of ateliers, churches, and stores to check on the quality and the subjects of the artefacts, as well as the fulfilment of the rules. Even though this regulation focused on contemporary artworks and creative industries, as did the statutes of other academies in Europe also, its range of actions was broad, and covered activities connected to heritage and the fine arts in the entire Duchy. It governed old "paintings and ancient sculptures" as well: the academy was responsible for supervising their state of preservation, assessing the need to restore, reshape, and repaint them. With this, both rulers and academics aimed "to preserve the good artworks, which deserve to last over time and escape destruction".

Based on a model of management that involved, to some extent, the protection of the local artistic corporations more than the protection of the artefacts, the decree of the Duchy of Milan diverged from the innovative concepts offered in the laws issued in other countries in these years. Observed from a comparative perspective, it appears to contrast in particular the procedural models fostered within the 1780 directive issued in the Grand Duchy of Tuscany.[84] Promoted by the Peter Leopold of Lorraine, son of Maria Theresa of Austria, this protocol took part in a broader reformation of both the local markets and the related customs duties pursued to relaunch Tuscany in the international scene. Peter Leopold's intention to modernise the country also concerned, inevitably, the abrogation of the old-century restrictions that the Medicis had introduced to control the outflow of paintings in Florence, Siena, Pisa, Pistoia, and Arezzo. Liberalising the excavations and the exports of artefacts in the capital and its provinces, meant that the Duchy was deprived of a valuable method to protect local heritage, as well as one of the oldest procedures existing in this field in Europe. It is interesting that Peter Leopold followed a model of liberalisation in Tuscany that was diametrically opposed to the severe limitations that his mother Maria Theresa had applied in Milan some years earlier. The innovative Enlightenment principles of liberty and tolerance that spread in second half

82 Johann Georg Christian von Lobkowitz (1686-1755) was a Bohemian prince and field marshal for the Holy Roman Empire; from 1743 to 1745 he was governor of the Duchy of Milan and Commandant of the imperial army in Italy. Wolf 1884, 50.

83 For this quote and the following ones, see Emiliani 1978, 153-159.

84 Emiliani 1978, 52-54.

of the 1700s might have strongly influenced the different attitude of Peter Leopold towards heritage.[85] Whatever the cause of such a divergence was, however, the systems prescribed to govern artefacts in both the Duchy of Milan and the Grand Duchy of Tuscany in the 1700s were destined to be surpassed by more functional and balanced models of protection. As will emerge in the next pages, the legal and administrative instrument that a few European states established to identify public heritage was to become the most successful of these models.

Fortune of a Paradigm

Among the procedures defined in the early modern centuries to govern artefacts, a few specific modus operandi require extended analysis, as the principles they are based upon gained growing importance for the development of heritage administration in the modern era. In particular, the general catalogue of heritage can be acknowledged as the instrument that introduced a first principle of prevention within the older methods of supervision and inspection, going beyond systems of punishment that were provided within the earliest regulations for safeguarding artefacts. Although both its configuration and organisation progressed substantially over time, the catalogue conceived in the early modern centuries embodied broad implications for heritage knowledge that have remained valid until today. Most importantly, the first examples of such a tool surpassed the idea of private inventories compiled for individual art collections and properties, and embraced all materials that were protected for the collective benefit, that is to say, state artefacts.

As emerged in the previous pages, the first ground-breaking model of a general catalogue of heritage was launched in Denmark in 1622. In its conception, the project involved significant benefits and consequences for the state's central administration, even though only a limited number of records were effectively submitted after the king's request. Stimulated by this initiative, Sweden introduced an all-encompassing register of protected artefacts soon after the publication of the *Placat* in 1666. Towards the end of that year, the regent and dean of the University of Uppsala, Magnus Gabriel de La Gardie [fig. 13],[86] together with the campus secretary Johan Hadorph,[87] announced guidelines to compile systematised reports on the artefacts that were scattered across the kingdom. Their protocol addressed "archbishops, bishops, and superintendents" in the Swedish counties, as well as religious ministers in the towns; while the latter were asked to list and describe the works located in their parishes, the former were in charge of collecting and revising reports from the communities under their jurisdictions, in order to standardise

85 Recent scholars acknowledged Peter Leopold as an enlightened monarch, who pursued welfare and advancement for the Grand Ducky of Tuscany; he was the first king ever to abolish dead penalty and torture in 1786. For a historical and cultural contextulisation of Peter Leopold and his reformations, see Baldacci 2000.

86 Magnus Gabriel de La Gardie (1622-1686) was a politician, *Rector Illustris* of the University of Uppsala from 1654, and member of the Regency from 1660 to 1672. Between 1644 and 1654, he was the favourite of Queen Christina of Sweden; he was her personal advisor and Great Treasurer of the State. Collijn 1933; Schück 1932; Ullgren 2015. See also Adlercreutz 2017; Mannoni 2021a.

87 Johan Hadorph (1630-1693) was secretary of the University of Uppsala from 1660. In 1667 he was appointed Director of the Swedish Academy of Antiquities and two years later became secretary of the National Archives. He had extensive knowledge on local antiquities and published several books of Swedish tales. Schück 1932.

them and send them to the central offices.[88] Obviously this extensive plan aimed to obtain methodical accounts of all the antiquities in Sweden, in order to allow subsequent – effortless – analysis of the data they contained. The idea of heritage fostered in the protocol was grounded basically on the definitions of antiquity provided in the *Placat*, further extended to include "liturgical books, chronicles, letters, notes from monasteries and cloisters, books containing legal texts, collections of tales and chants, [...] manuscripts, seals, and coins".[89] Even though these materials were not regarded as items worthy of protection, they could in fact provide important data in the campaign of cataloguing, as they contained evidence to aid understanding of the ancestral history of Swedish people. In this regard, it is noteworthy that the so-called *Placat II* of 1686 would also include "metal vessels, [...] objects that had been hidden in the earth in unruly times, [as well as] finds from lakebed or seabed" under protection.[90] Evidently, the categories of materials that were thought of as essential to identify Sweden and its history were being expanded step by step.

In 1667 the Board of Regents instituted a *Collegium Antiquitatis* – an Academy of Antiquities – within the University of Uppsala, entrusting to it the analysis and publication of the most significant Swedish antiquities based on information that was delivered in the reports.[91] Scholars have generally identified this institution as one of the oldest archaeological services in Europe.[92] It was composed of an exceptional team of collaborators, including a specialist in Gothic tales, two general assistants, a secretary, two draftsmen, two engravers, a typographer, an editor, and a messenger, alongside the foremost academics and antiquarians in charge. In the light of this, it is possible to affirm that the Swedish academy was one of the most efficient state institutions working to promote and disseminate antiquarian knowledge in the early modern centuries. The available information reveals that not only did it succeed in studying and publishing the data provided by numerous reports after the campaign of 1666-1667, but it also launched a new program of cataloguing for state heritage in 1690.[93]

Alongside the Swedish catalogue, one can position the so-called *Nota dei Quadri* (*Note of Paintings*) devised in the Republic of Venice towards the end of the early modern centuries. In broad terms, Venice was the only Old Italian State where the local administrative and judiciary systems were structured on common law; this meant that, while the local Senate did not issue any edict on heritage protection, the upkeep of public paintings and books was generally achieved by the concrete practices of cleaning and restoration. These procedures, however, proved to be insufficient. In 1773, the scholar and librarian

---

88 Tuneld 1960, VII-XII. I am grateful to the librarians of the University of Erlangen for allowing me to consult Tuneld's extremely rare volume. As mentioned in the Introduction, the translation of the 1666 protocol could not be achieved for the purposes of this volume.

89 Adlercreutz 2017, 9.

90 Adlercreutz 2017, 9. As mentioned in the Introduction, the translation of the 1686 *Placat II* could not be achieved for the purposes of this volume.

91 For the history of the Swedish Academy of Antiquities in these years, see Schück 1932. See also Adlercreutz 2017; Mannoni 2021a; Schnapp 1994, 176-177.

92 This observation and the following data are in Schnapp 1994, 176-177. Archaeology as a discipline developed only in the 1800s; in the 1600s, the analysis of old relics and the past chiefly followed the approaches of antiquarianism.

93 The results of these two campaigns of cataloguing are widely described in Tuneld 1960, VII-XX.

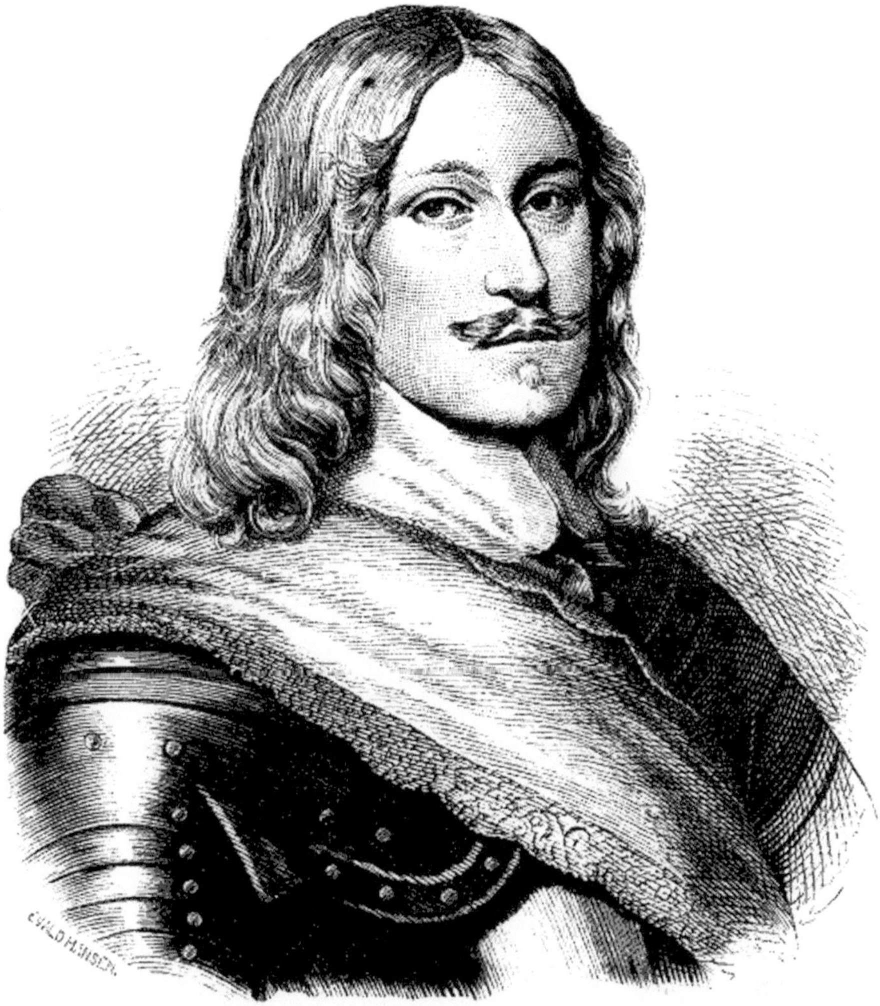

Figure 13. Unknown artist (E. Mansen?), *Magnus Gabriel de La Gardie*, litography, 1862-1887.

Anton Maria Zanetti [fig. 14] submitted a *memorandum* to the Tribunal of Inquisitors complaining about the miserable state and abandonment of "the public paintings existing in the palaces, churches, and other places" in the lagoon, including also monasteries, schools, and confraternities.[94] He explicitly condemned the widespread damage of these pieces, as well as their state of neglect and disrepair, taking into consideration the city's high level of humidity, and denounced the fact that several were missing altogether from their respective locations, "since they have been arbitrarily removed and sold for a little money to foreigners". In order to limit further losses of these works, and monitor their

94 Anton Maria Zanetti (1706-1778) was an art historian and Keeper of the Library of San Marco. He published several books; in his *Varie Pitture a fresco de' principali Maestri Veneziani* of 1760, and his *Della Pittura Veneziana e delle opere pubbliche de' Veneziani Maestri* of 1771, he already recorded the miserable state of neglect of Venetian paintings. For the role of Zanetti in setting up the Venetian catalogue, as well as this quote and the following ones, see Piva 2014, 83-114. See also Speroni 1988, 135-188.

state of preservation, Zanetti proposed an innovative program of protection based on their systematic cataloguing and regular inspection, to be entrusted to a specific officer. Within this plan, it can be observed, he formulated possibly the first ever concept of a catalogue for heritage that was specifically endangered. The subsequent steps that the State Inquisitors of Venice undertook were of crucial importance: they established the chair of Inspector of Public Paintings, with the assignment "to catalogue, supervise on the sales and relocations [of the artefacts], submit a report on their state of conservation every second month, as well as propose their restoration, and control the restorers".[95] Such a demanding and extensive task was, not surprisingly, assigned to Zanetti himself.

Within one year, Zanetti had listed all the "renowned paintings of the famous and distinguished professors" in Venice in a public register, that is, the worthy pieces which were endangered through loss or destruction. This record was structured on the basis of the artist, the subject, and the location of each item, following the topographic order of the Venetian *sestieri* – the city neighbourhoods.[96] In 1774, the plan was extended also to the Venetian provinces on the mainland: Brescia, Padua, Verona, and Bergamo. According to the procedures provided in the *Notes*, a copy of the relevant register was deposited in the institute where each painting was located; one individual there was to be responsible for its conservation, and assumed legal responsibility for the artwork in case of loss, illicit sale, or damage. It is fundamental that Zanetti's project coincided with a further substantial initiative in Venice, that is, the reformation of one of the oldest public workshops of restoration in Europe. Originally established at the end of the 1600s, this studio was completely reorganised under the direction of the manager and restorer Pietro Edwards in 1777.[97] Using this facility, after the extensive campaign of cataloguing, the Republic of Venice inaugurated a systematic program for the maintenance and restoration of all the public paintings belonging to the state.

A final model of catalogue that is worth mentioning was the record of the *Esatte Assegne* (*Exact Records*) introduced in the Papal States within the *Editto Doria Pamphilj* of 1802. Scholars have generally understood this decree as the final break between the old and the new understanding of heritage in Italy.[98] Indeed, together with several new practices of administration, it initiated an early form of control for art collectors in Rome, systematising the vagueness regarding private and public properties that had informed early modern laws. Art collectors were described in the edict as "the private owners of galleries containing statues and paintings, museums of sacred and profane antiquities, [...] and all the [...] proprietors of one or several ancient items or precious artworks": all were asked to submit a precise description of their possessions to the Chamber secretaries within one month after the edict was issued. As one might imagine, the efforts of the state to oversee private collections was not well received by the local aristocrats and art dealers, and several cases of breach were reported. For instance, Prince Camillo Borghese

95 For this quote and the following one, see Piva 2014, 101. After archival research, Piva confirmed that Zanetti also defined the duties of the Inspector of Public Paintings.

96 Speroni 1988, 157.

97 Pietro Edwards (1744-1821) became Director for the Restoration of Public Paintings in 1778; since 1771 he had devised new practices and trained specialists to achieve the optimal restoration of paintings in the public workshop in Venice. Conti 1988, 154-187.

98 Rossi Pinelli 1978. See also Emiliani 1978; Mannoni 2022a.

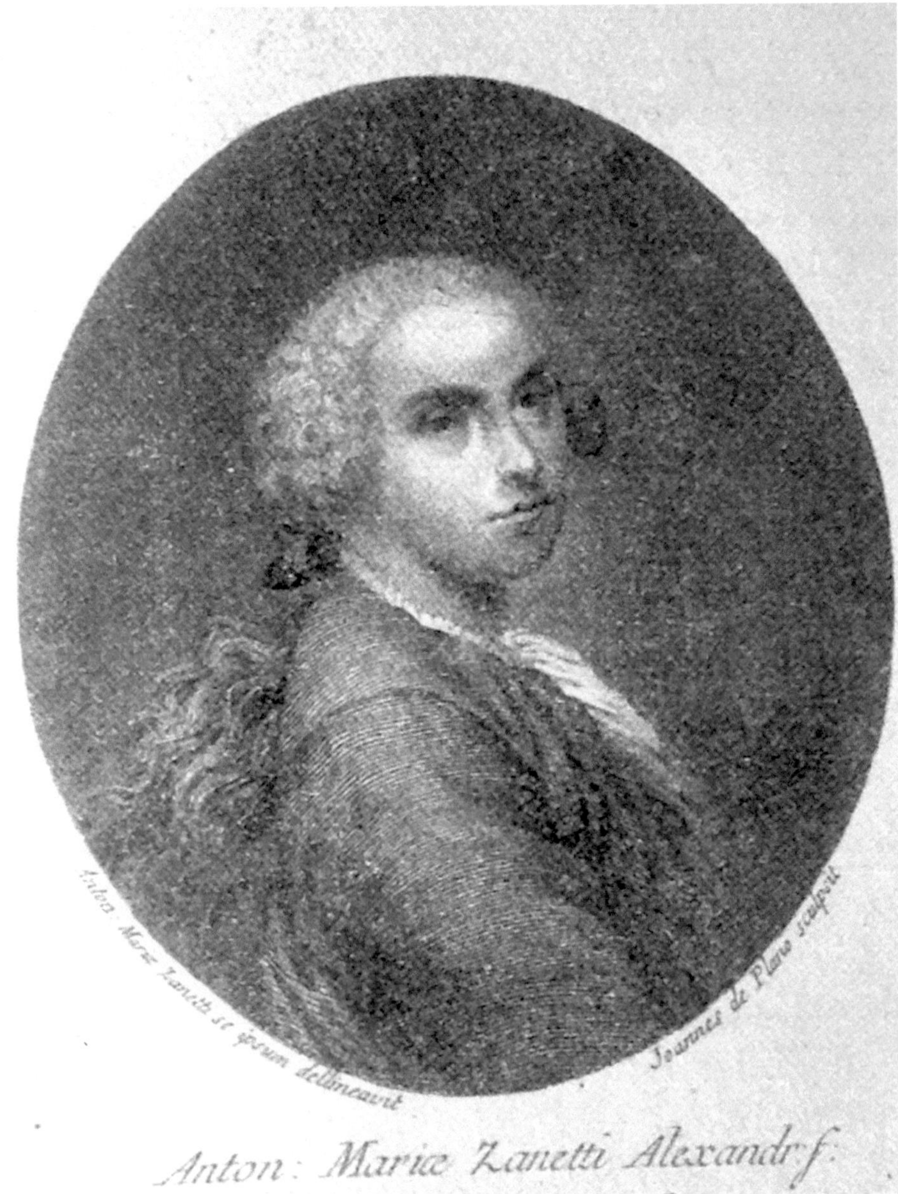

Figure 14. Unknown artist, *Anton Maria Zanetti the young*, engraving after a self-portrait, after 1778.

reported only "one statue without its head", although he had rich collections, while the art dealer Alexander Day refused to submit his note at all.[99] In spite of the strong resistance, however, more than 150 *Esatte Assegne* were presented to the papal office over the subsequent month, indicating that awareness on the collective advantage of protecting

99 Rossi Pinelli 1978, 38.

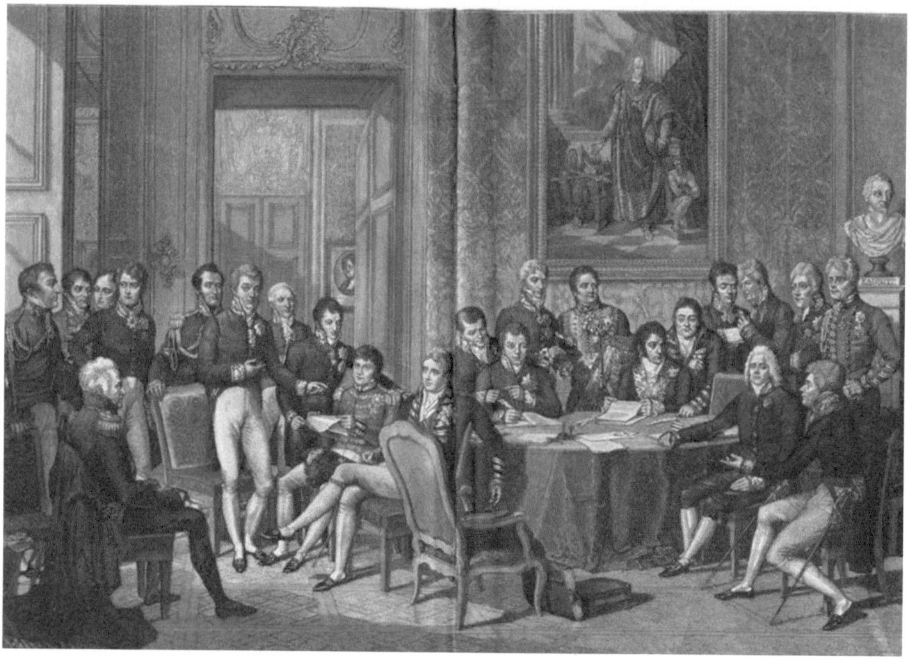

Figure 15. Jean Baptiste Isabey, *The Congress of Vienna*, engraving after a watercolour, 1815.

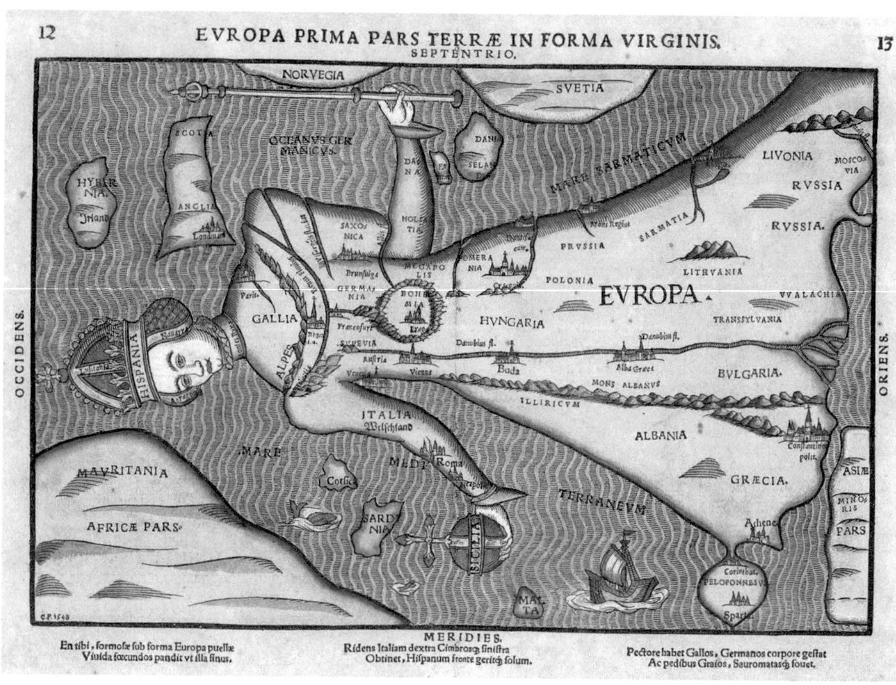

Figure 16. Heinrich Bünting, *Europa Prima Pars Terrae in Forma Virginis*, print, 1582.

artefacts – including private ones – was expanding more and more. From the perspective of our discourse, it can be affirmed that the issuing of the *Editto Doria Pamphilj* marked the conclusion of early modern legislation on the safeguarding of artefacts, and inaugurated modern approaches to the legal protection of heritage.

The end of the early modern era brought a profound change within the general understanding of heritage and its related symbolic value. Between the late 1700s and the early 1800s, the confiscations of artefacts carried out by Napoleon across Europe played a significant role in expanding the awareness of the need to defend local treasures, both among the governors and the common citizens. The subsequent refinement of codified law, together with the development of national states, transformed the idea of protection as well: in the 1800s, an increasing number of states adopted measures to supervise public and private artefacts, while concepts of heritage expanded to include new categories of objects and cultural expressions. In this framework, it is relevant that the Congress of Vienna of 1814-1815 deeply influenced the configuration of heritage protection not only within the individual states, but also in Europe *en bloc* [fig. 15]. Indeed, the decision of the allies to return the works confiscated by Napoleon to their pertinent countries can be interpreted as an early international rule on the customary restitution of heritage in post-war times. The Vienna resolution to "return [all of them] with no negotiation",[100] in particular, constituted the basis on which the 1954 Hague *Convention for the Protection of Cultural Property in the Event of Armed Conflict* would be founded.[101] In its wide impact on heritage safekeeping, the Congress of Vienna consolidated and raised to the highest level the legitimacy and the determination of each state to protect artefacts – principles that had gradually evolved in Europe during the early modern centuries [fig. 16].

100 For the quote and the negotiations on the return of the confiscated artefacts agreed during the Congress of Vienna, see Wescher 1988, 141-157.

101 See the Unesco webpage: http://www.unesco.org/new/en/culture/themes/armed-conflict-and-heritage/convention-and-protocols/1954-hague-convention/.

Part Two

Laws and Edicts in Early Modern European States

4

The Papal States

1
Etsi in Cunctarum orbis Provinciarum

Reintegratio antiqui officii et iurisdictionis magistrorum viarum Urbe eiusque districtus.

Summarium.
Exordium – 1. Causae huius dicti restituendi officii – 2. Restituitur – 3. Magistri creantur – 4. Qualis eorum sit iurisdictio – 5. Notarii eis dati – 6. Officialibus caeteris praecipitur ut eis obediant – 7. Syndicari et molestari in officio non debent – 8. Contrariorum derogatio.

Martinus episcopus servus servorum Dei, ad perpetuam rei memoriam, dilectis filiis nobilibus viris Baptistae Petri Matthaei, et Bocio de Stinobis, civibus Romanis, viarum Urbis nostrae Rom. magistri, salutem et apostolicam benedictionem.

(Exordium)
Etsi in cunctarum orbis provinciarum, iuxta commissum nobis desuper officium, decore atque florentia delectemur, dignum tamen non immerito reputamus et congruum, ut Urbis nostrae Rom., quam Principes apostolorum Petrus, et in sortem similem vocatus Paulus, tidei orthodoxae cardines, aliique victoriosi innumeri martyres sui sanguinis aspersione inundarunt, amplior nos cura perstringit, ut Urbs ipsa, quae divinis et humanis legibus perantea floruit, illiusque districius, nostris in temporibus, divina favente clementia, bonis assurgat moribus, et salutaribus in antea successibus commendetur.

(Causae huius dicti restituendi officii)
1. Cum itaque (sicut rei evidentia palam edocet) Urbs districtusque praedicti, quos paterno amplectimur affectu, ex defectu officii magistrorum, quod antiquitus pro viarum, stratarum, platearum et locorum aliorum tam publicorum quam privatorum, necnon aedificiorum lapideorum et ligneorum, parictum tignorum, banchorum, tectorum, tabulatuum, mignanorum, apothecarum et pontium, portarum, passorum, acquarum decuursum, canalium et meatuum, necnon urbanorum et rusticorum praediorum, pratorum, hortorum atque vinearum, finium, restaurationum, servitutum et libertatum administratione, institutum et ordinatum extitit, in praemissis et eorum singulis grandem deformitatem seu ruinam potius abhominabilem patiantur

et iacturam. Et (sicut accepimus) nonnulli ex civibus, habitatoribus et incolis Urbis et districtus praedicti, macellarii, videlicet, piscarii, sutores, palamantellarii, diversique artifices, loca ac etiam ergasteria Urbis inhabitantes, suasque inibi artes exercentes, viscera, intestina, capita, pedes, ossa, cruores, necnon pelles, carnes et pisces corruptos, resque alias foetidas atque corruptas in viis, stratis, plateis et locis publicis atque privatis huiusmodi proiicere atque occultare: nonnulli etiam ex civibus, habitatoribus et incolis eiusdem (quos aeque fatigat ambitio et repudianda conducit temeritas) mala malis invenientes, vias, stratas, plateas, loca publica, privata et ecclesiastica, ausu temerario atque sacrilego occupare, diripere, alienare et in usus proprios deducere, de illis quoque pro suo nutu disponere non verentur, intelligere nolentes, quantum huiusmodi sui excessus humanorum corporum sanitatem, aeris puritatem et enimarum salutem impediant.

(Restituitur)

2. Nos igitur praemissas deformitates et excessus huiusmodi sub dissimulatione ulterius praeterire non valentes, attendentes propterea, quod in eadem Urbe, multo temporis decursu, neglectum fuit, in usum plurimum pullulasse, et praemissis incommodis possetenus occurrere cupientes; officium magistratus huiusmodi, iuxta illius antiquam institutionem, auctoritate apostolica renovamus, suscitamus et reintegramus atque restituimus.

(Magistri creantur)

3. Vobis quoque, quos nostros et Urbis praedictae zelatores existere non ambigimus, quosque fides, legalitas et prudentia, circumspectio atque multiplicia virtutum merita apud nos efficaciter recommendavit, magistratus officium huiusmodi, usque ad nostrum beneplacitum, cum solitis ab antiquo iurisdictionibus, potestatibus, honoribus, privilegiis, libertatibus atque oneribus universis, et cum potestate ad opus vostrum quoties et iuxta modum, qui vobis videbitur, submagistros faciendi et ordinandi, eadem auctoritate conferimus, et de illo etiam vobis providemus; vos quoque in praemissis et ea quomodolibet concernentibus ac ab illis dependentibus et eis annexis, magistros facimus, constituimos, ordinamus, et etiam deputamus.

(Qualis eorum sit iurisdictio)

4. Ut exinde omnes et singulas deformitates et excessus, in praemissis vel circa ea, pro tempore quomodolibet occurrentes, absque cuiusvis vocatione seu citatione, sed per viam regiam, iuxta datam vobis a Domino prudentiam, etiam per demolitionem quorumcumque aedificiorum aut rerum aliarum, seu modum alium, quaecumque reparandi, corrigendi et commendandi, necnon praemissorum seu eorum occasione gravatos, ut praemittitur, absque lite, sed summarie, simpliciter et de plano (oppositione seu contradictione aut quacumque temporis etiam centenali praescriptione, legibus et consuetudinibus generalibus quibuscumque, caeterisque contrariis non obstantibus) relevandi, restituendi et etiam reponendi, contradictores quoque quoslibet et rebelles privandi, bandiendi, arrestandi, incarcerandi, atque omnia et singula faciendi et exercendi, quae magistri praedecessores vestri, qui fuerunt pro tempore, facere, gerere et exercere potuerunt seu etiam debuerunt, vobis, huiusmodi durante beneplacito, mandatum damus ac etiam potestatem.

(Notarii eis dati)

5. Et, ut officii vestri huiusmodi liberior et facilior sit exercitatio, Nardum de Bustachiis, procuratorem, necnon ipsum et Nicolaum de Mutis, nobiles viros cives romanos, notarios vestri officii, eadem auctoritate, facimus et ordinamus.

(Officialibus caeteris praecipitur ut eis obediant)

6. Mandantes exinde omnibus et singulis nostri Capitolii marescallis, caeterisque officialibus, ut vobis et submagistris vestris atque vestrum cuilibet, in similibus, quae vestri exercitationem officii concernunt, pareant et obediant pariter et intendant. Insuper quascumque excommunicationis aut interdicti sententias, poenas et multas alias per nos seu praedecessores nostros in magistros pro tempore existentes forsan promulgatas (quarum formam et tenorem volumus haberi pro expressis) auctoritate praedicta cassantes et irritantes.

(Syndicari et molestari in officio non debent)

7. Vobisque, et occasione per vos in vestro officio factorum, ordinatorum seu quomodolibet administratorum aut quavis occasione gerendorum, fundorum seu administrandorum nullibi locorum in causam trahi, syndicari aut alias quovis modo per quemcumque, etiam auctoritate apostolica, molestari valeatis, eadem auctoritate concedimus.

(Contrariorum derogatio)

8. Antedictis constitutionibus et ordinationibus apostolicis, necnon statutis et consuetudinibus Urbis, caeterisque contrariis non obstantibus quibuscumque, decernentes exinde irritum et inane quicquid contra praemissa seu aliquod praemissorum a quequam, quavis auctoritate, scienter vel ignoranter, contigerit attentari.

Nulli ergo etc.

Datum Romae apud Sanctos Apostolos, secundo kalendas aprilis, pontificatus nostri anno octavo.

Dat die 31 martii 1425, pont. Anno VIII.

2
Cum Almam Nostram Urbem

Pius Episcopus Servus Servorum Dei, ad perpetuam rei memoriam.

Cum Almam Nostram Urbem in sua dignitate, et splendore conservari cupiamus, potissime ad ea curam vigilem adhibere debemus, ut non solum Basilicae, ac Ecclesiae ejusdem Urbis, & pia, ac religiosa loca, in quibus plurimae Sanctorum reliquiae resident, in eorum miris aedificiis manuteneantur, et praeserventur; verum etiam antiqua, et prisca aedificia, et illorum reliquiae ad posteros maneant, cum eadem aedificia ornamentum, et decorem maximum afferant dictae Urbi, et monimenta veterum virtutum, et incitamenta ad illarum laudes assequendas, existant: et quod etiam magis considerandum est, ex ipsis aedificiis, ac aedificiorum reliquiis rectius intueri licet rerum humanarum fragilitatem, et quod nullo modo in illis sit canfidendum, cum eadem aedificia, quae maiores nostri cum eorum ingenti potentia, et sumptibus maximis, cum immortalitate certatura arbitrarentur, vetustate, et aliis sinistris casibus diminuta, et collapsa etiam esse cernantur. Ex praemissis

igitur, et aliis rationabilibus causis animum nostrum moventibus, dilectorum filiorum Corservatorum Camerae, et Capitum Regionum, ac Civium dictae Urbis supplicationibus inclinati, foelicis recordationis quorumdam Romanorum Pontificum praedecessorum nostrorum, qui aedificia ipsa dirui, vel destrui prohibuerunt, expresse vestigiis inhaerentes, ac Statutum antiquum in eadem Urbe vigens, quo etiam id fieri sub certis pecuniariis poenis prohibetur, ratum, et gratum habentes, ac auctoritate Apostolica, et ex certa scientia tenore praesentium, confirmantes , et approbantes, sub excommunicationis, ac pecuniariis in ipso Statuto expressis poenis, quas contrafacientes eo ipso incurrant, omnibus, et singulis, tam Ecclesiasticis, quam Saecularibus, cujuscumque praeeminentiae, dignitatis, status, ordinis, vel conditionis existant, etiamsi Pontificali, aut alia quavis Ecclesiastica, vel mundana dignitate praefulgeant, auctoritate, et scientia praedictis districtius inhibemus, ne quis eorum directe, vel indirecte, publice, vel occulte, aliquod aedificium publicum antiquum, seu aedificii antiqui reliquias, supra terram in dicta Urbe, vel ejus districtu existens, seu existentes, etiam si in eorum praediis rusticis, vel urbanis fuerint, demoliri, destruere, seu comminuere, aut rumpere, seu in calcem convertere, quoquo modo praesumant.
Quod si quis fuerit, qui contra prohibitionem hujusmodi venire praesampserit, dilectis filiis modernis, et pro tempore existentibus Conservatoribus Camerae dictae Urbis, qui pro praemissis per eorum officiales diligenter inquiri faciant, artifices, seu laboratores in opere demolitionis, seu devastationis hujusmodi inventos, carcerari, eorumque animalia, instrumenta, et res alias capi, et arrestari, confiscari faciendi, eosque, nec non illos, quorum nomine id egerint, ad multae solutionem compellendi plenam, et liberam auctoritate, et scientia praedictis, earumdem tenore praesentium concedimus facultatem.
Volumus autem, quod nullus praeter Romanum Pontificem, alicui in Praemissis licentiam dare valeat; huiusmodi vero licentia nisi per Bullas, vel Brevia Apostolica concessa fuerit, nullius existat roboris, vel momenti.
Non obstantibus constitutionibus, et ordinationibus Apostolicis, caeterisque contrariis quibuscumque.
Caeterum, ut praedicta omnia ad communem singulorum notitiam deducantur, ne de eis ignorantia praetendi, seu etian allegari possit, praesentes litteras per Urbem publice praeconizari, et valvis Capitolii dictae Urbis mandavimus, fecimusque affigi; decernentes auctoritate praefata, ut huiusmodi litterae publicatae, et ut praefertur affixae, omnes quos concernunt perinde arctent, ac si eis forent personaliter, et praesentialiter intimatae.
Cum non sit verisimile, apud eos remanere incognitum, quod tam patenter omnibus extitit intimatum.
Nulli ergo omnino hominum liceat, hanc paginam nostrae confirmationis, approbationis, inhibitionis, concessionis, voluntatis, et constitutionis infringere, vel ei ausu temerario contraire.
Si quis autem hoc attentare praesumpserit, indignationem omnipotentis Dei, ac Beatorum Petri et Pauli Apostolorum eius, se noverit incursurum.

Datum Romae apud Sanctum Petrum, Anno Incarnationis Dominicae Millesimo quadringentesimo Sexagesimo Secundo, quarto Kal. Maii, Pontificatus nostri anno quarto.

3
Cum Provida Sanctorum Patrum decreta

Sixtus Episcopus Servus Servorum, Dei ad futuram rei memoriam.

Cum provida Sanctorum Patrum decreta eos sacrilegos esse definiant, qui Ecclesias, et loca sacra Altissimo dedicata de vastant, ipsorumque diripiunt ornamenta, sicut et illos, qui de sacro sacrum auferre impia temeritate praesumunt, parique utrumque fagitium, ac duplici poena coerceant, decet merito, Nos quibus Ecclesiarum omnium cura dispositione superna commissa est, pro detestatione tanti criminis, proque statu prospero, venustate, et decore ipsarum Ecclesiarum in sua decentia debite conservandis, omni vigilantia, et attentione curare, ne perversorum crescente malitia, eaedem Ecclesiae, et sacra Dei templa, praecipue Almae Urbis, nostro conspectui anteposita, suis nudentur ornatibus, et huius sceleris nequissimi patratores, debitam recipiant ultionem.
Sane fide dignorum relatibus, non sine admiratione, ad nostrum pervenit auditum, quod nonnulli iniquitatis filii se inaniter Christianos esse profitentes, et a quorum oculis Dei timor, et reverentia Christianae Religionis abscessit, de Patriarchalibus, et aliis Sacratissimis Ecclesiis, et Basilicis dictae Urbis porphyreticos, marmoreos, et alios diversorum generum, et colorum lapides ad ipsarum usum, decorem, et ornatum deputatos ausu sacrilego abstulerunt hactenus, et in dies auferre, eosque ad diversa loca per se, vel alios asportare praesumunt, in gravem divinae Majestatis offensam, Ecclesiarum earumdem deformitatem, detrimentumque animarum suarum, periculum, et scandalum plurimorum.
Nos igitur sacrilegorum impios, et temerarios ausus huiusmodi, quantum nobis ex alto conceditur, reprimere cupientes, quamvis praemissorum occasione nonnullorum Praedecessorum nostrorum sanctiones, et prohibitiones variae emanaverint temporibus retroactis, quas in eo dumtaxat, quod de Ecclesiarum, et Sacrorum locorum ornamentis, atque lapidibus antedictis minime auferendis, prohibent, vel disponunt, seu illos, qui hujusmodi flagitiosissimos, ac pene in Christiano orbe inauditos excessus perpetrare, et in his sacrilegas manus iniicere praesumpserunt, excommunicationis sententia innodatos fore declarant, in suo robore volumus permanere, omnes, et singulos cujuscumque dignitatis, status, gradus, ordinis, vel conditionis fuerint, qui ex praedictis lapidibus, sive aliis ornamentis earumdem Ecclesiarum, sive Basilicarum dictae Urbis habuerint, aut in surripiendo, servando, et retinendo, auxilium praestiterint, vel favorem, nisi a die habitae praesentium litterarum notitiae, ea restituant cum effectu: scientes vero revelent, et ad notitiam nostram saltem per minores Poenitentiarios nostros deduci faciant, majoris excommunicationis sententia, a qua nisi in mortis articulo, et debita satisfactione praevia, a nullo praeterquam a Romano Pontifice absolvi possint, irretitos esse: Ecclesias vero, et loca alia quorum usibus, et ornatui illa deputata fuerint, aut forsan (quod absit) deputari contigerit in futurum, tamdiu Ecclesiastico interdicto subjacere, quamdiu ad loca, unde prius ablata fuere, absque diminutione aliqua fuerint reportata, harum serie declaramus.
Et insuper quisquis suae salutis immemor sacrilegii crimen huiusmodi committere praesumpserit in futurum, ultra censuras praedictas, Ecclesiae, sive Basilicae, a qua lapides, et ornamenta huiusmodi abstulerint, mediam libram auri pro recompensa sibi irrogatae injuriae, absque diminutione aliqua solvere teneatur.

Nulli ergo omnino hominum liceat, hanc paginam nostrae voluntatis, et declarationis infringere, vel ei ausu temerario contraire.
Si quis autem hoc attentare praesumpserit, indignationem omnipotentis Dei, ac Beatorum Petri, et Pauli Apostolorum ejus, se noverit incursurum.

Dat. Romae apud S. Petrum, Anno Incarnationis Dominicae Millesiimo quadringentesimo, septuagesimo quarto, septimo Idus Aprilis, Pontificatus Nostri Anno Tertio.

4
[Praefectum]

Raphaelo Urbinati.

Cum ad Principis Apostolorum phanum Romanum exaedificandum maxime intersit, ut lapidum, marmorisque copia, quavis abundare nos oportet, domi potius habeatur, quam peregre advehatur: exploratum autem mihi sit magnam ejus rei facultatem Urbis ruinas suppeditare, effodique passim omnis generis saxa fere ab omnibus, qui Romae, quique etiam prope Romam aedificare aliquid, vel omnino terram vertere parumper moliuntur: te, quo magistro ejus aedificationis utor, marmorum, et lapidum omnium, qui Romae, quique extra Romam denum millium passuum spacio posthac eruentur, Praefectum facio ea de caussa, ut quae ad ejus phani aedificationem idonea erunt, mihi emas.
Quare mando omnibus hominibus, mediocribus, summis, infinis, quae posthac marmora, quaeque saxa omnis generis intra ejus, quem dixi, loci spacium eruent, effodient, ut te earum rerum Praefectum de singulis erutis, effossisve quamprimum certiorem faciant.
Id qui triduo non fecerit, ei a centum usque ad trecentum numum aureorum, quae fibi videbitur, mulcta esto.
Praeterea quoniam certior sum factus, multum antiqui marmoris, et saxi, literis, monumentisque incisi, quae quidem saepe monumenta notam aliquam egregiam prae se ferunt, quaeque servari operae precium esset ad cultum literarum, Romanique sermonis elegantiam excolendam, a fabris marmorariis eo pro materia utentibus temere secari, ita ut inscriptiones aboleantur: mando omnibus, qui caedendi marmoris artem Romae exercent, ut sine tuo jussu, aut permissu lapidem ullum inscriptum, caedere, secareve ne audeant: eadem illi mulcta adhibita, qui secus atque jubeo fecerit.

Dat. sexto Cal. Sept. Anno tertio. Roma.

5
[Commissarium]

Ditecto Filio Latino Juvenali Mannecto, Civi Romano, Familiari, et Secretario Nostro Paulus PP. III. Dil. Fili salutem etc.

Inter ceteras Romani Pontificis curas, illam quoque memorandam arbitramur, ut Almae Urbis nostrae Romae, cui sedem primo universalis Imperii, deinde sanctae Christianae Religionis Deus concessit, cum religionis cultu etiam memoria veterum Monimentorum conservetur.
Pertinet enim ad Fidei nostrae dignitatem, et gloriam, quod illius Caput in loco, et capite tanti Imperii erectum est, digne quidem cum nullum in Terris Regnum, nulla Dominatio majoribus refulserit virtutibus, quas Deus sua clementia remunerans, mutato per rerum humanarum instabilitatem Imperio, substituit Religionem caelestem, ut hac fulgentius, quam terrena potestate corruscaret.
Quo magis postquam omnis Idolatriae cultus ab ipsa Urbe sublatus est, et Templa Idolis dicata in Dei nostri, et Sanctorum cultum abjerunt, debuissent antiqua Urbis Monimenta conservari, ut in ipsis Templis, ad aeternitatem, et splendorem aedificatis, divina magnificentius, et diuturnius celebrarentur, et ab invisentibus Urbis ruinas Deo laudes redderentur, qui tantas opes, et potentiam hominibus concessisset.
Verum, quod non sine summo dolore referimus, factum est, imo fit quotidie, ut praeter Gothorum, Vandalorum, atque aliorum Barbarorum, et Graecorum, ipsius quoque temporis injurias, nostra incuria, atque culpa, imo etiam dolo, atque avaritia veterum decora alta Quiritum acerentur, conterantur, obruantur, asportentur.
Illa est culpa, atque segnitia sinere caprificos, et hederas, aliasque arbores, et vepreta innasci, quibus marmora, et moles findantur, mox evertantur; domunculas etiam, et tabernas vetustis molibus applicari, quae sui ignobilitate veterum aedificiorum splendorem deforment, et quod multo damnabilius est, etiam statuas, signa, tabulas marmoreas, atque aeneas, porphyreticos, et numidicos, aliorumque generum lapides extra Urbem in alienas Terras, ac Civitates asportari.
Illa autem est avaritia, ac dolus, seu crimen potius, confringi passim, et comminui haec omnia, et in calcem coqui ad domos novas aedificandas, ut, nisi provideatur, non lon. issimo tempore Romam veterem Romae requiri necesse sit.
Quid? quod etiam in hujusmodi confractione, et comminutione Antiquitatis etiam interdum ossa Sanctorum Martyrum, in ruinis hujusmodi sepultorum, comminui, et violari contigit, fierique, ut cum Romanae majestatis laesione etiam sacrilegium misceatur: ad quae arcenda praeter officii nostri partes, etiam privatus in Patriam amor Nos urget, ut illius, ex qua sumus orti, decus, et majestatem conservare pro viribus cupiamus.
Proinde ad te, qui eadem Patriae caritate incensus, in qua ex nobili, ac vetusta Familia natus es, et studio Antiquitatum noscendarum, et perscrutandarum, sicut audivimus, et ipsi perspeximus, semper flagrasti, multumque in eo studio profecisti, quique Nobis tua virtute, fide, ingeniique praestantia admodum carus es, nostrae mentis oculos direximus, tibique hanc curam, quae Nobis summe cordi est, ut debet, demandandam statuimus, firma spe freti, te in gratiam nostram, in Patriae decus, in tuum studium, ei rei omni solertia, et vigilantia incubiturum esse.

Itaque te Commissarium super hoc nostrum generalem deputantes, plenissimam tibi facultatem auctoritate Apostolica tenore praesentium concedimus, intendendi, incumbendi, et curandi, ut omnia dictae Urbis, et Districtus ejus Monimenta, Arcus, Templa, Trophaea, Theatra, Amphitheatra, Circi, Naumachiae, Porticus, Columnae, Sepulchra, Epitaphia, Eulogia, Moles, Aquaeductus, Statuae, Signa, Tabulae, Lapides, Marmora, et denique quicquid nomine Antiquitatum, vel Monimentorum comprehendi potest, quantum fieri poterit, conserventur, atque a vepribus, virgultis, arboribus, praecipue hederis, et caprificis, omnino liberentur: neve his novae domus, aut parietes applicentur, neu ipsa diruantur, comminuantur, confringantur, in calcem coquantur, aut extra Urbem asportentur.
Contrafacientes autem poenis pecuniariis, ultra generalem excommunicationis sententiam, quam in eos post monitionem a te eis factam, in hic scriptis ferimus, tuo arbitrio imponendis, et ad opus tuae curationis hujusmodi applicandis, mulctandi, et puniendi, quaecumque ad hoc pertinentia, et tibi visa quibusvis nostro nomine sub poenis tibi visis praecipiendi, unum, seu plures loco tui, ubi opus fuerit, cum simili, vel limitata facultate subdeputandi, omniaque alia curandi, perficiendi, et exequendi, quae ad nostram hanc commissionem effectualiter adimplendam spectare cognoveris &c.

Datum Romae apud Sanctum Petrum &c. die 28. Novembris 1534. anno primo.

6
De officio Conservatorum

Lib. 1. Cap. XV.

Ad Officium Conservatorum ante omnia spectat vigilem, ac praecipuam curam pro Statu Sanctissimi Domini Nostri Papae, et Sanctae Romanae Ecclesiae, et pro Urbis tutela, et Civium quiete, ac Sanitate Conservanda semper habere; et quaecumque Ædificia, et opera publica, praesertim antiqua, inviolata, et illaesa custodire: Contra quoscumque interceptores aut violatores eorum acerrime insurgere, et inquirere, ac animadvertere: necnon ut in omnes Templorum, et Ecclesiarum ornamenta, aut lapides surripientes, aut corrumpentes diligenter inquiratur, et animadvertatur per eos, ad quos pertinet insistere, et curare, et ut Sacraria, et Reliquiae Sanctorum diligenter in Urbe custodiantur invigilare: Claves tabernaculi, ubi inclusa sunt Capita Beatorum Apostolorum Petri, et Pauli in Basilica Sancti Joannis Lateranensis, per eos custodiri solitas, apud se, vel alios deputatos retinere...
Reficiendorum Murorum, Pontium, Aquaeductuum, et omnium Ædificiorum publicorum sollicitam curam, diligentiamque habere, eaque frequenter visitare, et ne vitientur curare &c.

De antiquis Aedificiis non diruendis

Lib. III. cap. LXXXI.

Ne ruinis Civitas deformetur, et ut antiqua Ædificia decorem Urbis perpetuo repraesentent; nullus cujusvis status, aut conditionis, quaecumque antiqua Urbis Aedificia, tam ea, quae intra, quam quae extra Urbem sunt, etiam si intra propria praedia, vel possessiones

existant, quovis quaesito colore diruere aut diminuere, aut dirui, vel diminui facere audeat, vel praesumat.
Qui contrafecerit, poenam quingentorum aureorum incurrat, et Senator de hoc inquirere debeat.
[1580]

7
Prohibitione sopra l'estrattione di Statue di marmo o di metallo, Figure, Antichità e simili

Ippolito di S. Maria Nova Diacono Card. Aldobrandino della S. R. C. Camerlengo.
Ancorche per diversi Editti, e prohibitioni fatte in diversi tempi da altri Cardinali Camerlenghi nostri Antecessori sia stato prohibito l'estrarre da questa città di Roma e dallo Stato Ecclesiastico Figure, Statue, Antichità, Ornamenti, e lavori di marmo, metallo, e d'altre pietre senza loro e Nostra licenza. Nondimeno intendendosi, che da diversi si procura far l'estrattione di simili cose prohibite, et volendo Noi a ciò provedere di ordine espresso di N. Signore datoci a bocca e per l'autorità del nostro Uffitio di Camerlengato, non recedendo dalli sudetti Editti, e Prohibitioni sopra di ciò fatte da detti nostri Antecessori, anzi quelli confermando e rinovando con il presente di novo prohibiamo, ordiniamo, e commandiamo, che nessuna persona di qualsivoglia stato, grado, dignità, ordine, e conditione si sia ardischi e presumi estrahere, o fare estrahere da detta città di Roma, e suo territorio, per li luoghi dello Stato Ecclesiastico, ne da qualsivoglia luogo di detto Stato, per fuori di esso Stato, per Fiume, Mare, o per terra Figure, Statue, Antichità, Ornamenti, o lavori si antichi come moderni, di marmo, metallo, o d'altre pietre di qualsivoglia sorte, etiam in pezzi, senza Nostra licenza, sotto pena della perdita di esse e di scudi cinquecento, d'applicarsi per la metà alla R. C. A., un quarto all'accusatore, e l'altro all'essecutore, ed altre pene etiam corporali a nostro arbitrio, secondo la qualità dei casi.
Inoltre ordiniamo e commandiamo che cavandosi in luogo alcuno con la debita Nostra licenza, e trovandosi Statue, o alcuna delle cose sudette, o qualsivoglia altra cosa sì di qualsivoglia pietra, come di qualsivoglia metallo, debbano li patroni del luogo dove si sarà cavato, li cavatori, et altri che ne haveranno notizia, o almeno uno di loro, haverlo denunziato in termine di 24 hore a Noi o al nostro Auditore, o ne gli atti dell'infrascritto Nostro Notaro, e quelle trattenere da farne esito, donare, o vendere per quattro giorni dopo la denunzia; sotto le medesime pene, e se saranno cavatori, oltre le dette pene di tre tratti di corda.
Avertendo ogn'uno a non contravenire, perche contro gl'inobedienti si procederà alle sudette pene con ogni rigore non solo per inquisitione, ma si starà alla semplice relatione d'un testimonio degno di fede. Volendo inoltre che le prove fatte fuori dello Stato vaglino, e provino contro li trasgressori.
Dichiarando, che qualunque straordinario possa fare inventione delle fraudi delle sopradette cose, purchè faccia la denuntia nelli medemi atti.
Volendo e decretando, che il presente Editto affisso, e publicato nelli luoghi soliti di Roma, astringa ogni uno come li fusse personalmente intimato, et ogni cavatore, e patrone di vigne, et altri luoghi, dove si caverà, siano tenuti, et obbligati tenere affisso il presente Editto, sotto le medesime pene.

In fede. Dato in Roma nella Camera Apostolica li 5 di Ottobre 1624.
Hippolytus Card. Aldobrandinus Cam.
F. Canalius Aud. – Ant. Lamb. Cam. Apost. Gen. Comm.

8
Editto sopra l'estrattioni, e cave di Statue, Figure, Intagli, Medaglie. Inscrittioni di marmo, di mischio, metallo. Oro, Argento, Gioie, e cose simili antiche e moderne

Federico di SS. Vito e Modesto Diacono Card. Sforza della S. R. C. Procamerl., dalla Santità di N. Sig. specialmente deputato.
Essendoci venuto a notizia, che non ostante Bandi altre volte da nostri predecessori, e noi, fatti publicare contro quelli che cavano, e fanno cavare in luoghi publici, e privati vicino all'edificij, fabriche, mura, e ponti antichi, marmi, mischi, alabastri, platee, travertini, piperini, speroni, et altre diverse pietre, con pericolo, e ruina di detti edificij, e vie publiche, et in oltre cavano, e fanno cavare in diverse cave publiche, e private statue, torsi, bassi rilievi, teste, piedistalli, colonne, capitelli, inscrittioni, medaglie, carnei, et intagli di valore di marmo, metallo, gioie, di mischi, oro, et argento, o agate, e crugnole, amatisti, et altre diverse materie lavorate, e non lavorate, e che dette cose cavate, e ritrovate ben spesso, ancorche vi siano pene gravi, e prohibitioni fatte, e comminate in essi Bandi vendono, scanzano, trafugano, et ascondono in Roma, e fuori, senza saputa, e licenza nostra, scienza, et ordine de padroni dalli proprij luoghi, e proprie case ritrovate con danno publico, e particolare, e gravezza delle loro conscienze, e così privano, e spogliano quest'Alma Città di Roma, e li proprij padroni delle più belle cose, che in essa Città si ritrovino, così antiche, come moderne. Per tanto noi per ovviare a simili fraudi, e dare il debito castigo a delinquenti, d'ordine espresso di N. Sign. datoci a bocca, e per l'autorità del nostro officio di Pro-Camerlengato, non revocando l'altri Bandi sopra a ciò da nostri predecessori, e noi fatti, e publicati, anzi quelli quando faccia bisogno confermando, et approvando, ordiniamo, e commandiamo a tutte, e singole persone, tanto Ecclesiastiche, quanto Secolari di qualsivoglia stato, grado, ordine, e conditione, che non possino per l'avvenire guastare edificij, nè fabriche antiche, muraglie di travertini, marmo, piperini, et altra materia, così sopra a terra, come sotto terra, nè rompere, o cavare statue antiche, o altri ornamenti di qualsivoglia materia, nè tampoco cavare, o far cavare vicino a detti edificij, mura, fabriche, archi, ponti, cimiterij, o vie publiche in qualsivoglia luogo esistenti, senza nostra licenza, e con intervento di Leonardo Santi Commissario sopra le cave, et antichità da noi deputato, o altri in suo luogo da deputarsi.
Di più ordiniamo, e commandiamo, che per l'avvenire non si possa da persona alcuna tanto Ecclesiastica, come Secolare, come sopra vendere, nè estrahere, o fare estrahere fuora di Roma, nè dello Stato Ecclesiastico fuori d'esso alcuna sorte di statue, figure, bassi rilievi, colonne, vasi, alabastri, agate, diaspri, amatisti, o altri marmi, gioie, e pietre lavorate, e non lavorate, torsi, teste, fragmenti, pili, piedestalli, inscrittioni, o altri ornamenti, fregi, medaglie, carnei, o intagli di qualsivoglia pietra, overo metallo, oro, argento di qualsivoglia materia antica, o moderna, né meno figure, o pitture antiche, o altre opere in qualsivoglia cosa sculpite, depinte, intagliate, commesse, lavorate, o in altro

modo fatte, o che siano state novamente ritrovate in cave, o siano esistenti in Roma, e fuori di Roma, overo appresso qualsivoglia persona, o in qualunque luogo senza nostra licenza, e visione, a fede della qualità, e quantità, venditore, e compratore delle cose sudette fatta dal detto nostro Commissario, e data nell'atti dell'infrascritto nostro Notaro, et con la solita attergatione dell'altro nostro Commissario, sotto pena della perdita della robba, che sarà ritrovata, venduta, mandata ascosta, scanzata, trafugata, o incassata in Roma, o fuori di Roma senza licenza come sopra, e di 500 ducati d'oro di Camera d'applicarsi la metà alla Rev. Cam. Apostolica, un quarto all'accusatore, quale sarà tenuto secreto, e l'altro quarto al nostro Commissario, il quale possa procedere in simil materie per via d'inquisitioni, e denuntie avanti di noi, o nostro Auditore, e se gli darà fede con il suo giuramento, o un solo testimonio, et altre pene etiam corporali secondo la qualità delle persone, e delitti a nostro arbitrio, alle quali si procederà sommariamente con ogni rigore di giustitia.

In oltre dichiaramo, che nell'istesse pene incorreranno li compratori, e venditori delle sudette cose antiche se le venderanno, o compraranno senza nostra licenza per portare, o mandare fuori di Roma come sopra, non intendendo perciò ampliata, nè revocata la prohibitione da noi fatta in simil materie sotto li 5, e 9 di Ottobre 1624, e le pene in esse contenute s'applicaranno come sopra.

E perchè spesse volte li Cavatori, e Muratori, Operarij, Vignaroli, et altre simil persone sospette vendono, trafugano, rompono, e portano di nascosto via senza saputa delli padroni statue, teste, camei, intagli, medaglie, gioie, anelli, et altri lavori antichi di valore di qualsivoglia materia, come di marmo, alabastro, oro, argento, metallo, o di gioie, o d'altre pietre, e quelli rivendono a Ferravecchi, Scarpellini, Scultori, o Rivenditori, o Bottegari, senza scienza delli padroni delle proprie cose, e de luoghi proprij dove se ritrovano così di nascosto, come palese, gravando le loro conscienze. Però commandiamo, che nessuna persona sospetta come sopra espressa, possa vendere sotto pretesto d'haverle ritrovate, o havute in qualsivoglia modo alcuna delle sudette cose antiche, nè meno nissuno quelle comprare che passino il valore d'un scudo, se prima non ne darà notitia nell'atti dell'infrascritto nostro Notaro, overo al nostro Commissario della qualità, quantità, persona che vorrà vendere e comprare le cose sudette, sotto pena della perdita delle robbe, quale si restituiranno al proprio padrone, et altre pene a nostro arbitrio etiam pecuniarie d'applicarsi come sopra.

Prohibiamo anco, che non sia lecito ad alcun Falegname, Operario, e qualsivoglia altra persona far casse, o farne fare per incassare statue, et altre cose antiche di sopra espresse, overo moderne lavorate, o non lavorate, ne quelle incassare, ne Facchini, o Portatori, e Carrettieri portare, ligare, imballare, involtare, nè dette cose trasportare da un luogo all'altro, nè meno barcarolo o marinari possono mettere in Barche, o Vascelli casse, o balle, o involtini dove siano opere antiche, o moderne sudette senza che non siano viste dal nostro Commissario, e con nostra licenza come sopra, sotto le sudette pene, et altre etiam maggiori a nostro arbitrio.

Commandiamo et ordiniamo ancora, che nessun Castellano, Doganiere, Custode, Portiero, Guardiano di passo, Commissario del sigillo di Ripa lasci passare per mare, per fiume, ne per terra alcuna delle sudette opere antiche, o moderne che siano incassate, o senza cassa, o involtate, lavorate, o non lavorate di qualsivoglia materia, dipinta o scolpita, senza la nostra licenza, e sigillata col nostro sigillo sotto pena della privatione dell'offitio, e d'altre tanto corporali, quanto pecuniarie a nostro arbitrio.

Prohibiamo di più, che non sia lecito ad alcuno Carrettiere, Facchino, Portatore, Mulattiero di poter caricare, portare, far portare marmi, travertini, alabastri, paperini, statue, colonne, teste, figure, bassi rilievi, et altre cose lavorate, e non lavorate di qualsivoglia pietra, da qualunque cava, o edificio antico, e di qualsivoglia metallo, se prima non haveranno havuto la nostra licenza in scriptis come sopra, la quale se le darà gratis, e quella doveranno portare seco mentre porteranno, o lavoreranno simil materie, e mostrarla al detto nostro Commissario, o altri deputati se saranno da loro trovati, e ciò per evitare ogni fraude che si potesse commettere, sotto pena di tre tratti di corda da darseli subito, e di 25 scudi d'applicarsi come sopra, e perdita della detta robba.
Parimente non possa, nè debba alcun calcararo, cavatore, o altre simil persone, come Scarpellini, Scultori, Orefici, Fonditori, et altri guastatori rompere, guastare, spezzare per far calce, o portar via, né rivendere alcuna sorte di marmi scritti, lavorati, statue, figure, o altri ornamenti antichi, nè meno fondere, guastare, o ammaccare figure, medaglie, intagli di metallo, d'oro, d'argento antichi, che habbino figuratione, o memoria di cose antiche senza nostra licenza, o visione del nostro Commissario, o altri deputati, quale si darà gratis, sotto pena della perdita delle robbe, di 25 scudi d'applicarsi come sopra, et altre pene etiam corporali a nostro arbitrio.
E perchè fin hora da noi, o da altri si è dato, e si dan ben spesso licenze, e patenti di cavare, far cavare tesori, marmi, travertini, statue, pozzolana, et altre cose diverse dove è necessario l'intervento, et assistenza del sudetto nostro Commissario, o altri da deputarsi, quali attendono acciò non si cavi in luogo prohibito, e pregiudiciale a publichi edificii, vie, o cimiterij come di sopra si è espresso, commandiamo, et ordiniamo a qualsivoglia persona di qualsivoglia stato, grado, titolo, et ordine, e conditione che doppo la pubblicatione del presente Editto debba dar nota di dette licenze nell'offitio dell'infrascritto nostro Notaro, fra termine di dieci giorni, sotto pena della rivocatione di esse licenze, e che non possino per l'avvenire cavare senza la visione, o assistenza del detto nostro Commissario, o altro deputato sotto pena di 25 scudi d'applicarsi come sopra.
Che nessuna persona, che facci cavare in publichi, o privati luoghi con nostra licenza come sopra, sia se Scarpellino, Cavatore, o Padrone de' luoghi, possa vendere travertini, marmi, alabastro, statue, et altre cose sopra espresse, che ne prevenga la parte alla Rev. Camera, se prima non saranno vedute dal detto nostro Commissario, e misurate da periti da deputarsi da noi, e datone la parte che perviene a detta Camera a nostra dispositione, nè meno vendere piombo, metallo, oro, et argento, o nessun'altra cosa che ne pervenga la parte alla detta Camera, sotto pena della perdita delle robbe, di 100 scudi d'applicarsi come sopra, et altre pene etiam corporali a nostro arbitrio.
Prohibiamo anco a tutti Scultori, Scarpellini, Rivenditori, Cavatori, e Padroni di cave il poter vendere e comprare per l'avvenire alcuna sorte di statue, marmi lavorati, e non lavorati, figure, bassi rilievi, colonne, piedistalli, inscrittioni, medaglie, carnei, intagli, o altre cose antiche se prima non haveranno dato la nota nelli medemi atti dell'infrascritto nostro Notaro, della quantità, e qualità della robba che vogliano vendere, o comprare, affinche si possi sapere l'esito, e l'esistenza in Roma di dette robbe sopranominate, sotto le pene come sopra.
Di più ordiniamo, e commandiamo a qualsivoglia Cavatore, Vignarolo, Operario, Muratore, Scultore, Scarpellino, e qualsivoglia altro Padrone si sia di strade, cave, siti, luoghi, o botteghe dove siano dette cose antiche di sopra espresse, tanto in Roma, quanto fuori, che andando il nostro Commissario a vedere, e pigliare nota in detti luoghi dove siano statue,

figure, torsi, bassi rilevi, vasi, medaglie, camei, intagli, et altre cose d'oro, e d'argento, di metallo, marmo, o altra materia, di gioie lavorate, e non lavorate, debbano lasciarlo entrare, vedere, pigliarne, e darne nota di tutte le cose antiche, che loro haveranno, e prestarli ogni aiuto, e favore, e quelle cose ritenere senza vendere, o trasportare altrove per cinque giorni prossimi, et obedire a esso per simil causa, affinchè ne possi dare la debita denuntia a noi, o al nostro Auditore, nell'atti del nostro Notaro, avertendo ogn'uno a non contravenire sotto le sudette pene.

Che ogni scultore, operario, scarpellino, cavatore, padrone di cave, ferravecchi, rivenditori, e medagliari debbano tenere alle loro batteghe, cave, e luoghi dove saranno statue, o alcuna delle sudette cose a vendere, affisso il presente Editto: sotto pena di tre scudi per ciascuno ogni volta che non gli sarà trovato in luogo publico, acciò possa essere da ogn'uno visto, d'applicarsi come sopra.

Finalmente diamo, e concediamo ogni facoltà al detto nostro Commissario, straordinarij, e qualsivoglia altra persona, essecutore, e ministro di giustitia di poter cercare havendone notitia, e fare cercare in ogni luogo dove fossero statue, cose antiche di qualsivoglia materia, casse, barche, vascelli, valiscie, involti, e il simile possino anco fare Custodi, Guardiani, Barcaroli, Doganieri, con darne notitia a noi, overo al nostro Auditore, nell'atti del detto nostro Notato, quando fossero per estrahersi fuori di Roma senza nostra licenza, e si darà fede all'accusatore con un sol testimonio, et al nostro Commissario col suo giuramento. Commandiamo a tutti Bargelli, Essecutori, et altri Ministri di Giustitia, etiam Cursori, che in simil casi debbano darli, e prestarli ogn'aiuto, e favore, sotto pena della perdita dell'officij et altre a nostro arbitrio.

Notificando a tutti, che alle sudette pene sarà tenuto il Padrone per il ministro, et il ministro per il garzone, alle quali si procederà irremissibilmente con ogni rigore di giustitia; riserbando a noi l'arbitrio in ogni caso di poter sminuire, et accrescere le sudette pene secondo li casi che occorreranno.

Volendo, che il presente Editto, affisso, e publicato nelli luoghi soliti di Roma doppo tre giorni astringa ogn'uno come se li fosse personalmente intimato, e notificato.

In fede etc. Dato in Roma nella Camera Apostolica li 29 Gennaro 1646.
F. Card. Procamerarius
Lazarus Bottus Comm. Gen.
Iacobus Antonius Serperius Aud.

9
Prohibitione sopra l'estrattione di Statue di marmo o metallo, Figure, Antichità e simili

Palazzo del titolo della Basilica di S. Maria in Trastevere Prete Cardinale Altieri della S. R. C. Camerlengo.

Benchè per diversi Editti etc. (come nel n. 7). Pertanto noi volendo provedere, che non si faccino simili estrattioni, e fraudi e perciò dare il debito castigo a delinquenti, d'ordine espresso di N. S. datoci a bocca, e per l'autorità del nostro offitio di Camerlengato, non revocando gli altri bandi sopra tal materia da nostri Predecessori fatti, e publicati, anzi quelli, quando faccia di bisogno confermando et approvando, e specialmente quelli delli 5 Ottobre 1624, 24 Gennaio 1646 e 30 Agosto 1655. Col presente ordinamento e commandiamo a tutte e singole persone, tanto Ecclesiastiche, quanto Secolari di qualsivoglia stato, grado, ordine e condizione ancorche ricercasse speciale, e specialissima menzione, che non possino ne presumino per l'avvenire estrarre, e fare estrarre fuori di detto Stato, per fiume, mare, o per terra alcuna sorte di statue, figure, bassi rilievi, colonne, vasi, alabastri, agate, diaspri, amatiste, et altri marmi preziosi, gioie e pietre lavorate, e non lavorate, torsi, teste, fragmenti, pili, piedistalli, inscrittioni, o altri ornamenti, fregi, medaglie, camei, o intagli di qualsivoglia pietra, o vero metallo, oro, argento, di qualsivoglia materia antica, o moderna, ne meno figure, quadri, e pitture antiche, o altre opere in qualsivoglia cosa scolpite, dipinte, intagliate, commesse, lavorate, o in altro modo fatte, o che siano state nuovamente ritrovate in cave, o siano esistenti in Roma e fuori di Roma, o vero appresso qualsivoglia persona, o in qualunque luogo senza nostra licenza da darsi, e concedersi quanto alle cose antiche, in vigore solamente di special Chirografo di Sua Santità, e con visione e fede della qualità e quantità, Venditore e Compratore delle cose sudette fatta dal nostro Commissario sopra l'antichità, e cave, e data negl'atti dell'infrascritto nostro e della Reverenda Camera Apostolica Segretario e Cancelliere, e colla solita attergazione dell'altri nostri Commissarj attergatori delle licenze per acqua, e respettivamente per terra, sotto pena della perdita della robba, che sarà ritrovata, venduta, mandata, nascosta, scansata, trafugata, o incassata in Roma, o fuori di Roma per tutto lo Stato Ecclesiastico senza licenza come sopra, e di 500 ducati d'oro di Camera, d'applicarsi la metà alla R. C. Apostolica, un quarto all'accusatore, quale sarà tenuto secreto, e l'altro quarto al detto nostro Commissario, il quale possa procedere in simili materie per via d'inquisitioni, e denuntie avanti di noi, o nostro Auditore, e se li darà fede con il suo giuramento, o un solo testimonio, et altre pene etiam corporali secondo la qualità delle persone, e delitti a nostro arbitrio, alle quali si procederà sommariamente con ogni rigore di giustizia.

E perchè vi sono molte persone, che cavano e fanno cavare in luoghi publici e privati vicino all'edifitii, fabriche, mura e ponti antichi, marmi, mischi, alabastri, platee, travertini, peperini et altre diverse pietre con pericolo, e ruina di detti edifitii, e vie publiche, et inoltre cavano, e fanno cavare in diverse cave publiche, e private statue, torsi, bassi rilievi, teste, piedistalli, colonne, capitelli, inscrittioni, medaglie, camei, et intagli di valore di marmo, metallo, gioje, di mischi, oro, et argento, o agate, e crugnole, amatisti et altre diverse materie lavorate e non lavorate, e che dette cose, cavate e ritrovate ben spesso ancorchè vi siano pene gravi, e prohibitioni fatte e cominate in essi bandi, vendono scansano, trafugano, e ascondono in Roma, e fuori senza saputa e licenza nostra, scienza, et ordine de padroni delli propri luoghi, e proprie cose ritrovate, con danno publico e particolare, e gravezza delle loro coscienze, e cosi privano e spogliano quest'alma città di Roma, e li proprj padroni delle più belle cose, che in essa città si trovano così antiche come moderne; onde ordiniamo e commandiamo a tutte e singole persone sudette, che per l'avvenire non possino guastare edifitii, ne fabbriche antiche, muraglia de travertini, marmo, peperini, o altra materia sopra terra, ne rompere o cavare statue antiche, o altri ornamenti di qualsivoglia materia, ne tampoco cavare, o far cavare sotto terra vicino a detti edifitii, mura, fabriche, archi, ponti, cemeterii e vie publiche in qualsivoglia luogo esistenti senza nostra licenza, e con l'intervento del detto nostro Commissario da noi deputato, o altri in suo luogo da deputarsi.

Inoltre dichiariamo, che nell'istesse pene incorreranno li compratori, e venditori delle sudette cose antiche e moderne se le venderanno, o compreranno senza nostra licenza per portarle, o mandarle fuori di Roma come sopra, sotto le pene di sopra espresse.

E perchè spesse volte li cavatori, e muratori, operarii, vignaroli, et altre simili persone vendono, trafugano, rompono, e portano di nascosto via senza saputa delli padroni, statue, teste, camei, intagli, medaglie, gioje, anelli, et altri lavori antichi di valore, di qualsivoglia materia come di marmo, alabastro, oro, argento, metallo, o di gioje, o d'altre pietre, e quelli rivendono a ferravecchi, scarpellini, scultori, o rivenditori, o bottegari senza scienza delli padroni delle proprie cose, e de luoghi propri, dove si ritrovano così di nascosto, come palese. Però commandiamo, che nessuna persona come sopra espressa, possa vendere sotto pretesto di haverne ritrovate, o havuto in qualsivoglia modo alcune delle sudette cose antiche, ne meno nessuno quelle comprare, che passino il valore d'un scudo se prima non ne darà notizia nell'atti dell'infrascritto nostro Notato, ovvero al nostro Commissario della qualità, quantità, persona che vorrà vendere, e comprare le cose sudette sotto pena della perdita delle robbe, quale si restituiranno al proprio padrone, et altre pene a nostro arbitrio etiam pecuniarie d'applicarsi come sopra.

Prohibiamo anco, che non sia lecito ad alcun falegname, operario, e qualsivoglia altra persona far casse, o farne fare per incassar statue, et altre cose antiche di sopra espresse, o vero moderne lavorare o non lavorare, ne quelle incassare, ne facchini o portatori ligare, imballare, ne dette cose trasportare da un luogo all'altro, ne meno Barcarolo, o Marinari possano metterle in barche, o vascelli, casse o balle, o involtini, dove siano opere antiche, o moderne sudette senza che non siano viste dal nostro Commissario, e con nostra licenza come sopra sotto le sudette pene, et altre etiam maggiori a nostro arbitrio.

Commandiamo, et ordiniamo ancora, che nessuno Castellano, Doganiero, Custode, Portinaro, Guardiano di passo, Commissario del sigillo di Ripa, ne persona alcuna lasci passare per mare, per fiume alcuna delle sudette opere antiche, o moderne, che siano incassate, o senza cassa, o involtate, lavorate, o non lavorate, di qualsivoglia materia dipinta o scolpita senza la nostra licenza, e sigillata con nostro Sigillo sotto pena della privatione dell'offitio, e d'altre tanto corporali, quanto pecuniarie a nostro arbitrio.

Proibiamo di più che non sia lecito ad alcun carrettiero, facchino, portatore, mulattiero di poter caricare, portar marmi, travertini, alabastri, paperini, statue, colonne, teste, figure, bassirilievi et altre cose lavorate, e non lavorate di qualsivoglia pietra, da qualunque cava o edificio antico, e di qualsivoglia metallo, se prima non haveranno havuto la nostra licenza in scriptis come sopra; la quale se le darà gratis, e quella doveranno portare seco mentre porteranno o lavoreranno simil materie, e mostrarla al detto nostro Commissario o altri deputati, se saranno da loro trovati, e ciò per evitare ogni fraude, che si potesse commettere sotto pena di tre tratti di corda da darseli subito, e di venticinque scudi d'applicarsi come sopra, e perdita della detta roba. Parimenti non possa ne debba alcun calcararo, cavatore, o altre simili persone, come scarpellini, scultori, orefici, fonditori, et altri guastatori rompere, guastare, spezzare, far calce, o portar via o rivendere alcuna sorte di marmi scritti, lavorati, statue, figure o altri ornamenti antichi, ne meno fondere, guastare, o ammaccare figure, medaglie, intagli di metallo d'oro, d'argento antichi, che habbino figuratione o memoria di cose antiche senza nostra licenza, e visione del nostro

Commissario, o altri deputati, quale si darà gratis, sotto pena della perdita della roba, di scudi venticinque d'applicarsi come sopra, et altre pene etiam corporali a nostro arbitrio. E perche sinhora da Noi, o da altri si è dato, e si dan ben spesso licenza a patenti di cavare, e far cavar tesori, marmi, travertini, statue, pozzolana, et altre cose diverse, dove è necessario l'intervento e l'assistenza del sudetto nostro Commissario, o altri da deputarsi, quali attendino acciò non si cavi in luogo prohibito, e pregiudiziale a publici edificii, vie e cimiterii, come di sopra si è espresso, commandiamo et ordiniamo a qualsivoglia persona di qualsivoglia stato, grado, e condizione che dopo la publicatione del presente Editto, debba dar nota di dette licenze nell'offizio dell'infrascritto nostro Notaro fra termine di dieci giorni, sotto pena della rivocatione di esse licenze.

Che nessuna persona, che facci cavare in publichi, o privati luoghi con nostra licenza come sopra, sia se scarpellino, cavatore o patrone de luoghi possa vendere travertini, marmi, alabastro, statue et altre cose sopra espresse, che ne pervenga la parte alla Reverenda Camera se prima non saranno vedute dal detto nostro Commissario, misurate da Periti da deputarsi da noi, e datone la parte che perviene a detta Camera a nostra dispositione, ne meno vender piombo, metallo, oro et argento, o nessun'altra cosa, che ne pervenga la parte alla detta Camera, sotto pena della perdita delle robbe, di scudi dieci d'applicarsi come sopra et altre pene etiam corporali a nostro arbitrio.

Prohibiamo anco a tutti i scultori, scarpellini, rivenditori, cavatori, e padroni di cave il poter vendere, e comprare per l'avvenire alcuna sorte di statue, marmi lavorati, e non lavorati, figure, bassi rilievi, colonne, piedistalli, inscrittioni, medaglie, camei, intagli, o altre cose antiche se prima non haveranno dato la nota nelli medesimi atti dell'infrascritto nostro Notato della quantità e qualità della robba, che vogliano vendere o comprare, affinchè si possa sapere l'esito, e l'esistenza in Roma di dette robbe sopranominate, sotto le pene come sopra.

Di più ordiniamo, e commandiamo a qualsivoglia cavatore, vignarolo, operario, muratore, scultore, scarpellino, e qualsivoglia altro padrone si sia di statue, cave, siti, luoghi, o botteghe dove siano dette cose antiche di sopra espresse, tanto in Roma, quanto fuori che andando il nostro Commissario a vedere e pigliare nota in detti luoghi dove siano statue, figure, torsi, bassi rilievi, vasi, medaglie, camei, intagli, et altre cose d'oro, e d'argento, di metallo, marmo, o altra materia di gioje lavorate, e non lavorate, debbano lasciarl'entrare, vedere, pigliarne, e darne nota di tutte le cose antiche, che loro haveranno, e prestargli ogni ajuto, e favore, e quelle cose ritenere senza vendere o trasportare altrove per cinque giorni prossimi, et obedire ad esso per simil causa, afinchè ne possi dare la debita denunzia a Noi, o al nostro Auditore, negl' atti del nostro Notato, avertendo ogn'uno a non contravvenire sotto le sudette pene.

Che ogni scultore, operario, scarpellino, cavatore, padrone di cave, ferravecchi, rivenditori, e medagliati debbano tenere alle loro botteghe, cave e luoghi dove saranno statue, o alcuna delle sudette cose a vendere, affisso il presente Editto, sotto pena di tre scudi per ciascuno ogni volta, che non gli sarà trovato in luogo publico, acciò possa esser da ogn'uno visto, d'applicarsi come sopra.

Finalmente diamo e concediamo ogni facoltà al detto nostro Commissario, straordinarij, e qualsivoglia altra persona, esecutore, e ministro di giustizia, di poter cercare avendone notizia, e far cercare in ogni luogo dove fossero statue, cose antiche di qualsivoglia materia, casse, barche, vascelli, valisce, involti et il simile, possino anche fare custodi, guardiani,

barcaroli, doganieri, con darne notizia a noi, o vero al nostro Auditore, nell'atti del detto nostro Notare quando fossero per estraersi fuori di Roma senza nostra licenza, e si darà fede all'accusatore con un sol testimonio, et al nostro Commissario col suo giuramento. Commandiamo a tutti Barigelli, esecutori, et altri ministri di giustizia, etiam Cursori, che in simili casi debbano darli, e prestarli ogn'ajuto, e favore sotto pena della perdita dell'offitij et altre a nostro arbitrio.
Notificando a tutti, che alle sudette pene sarà tenuto il padrone per il ministro, et il mastro per il garzone, alle quali si procederà irremisibilmente con ogni rigore di giustizia, riserbando a Noi l'arbitrio in ogni caso, di poter sminuire, o accrescere le sudette pene secondo li casi che occorreranno.
Vogliamo ch'il presente editto affisso, e pubblicato ne' luoghi soliti di Roma, dopo tre giorni astringa ogn'uno come se li fosse personalmente intimato, e notificato.

In fede. Dato in Roma nella Cam. Apost. questo di 5 Febbr. 1686.
P. Card. Altieri Camer.
M. Zaccaria Aud. – S. Pilastri Comm. Gen.
Domenico Liberati Segr. e Canc. della R. C. A.

10
Prohibitione sopra l'estrattione di Statue di marmo, o metallo, Figure, Antichità e simili

Gio. Battista Spinola Diacono Card. di S. Cesareo della S. R. C. Camerlengo.
(Come al n. 8)
Dato in Roma nella Cam. Apost. questo di 18 Luglio 1701.

11
Editto sopra le Pitture, Stucchi, Mosaici, et altre Antichità, che si trovano nelle cave, Inscrizioni antiche, Scritture, e Libri manoscritti

Gio. Battista Spinola di San Cesareo Diacono Cardinale, della S. Romana Chiesa Camerlengo.
Premendo sommamente alla paterna carità, e zelo di N. Sig. che si conservino, quanto più si può, le antiche memorie, et ornamenti di quest'Alma Città di Roma, quali tanto conferiscono a promovere la stima della sua magnificenza, e splendore appresso le Nazioni straniere; come pur vagliono mirabilmente a confermare, et illustrare le notizie appartenenti all'Istoria così sagra, come profana; Quindi è che per espresso commandamento della Santità Sua datoci a bocca, e per l'autorità del nostro Offizio di Camerlengo rinovando, confermando, et ampliando li Bandi altre volte da Nostri Antecessori, e da Noi publicati, e particolarmente quello in data delli 18 Luglio 1701, con cui si proibisce l'estrazione di Statue, Pitture, Marmi, Metalli, Figure, Gemme, ed altre cose antiche, quale doverà inviolabilmente osservarsi, dichiariamo, et ordiniamo.
Che ritrovandosi sotto Terra nelle Cave, che si fanno, e faranno in avvenire con le debite licenze, Pitture, Stucchi, Pavimenti, Figure, o altri lavori di Mosaico, Monumenti, o sian

Sepolcri di qualsivoglia sorte, si debbano subito denuntiare al nostro Commissario delle Antichità, o sia Antiquario, che ora è Francesco Bartoli, nè possano guastarsi, e demolirsi senza la licenza, ch'egli darà gratis a nome Nostro, doppo d'aver fatto il disegno di quelle cose, che non si potranno conservare; Dichiarando che quest'ordine debba comprendere, et effettivamente comprenda non solo li Cavatori, Muratori, et altri Operarij, ma ancora li Padroni del Fondo, Affittuarij, Vignaroli, et ogn'altra persona interessata nella Cava, sotto pena di scudi 100 da applicarsi per la metà alla Reverenda Camera Apostolica, e per l'altra metà all'Accusatore, e anche sotto pena corporale da stendersi a pena grave afflittiva del corpo a nostro arbitrio secondo la qualità de casi, e delle persone.

E perche importa molto non meno per l'erudizione Ecclesiastica, che per la profana, di conservare le Inscrizioni antiche, che sono sopra terra, overo che si trovano sotto terra, scolpite, o impresse in pietra, o in qualsivoglia altra materia, ordiniamo, et espressamente proibiamo, che nessuna persona ardisca sotto qualsivoglia pretesto di muoverle dal luogo, in cui presentemente sono, o si troveranno in avvenire, e molto meno di segarle, romperle, o in altro modo guastarle per qualsivoglia uso, se prima non ne averà ottenuta speciale licenza in scritto da darsi in nome nostro da Monsig. Bianchini Cameriere d'Onore di N. Sig. a tal effetto deputato dalla Santità Sua, e contravenendo li Padroni, Scarpellini, Scultori, Muratori, Cavatori, e qualsivoglia altra persona, incorrano nella pena espressa nel precedente Capitolo.

In oltre vedendosi trascurata l'osservanza degl'antichi Bandi emanati per la conservazione de libri manoscritti, et altre scritture tanto publiche, quanto private, mentre varij Artefici, o altre persone, senza alcuna revisione, approvazione, o licenza si fanno lecito di comprare indifferentemente ogni sorte di scritture manoscritte da qualsivoglia persona, e convenendo con opportuno rimedio provedere a si grave disordine, dichiariamo, e proibiamo, che nissuna persona di qualunque grado, condizione, sesso, e qualità ardisca di vendere, o comprare sotto alcun pretesto qualsivoglia sorte di libri scritti a mano tanto Volgari, e Latini, quanto Greci, Ebraici, e di qualunque altra lingua cosi in carta pecora, come in carta bambacina, tanto intieri, quanto divisi, rotti, e sciolti, come pure Instromenti, Processi, Inventarij, Lettere, Bolle, Brevi, Diplomi, e qualunque altra sorte di carte, overo pergamene manoscritte, sotto che nome, o titolo siano, se non ne averà ottenuta particolar licenza in scritto dal Sig. Abbate Domenico Riviera Prefetto dell'Archivio Apostolico di Castel S. Angelo, overo dal Sig. Tomaso de Iulijs Custode dell'Archivio Segreto Vaticano, quali la daranno gratis in nome nostro, prima che si stabilisca la vendita, o almeno avanti, che si consegnino al Compratore le scritture, e libri sudetti, sotto pena a quelli, che contraverranno tanto nel comprare, quanto nel vendere senza licenza, come sopra, di esser tenuti in solido alla refezione di tutti li danni, et interessi, che per occasione di tale compra, e vendita patiranno li Padroni delle Scritture, o altri che in quelle abbiano interesse, et in oltre di tre tratti di corda da darseli subito in publico, e di scudi 200, da applicarsi alla R. C. A. de quali si promette, e si darà la metà a chi rivelarà le compre, e vendite di simili libri, e scritture fatte senza licenza, et esso rivelante sarà tenuto segreto.

Per l'istesse ragioni ordiniamo, e commandiamo a tutti i Librari, Pizzicatoli, Battilori, Cartolari, Dipintori, Cartolari, Tamburati, et altri Artegiani, che dentro il termine di otto giorni prossimi doppo la publicazione del presente Editto debbano aver notificato al sudetto Prefetto dell'Archivio di Castel S. Angelo, overo al Custode dell'Archivio Segreto

Vaticano quei libri, e scritture di sopra descritte, che si troveranno di avere nelle loro Botteghe, o altrove per uso, e servizio delle loro arti, e che non ardischino, nè presumano sotto qualsivoglia pretesto di sciogliere, dividere, rompere, o guastare detti libri, e scritture, tanto ad effetto di venderle, o valersene per legare altri libri, quanto per adoperarle ad uso delle loro Arti, senza licenza di detto Prefetto dell'Archivio di Castel S. Angelo, overo Custode dell'Archivio Segreto Vaticano, sotto le pene stabilite in detto secondo Capitolo, da eseguirsi irremissibilmente contro li trasgressori.
In tutti li casi di sopra espressi vogliamo, che s'intendano comprese anche le persone Ecclesiastiche tanto Secolari, quanto Regolari, et ogn'altra persona, quantunque privilegiata, e degna di speciale menzione; dichiarando che contro li disubbidienti si procederà rigorosamente, anche ex officio ad istanza del Fisco all'esecutione delle pene stabilite.

In fede etc. Dato in Roma in Cam. Apostolica questo di 30 Settembre 1704.
G. B. Spinola Camer.
Prospero Marefoschi Uditore
Silvio de Cavalieri Comm. Gen.

12
Prohibizione sopra l'estrazione di Statue di marmo, o metallo, Figure, Antichità e simili

Giovanni Battista Spinola del titolo di S. Cesareo della Santa Romana Chiesa Prete Cardinale Camerlengo.
Essendosi altre volte e con diversi altri Editti nostri e de' nostri Predecessori emanati e pubblicati, specialmente etc ... (come nel n. 8). Commettendosi giornalmente frodi, et inganni tra compratori e venditori con occultarsi da quelli l'intenzione dell'estrazzioni, e trasporti per fuori di Roma, e Stato Ecclesiastico di simili antichità, e colludendosi ben spesso tra di loro. Perciò per evitare simili frodi, et inganni, et il comodo di potere con facilità trafugare et occultare: Proibiamo a qualsivoglia persona tanto dimostrante in quest'Alma Città quanto forastiera, il poter stabilire la compra o vendita di statue, figure, antichità, et altre cose sudette, senza la nostra precedente licenza da darsi gratis con l'espressione de nomi, tanto del venditore, come del compratore, et anche del mezzano sotto la pena della perdita della robba stabilita, e contrattata e di sc. 500 da applicarsi, come sopra, ancorche non vi fosse intenzione di trasportar detta robba fuori di Roma e dello Stato Ecclesiastico.
Proibiamo anco etc ... (come nel n. 8). Dichiarando, che li Forastieri Ecclesiastici, e Secolari, tanto soggetti immediatamente, o mediatamente alla S. Sede, quanto stranieri, e sudditi d'altri Prencipi, saranno ligati e compresi nel presente nostro Editto, come se fossero stati alla pubblicazione di esso, o gli fosse stato personalmente intimato, senza che possano allegarne ignoranza veruna; ogni volta però, che apparisca della loro precedente dimora in Roma per lo spazio di un mese.
E per maggior notizia di tutti commandiamo, che li portinari delle Porte di Roma, e di Borgo, gli osti, albergatori, locandieri, et altri che ricattano, danno da mangiare, o alloggiano

particolarmente persone forestiere, sieno tenuti ed obbligati di tenere continuamente affisse le copie del presente Editto alle Porte della Città, ospizi, ostarie, locande, et alberghi loro respettivamente a vista d'ognuno, sotto pena di tre tratti di corda, e di sc. 25 per ciascuno, e ciascuna volta in caso di contravenzione.
Vogliamo finalmente che il presente Editto, affisso e publicato ne luoghi soliti di Roma, dopo tre giorni astringa ognuno come se gli fosse personalmente intimato e notificato.

In fede. Dato in Roma nella Camera Apostolica questo di 3 Aprile 1717.
G. B. Spinola Card. Camerl.
Faustino Crispotti Ud. – Gaspar Turchi Comm. Gen.
Antonio Gaetano Frosi, Segr. e Canc. della Rev. Cam. Apost.

13
Editto sopra li scalpellini, segatori di marmi, cavatori et altri

Annibale del Titolo di S. Clemente della S. R. C. Prete Card. Camerlengo.
Appartenendo alla nostra vigilanza il procuratore, che si conservino illese le opere, e memorie dell'antichità, dalle quali riceve tanto splendore quest'Alma Città di Roma, e suo Distretto; quindi è, che d'ordine espresso di Nostro Signore datoci a bocca, e per l'autorità del nostro Officio di Camerlengato, inerendo a gl'Editti pubblicati dai nostri Antecessori, e specialmente sotto li 18 Luglio 1701, e 8 Aprile 1717, e quelli confermando, ed approvando, coll'aggiunta ancora dei seguenti provedimenti: Ordiniamo, che nessuno di qualsivoglia grado, e condizioni possa cavare sotto terra in pubblici, o privati luoghi senza nostra espressa licenza in scritto, e in qualche luogo, quando si stimi da noi necessaria anche, senza l'assistenza del nostro Commissario sopra l'Antichità, o d'altra Persona da deputarsi a nostro arbitrio.
Secondo. Proibiamo a qualsisia Persona, ancorche avesse la nostra licenza per cavare, di farlo vicino agl'Edifizij, e Muraglie antiche, acciò non ne restino danneggiate.
Terzo. Ancora proibiamo il guastare qualunque Edifizio, o Fabrica, o altra opera antica sopra terra, ancorche lesa dal tempo, o rovinosa, senza nostra espressa licenza, e senza la precedente visita, ed inspezione del sudetto nostro Commissario.
Quarto. Ordiniamo, che ritrovandosi, o nel far Cave, o nel fare scassati di Vigne, o fondamenti di Fabriche, o per qualunque altro lavoro sotto terra, in luoghi tanto pubblici, quanto privati, Statue, o frammenti di esse, Torsi, Teste, Bassi rilievi, Piedistalli, Colonne, Capitelli, Inscrizioni, Vasi, Urne, ed altri ornamenti antichi di Pietra, Marmo, Terra cotta, Bronzo, o altro Metallo, debbano subito quelli, che le troveranno darne la notizia al predetto nostro Commissario, prima etiamdio di levare le sudette cose dal luogo, in cui saranno state trovate, acciò dal medemo siano subito visitate, e riconosciute, per assicurarsi ancora, che non si rompino, o offendino nel cavarle.
Quinto. Proibiamo a qualunque Scarpellino, Segatore di Marmi, o altri il segare, o far segare, o in altro modo rompere, o guastare qualunque pietra, o marmo, ove sia alcuna Inscrizione, o Basso rilievo, siccome ancora Colonne di qualsivoglia sorte, o tronchi di esse, quando questi riuniti insieme formino, o possino formare un intiera Colonna, senza la precedente visita del detto nostro Commissario, e nostra licenza in scritto, che sarà data gratis; siccome ancora senza alcun aggravio di spesa dovrà essere la visita, ed inspezione

da farsi in tutti i casi sopra espressi dal detto nostro Commissario, al quale in oltre proibiamo di ricevere cosa alcuna di recognizione, benchè minima, e spontaneamente offerta, sotto pena di privazione dell'Officio, ed altre a nostro arbitrio.
In ciaschedun caso poi di contravenzione alle sudette nostre proibizioni, ed ordini si procederà irremissibilmente alla pena, la quale sarà, oltre la perdita delle robbe sudette, di tre tratti di corda, e di scudi 25 da applicarsi per metà alla R. Cam. Apostolica, un quarto all'Accusatore che sarà tenuto segreto, ed un quarto al sudetto nostro Commissario, e si procederà ancora per via d'inquisizione, e in qualsivoglia altro modo più proficuo al Fisco.
Vogliamo finalmente, che il presente Editto affisso, e pubblicato ne' luoghi soliti di Roma astringa ogn'uno, come se gli fosse personalmente intimato, e notificato.

Dato in Roma nella Camera Apostolica questo dì 21 Ottobre 1726.
A. Card. Albani Pro-Camer.
G. Amadori Olim Lanfredini Auditore – N. Lana Comm. Gen.
Antonio Gaetano Frosi Segr. di Cam.

14
Prohibizione dell'estrazione delle Statue di marmo, o metallo, Pitture, Antichità e simili

Annibale per la Divina Misericordia Vescovo di Sabina Card. di S. Clemente della S. R. C. Camerlengo.
Benche con altri Editti da Noi, e nostri Antecessori in diversi tempi pubblicati, e specialmente sotto il di 5 Ottobre 1624, 29 Gennaro 1646, 30 Agosto 1655, 5 Febraro 1686, 18 Luglio 1701, 8 Aprile 1717, e 21 Ottobre 1726 sia stato proibito di estrarre, o far estrarre da Roma, e dallo Stato Ecclesiastico Statue di Marmo, o Metallo, Pitture, Antichità, e simili senza nostra precedente licenza; Sapendosi tuttavia, che più d'uno ardisce trasgredire gl'Ordini sudetti in grave pregiudizio del publico decoro di quest'Alma Città, a cui sommamente importa il conservarsi in essa le Opere illustri di Scoltura, e Pittura, e specialmente quelle, che si rendono più stimabili, e rare per la loro antichità, la conservazione delle quali non solo conferisce molto all'Erudizione si sagra, che profana, ma ancora porge incitamento ai Forastieri di portarsi alla medesima Città per vederle, ed ammirarle, e dà norma sicura di Studio a quelli, che applicano all'esercizio di queste nobili Arti, con gran vantaggio del publico, e del privato bene.
Quindi è, che d'ordine espresso di Nostro Signore datoci a bocca, e per l'Autorità del nostro Offizio di Camerlengato, non rivocando i mentovati Editti, anzi quelli espressamente rinovando, e confermando, specialmente proibiamo ad ogni Persona tanto Ecclesiastica, quanto Secolare di qualsisia stato, grado, e condizione, ancorchè richiedesse specialissima menzione di estrarre, o fare estrarre da Roma, e da qualsivoglia luogo dello Stato Ecclesiastico per Fiume, o per Mare, o per Terra, qualunque sorte di Statue, Figure, Colonne, Bassirilievi, Vasi, Urne, Dorsi, Teste, Camei, Intagli, Medaglie di tutte sorti, e Bronzi figurati, o altri ornamenti di Marmo, Pietra, Bronzo, o altro Metallo, e materia tanto antica, quanto moderna, siccome ancora Pitture, Mosaici, e Quadri, e altre simili Opere tanto antiche, quanto moderne senza nostra espressa licenza (che per le cose antiche non

si darà se non in virtù di special Chirografo di Sua Santità), e con precedente visione, e fede della qualità, e quantità delle cose sudette, da farsi dal nostro Commissario sopra all'Antichità, e colle altre condizioni, che vengono espresse ne mentovati Editti sotto pena della perdita della roba, che si estraesse senza la sudetta licenza, e di cinquecento ducati d'oro di Camera da applicarsi nella maniera, che verrà in appresso dichiarata, ed anche sotto altre pene corporali a nostro arbitrio, alle quali si procederà sommariamente con ogni rigor di giustizia.

E perche rispetto alli Camei, Intagli, Medaglie di tutte sorti, e simili Bronzi figurati, che sono frà le cose più pregevoli dell'antichità, e che rendono così cospicui li Musei di Roma si è da alcuni introdotto un segreto mercimonio, mediante il quale o vengono le cose sudette impunemente vendute, ed esitate fuori di Roma, e dello Stato Ecclesiastico, o con discredito del publico commercio alterate, e falsificate, e poi dai Mezzani, e Sensali vendute a Forastieri per prezzi esorbitanti, e lesivi, contravenendo nel primo caso alle reiterate proibizioni sopra ciò fatte da Noi, e nostri Antecessori, e nel secondo alla buona fede, che corrono i medesimi Forastieri; Perciò espressamente dichiariamo, che non solo verrà ad incorrere nelle pene di sopra comminate senza speranza di rimissione qualsivoglia Mezzano, Sensale, Cavatore, Vignarolo, o altra Persona, che averà alcuna parte nella detta vendita, e estrazzione fuori di Roma, e dello Stato, ma ancora ogni altro, che con gl'inganni sudetti in qualunque modo cooperasse alla mancanza della detta buona fede, o al discredito del publico Commercio.

Ed acciocche si ottenga con maggior sicurezza il fine, e l'effetto del presente Editto, ne alcuno ardisca trasgredirlo con la speranza di occultar facilmente le contravenzioni, e con ciò evitar le pene comminate; Perciò agl'Ordini dati ne precedenti Bandi aggiungiamo le seguenti dichiarazioni, e nuovi provedimenti cioè:

Primo, che in avvenire debba applicarsi alla Reverenda Camera Apostolica una sola terza parte della sudetta pena di ducati cinquecento d'oro di Camera, e dell'altre due terze parti una venga applicata all'Accusatore, e l'altra al nostro Commissario dell'Antichità nei casi, che si individueranno in appresso.

Secondo, che chiunque de Segretarij di Camera, o dei Ministri del nostro Tribunale riceverà la relazione, o denunzia di qualche Contravenzione sia obbligato a tener segreto l'Accusatore, o denunziante sotto pena della perdita del proprio Ufficio, e di altre pene anche corporali a nostro arbitrio.

Terzo, che non volendo l'Accusatore fidarsi d'altre Persone nella relazione, o denunzia possa farla a drittura in voce, o in scritto a Noi medemo, o al nostro Uditore, restando in tal caso a nostro carico non solo di tener segreta la di lui Persona, ma anche di prenderci Noi tutto il pensiero, acciò senza veruna sua ingerenza gli sia segretamente consegnata la terza parte delli detti ducati cinquecento d'oro di Camera.

Quarto, che i Falegnami, o altri Artefici di qualunque sorte, come anche i Facchini, Carrettieri, Marinari, Barcaroli, e simili Persone, quali avessero avuto alcuna parte nel far casse, imbarcare, o trasportare le cose sudette senza prima accertarsi della nostra licenza, e che per ciò fossero incorsi nelle pene comminate ne precedenti Bandi, se verranno a dar la denunzia, o relazione del Contrabando nel nostro Tribunale prima che sieno inquisiti per tal Causa nel medesimo, non solo ottenghino ipso facto la remission d'ogni pena incorsa, tanto pecuniaria, che corporale, ma sieno anche ammessi alla consecuzione della terza parte di detta pena pecuniaria, come tutti gl'altri Accusatori non colpevoli. E l'istesso

debba praticarsi con i Locandieri, Osti, Albergatori, e loro Garzoni, Serventi, o Familiari, che per qualsivoglia ragione fossero incorsi nelle medesime pene, ricordando, che a tenore de precedenti Bandi sarà tenuto il Padrone per il Ministro, ed il Mastro per il Garzone etc.
Quinto, che non essendovi l'Accusatore, o Denunziante, ma trovandosi a caso il Contrabando da Custodi, ed altri Officiali delle Porte, e dei Passi, o dagl'Esattori delle Gabelle publiche, e private, o finalmente anche da medesimi Esecutori debba applicarsi a loro quella terza parte della detta pena pecuniaria, che se vi fosse l'Accusatore o Denunziante sarebbe al medesimo dovuta.
Sesto, che quantunque debba esser cura, ed obbligo principale del sopradetto Commissario dell'Antichità il procedere alle inquisizioni, e denunzie de' Trasgressori, questo però non dovrà impedire, che tali diligenze passino pratticarsi ancora da altri; anzi espressamente comandiamo a tutti, e singoli Commissarii, Officiali, e Straordinarii di qualsivoglia Curia, e Tribunale, che soprintendono ad ogni altra sorte di Contrabandi il dover provedere alle dette inquisizioni, e denunzie, volendo che in tal caso debba applicarsi a' medesimi quella terza parte della pena, che sarebbe dovuta al detto nostro Commissario, se Egli avesse prevenuto gl'Offiziali delle altre Curie, e Tribunali nell'inquisizioni, o denunzie sudette. Che se poi in progresso della Causa, e Processo, che si farà ai Contraventori si credesse necessario prevalersi dell'opera di detto Commissario dell'Antichità, come già informato di tali materie, della pena, che dovrebbe conseguire la Camera Apostolica, acciocchè sempre restino intatte l'altre due terze parti spettanti a quelli, che avran dato le notizie, e fatta l'invenzione come si è detto sopra.
Settimo, che in tutta sorte di Contravenzioni agl'Ordini sudetti possa procedersi per via d'inquisizione, et ex Officio, e in ogn'altra miglior modo al Fisco più proficuo tanto nel caso, che la roba sudetta venisse attualmente frugata, quante anche dopo uscita da Roma, o dallo Stato; E a tenore de precedenti Bandi si darà fede all'Accusatore con un sol Testimonio, ed al nostro Commissario dell'Antichità col suo giuramento.
Ottavo, che sia permesso non solamente al detto nostro Commissario dell'Antichità, ma anche a tutti i Commissarii, Officiali, e Straordinarii delle altre Curie, e Tribunali, come pure ad ogn'altra Esecutore, e Ministro di giustizia di poter cercare, avendone notizia, e far cercare in ogni luogo dove fossero Statue, Pitture e cose antiche di qualsivoglia materia, che venissero estratte senza la detta nostra licenza, e di riconoscere, Carri, Barche, e simili Legni da trasporto per terra, e per acque, come anche di fare aprire Casse, Valige, e simili involti benchè coperti da qualsivoglia Arme, Insegna, o divise, e benchè le Persone, da cui la sudetta roba venisse accompagnata avessero qualunque sorte di Patenti, Familiarità Inibizioni, Privilegj, Indulti, ed Esenzioni. Volendo, che in simili casi tutti i Bargelli, Esecutori, ed altri Ministri di giustizia etiam Cursori debbino dare e prestare ogn'ajuto, e favore ai sudetti Commissarii Officiali etc. sotto pena della perdita de proprii Officii, e di altre pene anche corporali a nostro arbitrio.
Nono, che finalmente li Forastieri Ecclesiastici e Secolari tanto soggetti immediatamente, o mediatamente alla S. Sede, quanto Stranieri, e Sudditi d'altri Prencipi, dopo la permanenza di giorni quindici in Roma, restino compresi, e soggetti a questo nostro Editto come se gli fosse stato personalmente intimato, senza che possa suffragargli la scusa, o pretesto di soggezzione privativa a qualunque Curia, o Tribunale, bastando la loro trasgressione per renderli immediatamente soggetti alla nostra Giurisdizione, ed alle pene da Noi stabilite.

A fine poi che tutti abbiano più facilmente notizia di queste nostre Ordinazioni, comandiamo, che gl'Antiquari, li Portinari delle Porte di Roma gl'Osti, Albergatori, Locandieri ed altri, che ricettano, o alloggiano particolarmente Persone fuorastiere siano obbligate continuamente a (tenere) vista d'ognuno affisse le Copie del presente Editto, sotto pena di scudi venticinque in caso di Contravenzione.
Volendo, che il presente Editto affisso, e publicato, che sia ne' luoghi soliti di Roma astringa ognuno, come se gli fosse personalmente intimato.

Dato in Roma nella Camera Apostolica questo dì 10 Settembre 1733.
A. Vescovo Di Sabina Card. S. Clemente Cam.
F. G. Gaucci Uditore – N. Lana Commissario.

15
Proibizione della estrazione delle Statue di marmo, o metallo, Pitture, Antichità e Simili

Silvio del Titolo di S. Calisto Prete Cardinal Valenti della S. Romana Chiesa Camerlengo.
Importando sommamente al publico decoro di quest'Alma Città di Roma il conservarsi in essa le Opere illustri di Scoltura, e Pittura, e specialmente quelle, che si rendono più stimabili, e rare per la loro antichità, la conservazione delle quali non solo conferisce molto alla erudizione sì sacra, che profana, ma ancora porge incitamento a' Forastieri di portarsi alla medesima Città per vederle, ed ammirarle, e dà norma sicura di studio a quelli, che applicano all'esercizio di quelle nobili Arti con gran vantaggio del publico e privato bene. La Santità di Nostro Signore, a cui sta altamente a cuore la conservazione di queste nobili Arti, vuole onninamente, che si osservino le antiche, e provide Disposizioni fatte dai nostri Antecessori, togliendo di mezzo quegli infiniti abbusi, che sono stati prodotti e dal tempo, e dalla indolenza de subalterni Ministri; A tal'effetto si è degnata di espressamente comandarci in publicare il presente Editto.
Onde inerendo Noi alla suprema Volontà di sua Beatitudine, e in virtù del Nostro Uffizio di Camerlengato, rinuovando, e confermando in primo luogo gli Editti publicati da' Nostri Antecessori sopra la proibizione di estrarre dalla detta Città di Roma, e dallo Stato Ecclesiastico le cose predette; ed oltre più individualmente espresse nei mentovati Editti, cioè delli 5 Ottobre 1624, 29 Gennaio 1646, 30 Agosto 1655, 5 Febbrajo 1686, 18 Luglio 1701, 8 Aprile 1717, 21 Ottobre 1726, e 10 Settembre 1733. Proibiamo ad ogni Persona tanto Ecclesiastica, quanto Secolare di qualsivoglia stato, grado, e condizione, ancorchè richiedesse specialissima menzione, che non possa, nè presuma per l'avvenire estrarre, e far'estrarre fuori di Roma, Distretto, e suo Territorio per i Luoghi dello Stato, nè da qualsivoglia Luogo del medesimo per fuori di esso per Fiume, Mare, o Terra, sorta alcuna di Statue, Figure, Bassirilievi, Colonne, Vasi, Alabastri, Agate, Diaspri, Amatiste, ed altri marmi preziosi, Gioje, e Pietre lavorate, Dorsi, Teste, Frammenti, Pili, Piedestalli, Iscrizioni, o altri Ornamenti, Fregi, Medaglie, Carnei, Corniole, Monete, o Intagli di qualsivoglia Pietra, ovvero Metallo, Oro, Argento di qualsivoglia materia antica, o moderna, nè meno Figure, Quadri, Pitture antiche, o altre Opere in qualsivoglia cose scolpite, e dipinte, intagliate, comesse, lavorate, o in altro modo fatte, o che sieno state nuovamente ritrovate in Cave, o sieno esistenti in Roma, o fuori di

Roma, ovvero appresso qualsisia Persona, o in qualsisia Luogo, senza Nostra licenza da darsi, e concedersi, inquanto alle Cose rare, antiche, e di molto prezzo e valore, in vigore solamente di special Chirografo di Sua Santità, ed in quanto alle moderne, colla solita Nostra licenza, o di Monsignor Nostro Uditore, con preventiva visione, e fede della qualità, e quantità, Venditore, e Compratore delle Cose sudette, fatta dal Nostro Commissario sopra le Antichità, e Cave, e nella maniera, che quivi appresso spiegheremo, e data negli Atti dell'infrascritto Segretario, e Cancelliere della Reverenda Camera Apostolica, e colla solita attergazione degli altri Nostri Commissari attergatorj delle licenze per Acqua, e respettivamente per Terra, sotto pena della perdita della Roba, che sarà ritrovata, venduta, mandata, nascosta, scansata, trafugata, o incassata in Roma, o fuori di Roma per tutto lo Stato Ecclesiastico, senza licenza come sopra e di cinquecento Ducati d'oro di Camera, da applicarsi un terzo alla Reverenda Camera Apostolica, un terzo all'Accusatore, quale sarà tenuto segreto, e l'altro terzo al detto Nostro Commissario, o suoi Assessori, come stimeremo e giudicheremo meglio allora convenire.

E quantunque fin dall'anno 1726, fosse provveduto al buon regolamento delle Pitture, e Scolture tanto antiche, quanto moderne, colla deputazione di Persona, la quale col carattere di Commissario sopraintendente alle medesime dovesse invigilare per la osservanza di esso, con essergli stato a tal'effetto assegnato un onesto, e congruo provvedimento dalla Reverenda Camera Apostolica; nientedimeno colla sperienza si è riconosciuto, che l'opera di questo solo Ministro, sebbene coll'obbligo di tenere altra Persona idonea, e capace a tutte sue spese, non basta per ovviare alle continue fraudi, e disordini, che ne sono nati, e tutto giorno nascono in pregiudizio del publico bene; Abbiamo perciò destinato, come effettivamente destiniamo tre altre Persone col titolo di Assessori del sopradetto Commissario, assegnando a cadauna delle medesime la sua particolare incombenza, la quale sarà della Pittura ad uno, all'altro della Scoltura, ed al terzo degli Camei, Medaglie, Incisioni, ed ogni altra sorte di Antichità. Questi in conformità del loro titolo di Assessore, avranno la facoltà nei loro respettivi impieghi di visitare, e riconoscere tutte quelle materie, che vorranno semplicemente estraersi, facendone la loro visita, e relazione ad uso di arte, collo spiegarne e i pregi, e i difetti delle medesime. E perciò in avvenire per qualunque estrazione la Visita dovrà farsi dall'Assessore, il quale appiè della Supplica a Noi diretta dovrà stendere la sua Relazione, dopo di cui si sottoscriverà il Commissario, approvando quanto sarà stato da esso minutamente, e distintamente riferito col suo sentimento sopra il merito, e qualità della materia visitata, riservando però al Commissario la facoltà di visitare, e riconoscere egli stesso senza la dipendenza dell'Assessore. Questa Ricognizione, e Visita però intendiamo, e vogliamo, che sieno fatte gratis, e che non si possa ricevere emolumento alcuno a titolo ancora di dono, sotto pena della perdita dell'Offizio, da incorrersi ipso facto, ed altre ancora corporali a Nostro arbitrio.

Per la estrazione delle Statue tanto antiche, quanto moderne, vogliamo, che si prattichi il solito, che è di prendersi da Nostri Segretari di Camera le licenze nelle forme consuete, le quali dovranno esser prevenute dalla solita visita, ed approvazione del Commissario, coll'ordine Nostro, o di Monsignor Nostro Uditore in scritto per la necessaria spedizione.

E perciò, che spetta ai Quadri, ed ogni altra sorta di Pitture, ordiniamo, ed espressamente comandiamo, che tutti i Quadri, e Pitture antiche, e di ogni Autore ultimamente defonto con qualche riputazione, debbano esser soggette alle medesime Leggi, e Condizioni delle Statue, e di ogni altra sorta di Antichità, essendo Nostra precisamente, che nella estrazione di questi si pratichi ogni rigore, e che si osservino le solite regole del memoriale, visite, e spedizioni delle licenze da farsi da uno de' Segretari di Camera. Ma per tutti quei Quadri, e Pitture moderne non eccedenti il valore di scudi cento, e che si vogliano trasportare fuori di Roma per comodo delle vicine Ville, o nello Stato Ecclesiastico, ed anche fuori, ad effetto di dare maggior incitamento a i Professori, ed alla Gioventù, che si applica a questa nobil'Arte, basterà il semplice attestato dell'Assessore coll'approvazione del Commissario da farsi appiè della supplica, con che da Noi, o dal Nostro Monsignor Uditor se gli concederà la licenza per rescritto, e gratis in tutto.

Ad oggetto, che in avvenire ogniuno sappia il modo sicuro da tenersi nelle estrazioni da farsi o per acqua, o per terra; ordiniamo, che le Statue, Quadri, Marmi, ed altre Antichità di Metallo, e Pietre preziose si debbano visitare dall'Assessore a ciò deputato, secondo che saranno le materie da estrarsi, e ciò prima di essere imballate, o incassate. E se saranno cose, la estrazione delle quali, dopo la relazione fattane dall'Assessore coll'approvazione del Commissario, potremo permettere, o per acqua, o per terra, dovranno poi le casse, e balle, in cui saranno state collocate, trasportarsi nella Dogana di Ripetta, o di Ripa Grande, o di Terra respettivamente, e quivi alla presenza dei Ministri delle sudette Dogane essere di nuovo riconosciute dal medesimo Assessore, o pure dal Commissario per accertarsi della identità di quelle già da lui visitate, e per la estrazione delle quali si sarà ottenuta la Nostra licenza. Fatta poi questa seconda ricognizione, dovranno le medesime Casse, o Balle alla presenza dello stesso Assessore, o sia del Commissario sigillarsi col sigillo Nostro, o del Cardinal Camerlengo pro tempore, a Padiglione, il qual sigillo si custodirà da uno dei sudetti Ministri di Dogana, che a tal'effetto sarà da Noi deputato; E tutto ciò sotto le pene espresse di sopra, da incorrersi irremissibilmente in ogni caso di contravenzione, come fu ordinato con altro Editto sin sotto li 21 Ottobre 1726, al § 2.

Concediamo pienissima facoltà al Commissario di poter precedere contro gli Estrattori dolosi per via d'Inquisizione, e denunzia avanti di Noi, e Monsignor Nostro Uditore, alla deposizione del quale si darà fede con giuramento, e con un solo Testimonio; oltre le sudette pene della perdita della Roba, e de i cinquecento ducati d'oro di Camera, si aggiungneranno anche le corporali, secondo le qualità delle Persone, e Delitti a Nostro arbitrio, e si procederà con ogni rigore di giustizia, e sommariamente. Ed agli Assessori diamo semplicemente l'arbitrio, e facoltà di arrestare a nome Nostro tutte quelle cose, che fossero in disposizione di partire, o partissero attualmente senza Nostra licenza, dandone relazione al Commissario, ed a Monsignor Nostro Uditore, i quali procederanno in quel caso nelle forme prescritte e dal presente, e dagli antecedenti Editti, specialmente in quello publicato sotto li 21 Ottobre 1726 al § primo. E quando si verifichi la fraude, la terza parte della pena assegnata al Commissario sarà data all'Assessore.

E perchè vi sono molte Persone, che cavano, e fanno cavare in Luoghi publici, e privati vicino agli Edifizi, Fabriche, e Mura, e Ponti antichi, Marmi misti, Alabastri, Peperini, ed altre diverse Pietre con Pericolo, e rovina di detti Edifizi, e Strade publiche, ed in oltre cavano, e fanno cavare in diverse Cave publiche, e private Statue, Dorsi, Bassirilievi, Teste, Piedistalli, Colonne, Capitelli, Iscrizioni, Medaglie, Monete, Camei, ed Intagli di valore, e di Marmo, Metallo, Gioje, di Mischi d'Oro, e di Argento, o Agate, e Corniole, Amatisti, ed altre diverse materie lavorate, e non lavorate, e che le dette cose cavate, e ritrovate bene spesso, ancorche vi sieno pene gravi, e proibizioni fatte, e comminate in essi Bandi, vendono, scansano, trafugano, ed ascondono in Roma, e fuori di Roma, senza saputa, e licenza Nostra, scienza, ed ordine de' Padroni delli proprj Luoghi, e proprie cose ritrovate, con

danno publico, e particolare, e gravezza delle loro coscienze, e così privano, e spogliano quest'Alma Città di Roma, e li proprj Padroni delle più belle cose, che in essa Città si trovano, così antiche, che moderne.
Però ordiniamo, e comandiamo a tutte, e singole Persone sudette, che per l'avvenire non possano guastare Edifici, nè Fabriche antiche, muraglie di travertino, marmo, peperino, o altra materia sopra a terra, nè rompere, o cavare Statue antiche, o altri ornamenti di qualsivoglia materia, nè tampoco cavare sotto terra vicino a i detti Edifici, Muri, Fabriche, Archi, Ponti, e Cimiteri, Strade publiche in qualsivoglia luogo esistenti senza Nostra licenza, come pure fu ordinato in altra consimile Proibizione publicata li 8 Aprile 1717 nel § 2 e 3, qual licenza, quando sarà di Cave di Tavolozze, Peperini, Travertini, ed altre simili rustiche materie, dovrà riceversi dall'Offizio delle Strade, come sino al giorno di oggi si è praticato, proibendo al medesimo Offizio, e suoi Sostituti il fare qualunque altra sorte di licenze, e quando riguarderà Cave di Statue, Marmi etc., e di ogni altra estrazione di Quadri etc. vogliamo, che tutto spettino, e spettar debbono a Nostri soliti Segretari di Camera; Oltre le sudette licenze, vi dovrà intervenire il Commissario, o pure l'Assessore in quel modo, che da Noi si giudicherà più opportuno, o d'altri ancora in loro luogo da deputarsi da Noi.
Proibiamo di più, che non possa, nè debba alcun Calcararo, Cavatore, o altre simili Persone, come Scarpellini, Fonditori, ed altri Guastatori rompere, guastare, spezzare per far calce, o portar via, o rivendere alcuna sorte di Marmi scritti, lavorati, Statue, figure, o altri ornamenti antichi, nè meno fondere, guastare, o ammaccare Figure, Medaglie, Monete, intagli di Metallo d'oro, o di argento antichi, che abbiano figurazione, o memoria di cose antiche, senza nostra licenza, o di Monsignor nostro Uditore, e visione del nostro Commissario, e dell'Assessore sopra le antichità, la quale si darà gratis, sotto pena della perdita delle robe, e di scudi venticinque d'applicarsi come sopra, ed altre ancora corporali a nostro arbitrio, come pure fu proibito nella ridetta precedente Proibizione delli 8 Aprile 1717 al § 8.
E perchè sinora da Noi o da altri si sono date, e si danno bene spesso Licenze, e Patenti di cavare e far cavare Tesori, Marmi, Travertini, Statue, Pozzolana, ed altre cose diverse, nel cavo delle quali è necessario lo intervento, ed assistenza del sudetto nostro Commissario, o dell'Assessore, o altri da deputarsi, quali attendono, acciò non si cavi in luogo proibito, e pregiudiziale ai pubblici Edifizi, Strade, e Cimiteri, come di sopra si è espresso, comandiamo, et ordiniamo a qualunque Persona di qualsivoglia stato, grado, e condizione, che dopo la publicazione del presente Editto debba dar nota di dette Licenze nell'Offizio dell'infrascritto Segretario fra il termine di dieci giorni, sotto pena della rivocazione di dette Licenze, come fu ordinato ancora nella citata Proibizione del 1717 al § 9.
Che nessuna Persona, che faccia cavare in publici, o privati Luoghi con nostra licenza come sopra, siasi Scarpellmo, Cavatore, o Padrone de Luoghi, possa vendere Travertini, Marmi, Alabastri, Statue, ed altre cose sopra espresse, delle quali ne pervenga la parte alla Reverenda Camera, se prima non saranno vedute dal detto nostro Commissario, misurate da Periti da deputarsi da Noi, e datane la parte, che perviene a detta Camera a nostra disposizione. Nemeno vendere Piombo, Metallo, Oro, ed Argento, o nessun'altra cosa, di cui debbasene la parte alla detta Camera, sotto pena della perdita delle robe, e di scudi dieci da applicarsi come sopra, ed altre anche corporali a Nostro arbitrio, come dalla stessa citata Proibizione del 1717 al § 10.

Di più ordiniamo, e comandiamo a qualsivoglia Cavatore, Vignarolo, Operario, Muratore, Scultore, Scarpellino, e qualunque altro Padrone si sia di Statue, Cave, Siti, Luoghi, e Botteghe, dove sieno dette cose antiche di sopra espresse, tanto in Roma quanto fuori, che andando il nostro Commissario a vedere, e pigliar nota in detti Luoghi, dove sieno Statue, Figure, Dorsi, Bassirilievi, Vasi, Medaglie, Monete, Camei, Corniole, Intagli, ed altre cose d'Oro, e di Argento, di Metallo, o altra materia, di Gioje lavorate, o non lavorate, debbano lasciarlo entrare, vedere, pigliarne, e darne nota di tutte le cose antiche, che loro avranno, e prestargli ogni aiuto, e favore, e quelle cose ritenere senza stabilirne la vendita, o trasportarle altrove per cinque giorni prossimi, ed ubbidire ad esso per simile causa, affinchè ne possa darne la debita denunzia a Noi, o a Monsignor nostro Uditore negli atti dell'infrascritto Segretario, avvertendo ogniuno a non contravenire sotto le pene sudette, come fu ancora espresso in detta Proibizione del 1717 al § 12.
Proibiamo ancora a qualunque Falegname, Artefice, o altra Persona di far casse per portarvi le sudette cose, e quelle incassare; Siccome ancora a Facchini, Carrettieri, o altre Persone di legare, imballare, o trasportare le medesime cose, e Casse o Balle, ove sieno collocate senza che prima sieno state visitate, riconosciute, e sigillate dal nostro Commissario, ed ottenutane la nostra licenza, sotto pena di tre Tratti di Corda, e di scudi venticinque, da applicarsi come sopra, oltre la perdita delle sudette Casse, o Balle, per la quale pena pecuniaria sarà anche tenuto il Padrone per il Ministro, ed il Maestro per il Garzone, e si procederà anche per inquisizione, ed in ogni altro modo più proficuo al Fisco.
Come pure vogliamo, che le medesime proibizioni espresse si estendano anche contro i Barcaroli, e Marinari, i quali sotto qualunque pretesto si facessero lecito d'imbarcare, e ricevere sopra qualunque legno alcuna Cassa, o Balla, in cui sieno le robe sudette. E tanto, come dal citato Editto del 1726 al § 5 s'intenda ancora de Carrari, o Barrozzari.
Che i medesimi Falegnami, o altri Artefici di qualunque sorta, come anche i Facchini, Carrettieri, Marinari, Barcaroli, e simili Persone, le quali avessero avuta alcuna parte nel far Casse, imballare, imbarcare, o trasportare le sudette cose senza prima accertarsi della nostra licenza, e che perciò fossero incorsi nelle pene comminate nel presente Bando, se verranno a dare la denunzia, o relazione del Contrabando nel nostro Tribunale, prima che sieno inquisiti per tal causa nel medesimo, non solo ottengano ipso facto la remissione da ogni pena incorsa tanto pecuniaria, che corporale, ma sieno anche ammessi alla consecuzione della terza parte di detta pena pecuniaria, come tutti gli altri Accusatori non colpevoli, e lo stesso debba praticarsi con i Locandieri, Osti, Albergatori, e loro Garzoni, Serventi o Famigliari, che per qualsivoglia ragione fossero incorsi nelle medesime pene, ricordando, che a tenore de i precedenti Bandi, sarà tenuto il Padrone per il Ministro, ed il Maestro per lo Garzone.
Incarichiamo ancora strettamente a tutti i Custodi ed altri Ministri delle Porte, ed altri Luoghi di passo, sì per Terra, che per acqua, di non lasciar passare alcuna delle sudette robe, se non vedranno sopra le Casse, e Balle, o altri Involti, che le contengano, il predetto nostro sigillo, e se non sarà mostrata loro la nominata nostra licenza per la estrazione, sotto pena della privazione dell'Offizio, e di scudi venticinque, ed altre ancora corporali a nostro arbitrio, come fu proibito ancora nel altro citato Editto del 1726 al § 7.
Dichiariamo inoltre, che se le robe, le quali cadessero in commissum, saranno di Scolture, Statue, Marmi, Bronzi, Quadri, Pitture, Intagli, ed altra simile materia, la Santità di Nostro Signore, e Noi stessi coll'autorità del nostro Offizio ordiniamo, che in quanto alle Statue,

Marmi, e Bronzi s'intendano adesso per allora applicati alla Galleria di Campidoglio per le Statue, e riguardo a i Quadri, ed altre Pitture, all'altra Galleria ultimamente eretta nello stesso Campidoglio dalla munificenza di Nostro Signore, dove saranno unite, e custodite con l'altre a publico comodo, ed a perpetua gloria di Sua Beatitudine, che con tanta particolar cura si degna proteggere la conservazione di sì stimabili antiche opere; E per i Camei, Medaglie, ed altre simili antichità, queste cadute in commissum, si riporranno secondo le disposizioni, ed ordini della Santità Sua.

Dichiariamo ancora compresi in questo nostro Editto li Forestieri, benchè Ecclesiastici, Secolari, e Regolari, tanto soggetti immediatamente, o mediatamente alla Santa Sede, quanto stranieri, e Sudditi di altri Principi, che si trovano in Roma, e nello Stato Ecclesiastico, e vogliamo, che s'intendano subito astretti alla osservanza di esso. Quelli poi, che in avvenire vi verranno, dopo la permanenza di quindici giorni, senza che sia per suffragar loro l'allegata ignoranza del medesimo Editto. Siccome neppure debba giovare ad alcuno la scusa, o pretesto di soggetione privativa a qualunque Curia, o Tribunale, bastando la loro trasgressione per renderli immediatamente soggetti alla nostra Giurisdizione, ed alle pene da noi stabilite, come fu stabilito allora dalla precedente altra Proibizione delli 10 Settembre 1733 § Nono.

Oltre le concesse facoltà al detto nostro Commissario, diamo le medesime a tutti li Straordinari, Esecutori, e Ministri di Giustizia di poter cercare, avendone notizia, in ogni luogo, dove fussero Statue, Pitture, e cose antiche di qualsivoglia materia, riconoscere Barche, Carri, e simili Legni da trasporto per Terra, e per Acqua come anche di far aprire Casse, Valige, e simili Involti, benchè coperti da qualsivoglia Arma, Insegna, o Divisa, e benchè le Persone, dalle quali la sudetta roba venisse accompagnata, avessero qualunque sorta di Patenti, Famigliarità, Inibizioni, Privilegi, Indulti, ed Esenzioni. Ed il simile possano fare anche i Custodi, Guardiani, Barcaroli, Doganieri con darne notizia a Noi, o a Monsignor nostro Uditore, e negli atti dell'infrascritto Segretario, quando fossero per estraersi fuori di Roma senza la nostra licenza, e si darà fede all'Accusatore con un solo Testimonio, ed al nostro Commissario, o suo Assessore col loro giuramento. Comandiamo per tanto a tutti i Barigelli, Esecutori, ed altri Ministri di Giustizia, che in simili casi debbano dargli, e prestargli ogni ajuto, e favore, sotto pena della perdita degli Uffizi, ed altre a nostro arbitrio, come fu proibito nel precedente Editto delli 18 Luglio 1701 al § 9.

E perche rispetto alli Camei, Intagli, Monete, Medaglie, Corniole di tutte le sorte, e simili Bronzi figurati, che sono fra le cose più pregevoli dell'Antichità, e che rendono così cospicui li Musei di Roma, si è da alcun introdotto un segreto mercimonio, mediante il quale, o vengono le cose sudette impunemente vendute, ed esitate fuori di Roma, e dello Stato Ecclesiastico, o con discredito del publico Comercio alterate, e falsificate, e di poi da Mezzani, e Sensali vendute a i Forestieri per prezzi esorbitanti, e lesivi; contravenendo nel primo caso alle reiterate proibizioni sopra ciò fatte da i nostri Antecessori, e nel secondo alla buona fede, che corrono i medesimi Forestieri. Perciò espressamente dichiariamo, che non solo verrà ad incorrere nelle pene di sopra comminate, senza speranza di remissione, qualsivoglia Mezzano, Sensale, o Cavatore, Vignarolo, o altra Persona, che avrà parte nella detta vendita, ed estrazione fuori di Roma, e dello Stato, ma ancora ogni altro, che con gl'inganni sudetti in qualunque modo cooperasse alla mancanza di detta buona fede, o al discredito del pubblico Commercio, come fu proibito ancora con altro Editto delli 10 Settembre 1733 § 3.

Volendo inoltre, che chiunque de Segretari di Camera, o de Ministri del nostro Tribunale riceverà la relazione, o denunzia di qualche contravenzione, sia obbligato a tenere segreto l'Accusatore, o Denunziante, sotto pena della perdita del proprio Offizio, ed altre Corporali ancora a nostro arbitrio. E non volendo l'Accusatore fidarsi di altra Persona nella relazione, o denunzia, possa farla a dirittura in voce, o in scritto, o a Noi medesimi, o a Monsignor nostro Uditore, restando in tal caso a nostro carico non solo di tener segreta la di lui Persona, ma anche di prenderci Noi tutto il pensiero, acciò senza veruna sua ingerenza gli sia segretamente consegnata la terza parte delli detti scudi cinquecento: il che fu similmente ordinato col precedente Editto delli 10 Settembre 1733.

Notificando a tutti, che alle sudette pene si procederà irremissibilmente con ogni rigore di giustizia per inquisizione, ed in qualsivoglia altro modo più proficuo al Fisco, riservando a Noi l'arbitrio in ogni caso di poter diminuire, o accrescere le sudette pene, secondo li casi, che accaderanno.

A fine poi che tutti abbiano più facilmente la notizia di queste Nostre Ordinazioni, comandiamo, che li Portinari delle Porte di Roma, i Regattieri, gl'Osti, Albergatori, Locandieri, et altri, che ricettano, danno da mangiare, o alloggiano, particolarmente Persone forastiere siano obbligati di tenere continuamente affisse le copie del presente Editto alle Porte della Città, Ospizj, Osterie, Locande, et Alberghi loro respettivamente a vista d'ogn'uno, sotto pena di tre tratti di Corda, e di scudi 25 per ciascuno, e ciascuna volta in caso di contravenzione.

Vogliamo finalmente, che il presente Editto publicato, ed affisso che sia ne i Luoghi soliti di Roma, astringa ogni uno come se gli fosse personalmente intimato, e notificato.

Dato in Roma dalla Camera Apostolica, questo dì 5 Gennaio 1750.
S. Valenti Card. Camer.
G. M. Riminaldo Uditore – G. G. Rubini Comm. Gen.

16
Editto

Romualdo di S. Maria ad Martyres Diacono Card. Braschi Onesti, della S. R. C. Camerlengo.
L'abuso da qualche tempo introdotto in pregiudizio dei diritti Fiscali circa la escavazione, e reperizione di Statue, e di qualunque monumento di antichità, come anche di Marmi, di Metalli, di Gemme pretiose, di Tesori, e di tutt'altro nascosto nelle viscere della Terra, e sotto la rovina degli antichi Edifici, che appartiene al Sovrano diritto di Regalia, ha richiamato la cura, e vigilanza della Santità di Nostro Signore a premettere l'abolizione, e ritiro di tutte, le licenze fino ad ora concedute, per prescrivere in seguito le opportune providenze. Noi pertanto per ordine espresso della Santità Sua datoci a bocca, e per l'autorità del Nostro Officio di Camerlengato ordiniamo, commandiamo a tutte e singole Persone tanto Ecclesiastiche, quanto Secolari di qualsivoglia stato, grado, ordine, e condizione, ancorchè ricercassero speciale, e specialissima menzione, che dal giorno della pubblicazione del presente Editto debba intendersi rivocata, ed abolita qualunque licenza, che sia stata fino ad ora accordata di cavare, e far cavare nei Luoghi publici, e privati, ed anche nei Terreni o di propria libera pertinenza, o posseduti per qualunque titolo, niuno affatto eccettuato, ancorchè avesse

bisogno di speciale menzione; E perciò si proibisce a ciascuno, che da ora innanzi non abbia ardire d'intraprendere, e proseguire alcuno scavo senza una nuova licenza, che sarà munita delle cautele, e riserve proporzionate ai diritti del Principato, ed all'interesse della Reverenda Camera, avvertendo fin da ora, che adesivamente agli Editti altre volte emanati dai Cardinali Camerlenghi Nostri Predecessori, sarà proibito di estrarre, e far estrarre da questa Alma Città di Roma, e dallo Stato Ecclesiastico per Fiume, Mare, o per Terra qualunque sorta di Statue, Colonne, Pietre, e Marmi preziosi lavorati, e non lavorati, ed altra qualsiasi cosa, che sarà ritrovata nei scavi da permettersi, non potendosi allegare alcuna scusa, o protesto della credulità concepita, per la condiscendenza usata nei passati tempi.

Avverta perciò ognuno di obedire esattamente a quanto viene ordinato nel presente Editto, giacchè in caso di qualunque contravenzione, o nel cavare senza nuova licenza, o nel fare qualche fraudolenta estrazione, oltre la perdita della robba o ritrovata nei Cavi, o sorpresa nella tentata estrazione, il Delinquente incorrerà la pena di Scudi trecento d'applicarsi per metà all'Accusatore, che sarà tenuto segreto, e per l'altra metà alla Reverenda Camera; ed altre pene anche corporali a Nostro arbitrio, da misurarsi secondo le circostanze dei casi.

Dato in Roma nella Camera Apostolica questo dì 21 Agosto 1801.
R. Card. Braschi Onesti Camerlengo
P. Ferrari Uditore – G. Pecci Comm. Gen. della R. C. A.

17
Editto Doria Pamphilj

Giuseppe del Titolo di S. Cecilia Prete Cardinal Doria Pamphilj della S. R. C. Pro-Camerlengo.
Mentre la Santità di Nostro Signore Papa Pio VII. estende le sue Paterne cure a tutti gli oggetti delle Arti produttrici, e di manifattura, per aumentare con i loro prodotti la opulenza, e la prosperità dei suoi amatissimi Sudditi, non perde di vista un altro ramo d'industria, che quasi proprio, e particolare di questa Popolazione, e di questo suolo non che concorre, e gareggia con quelli, ma ne supera l'attività e la influenza non meno nel promuovere i vantaggi, che nell'accrescere il decoro, e la celebrità di questa Metropoli, ed anche dello Stato. Riconoscendo la Santità Sua nelle produzioni delle Belle Arti, che nate nella Grecia hanno da tanti secoli trasportato, e fissato il loro proprio, e quasi unico domicilio in Roma, uno dei pregi più singolari, che distingue da tutte le altre questa Città, ed insieme una delle più utili, e più interessanti occupazioni dei suoi Sudditi, e di tutti quelli, che vi concorrono, ha rivolti efficacemente i suoi pensieri a procurare, che i Monumenti, e le belle opere dell'Antichità, che servono di alimento alle Arti stesse, e di esemplare, di guida, e di eccitamento a quelli, che le professano, si conservino quasi i veri Prototipi, ed esemplari del Bello, religiosamente per ornamento, e per istruzione publica, e si aumentino ancora con il discuoprimento di altre rarità, che in qualche parte compensino la perdita di quelle, che le vicende dei tempi ci hanno involate. A questo oggetto della conservazione dei Monumenti, che esistono, e del discuoprimento dei nuovi; ed all'altro egualmente d'incoraggiare, ed animare le Arti del Disegno, e quei, che si dedicano alle medesime, ha stabiliti i più energici, ed opportuni provedimenti con ispecial Chirografo segnato il primo Ottobre, a noi diretto per l'esecuzione, del tenore seguente, cioè:

Rmo Card. Giuseppe Doria Pamphilj Pro-Camerlengo.

La conservazione dei Monumenti, e delle produzioni delle Belle Arti, che ad onta dell'edacità del tempo sono a noi pervenute, è stata sempre considerata dai Nostri Predecessori per uno degli oggetti i più interessanti, ed i più meritevoli delle loro impegnate providenze. Questi preziosi avanzi della culta Antichità forniscono alla Città di Roma un ornamento, che la distingue ma tutte le altre più insigni Città dell'Europa; somministrano i Soggetti li più importanti alle meditazioni degli Eruditi, ed i modelli, e gli esemplari i più pregiati agli Artisti, per sollevare li loro ingegni alle idee del bello, e del sublime; chiamano a questa Città il concorso dei Forastieri, attratti dal piacere di osservare queste singolari Rarità; alimentano una grande quantità d'Individui impiegati nell'esercizio delle Belle Arti; e finalmente nelle nuove produzioni, che sortono dalle loro mani, animano un ramo di commercio, e d'industria più d'ogni altro utile al Pubblico, ed allo Stato, perchè interamente attivo, e di semplice produzione, come quello che tutto è dovuto alla mano, ed all'ingegno dell'Uomo. Nel vortice delle passate vicende, immensi sono stati li danni, che questa Nostra dilettissima Città ha sofferti nella perdita dei più rari monumenti, e delle più illustri Opere dell'Antichità. Lungi però dall'illanguidirsi per questo, si è anzi maggiormente impegnata la Paterna Nostra sollecitudine a procurare tutti i mezzi, sia per impedire che alle perdite sofferte nuove se ne aggiungano, sia per riparare con il discuoprimento di nuovi Monumenti alla mancanza di quelli, che sonosi perduti. Sono state queste le riflessioni, che dappresso all'illustre esempio, che la S. M. di Leone X, diede nella persona del gran Raffaello d'Urbino, ci hanno recentemente determinati ad eleggere l'incomparabile Scultore Canova, emolo dei Fidia, e dei Prassiteli, come quello lo fù degli Apelli, e dei Zeusi, in Ispettore generale di tutte le Belle Arti, e di tutto ciò, che alle medesime appartiene; ed a Lui durante la sua vita abbiamo conferite, colla sola dipendenza da Voi, le più estese, e superiori facoltà per invigilare sopra tutto quello, che può influire al mantenimento, ed alla felice propagazione delle Arti del Disegno, e di quelli, che le professano. Queste stesse riflessioni, facendoci sempre più conoscere di quanto interesse sia per i vantaggi dei Nostri amatissimi Sudditi, per il pubblico bene, unico scopo delle incessanti Nostre sollecitudini, e per il decoro, e per la celebrità di questa Nostra Metropoli il procurare tutti i mezzi onde conservare, ed accrescere a comune istruzione, i Monumenti dell'Antichità, bei modelli delle Arti, ed animare insieme i benemeriti cultori delle medesime, hanno richiamata la Nostra attenzione a rinnovare le antiche, ed aggiungere nuove energiche, ed efficaci providenze dirette a questi interessantissimi oggetti. Inerendo quindi alle Costituzioni dei Nostri Predecessori, e segnatamente all'Editto del Cardinal Silvo Valenti, Vostro Predecessore nella dignità di Camerlengo dei 5 Gennajo 1750, pubblicato di ordine della Santa Memoria di Benedetto XIV, di Nostro Moto proprio, certa scienza, e pienezza della Nostra Sovrana, ed Apostolica Potestà, ordiniamo, e prescriviamo ciò, che siegue.

1. In primo luogo vogliamo, che sia affatto proibita da Roma, e dallo Stato l'estrazione di qualunque Statua, Bassorilievo, o altro simile lavoro rappresentante figure Umane, o di Animali, in Marmo, in Avorio, ed in qualunque altra materia, ed altresì di Pitture antiche, Greche, e Romane, o segate, o levate dai muri, Mosaici, Vasi detti Etruschi, Vetri, ed altre opere colorite, ed anche di qualunque opera d'intaglio, Vasi antichi, Gemme e Piere incise, Camei, Medaglie, Piombi, Bronzi, e generalmente di tutti quelli lavori, o di grande, o di piccolo Modello, che sono conosciuti sotto il nome di antichità,

pubbliche, o private, Sacre, o Profane, niuna eccettuata, ancorchè si trattasse di semplici frammenti, da' quali ancora grandi lumi ricevono le Arti, e gli Artisti; ed eziandio di qualunque antico Monumento, cioè di Lapidi, o Iscrizioni, Cippi, Urne, Candelabri, Lampadi, Sarcofagi, Olle Cinerarie, ed altre cose antiche di simil genere, e di qualunque materia siano composte, comprese anche le semplici Figuline. Questa proibizione vogliamo, che si estenda ancora alle opere asportabili di Architettura, cioè Colonne, Capitelli, Basi, Architravi, Fregi, Cornici intagliate, ed altri ornamenti qualsivogliano di antiche Fabriche, ed anche alle Pietre dure, Plasme, Lapislazuli, Verdi, Rossi, Gialli antichi, Alabastri Orientali, ancorchè grezzi, e non lavorati, Porfidi, Graniti, Basalti, Serpentini, ed alti simili, fuori del semplice Marmo bianco.

2. La stessa generale proibizione di estrarre, vogliamo che si estenda anche alle Pitture in Tavola, o in Tela, le quali sieno opere di Autori Classici, che hanno fiorito dopo il risorgimento delle Arti, o interessino le Arti stesse, le Scuole, la erudizione, o in fine per altre ragioni siansi rese celebri; incaricando sotto la loro più stretta responsabilità le persone destinate a presiedere alle Belle Arti, a non permettere, che si confondano queste opere, di cui non sarà mai permessa l'estrazione, con le altre, che con le cautele, e licenze da riferirsi in appresso, potranno estrarsi.

3. Ad oggetto poi, che questa proibizione assoluta di estrazione riguardo agli oggetti descritti abbia la sua piena, ed inviolabile esecuzione in ogni tempo, e restino radicalmente estirpati gli abusi, che nei tempi passati hanno deluse le più accurate providenze dei Nostri Antecessori; proibiamo a chiunque, ed anche a Voi, di concedere in avvenire qualunque licenza di estrarre gli oggetti suddetti; assoggettiamo a questa proibizione le persone tutte, di qualunque privilegio fornite, e di qualunque Dignità decorate, compresi anche li Rmi Cardinali benchè Titolari, Protettori di Chiese, ed altri privilegiatissimi, ancorchè richiedessero per essere compresi specifica, ed individuale menzione, ed ancorchè fossero rivestiti di qualsivoglia carattere, quanto più si possa concepire eminente; vogliamo che anche i Possessori Esteri degli enunciati oggetti esistenti in Roma, sieno alla stessa proibizione sottoposti; come ancora, che la medesima comprenda per tutti gli effetti anche li Forastieri, che non abbiano fissato domicilio alcuno in Roma.

4. Quelli poi, che estrarranno da Roma, o dallo Stato, o per la via di Mare, o per quella di Terra gli oggetti anzidetti, come ancora quelli, che scientemente gli avranno a loro venduti, ed i Sensali, e complici della vendita, oltre la perdita degli oggetti stessi, saranno ciascuno singolarmente soggetti alla multa pecuniaria di Cinquecento Ducati d'Oro di Camera, e cumulativamente ad altre Pene afflittive del corpo a Vostro arbitrio, da estendersi fino alla Galera per cinque Anni, secondo la qualità delle persone, la importanza dell'oggetto, e la malizia, che avrà accompagnata la fraudolenta estrazione. Anche quelli, che avranno prestato mano alla estrazione, cioè i Facchini, Falegnami, ed altri Artefici, da cui siansi scientemente formate le Casse, Imperiali, ed ogni simile continente, atto a rinchiudere il Contrabando, o che avranno fatto l'Incassatura, o l'Imballaggio, i Carrettieri, Mulattieri, Barcaroli, ed altri Condottieri, che avranno dato mano al trasporto, si considereranno tutti per complici dell'estrazione; bastando in loro ad indurre la malafede l'atto stesso della estrazione vietata, e la mancanza della non mai concedibile licenza e come tali, oltre alla perdita dei respettivi Ordegni Animali, ed Istromenti, Carci, Barche inservienti ai trasporto,

ed alla estrazione, incorreranno anche la pena di Ducati dieci in quanto agli Artieri, e Facchini; e di Ducati cento rispetto ai Condottieri, oltre le pene Corporali, che riserviamo al Vostro arbitrio.

5. Sarà però permessa la Vendita, ed il commercio di tutti gli accennati Monumenti, ed oggetti di Arti liberamente, se seguirà dentro Roma, e con la Vostra licenza nel caso di trasportarli ad altro Luogo dello Stato, la quale licenza concederete premessa sempre la visita dell'Ispettore delle Belle Arti, e del Commissario delle Antichità, e in luogo di quest'ultimo dei suoi Assessori, e con obligare l'Asportante a dare idonea Cauzione di riportare dentro un termine, che gli farete prescrivere, il documento in forma provante, di avere recato, e collocato l'oggetto asportato nel luogo della sua destinazione dentro lo Stato; e mancando, sarà tenuto non solo alla Convenzionale, ma ben anche ad alte pene corporali a Vostro arbitrio.

6. Provveduto così alla conservazione delle Opere, che devono rimanere perennemente ad ornamento insieme della Città, e per servire allo Studio, ed alla Istruzione degli Artisti, e degli Eruditi, per animare maggiormente le Arti, ed i loro Cultori, vogliamo, che tutte le Produzioni di Autori viventi, sia in Scultura sia in Pittura, o in altri oggetti di Belle Arti, possino vendersi, ed estrarsi anche fuori di Stato, e che ugualmente estrarre si possano le pitture di Autori morti, purchè non siano del pregio, e della Classe descritta di sopra, premessa però sempre la licenza da darsi in iscritto da Voi, e dai Vostri Successori, alla quale dovrà immancabilmente precedere la visita, e la relazione dell'Ispettore, e del Commissario sudetto, e di uno de' suoi Assessori, il tutto da darsi gratis, e senza alcun pagamento. E ad effetto che i sudetti Assessori, sempre con la totale dipendenza, e subordinazione all'Ispettore, e Commissario delle Antichità, esercitino il loro Ufficio con maggior puntualità, ed esattezza, abbiamo ordinato, che sia dato loro un Onorario fisso di Scudi Venti per Mese; proibendo però ad essi di ricevere qualunque cosa, anche a titolo di ricognizione, e di gratificazione volontaria; ed abolendo qualunque esazione si facesse da loro a titolo di Stima, di Regalia, di Propina, o per qualunque altro motivo. Li avvertirete poi, che qualunque negligenza nell'esercizio del loro importante Officio, sarà irremissibilmente punita con la perdita dell'impiego; e qualunque contravenzione sarà oltre questa castigata ancora con pene corporali anche gravi, e gravissime a Vostro arbitrio; e ciò senza togliere le pene, che potessero meritare per loro stessi i delitti, i quali venissero a cumularsi, e congiungersi con la contravenzione, e la delinquenza in Officio.

7. Collimando sempre allo stesso oggetto della conservazione delle preziose memorie dell'Antichità, proibiamo a chiunque di mutilare, spezzate, o in altra guisa alterare, e guastare le Statue, Bassirilievi, Cippi, Lapidi, o altri antichi Monumenti, e molto più lo squagliare li Metalli antichi figurati, o anche di semplice ornato, le Medaglie di ogni sorte, le Iscrizioni in Metalli, e qualunque altra cosa di simil genere, ancorchè tali Monumenti non fossero che frammenti dando a Voi facoltà di punire li Contraventori, o con pene pecuniarie, o anche con pene afflittive del Corpo, da estendersi fino all'Opera per un Anno, secondo il Vostro prudente arbitrio. Sarà poi cura speciale dell'Ispettore delle belle Arti, e del Commissario l'invigilare acciò non seguino tali abusi; acquistando anche quando occorra gli oggetti per i publici Musei: e nel solo caso, in cui eglino crederanno, che questi non siano di alcun momento, e che si

possino senza danno convertire in altri usi, loro unitamente, e non divisamente sarà permesso di dare le opportune licenze per isquagliarli, o adoperarli in altra guisa.

8. Rinnovando la Costituzione della San. Mem. di Pio II. *Cum Almam Nostram Urbem* del 1462, proibiamo sotto le stesse pene a chiunque di demolire o in tutto, o in parte, qualunque avanzo di antichi Edificj o dentro, o fuori di Roma, ancorchè esistenti nei Predj o Urbani, o Rustici, di privata sua, o altrui proprietà; riservando a Voi per via di visita dell'Ispettore, e del Commissario la facoltà di accordare la licenza per ruinare quelli Ruderi, la conservazione delli quali si conoscesse non essere di alcuna importanza nè per le Arti, nè per la Erudizione. Inculcherete poi seriamente in Nostro nome tanto ai Conservatori del Nostro Popolo Romano, quanto all'Ispettore, e Commissario sudetto delle Antichità d'invigilare tanto per la osservanza di questa Nostra prescrizione, quanto perchè siano le antiche Fabriche ristaurate, ripulite nelle occorrenze, e conservate colla maggiore esattezza.

9. Richiamando del pari al suo pieno vigore l'altra Costituzione della S. M. di Sisto IV. Nostro Predecessore, che comincia *Quam provida*, dell'Anno 1474, sotto le stesse pene nella medesima contenute, e sotto altre o Pecuniarie, o Corporali a Vostro arbitrio, proibiamo di togliere dalle Chiese pubbliche, e Fabriche annesse, compresi anche i semplici Oratorj, Marmi antichi scolpiti, o lisci di qualunque sorte, Iscrizioni, Mosaici, Urne, Terre cotte, ed altri ornamenti, o Monumenti di qualunque specie, esposti alla publica vista, o ascosi, e sepolti; sottoponendo alle stesse pene i Venditori, i Compratori, ed i Cooperatori. Ed acciò abbia questa proibizione il suo pieno effetto, togliamo ai Rettori, o Amministratori di dette Chiese, di qualunque grado, e dignità, e di qualunque Privilegio muniti, compresi anche i Rmi Cardinali Titolari, e Protettori, e i Patroni o Laici, o Ecclesiastici, le Congregazioni de' Vescovi, e Regolari, del Concilio, della Disciplina Regolare, ed altre, e lo stesso nostro Rmo Card. Vicario, la facoltà di accordare sotto qualunque pretesto alcuna licenza di levare dal loro luogo, e molto più di distrarre i detti ornamenti delle Chiese, e Fabriche annesse, la quale facoltà riserviamo a Voi solo; previo però sempre l'esame, e la relazione dell'Ispettore delle Belle Arti, e del Commissario delle Antichità.

10. La stessa proibizione vogliamo, che abbia luogo per i Quadri delle Chiese, i quali non solo non potranno togliersi dal luogo in cui sono collocati, o alienarsi; ma neanche farsi ristaurare o sul luogo, o fuori, e neppure levarsi per copiarli senza la intelligenza, e consenso dell'Ispettore delle Belle Arti, e del Commissario delle Antichità, che ne dovranno a Voi fare la relazione.

11. Acciò poi le Nostre providenze non restino deluse, o defraudate, ordiniamo, che tutti i Privati, che hanno Gallerie di Statue, e di Pitture, Musei di Antichità Sacre, o Profane, o semplici raccolte dell'uno, e dell'altro genere, ed anche quelli, che senza avere o Gallerie, o Musei, o Raccolte, hanno attualmente presso di loro uno, o più oggetti antichi, o in altro modo pregievoli di Arte, particolarmente in genere di Scultura, o di Pittura in Roma, e in tutto lo Stato, debbano dare un'esatta assegna, distinguendo ciascun pezzo, dentro il termine di un Mese in Roma negli Atti di uno de' Segretarj della Nostra Camera, che Voi destinerete, e nello Stato presso il Cancelliere della Comunità dentro il termine di due Mesi da computarsi dalla data dell'Editto, che Voi publicherete. In seguito si farà ogni anno, e anche più sovente, credendolo Voi opportuno, in Roma la visita dall'Ispettore delle Belle Arti, e dal Commissario delle

Antichità, ovvero dagli Assessori, previa però sempre la intelligenza dell'Ispettore medesimo; e nello Stato, dalle persone, che da Voi si destineranno per riconoscere se si conservano gli oggetti assegnati presso i Possessori; e rispettivamente nel caso, che ne abbiano disposto, per sapere quale disposizione abbiano data ai medesimi. Chiunque o non darà nel termine prefisso l'assegna, o la darà mancante, perderà gli oggetti non assegnati, se saranno di libera sua proprietà, o ne pagherà il loro valore se saranno fideicommissarj, e gli oggetti in questo caso rimaranno sempre nella stessa maniera vincolati. Chi poi nelle visite ricuserà di dare preciso sfogo alle disposizioni prese degli oggetti mancanti, o dandolo non si verificherà, ovvero lo darà vago, e tale, che non ammetta verificazione, si considererà per Contraventore alle Leggi della proibita estrazione, e come tale sarà punito.

12. Niuno, che accomoderà Strade publiche, o vicinanze sia in Città, sia in Campagna, ardirà sotto le pene comminate ai Devastatori dei publici Monumenti, di demolire gli Edifizj antichi vicini per toglierne i Materiali: e siccome avviene, che lavorando nelle Strade per allargarle, o mutar loro direzione, spesso gli Operaj trovano Sepolcri, ed antiche Fabriche, che devastano, oppure oggetti di Belle Arti, che distruggono, o si appropriano, o alienano a loro vantaggio contro ogni ragione, essendo queste cose riservate al Principe; perciò vogliamo, che chiunque caderà in questi delitti, sia punito con le stesse pene comminate contro i Devastatori dei publici Monumenti; e le Antichità ricuperate dalle loro mani, o da chi con qualunque titolo le riterrà, vogliamo che siano applicate ai publici Musei.
13. Chiunque, sia Padrone, sia Lavorante, che nel cavare i fondamenti delle Case, o fare scassati, o altri lavori nelli Terreni troverà cose antiche asportabili, sarà tenuto darne subito la denuncia in Roma presso il Segretario di Camera, che sarà da Voi deputato; e nelle Provincie negli Atti della Cancelleria Locale; e non dandola dentro dieci giorni dalla seguita ripetizione, sarà punito con la perdita della roba trovata, e con altre pene a Vostro arbitrio, da aumentarsi maggiormente quando all'omessa denuncia si unisse la fraudolenta alienazione. Sarà poi in libertà Vostra, e dell'Ispettore delle Belle Arti, e del Commissario delle Antichità di fare per i publici Musei acquisto dell'oggetto denunciato, a prezzi ragionevoli; per la qual causa dovrà dopo la denuncia passare il termine di un Mese, prima che il possessore possa disporne. La stessa denuncia dovrà darsi, se si troveranno, cavando come sopra, avanzi di Case antiche, o altre Fabriche Romane, ancorchè non vi si trovino oggetti di Antichità.
14. Niuno potrà neppure nei suoi privati fondi fare Scavi per ritrovare Antichità, e Tesori nascosti, senza Vostra particolar licenza, in cui si preserveranno sempre i soliti diritti Fiscali sulla porzione degli oggetti ritrovati; ottenuta la licenza, si dovrà avvertire dallo Scavatore, e dal Deputato assistente, l'Ispettore delle Belle Arti, ed il Commissario delle Antichità del giorno preciso, in cui si comincia lo Scavo. Sarà poi in loro libertà o per sé medesimo, o per mezzo dell'Assessore della Scultura, o trattandosi di Scavi lontani da Roma, di altre Persone, che da Voi saranno destinate, di assistere allo Scavo medesimo, quando a Voi parerà: su di che v'incarichiamo di usare la maggiore vigilanza. Si dovrà dare dallo Scavatore una esatta denuncia degli oggetti ritrovati, presso il Segretario di Camera da Voi destinato in Roma, e nelle Provincie presso il Cancelliere della Comunità; e trovandosi quella mancante, sarà l'uno, e l'altro punito a misura della commessa infedeltà. Chiunque intraprenderà Scavi senza la Vostra licenza, o non eseguirà la

succennata prescrizione, oltre la perdita della roba in caso, che l'abbia trovata, caderà nella pena di Cinquecento Ducati d'oro, ancorchè nulla avesse rinvenuto.

15. Vogliamo, che per la esecuzione di queste ordinazioni, e di altre, che sopra questa materia sono state promulgate dai Nostri Predecessori, le quali intendiamo, che seguitino ad avere il loro vigore in tutte le parti, nelle quali non si oppongono al presente Nostro Chirografo, Voi, ed i Vostri Successori abbiate una piena, e privativa giurisdizione esclusivamente da qualunque altro Tribunale ancorchè Camerale; con il che per altro non intendiamo d'impedire, anzi vogliamo animare i Capi di qualunque Tribunale, ed azienda, ed i loro Ministri, ed Esecutori, a cooperare, ed a dare ogni ajuto per lo scuoprimento, ed arresto dei Contrabandi, e per l'apprensione dei Contraventori; tutto riferendo in appresso al Vostro Tribunale. Ed acciò che in tutto quello, che riguarda le Belle Arti si usi la massima vigilanza, vogliamo che Voi, in figura di supremo, ed indipendente Magistrato, abbiate una assoluta giurisdizione, vigilanza, e presidenza sopra le Antichità Sacre o Profane, sopra le Belle Arti, e quei, che le professano, sopra gli oggetti delle medesime, non solo in Roma, ma anche nello Stato Ecclesiastico, e sopra le Chiese, Accademie non addette a Nazioni estere, ed altre Società relative alle Arti medesime, niente affatto eccettuato, e con piena indipendenza da qualunque persona ornata di qualunque Dignità anche Cardinalizia, e fornita di qualunque giurisdizione, e privilegio, cosicchè neppure si eccettuino i Rmi Cardinali, Vescovi, Abbati, Titolari, e Protettori delle Chiese; con darvi anche facoltà di rinnovare Editti, di promulgarne dei nuovi, e di prendere tutte quelle providenze, che di tempo in tempo crederete opportune, perché le Belle Arti prosperino maggiormente, e gli Amatori siano più animati a coltivarle.

16. Comandiamo che contro quelli, che contraverranno alle presenti, o ad altre antiche prescrizioni, si possa da Voi per mezzo dei vostri Ministri procedere sommariamente, e con le facoltà Economiche, ed anche per inquisizione, e per Officio, ancorchè gli oggetti, sui quali cade la Inquisizione, più non esistessero; nel qual caso vogliamo che oltre le pene comminate nei rispettivi casi, se ne debba dai Contraventori pagar il prezzo alla stima, anche di credulità, e di affezione, che ne farà l'Ispettore delle Belle Arti, ed il Commissarío delle Antichità: con accordarvi la facoltà di procedere alla condanna con il detto anche di un sol Testimonio, unito a quello del Denunciante, o ad altri amminicoli; tolto di mezzo ogni ricorso, inibizione, ed appellazione, che non fosse stragiudizialmente segnata di Nostro propria mano.

17. Mentre poi Noi raccomandiamo con il maggior fervore del Nostro spirito alla Vostra vigilanza l'adempimento di queste Nostre disposizioni, non lasciamo di occuparci seriamente, per quanto le circostanze dei tempi, e le forze del Nostro Erario lo permettono, a rinvenire tutti i mezzi onde riparare coll'acquisto di nuovi oggetti preziosi, alle perdite sofferte nei publici Musei, ai quali perciò applichiamo per la porzione spettante al nostro Erario, tutti i Monumenti, che si devolveranno al medesimo, e tutte le pene, eccettuata la porzione dovuta secondo le vigenti Leggi al Denunciante, ed agli Esecutori. Nello stesso tempo, e per la stessa causa proporzionando l'importanza dell'oggetto alle scarse forze del Nostro Erario, abbiamo destinata la somma annua di Piastre diecimila per l'acquisto delle cose interessanti in aumento dei Nostri Musei; sicuri che la spesa diretta al fine di promuovere le Belle Arti, è largamente compensata dagl'Immensi vantaggi, che ne ritraggono i Sudditi,

e lo Stato la di cui causa non può essere da quella dell'Erario disgiunta; ed animati ancora dalla giusta considerazione di aprire un esito ai Possessori, e dai Raccoglitori di cose antiche, delle quali la Estrazione è affatto proibita. Maggiore poi è anche il Nostro impegno, d'incoraggiare quei che professano le Belle Arti con premj, e con onori proporzionati al loro merito, e di agevolare loro tutte le strade per giungere alla perfezione nell'esercizio della loro nobile professione, la quale nell'unire l'utile al dilettevole, forma l'ornamento della Nostra Città, l'ammirazione di quei, che vi concorrono, ed il vantaggio di moltissimi Nostri Sudditi, che vi si occupano. Sarà dunque Vostra cura, che questa Pagina della Nostra volontà abbia il suo pieno effetto.

Volendo, e decretando, che al presente Nostro Chirografo, benché non esibito, nè registrato in Camera, e ne' suoi Libri, non possa mai darsi, nè opporsi di sumezione o orrezione, nè di alcun altro vizio, o difetto della Nostra volontà, ed intenzione, nè che mai sotto tali, o altri pretesti, quantunque validi, e validissimi, e giuridici anche di Jus quesito, o pregiudizio del terzo, possa essere impugnata, revocata, o moderata, ridotta *ad viam juris*, e concedersi contro di essa l'*Aperitione oris* o altro qualunque rimedio; e che così, e non altrimenti debba sempre, ed in perpetuo giudicarsi, definirsi, ed interpretarsi da qualsivoglia Giudice, o Tribunale, benché Collegiale, Congregazione, anche di Rmi Cardinali, Legati a Latere, Vice Legati, Camerlengo di S. Chiesa, Tesoriere, Rota, Camera, e qualsivoglia altro; togliendo loro ogni facoltà, e giurisdizione di definire, ed interpretare in contrario. Dichiarando Noi fin d'adesso preventivamente nullo, irrito, ed invalido tutto ciò, che da ciascuno di essi con qualsivoglia autorità, scientemente, o ignorantemente fosse in qualunque tempo giudicato, o si tentasse di giudicare contro la forma, e disposizioni del presente Nostro Chirografo, quale vogliamo che vaglia, e debba avere sempre, ed in perpetuo il suo pieno effetto, esecuzione, e vigore, colla semplice Nostra sottoscrizione, benchè non ci siano state chiamate, sentite, o citate qual si siano Persone ancorchè Privilegiate, Privilegiatissime, Ecclesiastiche, e Luoghi Pii, che avessero, e pretendessero avervi interesse, e per comprenderle fosse bisogno di special menzione. Non ostante la Bolla di Pio IV. *de Registrandis*, la regola della Nostra Cancelleria *de Jure quaesito non tollendo*, e non ostante ancora tutti, e qualsisiano Chirografi, Brevi, Ordinazioni, e Costituzioni Apostoliche Nostre, e dei Nostri Predecessori, Bandi, Editti, in virtù di essi, ed in qualunque modo emanati, affissi, e pubblicati, Leggi, Statuti, Riforme, Stili, e Consuetudini, e qualunque altra cosa, che facesse, o potesse fare in contrario. Alle quali tutte, e singole, avendone il tenore qui per espresso, e di parola in parola inserto, e registrato, e supplendo colla prenezza della Nostra Potestà Pontificia ad ogni vizio, o difetto qualunque sostanziale, e formale, che vi potesse intervenire per questa sola volta; e per la piena, e totale Esecuzione di quanto si contiene nel presente Nostro Chirografo, ampiamente, ed in ogni più valida forma Deroghiamo.

Dato dal Nostro Palazzo Apostolico Quirinale questo di primo Ottobre 1802.
Pius PP. VII.

Acciò dunque le benefiche providenze ordinate da Sua Beatitudine con il surriferito Chirografo abbiano la loro piena esecuzione, e produchino quegli utili effetti, che la Santità Sua si è proposti della conservazione, ed accrescimento dei Monumenti, e delle Opere antiche; e dell'incoraggimento, e propagazione delle Belle Arti, dopo avere analogamente alle facoltà nel medesimo accordateci destinato l'Officio del Segretario di Carnera Francesco Gregorj in Roma, e nelle Provincie le rispettive Cancellerie dei Governatori Legali, per ricevere le assegne, ed eseguire tutti quegli Atti, che trovansi nel sudetto Chirografo prescritti, vogliamo, ed ordiniamo, acciò niuno possa allegare ignoranza delle Sovrane disposizioni, che le medesime si deducano a notizia del Publico con il presente Nostro Editto, il quale affisso, e publicato nei Luoghi soliti di questa Dominante, e delle Provincie sudette obligherà ciascuno nella Città medesima, e nello Stato come se fosse stato a tutti personalmente intimato. Ed affinchè in avvenire possa egualmente essere a notizia di tutti, nè possa mai in tempo alcuno allegarsene ignoranza; ordiniamo, che lo stesso Editto si tenga, e conservi perpetuamente affisso presso il sudetto Segretario di Camera in Roma, e nello Stato presso le dette Cancellerie: rendendone responsabile non solo i Cancellieri, ma anche i respettivi Governatori delle Città, e Paesi. Avverta pertanto ognuno di uniformarsi esattamente alle prescrizioni ordinate nel preinserto Chirografo, e publicate con il presente Nostro Editto; giacchè contro quelli, che contraverranno, si procederà irrimissibilmente alla esecuzione delle pene nel medesimo contenute.

Dato in Camera Apostolica questo di 2 Ottobre 1802.
G. Card. Doria Pamphilj Pro-Cam.
P. Ferrari Udit. - G. Pecci Comm. Gen. della R. C. A.

18
Notificazione

Giuseppe del Titolo di S. Cecilia Prete Card. Doria Pamphilj della S. R. C. Pro-Camerlengo.
Quantunque con altri Editti de Nostri Antecessori siansi sempre vietati gli scavi di qualunque materia presso le Mura di questa Dominante, affine di preservarle da ogni pregiudizio, nulla di meno essendoci giunto a notizia, che ad onta di sì provvide Leggi ardisca taluno di cavare Arena, Terra, o Creta in vicinanza delle Mura stesse non senza pregiudizio di arrecargli li temuti danni; Quindi è, che a rimovere affatto un sì grave disordine, richiamando alla piena, e puntuale osservanza gli Editti succennati, e specialmente quelli emanati li 8 Aprile 1717, li 2 Ottobre 1726, li 10 Settembre 1733, e li 5 Gennaro 1750.
Proibiamo espressamente a qualunque persona di qualunque grado, e condizione il cavare, o far cavare sotto qualsivoglia pretesto, o quesito colore nelle vicinanze delle Mura circondarie di Roma Arena, Terra, Creta, o qualunque altra materia sotto pena della formale carcerazione, di 500 Ducati di oro di Camera, ed altre eziandio Corporali ad arbitrio nostro, e dei nostri Successori, secondo la qualità del fatto, e delle persone in via sommaria, anche per inquisizione con ogni rigore di giustizia.

Vogliamo in oltre, che li Custodi, e Rincontri delle Porte invigilino alla esatta osservanza di somigliante divieto, ed altrettanto faccia il Revisore, o sia Ispettore delle mure, a di cui carico rimarrà di minutamente osservare, se avvenga ogni più tenue trasgressione: Anzi sorprendendo qualche Refrattario nell'atto di essa, dovrà egli andare alla Porta più vicina, prender la Forza, che in questo caso non gli sarà negata, farlo arrestare, e tradurre al nostro Tribunale, onde sia giudicato nella forma di sopra espressa. E qualora trovi eseguita la mal'opera senza il Contraventore, dovrà usare tutte le possibili ricerche per venirne in cognizione, con dedurlo a nostra notizia, e così procedere nella maniera stabilita.
Ognuno pertanto conosca subito trasfuso in se il debito di uniformarsi inviolabilmente al prescritto fin'ora, poichè la presente affissa, e publicata che sia nei Luoghi soliti, e alle Porte di questa Capitale obbligherà tutti, come se fosse stata loro personalmente intimata.

Data in Camera questo dl 7 Gennaro 1803.
G. Card. Doria Pamphilj Pro-Cam.
P. Ferrari Udit. – G. Pecci Comm. Gen. della R. C. A.

1
[...] In all the Provinces

Reinstatement of the ancient office and jurisdiction of the road masters of the City and its district.

Summary.
Preamble – 1. Reasons for reinstating such an office – 2. On its reinstatement – 3. Establishment of the Masters – 4. On their jurisdiction – 5. Appointment of their Secretaries – 6. Prescription to the other officials to obey them – 7. On the need to not criticise and bother them during the execution of their duties – 8. Abolition of the conflicting [regulations].

Martin Bishop servant of God's servants, in eternal memory, addressing his beloved sons and noblemen Battista Pietro Mattei and Baccio de Stinchi, Roman citizens, and Road Masters of the City of Rome, wishing them health and apostolic blessing.

(Preamble)
In accordance with the functions entrusted to us from above, we are delighted about the adornment and prosperity of the world's provinces. Nevertheless, a greater commitment towards our City of Rome should be taken into account, in consideration of the Princes of the Apostles and cornerstones of the orthodox faith Peter and Paul, as well as other martyrs, who have effused [the city] with their blood. We believe it would be commendable and appropriate for this meritorious City and its district, which in the past have flourished thanks to divine and human deeds, to continue to prosper and improve in our time. The favor of the divine clemency, as well as the public decency, will indeed add value to the beneficial glories of the past.

(Reasons for reinstating such an office)

1. As evidence plainly proves, the City and the above-mentioned district, embraced within fatherly love, have been suffering for a long time because of the absence of the Masters related to this office. Their duty of administering roads, streets, squares, and other public and private places, as well as buildings made of stone and wood, walls made of beams, benches, roofs, floors, terraces, storages and staircases, gates, passages, watercourses, canals, and pipe drains, and also urban and rustic parcels, lawns, vegetable gardens, and vineyards, together with their task of supervising borders, restorations, the rights of way and the related authorisation – are thus re-established and ordered. Such reinstatement is permitted and allowed according to each individual case in order to contrast the tolerance of any reprehensible and detrimental ugliness and ruin. Indeed, as we have been informed, there are several citizens, tenants, and dwellers who indulge in such destructions, as well as butchers, fishermen, shoemakers, tanners, several artisans who own workshops, and city inhabitants who practice their professions; they all conceal intestines, bowels, heads, feet, bones, blood, as well as leathers, fleshes, rotten fishes, and other filthy spoiled materials in streets, roads, squares, and both public and private spaces. Furthermore, there are several citizens, tenants, and dwellers who indulge in their recklessness and vanity, going from bad to worse and persevering sacrilegious provocations; they occupy, ravage, sell, employ for their uses and wills streets, roads, squares, as well public, private, and ecclesiastic places. They do not understand how badly their dissipations impair the human body's health, the air's purity, and the spirit's well-being.

(On its reinstatement)

2. As we cannot ignore these distortions and excesses any longer; as we have overlooked the fact that these have been spreading across the City, becoming an actual habit; as we sincerely wish to fix the related damages; with our apostolic authority, we renew, reestablish, and reinstate the office of such a Master, according to its ancient institution.

(Establishment of the Masters)

3. With no hesitation, we appoint you, enthusiasts of ourselves and our City, compelling proofs of faith, legality, prudence, caution, and several virtues. We confer on you the responsibility of this office, until our approval ceases, together with its ancient jurisdictions, powers, honors, privileges, faculties, and all the duties; together with the authority to appoint the Vice-masters to support you, at any time and opportunity, and to bestow on them your same powers. We assign, entrust, and order you, designates Masters, the above-mentioned duties, as well as any other function depending on and relating to these.

(On their jurisdiction)

4. For all the duration of your appointment, we grant you the following mandates and powers: to adjust, correct, and repair each and every related alteration and excess mentioned above, in any way and time you deem suitable; to sue anyone or undertake legal action, in accordance to God's prudence, in the case that buildings and similar constructions are demolished, or of other misdemeanors; to mitigate, appease and resettle the excesses that derive from both the above-mentioned cases and arguments, or other controversies; to banish, arrest, incarcerate, deprive of their freedom any other rebel and offender; and finally, to implement and execute every authority that falls under the functions, exercises, and management of the previous Masters.

(Appointment of their Secretaries)

5. In order to facilitate and ease such a substantial responsibility, with the same authority, we appoint as your office Secretaries the prosecutor Nardo de Bustacchi and Nicola de Muti, both noble Roman citizens.

(Prescription to the other officials to obey them)

6. We order to each and every Marshal of our Capital, as well as the other officials, to obey, follow, and comply with you and your Vice-masters, as concerns any aspect related to the implementation of your duties. Furthermore, with the above-mentioned authority, we nullify and invalidate any past sentence of excommunication or interdiction enforced against the Masters by our Predecessors.

(On the need to not criticise and bother them during the execution of their duties)

7. With the same above-mentioned authority, we also declare that you, being operators, coordinators, and administrators of rightful duties, shall be exempted from trials and liberated from criticisms and inconveniences coming from anyone, even if these are persons invested with apostolic authority.

(Abolition of the conflicting [regulations])

8. It might occur that these constitutions and ordinances, as well as the City's statutes and customs, are disregarded, in spite of any effort to the contrary; therefore, we declare that any opposition to all these principles, or any of them, carried out deliberately or under any authority, shall be vain and invalid.

To anyone, therefore, etc.
Issued in Rome, in the SS. Apostles, on the second day before April's calends.
Eighth year of our pontificate.
31 March 1425.

2
[...] Our Soul-Nourishing City

Bishop Pius II, Servant of God's Servants. In perpetual memory of the event.

The desire to preserve Our Soul-Nourishing City's dignity and splendor compels Our utmost vigilance in maintaining and protecting the City's Basilicas, Churches, Shrines, and Holy grounds, and its ancient buildings and remains for the generations to come.
Indeed, such edifices adorn and honor the City, as do the memories of ancient Virtues and Glories that We so eagerly wish to foster and perpetuate.
Furthermore, since said edifices and remains help us to perceive the fragility of all human deeds better, because these ruins may no longer be relied upon, although our ancestors' mighty finances and investments prove that they were intended for immortality.
Nonetheless, time and calamities have had the upper hand.
Therefore, given the above and other reasons that torment Our soul;
Accepting the pleas by Our beloved Conservators of the Chamber, Lords of the Regions, and Citizens of the Urbs;

In keeping with some of Our most celebrated Predecessors' determination to preserve and maintain such constructions;
In confirmation of the ancient Statute currently in force in the City, which forbids all wrecking and demolishing under pain of strict financial sanctions;
By Our Apostolic authority and in full knowledge of the above-stated;
We confirm and approve the Statute under pain of excommunication and other financial penalties specified in the Statute itself.
Regardless of their grade, dignity, standing, order, or condition, all transgressors – both the Clergy and the Lay – including those invested with the Pontifical dignity or any other Ecclesiastical or Lay dignity, shall be punished by said penalties and sanctions.
Furthermore, by the authority and knowledge mentioned above, We strictly ban all persons from claiming the right to wreck, destroy, shatter, break, or lime ancient public edifices and remains – either directly or by proxy, openly or covertly — that still stand in the City and its District – both in the countryside and the Urbs.
By the authority and knowledge mentioned above, in the event of any transgressions, the beloved Conservators of the Urban Chamber that direct the investigations and inquiring officers are now entitled to:
Incarcerate any prospective ringleaders and perpetrators caught in the act; Confiscate their pack animals, tools, and other such possessions; Arrest and detain both perpetrators and ringleaders; Impose the full payment of the financial penalty.
Moreover, no one but the Roman Pontiff may grant any such permission. Indeed, such authorisations shall only be issued through Bulls and Apostolic Briefs. No other person has the Power or Right to take such action.
No counteractive Constitution, Apostolic Act, or Ordinance may ever be promulgated.
To ensure that all are informed, and no one may claim ignorance, We have notified the Proclaimers and had the here present Letter affixed in all of the City's public venues, including the Capitolium door.
By the authority referenced above, We acknowledge that every person concerned is to be considered bound by this Letter as if informed personally. Indeed, it is doubtful that anyone could still be unaware of such a publicised law.
Therefore, this present Paper bearing Our Confirmation, Approval, Prohibition, Concession, Will, and Constitution may not be violated or disregarded by anyone.
Those who dare do so shall bring upon themselves the wrath of God Almighty and His Apostles, the Blessed Peter and Paul.

Issued in Rome at Saint Peter's, on May 4th, in the year of the Incarnation 1462. Year IV of Our Pontificate.

3
[...] Our Holy Fathers' wise decrees

Bishop Sixtus, Servant of God's Servants. In perpetual memory of the event.

Inasmuch as Our Holy Fathers' wise decrees condemn as sacrilegious those who ruin, despoil, or plunder the Lord's Churches and holy grounds to steal their sacred ornaments and ravage their furnishings; and
Because such crimes lead to doubled penalties;
Since We are the supreme custodians of all Churches and wish to express Our most profound reproach towards such serious crimes;
To safeguard Our Churches' prosperity, perfection, decoration, and dignity;
We decree that the fullest attention and care be paid to prevent God's Churches and holy temples, especially those in the Soul-Nourishing City, from being despoiled by such malicious thugs. All the perpetrators of such crimes shall incur due punishment.
Much to Our surprise, someone's reliable reports have informed Us of several children of iniquity that falsely profess to be Christians and show no fear of the Lord nor respect for the Christian Religion, the Patriarchal Churches and Basilicas, and the City's other consecrated Churches. These sinners have dared plunder a number of scarlet red marbles, along with other marbles of different colours, that had been intended for the Churches' decoration and adornment. Moreover, they now smuggle and transfer booty daily, both by themselves and with the aid of others, thus offending the Lord, disfiguring Churches, damning their souls, and jeopardising the lives of many.
Therefore, because We strongly wish to counter these sinners' sacrilegious acts as much as possible, if God wills it; and
Despite the sanctions and prohibitions promulgated by Our Predecessors, whose applicability We now confirm; which
Prohibit the plunder of the ornaments and marbles mentioned above from all Churches and holy grounds; and
Provide for the excommunication of those who dare indulge in such shameful crimes, the like of which was unheard of before;
We decree that all the persons, regardless of their dignity, status, grade, order, or condition, who;
Are found in possession of such stones and other ornaments from Churches and Basilicas in the City; or
Have aided or supported the plunderers in stealing, concealing, and storing the booty;
Must return the loot, as of the Publication of the present Letter.
All the transgressors who fail to confess and inform Us through our minor Penitentiaries shall be sentenced to excommunication. The Roman Pontiff retains the right to acquit the offenders on the point of death and upon monetary compensation.
Furthermore, the Churches and holy grounds that were, or might have been, adorned by the stones in question, shall be subjected to ecclesiastical interdiction. This Ecclesiastical forbiddance shall be effective until the return, albeit partial, of the loot to the locations from which they were removed.

Moreover, those who commit such crimes in disregard of their salvation must pay half a Libra of gold to the Church or Basilica from which they have plundered the stones or ornaments, as compensation for the offense.
Therefore, all persons are banned from shredding or contradicting the present Paper that bears Our will and decree.
Those who dare do so shall bring upon themselves the wrath of God Almighty and His Apostles, the Blessed Peter and Paul.

Issued in Rome at Saint Peter's, on April 25th, in the year of the Incarnation 1474. Year III of Our Pontificate.

4
[Appointment of a Prefect for the Marbles]

To Raphael from Urbino.[102]

Because, for the construction of the Roman Temple of the Prince of the Apostles (Saint Peter's Basilica), it is of the utmost importance that a large amount of stone and marble, which should nonetheless be kept in stock at all times, be stored in town rather than imported from outside;
And since I must consider the opportunity offered by the City's Ruins, the stones of all kinds that are continually dug out on construction sites within and beyond Rome, and the stones that are temporarily unearthed;
I appoint you, my current Superintendent for this construction, its marbles, and all the stones in Rome and within ten thousand steps of it, as Prefect in the purchase of the marbles needed henceforth for the construction of the Temple.
Therefore, I command that all the common diggers, regardless of their level of experience, must immediately report the amount and type of marbles and stones they unearth or excavate within the radius indicated above.
As Prefect to the assignments mentioned above, you shall ensure that all transgressors be fined from one hundred up to three hundred golden crowns, as deemed appropriate.
Furthermore, because I am aware that several marbles and engraved stones represent monuments to be cherished for the sake of the Humanities and Roman Language; and that The marble workers that use them as raw material saw and erase the inscriptions indiscriminately;
Therefore, I command that all the marble cutters in Rome must refrain from cutting or sawing engraved stones without your order or permission. All transgressors shall be punished as specified above.

Issued in Rome on September 26th, Year III [1515].

---

102 Raffaello da Urbino (1483-1520). Variations: Raffaello Sanzio, Raphaele Urbinas.

5
[Appointment of a Commissary of Antiquities]

To my Treasured Son Latino Giovenale Manetti, Roman Citizen, Relative, and Personal Secretary – Pope Paul III.

Treasured son, I send you my greetings, etc. Among the many duties of the Roman Pontiff and along with the safeguard of Religion, We believe one must always count the preservation of Our Soul-Nourishing City's Monuments. Let us not forget that the Lord elected the City of Rome as the Seat of the Universal Empire and, subsequently, of the Holy Christian Religion.
Since Our Faith's Representative rightfully sits in the capital of such a grand Empire; and
Because there is no other Kingdom on Earth as virtuous and blessed by God as this one; and
As the Empire has changed so profoundly, due to the instability of all human pursuits;
Therefore, Our Sacred Faith and Divine Religion gleam and shine more than any existing secular power.
After eradicating Idolatry from Our City and converting all Pagan Temples to the cult of God and the Saints, it became Our priority to safeguard the Urbs' Monuments' everlasting splendor. Consequently, We acted to foster the magnificence and frequency of the Sacred Services for all those wishing to visit the City's Ruins to praise the Lord that has bestowed such wealth and power on humanity.
However, due to Our negligence and meanness, We are bitterly reminded of Our responsibility in the shattering, liming, burial, and removal of the Quirites' ancient glories by Goths, Vandals, other Barbarians, Greeks, and contemporary raiders, which concurred with the ravages of time.
Namely, We are to blame for letting the marbles be cracked and overturned by wild fig-trees, ivies, and other weeds;
For allowing the construction, over the old rocks, of shacks and huts that disfigure the ancient buildings' magnificence; and mostly
For turning a blind eye to the smuggling of Statues, insignia, marble and bronze slabs, or scarlet, Numidian, and other coloured stones.
If the proper measures are not taken soon, it will eventually be impossible to find the olden Rome amidst the new houses built with the antiquities shattered, cracked, smashed, and limed for construction, out of avarice and ill will. What is more, there have been reports of bones of the Saint Martyrs being smashed along with the other stones unearthed from the ancient ruins, thus adding sacrilege to the lese-majesty of the Roman antiquities.
To prevent the recurrence of such crimes, in keeping with Our Office's duties, Our love for the Homeland moves Us to preserve the honor and majesty of She who gave birth to Us children with all the strength We have.
Therefore, it is to you;
Who, born to a noble and ancient Family, loves the Homeland as much as we do, and has studied and retrieved antiquities with such outstanding dedication;
Who, We are told and have noticed, has progressed so well in such matters;
Whom We love so fondly for your virtue, fidelity, and supreme ingenuity;

It is to you that We directed Our eyes and mind, choosing to entrust you with such a critical assignment that We understandably have at heart;
We rest assured that you will spend every effort to win Our praise, for your Homeland's sake and the call of duty.
Therefore, We appoint you general Commissary, by Our Apostolic Authority, in keeping with the decrees in force. Moreover, We grant you full powers to adjudicate, direct, and act in a spirit of conservation and respect, to remove all of the bushes, shrubs, plants, ivies, and, most importantly, caprifigs that invade our City and its district from the:
Monuments, Arches, Temples, Memorials, Theaters, Amphitheaters, Circuses, Naumachiae, Porticoes, Columns, Sepulchers, Epitaphs, Eulogies, large Stones, Aqueducts, Statues, Figures, Panels, Gemstones, Marbles, and any other items that fall within the category of "Antiquities and Monuments"; and
We encourage you to prohibit the construction of new walls and habitations that lean into such Antiquities and Monuments. Furthermore, such Antiquities and monuments may never be demolished, cut into pieces, shattered, baked in limestone, nor transported outside the City.
Moreover, We authorise you to punish all transgressors by monetary fines or excommunication. The latter shall follow the official reprimand set forth in this Letter;
You shall reserve the right to inflict such penalties on all persons at will, including members of your administration;
You shall act on Our behalf as you deem best, imposing the penalties you believe are most befitting;
You shall appoint one or more Representatives, when necessary, bestowing on them powers equal or inferior to yours;
You shall administer, enforce, and complete all the assignments that, in your view, concern the accomplishment of Our present Commission.

Issued in Rome at Saint Peter's, on November 28th, 1534. Year I.

6
The office of the Conservators

Vol. I. Chap. XV.

Primarily, the office of the Conservators must always be vigilant and careful for the sake of Our Holy Lord, the Pope, and Our Holy Roman Church, the City and citizens' serenity, and public security.
Furthermore, it must preserve all Buildings and public infrastructures, notably the ancient ones. Accordingly, its supervisors must also be vigilant and careful, prosecuting and investigating every theft and wreckage of Temple and Church ornaments and stones, or safeguarding the Saints' Memorial Monuments and Relics.
Moreover, the Conservators must guard the keys to the chapel in the Saint John Lateran Basilica, where the heads of Saint Peter and Paul are kept, either directly – as is customary – or by proxy; and

Oversee the maintenance of Walls, Bridges, Aqueducts, and Public Buildings in need of restoration. Also, the Conservatories must frequently visit and supervise such sites to preserve them from wreckage.

Ancient Buildings not to be demolished

Vol. III. Chap. LXXXI.

Ruins shall not disfigure Our City. Quite the contrary, the ancient buildings must at all times prove the City's decorum.
Regardless of their position, condition, or motivation, no citizen may destroy or wreck – either directly or by proxy – any sort of urban building situated both within and beyond its boundaries. Such prohibition also applies to edifices located within one's property or estate.
All transgressors shall be punished by five hundred aurei. Also, the Senator in office is compelled to run an inquiry.
[1580]

7
Prohibition against the export of Statues of marble and metal, Figures, Antiquities, and the like

Cardinal Ippolito Aldobrandini, Dean of Santa Maria Nuova, Chamberlain of the Holy Roman Church.
Several Edicts and prohibitions issued at different times by our Predecessors have banned the export of Figures, Statues, Antiquities, Ornaments, works in marble, metal, and other stone outside the city of Rome and the State of the Church without their and Our authorisation.
However, since many have taken action to export such items in violation of the existing laws, We wish to fulfil Our Lord's direct orders and counter these incidents through the authority of the Office of Chamberlain, without withdrawing from said Edicts and Prohibitions issued by our Predecessors.
On the contrary, We hereby reaffirm and renew the bans, commanding that no person of any state, grade, dignity, order, and condition may export – either directly or by proxy – Figures, Statues, Antiquities, Ornaments, or works – either ancient or modern – in marble, metal, or stone of any kind – both integer and in pieces, without Our license. Said ban applies to the city of Rome, its territory, and all locations within the State of the Church and extends to all transportation by River, Sea, or Land. All offenders will be punished by the confiscation of the items and a fine of five hundred crowns. Half the sum will be allotted to the Reverend Apostolic Chamber; one-quarter is for the accuser, the other fourth for the executor. Any other penalty, including corporal punishment, remains at our discretion, depending on the case's gravity.
Furthermore, We command that any excavations performed under Our license that should produce Statues, or other items among the ones listed above, or any objects in stone and metal of all kinds, must be reported within 24 hours after the discovery either

by the owners of the estate where the excavation was carried out, the diggers, or any other person informed.
The finding must be notified to either Us or our Auditor, or recorded for Our Notary mentioned below, refraining from donating, selling, or disposing of the item within four days after the report, under the punishment mentioned above with an additional three strappados for the diggers.[103]
All prospective offenders are warned that the penalties mentioned above will be imposed strictly not only upon investigation but also through the testimony of any witnesses deemed trustworthy. Evidence collected outside the State will be presented and used in a court of law.
The misdemeanors mentioned above may be detected by any person, provided the denouncement is enclosed in the proceedings.
The present Edict will be affixed and published in Rome's usual venues, and everyone will be held accountable as if they were informed personally. All diggers and owners of vineyards and other locations must publicly display this Edict under the penalties mentioned above.

In faith. Issued in Rome, at the Apostolic Chamber, on October 5th, 1624.
Chamberlain Cardinal Ippolito Aldobrandini
Auditor F. Canali
General Commissary of the Apostolic Chamber Antonio Lamberti

8
Edict on the export and excavation of Statues, Figures, Carvings, Medallions, inscriptions in marble, inlaid marble, metal, Gold, Silver, Jewels, and similar ancient and modern items

Federico Sforza, Dean Cardinal of Saints Vitus and Modestus, Pro-Chamberlain of the Holy Roman Church, specially appointed by Our Lord His Holiness.
Notwithstanding the Notices already issued by our predecessors and Ourselves against those who dig – either directly or by proxy – in public and private spaces, near buildings, construction sites, walls, and ancient bridges, in search of works in marble, inlaid marble, alabaster, slab, travertine, peperino, spur, and other stone, to the risk and detriment of said buildings and public thoroughfares; and
Notwithstanding the Notices against those who dig – either directly or by proxy– in public and private quarries, in search of statues, busts, bas-reliefs, heads, pedestals, columns, capitals, inscriptions, medallions, cameos, and precious carvings on marble, metal, precious stone, inlaid marble, gold, silver, agate, crugnola stone, amethyst, and other stones – both wrought and uncut; and
Notwithstanding the severe punishments and the prohibitions published in said Notices to counter said diggings, which are often retrieved as well;

103 The strappado was a form of torture, employed from the Middle Ages. It was also known as "reverse hanging".

Nevertheless, We are informed that many items are sold, smuggled, stolen, and cached, both in Rome and beyond, without due notification, license, and consent by the owners of the spaces and homesteads involved. Consequently, such conduct leads to the public and private detriment, crises of conscience, and the ransacking of the ancient and modern assets in our Soul-Nourishing City of Rome.

Therefore, to rectify the misdemeanors and punish all offenders adequately, by Our Lord's spoken order and through the authority of the office of Pro-Chamberlain, pursuant to all previous Notices and in confirmation of the ones issued by our predecessors and Ourselves that are relevant;

We hereby command that all persons – both Ecclesiastical and Lay – of any state, grade, order, and condition refrain from wrecking buildings, ancient construction sites, walls in travertine, marble, peperino, and other materials, both over and underground, either directly or by proxy;

Furthermore, it is forbidden to break or excavate ancient statues and other antiquities of any material or dig near said buildings, walls, construction sites, arches, bridges, cemeteries, or thoroughfares without Our permission or the patronage of either the Commissary for quarries and antiquities Leonardo Santi – who was appointed by Us directly – or his prospective deputy.

Moreover, all Ecclesiastical and Lay persons, as specified above, are banned from selling or exporting – either directly or by proxy, outside Rome and the Papal State – any type of statue, figure, bas-relief, column, vase, alabaster, agate, jasper, amethyst;

Other marble, precious stones, wrought stones, uncut stones, busts, heads, fragments, pillars, pedestals, inscriptions;

Other ornaments, friezes, medallions, cameos, or carvings made on any sort of stone, metal, gold, silver both ancient and modern;

Figures, ancient paintings, or other works sculpted in any material, painted, carved, assembled, crafted, or otherwise created, that are either found in quarries, located within Rome or beyond, in any person's possession, or in any other place.

Therefore, the sale and export of said items are restricted to those issued with our license. Subsequently, our Commissary will oversee transactions between purchasers and sellers – which will also be registered by our Notary mentioned above and countersigned by our other Commissary. Moreover, the former Commissary will certify the quality and quantity of the items in question.

All the items found, sold, concealed, withheld, smuggled, or purchased without a license, within or beyond Rome, will be confiscated as specified above. All offenders will be fined 500 Chamber golden ducats. Half of the sum will be allotted to the Reverend Apostolic Chamber; one-fourth is for the accuser, whose identity will be kept secret; one-fourth is for our Commissary. Furthermore, the Commissary has the right to perform investigations, press charges on behalf of ourselves or our Auditor, testify under oath to substantiate allegations, and act upon the testimony of even just one witness. All penalties, including corporal punishment, will be imposed depending on the offenders' social standing and will be carried out rigorously.

Moreover, We hereby uphold the prohibitions issued on October 5th and 9th, 1624, and decree that the penalties contained therein to contrast the unlicensed sale, purchase, and export of goods outside Rome, will remain unchanged and be implemented as specified above.

Since Diggers, Stonemasons, Builders, Vintners, and other suspicious professionals often sell, steal, break, and smuggle statues, heads, cameos, carvings, medallions, precious stones, rings, and other valuable antiquities made of any kind of material, as well as marble, alabaster, gold, silver, metal, precious stone or different types of stone; and
Since said professionals often sell the items mentioned above to Iron Dealers, Stonecutters, Sculptors, Retailers, or Shopkeepers, and do not inform the lawful owners of the goods and sites in question;
Therefore, We ban all such suspicious professionals from selling any said antiquities found or owned under any pretense whatsoever. Accordingly, the sale of items that exceed one crown's value is subject to our Notary's preliminary registration, the Commissary's appraisal of the items' quality and quantity, and his identification of the seller and purchaser.
All offenders will be punished by the confiscation of the goods in question, which will be returned to the lawful owners, and by other discretionary penalties – including monetary fines – to be implemented as specified above.
Furthermore, We ban all Carpenters, Laborers, and other such professionals from crafting chests – either directly or by proxy – to package statues and other antiquities listed above, as well as modern items – both wrought and uncut; and
All Porters, Bearers, and Carters from transferring, fastening, packing, bundling, and transporting said items; and
All boatmen and sailors from embarking chests, bundles, and parcels containing ancient or modern artworks on Boats and Vessels, without our Commissary's supervision and our license, as specified above, under the same punishment, or subject to stricter penalties at our discretion.
Moreover, We ban all Castellans, Customs Officers, Keepers, Gatekeepers, Border Officers, and Commissaries of the seal of the port of Ripa from allowing the transit on rivers, by sea, and land, of the ancient and modern artworks listed above without a license sealed with our stamp. The restrictions include items transported in chests, without a chest, bundled, wrought, uncut, of any material, painted, or sculpted. All offenders will be punished by the confiscation of the items in question, as well as corporal and monetary penalties at our discretion.
Additionally, We ban all Carters, Porters, Bearers, and Muleteers from packing or transporting – either directly or by proxy – marble, travertine, alabaster, peperino, statues, columns, heads, figures, bas-reliefs, and any other wrought or uncut stone from any quarry or ancient building, and of any metal, without a license in writing as specified above. The license is free of charge and must be kept at hand by those who transport or cut the goods listed and produced on our Commissary or other appointees' request to prevent any misdemeanor. All offenders will be punished by three strappados, to be dealt on the spot, a fine of 25 crowns imposed as specified above, and the confiscation of the items in question.
Accordingly, all limestone workers, diggers, Stonecutters, Sculptors, Jewelers, Casters, and other wreckers are banned from breaking, wrecking, and shattering to produce mortar, for transportation, or resale without our permission or the supervision of the Commissary or other appointees. Said license is free of charge. The interdicted items include wrought marble, marble bearing inscriptions, statues, figures, and other ancient ornaments. It is also forbidden to melt, wreck, or dent figures, medallions, carvings on ancient metal, gold, or silver, bearing representations or records of ancient events without the permission

and supervision mentioned above. All offenders will be punished by the confiscation of the items, a fine of 25 crowns to be imposed as specified above, and other discretionary penalties – including corporal punishment.

Since, so far, We and others have often issued permits and licenses to excavate – either directly or by proxy – treasures, marble, travertine, statues, pozzolana, and similar items that require the intervention and assistance of our Commissary or other prospective appointees to ensure that no unauthorised excavations are conducted on unauthorised sites or near public buildings, thoroughfares, or cemeteries that might be damaged, as described above;

Therefore, We command that, within ten days of this Edict's publication, every person issued with a license, regardless of their state, grade, title, order, and condition, must report to our Notary's office stating which permits are currently in their possession. All transgressors will be punished by the cancelation of said licenses; any future excavation will be subject to the supervision and assistance of our Commissary or other appointees and punished by a fine of 25 crowns in case of infringement, to be imposed as specified above.

No Stonecutter, Digger, or Estate Owner issued with our license and excavating by proxy on public or private land, may sell travertine, marble, alabaster, statues, and the other items listed above, without our Commissary's supervision and measurements. Furthermore, a due portion of the finds must be allotted to the Reverend Chamber and put at our disposal, as estimated by our appointed appraisers. This restriction extends to the sale of lead, metal, gold, silver, and any other item partly allotted to the Chamber. All transgressors will be punished by the confiscation of the items, a fine of 100 crowns, to be imposed as specified above, and corporal penalties at our discretion.

We hereby ban all Sculptors, Stonecutters, Retailers, Diggers, and Quarry Owners from selling and purchasing any statue, wrought marble, raw marble, figures, bas-reliefs, columns, pedestals, inscriptions, medallions, cameos, carvings, or other antiquities without notifying our Notary of the items' amount and quality, in order to register the transfer of ownership and ascertain the existence of similar specimens in Rome, under the penalties specified above.

Moreover, all Diggers, Vintners, Stonecutters, Builders, Sculptors, and Owners of thoroughfares, quarries, sites, locations, or workshops where the items mentioned above are stored – both within Rome and beyond – must receive our Commissary;

Furthermore, the Commissary must always be allowed to view, inspect, locate, and record the statues, figures, busts, bas-reliefs, vases, medallions, cameos, carvings, items in gold, silver, metal, marble, and other materials, as well as the precious stones – both wrought and uncut. Therefore, it is said professionals' duty to welcome and help the Commissary in his work's performance and refrain from selling or transferring the items in question for five days. Accordingly, said professionals must obey the Commissary in reporting the finds to us, our Auditor, or on the Notary's record, under the penalties mentioned above.

All sculptors, builders, stonecutters, diggers, quarry owners, iron dealers, retailers, and medallion casters must affix this Edict in their workshops, quarries, and locations where the statues and the other items are kept for sale. All transgressors will be punished by a fine of three crowns every time they do not comply with the affixation order, under the penalties mentioned above; the Edict must, therefore, be made visible to all.

Finally, We invest our Commissary, special collaborators, executors, and ministries of justice with the authority to act on any reports filed, searching the locations where the statues, antiquities of any material, chests, boats, vessels, luggage, bundles, and the like may have been stored by Keepers, Watchmen, Boatmen, and Customs Officers. Subsequently, We must be informed, together with our Auditor, and in our Notary's records, of any unlicensed export heading out of Rome. The presence of one witness and the Commissary's sworn statement will suffice to validate the accuser's testimony. We command that all Captains of Justice, Executors, Ministers of Justice, and Heralds help and favor the Commissary, under pain of losing their appointment, and further penalties at our discretion.

All be warned that the penalties described above will be imposed strictly and irreversibly holding private Owners accountable for the Ministers' misdemeanors, and Masters for their Servants'. We reserve the right to act discretionally to increase or decrease penalties depending on each case.

This Edict must be published and affixed in Rome's customary venues within three days of its issuance, after which everyone will be considered as informed and accountable. In faith etc.

Issued in Rome, at the Apostolic Chamber, on January 29th, 1646.
Pro-Chamberlain Cardinal Federico
General Commissary Lazzaro Botto
Auditor Jacopo Antonio Serperio

9
Prohibition against the export of Statues of marble and metal, Figures, Antiquities, and the like

Palace of the title of the Basilica of Santa Maria in Trastevere, Cardinal Priest Altieri, Chamberlain of the Holy Roman Church.

Despite the numerous Edicts etc. (as in no. 7), We wish to counter all illegal exports and misdemeanors, punishing all offenses effectively, pursuant to Our Lord's spoken wishes and through the authority of the Office of Chamberlain. Consequently, We do not withdraw from the previous notices issued and published on such matters by our Predecessors – which indeed we uphold when relevant – and make particular reference to the ones published on October 5th, 1624, January 24th, 1646, and August 30th, 1655.

We hereby ban all persons, both Ecclesiastical and Lay, of any state, grade, order, and condition, none excluded, from performing or demanding to perform exports – either directly or by proxy – headed out of the State. The ban applies to all transports by river, sea, or land and pertains to all types of statues, figures, bas-reliefs, columns, vases, alabaster, agate, jasper, amethysts, and other precious marble, jewels, wrought stones, and uncut stones; as well as Busts, heads, fragments, pillars, pedestals, inscriptions, and other ornaments, friezes, medallions, cameos, or carvings on any type of stone, metal, gold, silver, or of any ancient or modern material;

Figures, paintings, ancient depictions, or other works sculpted in any material, painted, carved, assembled, crafted, or otherwise created, which have been recently found in quarries or are within or beyond Rome in any person's possession or any location. The restriction applies to all the persons not in possession of a license issued by us, in compliance with His Holiness' special Chirograph. Accordingly, our Commissary for antiquities and quarries will draft a sworn statement specifying the Purchaser and Seller and assessing the items' quality and quantity. The Commissaries responsible for the documentation regarding waterway and land transportation will attach the statement to the documents issued by the Secretary and Chancellor of the Reverend Apostolic Chamber. All transgressors without a license issued as specified above will be punished by the confiscation of the items found, sold, shipped, concealed, withheld, stolen, or cached within or beyond Rome and the Papal State. A fine of 500 golden ducats will also be imposed: half of the sum will be allotted to the Reverend Apostolic Chamber; one-quarter is for the accuser, whose identity will be kept secret; one-fourth is for our Commissary mentioned above. Furthermore, the Commissary has the right to perform investigations, press charges on behalf of ourselves or our Auditor, testify under oath to substantiate allegations, and act upon the testimony of even just one witness. All penalties, including corporal punishment, will be imposed depending on the offenders' social standing and will be carried out rigorously.

Since many dig – either directly or by proxy – in public and private spaces, near buildings, construction sites, walls, and ancient bridges, in search of works in marble, inlaid marble, alabaster, slab, travertine, peperino, and other stone, to the risk and detriment of said buildings and public thoroughfares; and

In public and private quarries, in search of statues, busts, bas-reliefs, heads, pedestals, columns, capitals, inscriptions, medallions, cameos, and precious carvings on marble, metal, precious stone, inlaid marble, gold, silver, agate, crugnola stone, amethyst, and other stones – both wrought and uncut; and

Notwithstanding the severe punishments and the prohibitions published in said Notices to counter said diggings, which are often retrieved as well;

Nevertheless, We are informed that many items are sold, smuggled, stolen, and cached, both in Rome and beyond, without due notification, permission, and consent by the owners of the spaces and items involved. Consequently, such conduct leads to the public and private detriment, crises of conscience, and the ransacking of the most beautiful ancient and modern assets in our Soul-Nourishing City of Rome.

Therefore, We ban all the persons mentioned above from ruining land structures such as buildings, ancient construction sites, walls in travertine, marble, peperino, or other materials; and

Wrecking or excavating ancient statues and other ornaments in any material, or excavating – either directly or by proxy – near said buildings, walls, construction sites, arches, bridges, cemeteries, and public thoroughfares in any place without our permission and the supervision of our Commissary or other appointees.

Moreover, all sellers and purchasers who trade and ship said ancient and modern items outside Rome will be punished by the same penalties, as mentioned above.

Since Diggers, Stonemasons, Builders, Vintners, and other suspicious professionals often sell, steal, break, and smuggle statues, heads, cameos, carvings, medallions, precious stones, rings, and other valuable antiquities made of marble, alabaster, gold, silver, metal, precious stone or different types of stone; and

Since said professionals often sell the items mentioned above to Iron Dealers, Stonecutters, Sculptors, Retailers, or Shopkeepers, and do not inform the lawful owners of the goods and sites where the finding took place either covertly or openly;

Therefore, We ban all such persons from selling and purchasing any said antiquities found or owned under any pretense whatsoever. Accordingly, the sale of items that exceed one crown's value is subject to our Notary's preliminary registration, the Commissary's appraisal of the items' quality and quantity, and his identification of the seller and purchaser.

All offenders will be punished by the confiscation of the goods in question, which will be returned to the lawful owners, and by other discretionary penalties – including monetary fines – to be implemented as specified above.

Furthermore, We ban all Carpenters, Laborers, and other such professionals from crafting chests or Lighting – either directly or by proxy – to package statues and other antiquities listed above, as well as packing modern items – both wrought and uncut; and

All Porters and Bearers, from fastening, packing, bundling, and transporting said items; and

All boatmen and sailors from embarking chests, bundles, and parcels containing said ancient or modern artworks on Boats and Vessels, without our Commissary's supervision and our permission, as specified above, under the same punishment, or subject to stricter penalties at our discretion.

Moreover, We ban all Castellans, Customs Officers, Keepers, Gatekeepers, Border Officers, Commissaries of the seal of the port of Ripa, and any other person from allowing the transit on rivers, by sea, and land, of the ancient and modern artworks listed above without a license sealed with our Stamp. The restrictions include items transported in chests, without a chest, bundled, wrought, uncut, of any material, painted, or sculpted. All offenders will be punished by revoking their appointment as well as corporal and monetary penalties at our discretion.

Additionally, We ban all Carters, Porters, Bearers, and Muleteers from packing or transporting – either directly or by proxy – marble, travertine, alabaster, peperino, statues, columns, heads, figures, bas-reliefs, and any other wrought or uncut stone from any quarry or ancient building, and of any metal, without a license in writing as specified above. The license is free of charge and must be kept at hand by those who transport or cut the goods listed and produced on our Commissary or other appointees' request to prevent any misdemeanor. All offenders will be punished by three strappados, to be dealt on the spot, a fine of twenty-five crowns imposed as specified above, and the confiscation of the items in question.

Accordingly, all limestone workers, diggers, Stonecutters, Sculptors, Jewelers, Casters, and other such wreckers are banned from breaking, wrecking, or shattering to produce mortar; from transportation or resale without our permission or the supervision of the Commissary or other appointees. Said license is free of charge. The interdicted items include wrought marble, marble bearing inscriptions, statues, figures, and other ancient ornaments. Melting, wrecking, or denting figures, medallions, carvings on ancient metal, gold, or silver, that bear representations or records of ancient events is subject to the permission and supervision mentioned above. All offenders will be punished by the confiscation of the items, a fine of 25 crowns to be imposed as specified above, and other discretionary penalties – including corporal punishment.

Since, so far, We and others have often issued permits and licenses to excavate – either directly or by proxy – treasures, marble, travertine, statues, pozzolana, and similar items that require the intervention and assistance of our Commissary or other prospective appointees to ensure that no unauthorised excavations take place on forbidden grounds or near public buildings, thoroughfares, or cemeteries that might be damaged, as described above;
Therefore, We command that, within ten days of this Edict's publication, every person issued with a license, regardless of their state, grade, and condition, must report to our Notary's office stating which permits are currently in their possession. All transgressors will be punished by the cancelation of said licenses.
No Stonecutter, Digger, or Estate Owner issued with our license and excavating by proxy on public or private land, may sell travertine, marble, alabaster, statues, and the other items listed above, or allocate a due portion to the Reverend Chamber without our Commissary's supervision and measurements performed by Appraisers appointed by us. Subsequently, a due portion of the finds must be allotted to said Chamber and put at our disposal. This restriction extends to the sale of lead, metal, gold, silver, and any other item partly allotted to the Chamber. All transgressors will be punished by the confiscation of the items, a fine of ten crowns, to be imposed as specified above, and corporal penalties at our discretion.
We hereby ban all Sculptors, Stonecutters, Retailers, Diggers, and Quarry Owners from selling and purchasing statues, wrought marble, raw marble, figures, bas-reliefs, columns, pedestals, inscriptions, medallions, cameos, carvings, or other antiquities without notifying our Notary of the items' amount and quality, under the penalties specified above. The Notary will thus register the transfer of ownership and ascertain the existence of similar specimens in Rome.
Moreover, all diggers, vintners, laborers, stonemasons, sculptors, stonecutters, and owners of statues, quarries, sites, locations, or workshops where the ancient items mentioned above are stored – both within Rome and beyond – must receive our Commissary;
Furthermore, the Commissary must always be allowed to view, inspect, locate, and record the statues, figures, busts, bas-reliefs, vases, medallions, cameos, carvings, items in gold, silver, metal, marble, and other materials, as well as the precious stones – both wrought and uncut. Therefore, said professionals' duty is to welcome and help the Commissary in his work's performance and refrain from selling or transferring the items in question for five days. Accordingly, said professionals must obey the Commissary in reporting the finds to us, our Auditor, or on the Notary's record, under the penalties mentioned above.
All sculptors, laborers, stonecutters, diggers, quarry owners, iron dealers, retailers, and medallion casters must affix this Edict in their workshops, quarries, and locations where the statues and the other items are kept for sale. All transgressors will be punished by a fine of three crowns every time they do not comply with the affixation order, under the penalties mentioned above; the Edict must, therefore, be made visible to all.
Finally, We invest our Commissary, special collaborators, executors, ministries of justice, and any other person involved with the authority to act on any reports filed and search the locations where the statues, antiquities of any material, chests, boats, vessels, luggage, bundles, and the like may have been stored by keepers, watchmen, boatmen, and customs officers. Subsequently, We must be informed, together with our Auditor, and in our Notary's records, of any unlicensed export heading out of Rome. The presence of one witness and the Commissary's sworn statement will suffice to validate the accuser's testimony. We

command that all captains of justice, executors, ministers of justice, and heralds help and favor the Commissary, under pain of losing their appointment, and further penalties at our discretion.
All be warned that the penalties described above will be imposed strictly and irreversibly, holding the private owners accountable for the ministers' misdemeanors and masters for their servants'. We reserve the right to act discretionally to increase or decrease penalties depending on each case.
This Edict must be published and affixed in Rome's customary venues within three days of its issuance, after which everyone will be considered as informed and accountable.

In faith. Issued in Rome, at the Apostolic Chamber, on February 5th, 1686.
Pro-Chamberlain Cardinal Paluzzo Altieri
Auditor Michelangelo Zaccaria – General Commissary S. Pilastri
Secretary and Chancellor of the Reverend Apostolic Chamber Domenico Liberati

10
Prohibition against the export of Statues of marble and metal, Figures, Antiquities, and the like

Giovanni Battista Spinola, Dean Cardinal of San Cesareo (in Palatio), Chamberlain of the Holy Roman Church.
(As referenced in no. 8)
Issued in Rome, at the Apostolic Chamber, on July 18th, 1701.

11
Edict on the Pictures, Stuccoes, Mosaics, and other Antiquities found in quarries, ancient Inscriptions, Writings, and Manuscripts

Giovanni Battista Spinola, Dean Cardinal of San Cesareo (in Palatio), Chamberlain of the Holy Roman Church.
Since Our Lord, in all his fatherly charity and zeal, cares deeply about the conservation of our ancient mementos, which promotes our Soul-Nourishing City of Rome's fame among all foreign Nations; and
As its ornaments serve the purpose of confirming and illustrating both the sacred and profane History magnificently;
Therefore, by the spoken command of His Holiness, through the authority of the Office of Chamberlain, pursuant to all previous Notices, in confirmation and extension of the ones issued by Our Predecessors and Ourselves; and
With particular reference to the Edict issued on July 18th, 1701, against the export of Statues, Pictures, Marble, Metals, Figures, Gemstones, and other antiquities, which is hereby upheld;
We command that all Paintings, Stuccoes, Flooring, Figures, Mosaics, Monuments, and Sepulchers that are Buried in Quarries and retrieved under license, must be immediately

reported to our current Commissary for Antiquities, the Antiquarian Francesco Bartoli. The artefacts' damage and destruction are subject to his permission, which is issued on Our behalf and free of charge, upon presentation of a drawing of the items that cannot be preserved.

The present Order is directed at Diggers, Stonemasons, Builders, Land Owners, Tenants, Vintners, and any other person involved in Quarries, under pain of 100 crowns. Half the sum will be allotted to the Reverend Apostolic Chamber, whereas the other half is for the Accuser. We retain the right to inflict corporal punishment discretionally, depending on the case's gravity and the person's standing.

Since the conservation of ancient Inscriptions is of the utmost importance for both the Ecclesiastical and lay erudition, whether they are over or underground, sculpted, engraved on stone or other material;

Therefore, We ban all persons from removing the artefacts from their present or future location for any reason, or sawing, breaking, or damaging them for any purpose without a special license written and issued on behalf of Monsignor Bianchini, Our Lord's Honorable Chamberlain, who was appointed by His Holiness personally. All Owners, Stonecutters, Sculptors, Stonemasons, Diggers, and all other professionals will be punished by the penalties mentioned in the preceding Chapter.

Furthermore, as the ancient Notices issued to preserve manuscripts and other public and private writings often go disregarded, while several Artisans and other professionals are allowed to purchase all sorts of manuscripts indiscriminately, without any supervision, approval, or permission, from all kinds of sellers; and

Wishing to address these severe misdemeanors effectively, We ban all persons, regardless of their grade, condition, gender, and standing, from selling or purchasing, for any purpose whatsoever, all handwritten books in either Vernacular, Latin, Greek, or Hebrew, bound in parchment or cotton paper, either whole, divided, torn, or loose; and

Tools, Proceedings, Inventories, Letters, Bulls, Briefs, Charters, and any other sheet of paper or scroll bearing any name or title, without a written license by the Abbot Domenico Riviera, Prefect of the Apostolic Archive of Castel Sant'Angelo, or Tommaso Di Giulio, Custodian of the Vatican Secret Archive. The license is issued on our behalf, free of charge, and prior to the sale or, at most, the delivery of said writings and books to the Purchaser. All unlicensed sales and purchases will be punished by the penalties mentioned above and the compensation *in solidum* with an interest of any damage caused to the Writings' Owner or other parties involved. Additionally, transgressors will be dealt three strappados on the spot in public and fined 200 crowns; half the sum will be allotted to the Reverend Apostolic Chamber, whereas the other half is for the informer who revealed the unlicensed trade of such books and writings and whose identity must be kept secret.

For the same reasons, We command that all Booksellers, Herbalists, Beaters, Paper Dealers, Painters, Bookbinders, and other Artisans must notify the Prefect of the Archive of Castel Sant'Angelo, or the Custodian of the Vatican Secret Archive of any such books and writings in their possession, custody, or disposal. The notification must take place within eight days of the issuance of the present Edict.

Moreover, all such professionals are banned from unbinding, dividing, tearing, or ruining said books and writings, whether for resale, to bind new books, or use them in their Jobs, without a license by the Prefect of the Archive of Castel Sant'Angelo or the Custodian of the Secret Vatican Archive, under the pains specified in Chapter Two, which will be imposed strictly.

Furthermore, We wish to clarify that all the restrictions and penalties mentioned above also apply to the Secular and Regular Ecclesiastical persons, along with all other persons, regardless of their privilege and notability. All penalties will be carried out rigorously and *ex officio* at the instance of the Revenue Office.

In faith etc. Issued in Rome, at the Apostolic Chamber, on September 30th, 1704.
Chamberlain Giovanni Battista Spinola
Auditor Prospero Marefoschi
General Commissary Silvio de Cavalieri

12
Prohibition against the export of Statues of marble and metal, Figures, Antiquities, and the like

Giovanni Battista Spinola, Cardinal Priest of the title of San Cesareo (in Palatio), Chamberlain of the Holy Roman Church.
Whereas several previous Edicts have been issued and published by Ourselves and our Predecessors, particularly etc. (as in no. 8); and
Whereas frauds and deceptions between purchasers and sellers occur daily, whenever these parties collude in exporting antiquities outside Rome and the Papal State;
To avoid such frauds and deceptions and counter theft and contraband;
Therefore, We ban both this Soul-Nourishing City's residents and all foreigners from trading statues, figures, antiquities, and the other items mentioned above without a license issued by Us, free of charge, and bearing the purchaser, buyer, and intermediary's names. All transgressors will be punished by the confiscation of the items traded, and a fine of 500 crowns, to be imposed as specified above, albeit lacking the intention to export the goods outside Rome and the Papal State.
Furthermore, etc. (as in no. 8). All Aliens, Clergy, and Laypeople subject to the Holy See both directly and indirectly, as well as all foreigners and other Princes' subjects, who have resided in Rome for at least one month, are hereby bound and engaged in the present Edict, acknowledge its publication and compulsoriness, and may not plead ignorance.
To better inform the public, We order that all gatekeepers at the Gates of Rome and Borgo, innkeepers, tavern keepers, hotel managers, and other professionals providing room and board for foreigners must at all times keep a copy of the present Edict affixed at the City's Gates, hostels, taverns, inns, and hotels for everyone to read. All transgressors will be punished by three strappados and a 25-crown fine each, to be imposed upon detection.
Finally, the present Edict must be affixed in Rome's usual venues and considered personally binding and acknowledged as of three days after publication.

In faith. Issued in Rome at the Apostolic Chamber on April 3rd, 1717.
Chamberlain Cardinal Giovanni Battista Spinola
Auditor Faustino Crispotti – General Commissary Gaspare Turchi
Secretary Antonio Gaetano Frosi, Chancellor of the Reverend Apostolic Chamber

13
Edict on stonecutters, marble cutters, diggers, and the like

Annibale, Cardinal Priest of the title of San Clemente, Chamberlain of the Holy Roman Church.

Whereas it falls within Our duty to ensure that the ancient artworks and mementos, which adorn the Soul-Nourishing City of Rome and its District, be preserved intact; and

Whereas We abide by our Lord's spoken orders through the authority of the Office of Chamberlain and act in confirmation and extension to the Edicts issued by our Predecessors – with particular reference to the ones issued on July 18th, 1701, and April 8th, 1717;

We ban all Persons, regardless of their grade and condition, from excavating in public and private locations without our written permission. Where relevant, our Commissary for Antiquities or another Person appointed by us will provide assistance.

Second, We ban all Persons issued with an excavating license from digging near Buildings and ancient Walls, in order not to damage them.

Third, no Buildings, Construction Sites, and other edifices over ground, including those eroded by time or in ruins, may be demolished without our permission and our Commissary's inspection and supervision.

Fourth, all Statues and fragments, Busts, Heads, Bas-reliefs, Pedestals, Columns, Capitals, Inscriptions, Vases, Urns, and other ancient ornaments in Stone, Marble, Terracotta, Bronze, and other Metals, which are found while digging Quarries, allotting Vineyards, and laying foundations on Construction Sites, must be reported to our Commissary immediately, prior to the items' removal. Therefore, the Commissary will inspect and assess the items to avoid damage and rupture during the excavation works.

Fifth, all Stonecutters, Marble Cutters, and other such professionals are banned from cutting – either directly or by proxy – any stone and marble bearing inscriptions, Bas-reliefs, Columns, and stumps of all sorts without our Commissary's preliminary inspection and our written permission, which is issued free of charge. Said inspection will also be performed gratis in all the cases mentioned above, as our Commissary is expressly instructed not to accept offerings of any sort and proportion. All transgressions will be punished by dismissal and sanctioned at our discretion.

All penalties for the transgression of the orders and prohibitions mentioned above will be imposed strictly and irreversibly, under pain of the items' confiscation, three strappados, and a fine of 25 crowns. Half of the sum will be allotted to the Reverend Apostolic Chamber; one-fourth is for the Accuser, whose identity will remain secret; one-fourth is for our Commissary. The investigation will be carried out as is most convenient for the Revenue Office.

Finally, the present Edict must be affixed and published in Rome's usual venues, and everyone will be held accountable as if they were informed personally.

Issued in Rome at the Apostolic Chamber on October 21st, 1726.
Pro-Chamberlain Cardinal Annibale Albani
Auditor Giacomo Amadori, formerly Lanfredini – General Commissary Nicola Lana
Secretary of the Chamber Antonio Gaetano Frosi

14
Prohibition against the export of Statues of marble and metal, Paintings, Antiquities, and the like

Annibale, Cardinal of the title of San Clemente, Chamberlain of the Holy Roman Church, Bishop of Sabina by God's Mercy.

Despite the previous Edicts issued by our Predecessors and Ourselves - especially the ones of October 5th, 1624, January 29th, 1646, August 30th, 1655, February 5th, 1686, July 18th, 1701, April 8th, 1717, and October 21st, 1726, prohibiting the unlicensed export – either directly or by proxy – of Statues of Marble or Metal, Paintings, Antiquities, and the like outside Rome and the Papal State;

Whereas We have been informed that many transgress said Orders and undermine the public decor of our Soul-Nourishing City; and

Whereas the City's primary concern is to preserve its illustrious Works of Sculpture and Painting, especially those which are outstandingly valued and rare because of their antiquity; and

Whereas its tradition contributes to both the Sacred and Lay Erudition encouraging countless Foreign Visitors, as well as Students of the Arts who can learn the canons that benefit all communities and individuals greatly;

Therefore, by Our Lord's spoken order, through the Authority of the Office of Chamberlain, and in confirmation and extension of the precedent Edicts, We ban all Persons, both Ecclesiastical and Lay, of any state, grade, and condition, including all special titles, from exporting any type of Statue, Figure, Column, Bas-relief, Vase, Urn, Bust, Head, Cameo, Carving, Medallion, Bronze figurine, ornament of Marble, Stone, Bronze, or other Metals, as well as ancient or modern materials, Depictions, Mosaics, Paintings, and similar ancient and modern Works without our direct permission and our Commissary for Antiquities' preliminary inspection and assessment of the items' quality and quantity. The authorisation for the ancient items may be issued only by His Holiness' special Chirograph. The ban applies to all transportation by River, Sea, or Land.

All transgressors will be punished by the confiscation of the items exported without a license; five hundred Chamber golden ducats, to be applied as mentioned below; corporal punishment established at our discretion and carried out rigorously.

Whereas Cameos, Carvings, Medallions of all kinds, and Bronze figurines represent the most valuable ancient assets displayed in Rome's Museums; and

Whereas several Intermediaries and Mediators illegally trade, sell, and export said items outside Rome and the Papal State at exorbitant prices for the Foreigners involved; or alter and forge articles to the public's detriment; and

Whereas, in the former case, said offenders act in violation of the repeated prohibitions issued by our Predecessors and Ourselves, and, in the latter, they defraud Foreigners by deception;

Therefore, We command that all Intermediaries, Mediators, Diggers, Vintners, and other Persons taking part in said trades and exports outside Rome and the Papal State, as well as all those who act deceptively or cooperate in circumventing Foreigners or discrediting public Commerce, will be punished irreversibly as specified above.

Furthermore, to better enforce the present Edict and ensure that no one will elude its regulations or escape its penalties, We hereby add the following amendments and measures to the Orders issued in the preceding Notices.
First, the Reverend Apostolic Chamber will only be allotted one-third of the mentioned five hundred Chamber golden ducats imposed as a fine; the remaining two-thirds are for the Accuser and our Commissary for Antiquities, respectively, in the cases outlined below.
Second, if any Secretary of the Chamber or Minister of our Tribunal receives charges and reports of Transgression, they must keep the Accuser's identity secret, under pain of losing their Appointment and further penalties at our discretion, including corporal punishment.
Third, if the Accuser does not trust other Persons to take their report, the charges they press may be addressed either to Us directly or to our Auditor – be it verbally or in writing. In such cases, We reserve the right to keep their identity secret and conduct the investigation personally. Notwithstanding, the Accuser will be awarded one-third of the five hundred Chamber golden ducats.
Fourth, all the Carpenters and Artisans of all kinds, such as Porters, Carters, Sailors, Boatmen, and the like who packed, embarked, or transported said items without verifying our license's issuance are liable for punishment as specified in the precedent Notices. However, said professionals may clear themselves, *ipso facto*, from both the fines and corporal punishments by reporting the Contraband to our Tribunal or pressing charges before being incriminated. Furthermore, such a course of action will entitle said professionals to one-third of the fine imposed, on a par with the guiltless Accusers.
The same applies to Hotel Managers, Innkeepers, Tavern Keepers, Subordinates, Servants, or Family Members liable for said penalties; Private Owners will be held accountable for the Ministers' misdemeanors and Masters for their Servants', pursuant to the precedent Notices.
Fifth, in the absence of an Accuser or Denouncer, one-third of the fine will be allotted to the Keepers, Gatekeepers, Border Officers, public and private Tax Collectors, or Agents who reported the Contraband.
Sixth, the Commissary for Antiquities' primary concern and duty is to investigate and file charges against Transgressors. However, such offices may also fall upon other persons. Therefore, We command that all Commissaries, Officers, and Special Collaborators superintending Contraband cases in our Curiae and Tribunals must oversee the proceedings and divert one-third of the fine to said individuals. The allocated sum will consist of the money otherwise destined for the first Commissary, and it will be allotted among the Curiae and Tribunals' Officers to launch said investigation or press charges.
If the Commissary for Antiquities' intervention becomes necessary during the Proceedings or Trial against the Transgressors, he will receive one-third of the fine destined for the Apostolic Chamber as compensation for his expertise. Notwithstanding, the remaining two-thirds are for the informants, as mentioned above.
Seventh, all the Transgressions to the Orders mentioned above will be investigated and prosecuted *ex officio* to benefit the Revenue Office when the items are stolen and smuggled outside Rome or the State. Pursuant to the precedent Notices, the presence of one witness and the Commissary for Antiquities' sworn statement will suffice to validate the Accuser's testimony.

Eighth, in addition to our Commissary for Antiquities, all the Commissaries, Officers, Special Collaborators, Executors, and Ministers of Justice from other Curiae and Tribunals may act upon testimonies – either directly or by proxy – and search for Statues, Paintings, and antiquities of any type extracted without our permission.
Furthermore, said officials may stop and search all Carts, Boats, Watercraft, and Land Vehicles; and
Search all Chests, Luggage, and bundles, notwithstanding the Coats of Arms, Emblems, uniforms, Permits, Families, Privileges, Concessions, and Exemptions of the persons involved in the transportation.
For such cases, We command that all Captains of Justice, Executors, Ministers of Justice, and Heralds help and favor the Commissary, under pain of losing their appointment, and further penalties at our discretion.
Ninth, all Aliens, Clergy, and Laypeople subject to the Holy See both directly and indirectly, as well as all Foreigners and other Princes' subjects, who have resided in Rome for at least fifteen days, are hereby bound and engaged in the present Edict, acknowledge its publication and compulsoriness, and may not plead ignorance. Notwithstanding the exclusive subjection to other Curiae or Tribunals, all transgressors fall, *ipso facto*, under our Jurisdiction and are liable to the penalties We have established.
To ensure that all members of the public may easily access our Orders' contents, We command that all Antiquarians, Gatekeepers at the Gates of Rome, Innkeepers, Hotel Managers, Tavern Keepers, and other professionals providing room and board, especially for foreigners, must at all times keep affixed a copy of the present Edict. All Transgressors will be punished by a fine of twenty-five crowns.
The present Edict will be affixed and published in Rome's usual venues, and everyone will be held accountable as if they were informed personally.

Issued in Rome at the Apostolic Chamber on September 10th, 1733.
Chamberlain Albani, Bishop of Sabina, Cardinal of San Clemente
Auditor F. G. Gaucci – Commissary Nicola Lana

15
Prohibition against the export of Statues of marble and metal, Paintings, Antiquities, and the like

Silvio Valenti, Cardinal Priest of the title of San Callisto, Chamberlain of the Holy Roman Church.
Whereas the public decor of our Soul-Nourishing City of Rome thrives and flourishes on the illustrious Works of Sculpture and Painting, especially the rarest and most valuable antiquities; and
Whereas these assets' conservation stimulates both the sacred and profane erudition remarkably, encouraging Foreigners to visit the City and admire its beauties. And because it represents a model for students of the Arts who benefit our community and private citizens; and

Whereas Our Holy Father wishes to protect the noble Arts, pursuant to the ancient Measures issued by our sensible Predecessors, and respond to the countless abuses produced by time and brought forth by our subordinate Ministers' negligence;
Therefore, We have been ordered to publish the following Notice.
In keeping with His Holiness' Will, through the authority of the Office of the Chamberlain, in confirmation and renewal of Our Predecessors' Notices regarding the prohibition to export the items mentioned outside the City of Rome and the Papal State; and
With particular reference to the Notices of October 5th, 1624; January 29th, 1646; August 30th, 1655; February 5th, 1686; July 18th, 1701; April 8th, 1717; October 21st, 1726; September 10th, 1733;
All persons – both Ecclesiastical and Lay – of any state, grade, and condition, including those with special titles, are banned from performing or demanding to perform exports – either directly or by proxy – headed out of Rome's urban area, District, Territory, and the Papal State. The ban applies to all transports by River, Sea, and Land and pertains to all types of Statues, Figures, Bas-reliefs, Columns, Vases, Alabaster, Agate, Jasper, Amethysts, and other precious marble, Jewels, and Wrought Stones; as well as
Busts, Heads, Fragments, Pillars, Pedestals, Inscriptions, and other Ornaments, Friezes, Medallions, Cameos, Cornelian stones, Coins, or carvings on any type of Stone, Metal, Gold, Silver, or of any ancient or modern material; and
Figures, Paintings, Ancient Depictions, or other Works sculpted in any material, painted, carved, assembled, crafted, or otherwise created, which have been recently found in Quarries or are within or beyond Rome in any Person's possession or any Location, without a License issued by us.
With regard to rare, antique, upscale, and valuable Items, said License may be issued by His Holiness' special Chirograph exclusively. Respecting modern Items, the usual License issued by Us or Our Monsignor Auditor will suffice. In the latter case, Our Commissary for Antiquities and Quarries will draft a sworn statement specifying the Purchaser and Seller and assessing the items' quality and quantity as specified below. Subsequently, the other Commissaries responsible for the documentation on Waterway and Land transportation will attach the statement to the documents issued by the Secretary and Chancellor of the Reverend Apostolic Chamber.
All transgressors without a license issued as specified above will be punished by the confiscation of the items found, sold, shipped, concealed, withheld, stolen, or cached within or beyond Rome and the Papal State. A fine of five hundred Chamber Golden Ducats will also be imposed: one-third of the sum will be allotted to the Reverend Apostolic Chamber; one-third is for the Accuser, whose identity will be kept secret; one-third is for our Commissary mentioned above or his Assessors, as deemed befitting.
Despite the efficacy of the 1726 regulations on Paintings and ancient and modern Statues, and the appointment of a Person serving as superintending Commissary, whose compensation was expressly set at an honest and adequate level by the Reverend Apostolic Chamber;
Nevertheless, time and experience have shown how the endeavor of this one Minister only – in spite of his obligation to appoint a suitable Adjutant at his own expense — is not sufficient to counter the frauds and misconducts that harm our community daily;
Therefore, We hereby appoint three other Persons as said Commissary's Assessors, each of whom will be tasked respectively with Painting; Sculpture; Cameos, Medallions,

Engravings, and any other Antiquity. Pursuant to their title, the Assessors will have the power to inspect and assess the items to be excavated, visit the sites in question, and produce reports on the items' artistic qualities and flaws.

Furthermore, all excavations will henceforth be subject to the Assessor's Visit and Report, which will then be attached to the Petition directed to Us. Subsequently, the Commissary will countersign said documents, stating his approval of the assessment performed, its conformity, and the items appraised. However, the Commissary reserves the right to perform visits and examinations personally and independently of the Assessor. Said Examinations and Visits will be conducted free of charge. All forms of allowance and contribution are hereby forbidden, under pain of losing one's Appointment – to be imposed *ipso facto*, and further penalties at Our discretion, including corporal punishment.

As for the excavation of ancient and modern Statues, We command that, as is the custom, Our Secretaries of the Chamber issue the licenses after the Commissary's routine visit and approval, upon receiving orders regarding shipment from Us or Our Monsignor Auditor.

As for Paintings and Depictions of all kinds, We command that all Paintings and ancient Depictions created by artists of any importance that have recently died must be subject to the Laws and Conditions of Statues and Antiquities of all sorts. Therefore, We firmly order that all exports be performed with the greatest care, following the procedures specified in the memorandum and after the visits and conferral of the licenses issued by the Secretaries of the Chamber.

However, for all modern Paintings and Depictions destined for exportation, whose value does not exceed one-hundred crowns, it will suffice for them to have the Assessor's certificate enclosed, along with the Commissary's approval and attached to the petition for the written license issued by Us or Our Monsignor Auditor.

Said procedure, which is free of charge, is intended to favor the Professors and Youths engaged in this noble Art.

Henceforth, to ensure that all are informed on how to perform excavations on land or water safely, We command that all Statues, Paintings, Marbles, and other Antiquities of Metal and Gemstone must be inspected by the competent Assessor, depending on the items to be extracted, prior to their packing or casing.

All authorised items reported, approved by the Commissary, and excavated must then be shipped to the Customs in either Ripetta, Ripa Grande, or by Land. There the Customs Ministers will vouch for the Assessor and Commissary's second identification of the goods mentioned above and authorised by Us. Subsequently, in the presence of the mentioned Assessor and Commissary, the Chests or Bundles in question must be sealed with Our stamp, or the interim Chamberlain Cardinal's, in Padiglione. The stamp must be kept by one of the Customs Ministers mentioned above and appointed to the task by Us personally.

All transgressors will be punished as specified above, strictly and irreversibly, as ordered in § 2 of the Notice issued on October 21st, 1726.

Furthermore, Our Commissary is hereby fully entitled to prosecute all malicious Excavators, launch investigations, and press charges to Us and Our Monsignor Auditor. The presence of one Witness and the Commissary's sworn statement will suffice to validate the testimony in question. All Transgressors will be punished by the penalties mentioned above, namely the Items' confiscation, a fine of five hundred Chamber golden ducats, and corporal punishments at our discretion, to be inflicted according to the Persons' social

standing and the Crime's seriousness. The penalties described above will be imposed strictly and summarily.
The Assessors have the right to stop all the shipments due to leave or departed without Our permission. Upon receiving the Assessor's report, the Commissary and Our Monsignor Auditor will take action pursuant to the present and precedent Notices, with particular reference to the one issued on October 21st, 1726, § 1.
In such cases, upon detecting fraud, the one-third of the fine destined for the Commissary will, alternately, be allotted to said Assessor.
Moreover, whereas many still dig – either directly or by proxy – in public and private Spaces, near Buildings, Construction Sites, Walls, and ancient Bridges, in search of Inlaid Marble, Alabaster, Peperino, and other Stone, to the Risk and detriment of said Buildings and public Thoroughfares; and
Whereas many dig – either directly or by proxy – in public and private Quarries, in search of Statues, Busts, Bas-reliefs, Heads, Pedestals, Columns, Capitals, Inscriptions, Medallions, Coins, Cameos, and precious Carvings on Marble, Metal, Precious Stone, Inlaid Gold, Silver, Agate, Crugnola Stone, Amethyst, and other materials – both wrought and uncut; and
Notwithstanding the severe punishments and the prohibitions published in said Notices to counter said diggings, which are often retrieved as well;
Whereas many items are sold, smuggled, stolen, and cached, both in Rome and beyond, without due notification, permission, and consent by Us and the Owners of the Spaces involved and items found;
Consequently, such conduct leads to the public and private detriment, crises of conscience, and the ransacking of the most beautiful ancient and modern assets in our Soul-Nourishing City of Rome;
Therefore, We command that all the Persons mentioned above refrain from wrecking Buildings, ancient Construction Sites, walls in travertine, marble, peperino, and other materials, both over and underground;
Furthermore, it is forbidden to break or excavate ancient Statues and other ornaments of any material or dig near said Buildings, Walls, Construction Sites, Arches, Bridges, Cemeteries, public Thoroughfares, or any different location without Our permission, as laid down in the Prohibition issued on April 8th, 1717, § 2 and 3. In the case of Quarries of Slab, Peperino, Travertine, and other such raw materials, the license will be granted by the Thoroughfare Office as per the procedure.
However, said Office and its Substitutes may not license the excavation of Statues, Marble, Paintings, etc. As is the custom, the management of such matters will be assigned to Our Secretaries of the Chamber, Commissary, Assessors, or other deputies appointed by Us, as deemed befitting.
Moreover, We ban all Limestone Workers, Diggers, and other Persons such as Stonecutters, Casters, and other Wreckers from breaking, wrecking, shattering to produce mortar, ship, or resell any kind of inscribed Marble, wrought Marble, Statue, figure, and other ancient ornaments; and
Melting, wrecking, or denting Figures, Medallions, Coins, carvings on ancient Metal, Gold, or Silver, bearing representations or records of ancient events without a license by Us or our Monsignor Auditor, and the supervision of our Commissary and Assessor for antiquities. Said license will be issued free of charge. All transgressions will be punished

by the confiscation of the items, a fine of twenty-five crowns to be imposed as specified above, and other discretionary penalties – including corporal punishment, as indicated in the Prohibition issued on April 8th, 1717, § 8.

Since, so far, We and others have often issued Licenses and Permits to excavate – either directly or by proxy – Treasures, Marble, Travertine, Statues, Pozzolana, and similar items that require the intervention and assistance of our Commissary, Assessor, or other prospective appointees to ensure that no unauthorised excavations are conducted on unauthorised sites or near public Buildings, Thoroughfares, or Cemeteries that might be damaged, as described above;

Therefore, We command that, within ten days of this Edict's publication, every Person issued with a License, regardless of their state, grade, and condition, must report to our Secretary's Office stating which Licenses are currently in their possession. All transgressors will be punished by the cancelation of said licenses, as ordered in the Prohibition issued in 1717, § 9.

No Stonecutter, Digger, or Estate Owner issued with our license and excavating by proxy on public or private Land, may sell Travertine, Marble, Alabaster, Statues, and the other items listed above, without our Commissary's supervision and Our appointed Appraisers' measurements. Furthermore, a due portion of the finds must be allotted to the Reverend Chamber and put at our disposal, as estimated by our Appraisers. This restriction extends to the sale of Lead, Metal, Gold, Silver, and any other item partly allotted to the Chamber. All transgressors will be punished by the confiscation of the items, a fine of ten crowns, imposed as specified above, and corporal penalties at Our discretion, as in the Prohibition issued in 1717, § 10.

Moreover, all Diggers, Vintners, Laborers, Stonemasons, Sculptors, Stonecutters, and Owners of Statues, Quarries, Sites, Locations, or Workshops where the ancient items mentioned above are stored – both within Rome and beyond – must receive our Commissary;

Furthermore, the Commissary must always be allowed to view, inspect, locate, and record the Statues, Figures, Busts, Bas-reliefs, Vases, Medallions, Coins, Cameos, Cornelian Stones, Carvings, items in Gold, Silver, Metal, and other materials, as well as the Precious Stones – both wrought and uncut. Therefore, said professionals' duty is to welcome and help the Commissary in his work's performance and refrain from selling or transferring the items in question for five days. Accordingly, said professionals must obey the Commissary in reporting the finds to us, our Monsignor Auditor, or on the Secretary's record, under the penalties mentioned above, as specified in the Prohibition issued in 1717, § 12.

All Carpenters, Artisans, and other Persons are banned from crafting chests to pack and ship the items mentioned above. Similarly, all Porters, Carters, and other Persons are banned from fastening, bundling, or transporting items, Chests, and Bundles that have not been licensed by Us and inspected, identified, and sealed by our Commissary. All transgressors will be punished by the confiscation of the Chests and Bundles, three Strappados, and a fine of twenty-five crowns, as specified above. The fine will be imposed holding Private Owners accountable for the Ministers' misdemeanors and Masters for their Servants'. The investigation will be carried out as is most convenient for the Revenue Office.

Furthermore, all Boatmen and Sailors are banned from embarking Chests and Bundles containing the items mentioned above under any pretext.

§ 5 of the Notice issued in 1726 applies to Charioteers and Wagoners as well.

All the Carpenters and Artisans of all kinds, such as Porters, Carters, Sailors, Boatmen, and the like who crafted Chests and packed, embarked, or transported said items without verifying our license's issuance are liable for punishment as specified in the present Notice. However, said professionals may clear themselves, *ipso facto*, from both the fines and corporal punishments by reporting the Contraband to our Tribunal or pressing charges before being incriminated. Furthermore, such a course of action will entitle said professionals to one-third of the fine imposed, on a par with the guiltless Accusers. The same applies to Hotel Managers, Innkeepers, Tavern Keepers, Subordinates, Servants, or Family Members liable for said penalties; Private Owners will be held accountable for the Ministers' misdemeanors and Masters for their Servants'.

Moreover, We ban all Keepers and Ministers of Gates and Turnpikes from allowing the transit by water and Land of the items mentioned above if the Chests, Bundles, and Packages in question do not bear our seal. The restrictions extend to those who fail to produce our export license. All offenders will be punished by the confiscation of the license itself, a fine of twenty-five crowns, and corporal penalties at our discretion, as specified in the Notice issued in 1726, § 7.

Additionally, if the items confiscated are Sculptures, Statues, Marbles, Bronzes, Paintings, Depictions, Carvings, and the such like Our Holy Father and We, through the authority of our Office, command that the Statues, Marbles, and Bronzes must be dispatched to the Capitoline Gallery of Statues. The Paintings and Depictions will also be consigned to the Capitoline Gallery, which was recently built thanks to His Holiness' munificence, and stored there with other artworks for the public's benefit. Praise be to His Beatitude, who strives to protect these estimable ancient artworks. The remaining Cameos, Medallions, and other such confiscated antiquities will be stored in keeping with His Holiness's commands.

Furthermore, all Aliens, Clergy, Regular Clergy, and Laypeople subject to the Holy See both directly and indirectly and all foreigners and other Princes' subjects, who have resided in Rome or the Papal State for at least fifteen days, are hereby bound and engaged in the present Edict, acknowledge its publication and compulsoriness, and may not plead ignorance. Notwithstanding the exclusive subjection to other Curiae or Tribunals, all transgressors fall under our Jurisdiction and are liable to the penalties established conclusively in the Prohibition issued on September 10th, 1733, § 9.

The powers assigned to our Commissary to act upon reports, inspecting sites bearing Statues, Depictions, and antiquities of any kind; and

Identify Boats, Carts, Watercraft, and Land Vehicles; and

Search all Chests, Luggage, and Bundles, notwithstanding the Coats of Arms, Emblems, Uniforms, Permits, Families, Restrictions, Privileges, Concessions, and Exemptions of the persons involved in the transportation;

Are hereby extended to Special Collaborators, Executors, and Ministers of Justice.

The same applies to Keepers, Watchmen, Boatmen, and Customs Officers whose duty is to notify Us or our Monsignor Auditor and record the outcome of their searches and inspections for the Secretary mentioned below whenever they detect unlicensed exports heading out of Rome. The presence of one witness and the Commissary's sworn statement, or that of his Assessor, will suffice to validate the Accuser's testimony. We command that all Captains of Justice, Executors, and other Ministers of Justice must help and favor the Commissary, under pain of losing their Appointment, and further penalties at our discretion, as specified in the Notice issued on July 18th, 1701, § 9.

Moreover, whereas several Cameos, Carvings, Coins, Medallions, Cornelian Stones, and Bronze Figures have been secretly traded and smuggled outside Rome and the Papal State; and

Whereas these artworks have been frequently altered, forged, and sold to Foreigners at exorbitant prices by all sorts of Intermediaries and Mediators, to the detriment of public Commerce; and

Whereas such Ancient items are often among the finest works kept in Rome's Museums; and

Notwithstanding our Predecessors' repeated Prohibitions, in the former case, and the Foreigners' good faith, in the latter;

Therefore, all Intermediaries, Mediators, Diggers, Vintners, and any other Person involved in the trade and export outside Rome and the State; or

In the deceptions, frauds, and detrimental enterprises mentioned above;

Be warned that they will be punished irreversibly, pursuant to the penalties mentioned above, as specified in the Notice issued on September 10th, 1733, § 3.

Furthermore, upon collecting charges or receiving reports of transgressions, our Tribunal's Secretaries of the Chamber and Ministers must keep the Accuser or Plaintiff's identity secret, under pain of losing their Appointment, and other Corporal Punishments at our discretion. However, if the Accuser does not trust other Persons to take their report, the charges they press may be addressed either to Us directly or to our Monsignor Auditor – be it verbally or in writing. In such cases, We reserve the right to keep their identity secret and conduct the investigation personally. Notwithstanding, the Accuser will be awarded one-third of the five hundred ducats mentioned above, as specified in the Notice issued on September 10th, 1733.

All be warned that the penalties mentioned above will be imposed strictly and irreversibly through investigation or any other procedure deemed convenient for the Revenue Office. We reserve the right to act discretionally to increase or decrease penalties depending on each case.

To better inform the public about Our Directives, We order that all Gatekeepers at the Gates of Rome, Second-hand Retailers, Innkeepers, Tavern Keepers, Hotel Managers, and other professionals providing room and board for Foreigners must at all times keep a copy of the present Edict affixed at the City's Gates, Hostels, Taverns, Inns, and Hotels for everyone to read. All transgressors will be punished by three Strappados and a 25-crown fine each, to be imposed upon detection.

Finally, the present Edict must be affixed in Rome's usual venues and considered personally binding and acknowledged.

Issued in Rome at the Apostolic Chamber on January 5th, 1750.
Chamberlain Cardinal Silvio Valenti
Auditor Giovanni Maria Riminaldi
General Commissary Giovanni Giuliano Rubini

16
Edict

Romualdo Braschi Onesti, Cardinal Dean of Santa Maria ad Martyres, Chamberlain of the Holy Roman Church.
Whereas the repeated violation of the Revenue Office's rights over the excavation and discovery of Statues and other antiquities such as Marbles, Metals, Precious Stones, Treasures; and
All the other things buried which are in the bowels of the Earth or under ancient Buildings and fall within Our Lord's Regalian Rights;
Has prompted His Holiness to revoke and void all the licenses issued so far and take the following measures.
Therefore, by Our Lord's spoken order and through the authority of the Office of Chamberlain, We command to all Persons — both Ecclesiastical and Lay – of any state, grade, order, and condition, including those who request special exemptions; that
As of the date of this Edict's publication, all the licenses for the excavation – both direct and by proxy – in both public and private Sites, including Estate owned freely, in whatever capacity, or due to exemption, are hereby revoked without exception.
Furthermore, all excavations are henceforth subject to the issuance of a new license that safeguards the Princedom and Reverend Chamber's interests and rights.
Moreover, in confirmation of Our Predecessors' Edicts, all exports of Statues, Columns, precious Stones, and Marbles – both wrought and uncut – and any other item, heading out of the Soul-Nourishing city of Rome and the Papal State by River, Sea, or Land, are hereby banned. Unlike the past, when lenience was the norm, transgressors may no longer plead ignorance or make excuses.
This Edict must be followed strictly. All transgressions, excavations, and fraudulent exports performed without a newly issued license will be punished by the confiscation of the items found or exported and a fine of three hundred Crowns. Half of the sum will be allotted to the Accuser, whose identity will remain secret; the other half is for the Reverend Chamber. We reserve the right to inflict corporal punishments at our discretion, depending on the case's gravity.

Issued in Rome at the Apostolic Chamber on August 21st, 1801.
Chamberlain Cardinal Romualdo Braschi Onesti
Auditor P. Ferrari – General Commissary of the Reverend Apostolic Chamber Giuseppe Pecci

17
Edict Doria Pamphilj

Giuseppe Doria Pamphilj, Cardinal Priest of the Title of Santa Cecilia, Pro-Chamberlain of the Holy Roman Church.
Whereas Our Lord Pope Pius VII extends his Paternal care to all of the productive Arts and handicrafts to increase his beloved Subjects' wealth and prosperity;

Whereas He does not forget that branch of the industry so peculiar to our People and land as to outpace all the other sectors in benefiting this Metropolis and State's decorum and fame;
Whereas His Holiness acknowledges the unique importance and significance of the Fine Arts – which were born in Greece and came to establish themselves in our City permanently and almost exclusively, over the last few centuries – in providing employment for all our Subjects and professionals involved; and
Whereas He has proactively worked to ensure the conservation of the Monuments, Fine Antiquities, and Archetypes that have so effectively served as models, guides, and exemplars for contemporary Art, Beauty, Religious ornaments, and public education; and
Whereas He has fostered the discovery and retrieval of ever new rarities, which may compensate for the loss of the artworks swept away by events;
Therefore, for the conservation of the existing Monuments and the discovery of new works of art to encourage and animate the Arts of Drawing and its masters as of October the first, in conjunction with his special Chirograph, His Holiness has taken vigorous measures directing us as follows.

Pro-Chamberlain Cardinal Rino Giuseppe Doria Pamphilj.
Surely, Our Predecessors' most felt concern was, quite invariably, the conservation of the most outstanding Monuments and works of the Fine Arts that have defied age and time to be contemplated in all their original beauty. Indeed, the precious remains of the cultivated Antiquity endow the City of Rome with an ornament that sets her apart from all the other grand Cities of Europe. They provide our Scholars with Themes upon which to reflect; they present our Artists with models and exemplars from which to seek inspiration in the pursuit of the beautiful and the sublime; they summon scores of Foreigners who revel and rejoice in beholding such unique rarities; they grant sustenance for countless Individuals employed in the practice of the Fine Arts; finally, they represent the lifeblood of our State and Community's commerce and industry since the new works created are a clean and easy surplus – as is the case with all the crafts produced by Man's ingenuity.
A maelstrom of harmful events brought to the irreversible loss of this Beloved City's rarest monuments and Works of Antiquity. Nonetheless, on no account has Our Holy Father dwelled on the misfortunes of the past. Quite the contrary, He has renewed his efforts in procuring the means to counter any further losses and foster the discovery of new Monuments to make up for all the precedent dispossessions.
Therefore, after such reflections and following the example set by His Holiness Leo X and his magnificent appointee Raphael from Urbino, We have determined as follows;
We hereby elect the incomparable Sculptor Canova[104] – the truest descendant of Phidias, Praxiteles, and their masters, Apelles and Zeuxis – as General Inspector for the Fine Arts and all that pertains to them.
Accordingly, he will act as the supreme inspector for the maintenance and promotion of the Arts of Drawing and their adepts, answering to no one else than Yourself.
Furthermore, having considered how beneficial it is for Our beloved Subjects, the common good, the public decorum, and Our Metropolis' fame, We have concluded that all of Our efforts must be aimed at preserving the Ancient Monuments, fostering the Fine Arts'

104 Antonio Canova (1757-1822).

models, and supporting its masters. Consequently, the olden acts must be extended and upheld by new energetic measures.

Therefore, pursuant to Our Predecessors' Legislation, namely to the Edict issued on January 5th, 1750, by Your Predecessor Chamberlain Cardinal Silvio Valenti and published by Order of the Lamented Benedict XIV, We command, *motu proprio*, as follows.

1. First of all, We ban the export outside Rome and its State of Statues, Bas-reliefs, and any other work representing Humans or Animals which is made of Marble, Ivory, and any other material; and
   ancient Mural Paintings – both Greek and Roman – that have been sawed off or removed from walls, Mosaics, Etruscan Vases, Glassware, and other stained works; and
   all sorts of carvings, ancient Vases, Gemstones, Carved Stones, Cameos, Medallions, Leads, Bronzes, and all of those small or large-scale works that are known as *antiquities*; and
   public, private, Sacred, and Profane crafts, including fragments that might inspire the Arts and Artists; and
   all ancient Monuments, namely Gravestones, Inscriptions, Stelae, Urns, Candleholders, Chandeliers, Sarcophagi, Funerary Jugs, and the such like including plain Figurines, made of any material; and
   Removable Architectural items such as Columns, Capitals, Bases, Architraves, Friezes, engraved Frames, and other ornaments from ancient Construction Sites; and Hard Stones, Soft Stones, antique Lapis Lazuli, either Green, Red, or Yellow, Oriental Alabaster – both wrought and uncut – Porphyry, Granite, Basalt, Serpentine, and the such like, except for plain white Marble.
2. Said prohibition also applies to Panel and Canvas Paintings created by Classical Artists that flourished after the renaissance of the Arts, and Paintings that may be of interest for the Arts, Schools, erudition, or other illustrious reasons. Accordingly, the persons in charge of directing the Fine Arts will be responsible for protecting said artworks against the export and mistaking of these artworks for items that may be – cautiously – licensed for export.
3. To ensure the fullest extension and effectiveness of said prohibition and counter any possible transgression that may have circumvented Our Predecessors' acts;
   We hereby ban all persons, including Yourself, from issuing any sort of license to export the items mentioned above. Said prohibition applies to all persons, notwithstanding their privileges and Dignities, including Reverend Cardinals of Titles, Patrons of Churches, and the illustrious exempts. Special requests or individual mentions of all kinds may not be considered exceptions, regardless of their eminence.
   Finally, said prohibition applies to all Foreign Owners of the items mentioned above – both residents and aliens.
4. All the persons found exporting said items outside Rome and its State by Sea and Land, and those who have sold the items, worked as Mediators, or served as accomplices will be punished by the confiscation of the works in question, a fine of Five Hundred Golden Ducats of the Chamber, and other corporal penalties at Your discretion. A Prison sentence of up to five Years may also be imposed depending on the person's quality, the item's importance, and the malice involved in the misdemeanor. Furthermore, all the

Porters, Carpenters, and other Artisans who cooperated by crafting Chests, Luggage Racks, Trunks, Bundles, and other containers used for the Contraband; and
the Carters, Muleteers, Boatmen, and other Drivers that took part in the transportation;
Will all be considered accomplices in the export.
The maliciousness of their intent will be proven by the very act of exporting forbidden goods without a license. Therefore, We will impose an additional fine of ten Ducats for the Artisans and Porters, and one hundred Ducats for the Drivers, along with the confiscation of the Draft Livestock and Corporal penalties at Your discretion.

5. The Monuments and Artworks' Sale and trade will be allowed freely within Rome and subject to Your license when the items are transported to new Locations within the State. The issuance of the said license must be preceded by a scrutiny performed by the Inspector for the Fine Arts and the Commissary for Antiquities. In the absence of the former, the examination will be carried out by his Assessors. The Removing party must provide Securities for the timely return of a form attesting to the item's delivery to the Location indicated within the State. Failure to comply will result in the Customary penalties together with corporal punishments at Your discretion.
6. Having thus ensured the Artworks' Conservation, which must at all costs remain in the City for its eternal ornament, to foster our Artists and Scholars' Studies and Erudition, and stimulate the Arts and their Masters We command as follows.
   All the Works crafted by living Artists – either of Sculpture, Painting, or other Fine Arts – may be sold and exported outside the State. Accordingly, the deceased Artists' works may be sold as long as they do not fall within the Categories mentioned above and are of lesser quality. Indeed, their trade is subject to Your license or that of Your Successors and will be preceded by the Inspector, Commissary, and Assessors' evaluation and report, all of which will be performed free of charge. To guarantee the Assessors' accuracy in the performance of their duties, notwithstanding their complete dependence on the Inspector and Commissary, We command that they be granted a Retainer fixed at Twenty Crowns a Month. Consequently, the Assessors are banned from accepting any form of reward, gratuity, Down payment, Contribution, Gift, and the such like. You must then warn each of them that any kind of negligence in exercising their essential duties will be punished strictly by revoking their Appointment. Moreover, all transgressions will be punished by corporal penalties whose severity will be at Your discretion, together with any other cumulative penalties that may have added to said transgressions and abuse of Office.
7. With reference to the conservation of Antiquities, We ban all persons from mutilating, chipping, altering, or spoiling Statues, Bas-reliefs, Stelae, Gravestones, and other ancient Monuments; and from fusing ancient Metals bearing figures or ornaments, Medallions of all kinds, Metal Inscriptions, and the such like including fragments. Therefore, You will retain the right to punish all Transgressors by fines or Corporal penalties at Your prudent discretion, including One-year-long forced labor sentences. Furthermore, it is the Inspector for the Fine Arts and Commissary's duty to ensure that said abuses do not occur by purchasing the items that might be valuable for public Museums whenever needed and authorising the melting or reallocation of all the artworks deemed of lesser quality. The issuance of such licenses is subject to said officers' unanimous consent.

8. Renewing the Constitution granted by the Holy Memory of Pius II, *Cum Almam Nostram Urbem*, dated 1462, and by the same penalties, We hereby ban all persons from demolishing or ruining the remains of ancient Buildings both within and beyond Rome, including the Urban and Rural Estates of second or third-party ownership. Accordingly, You will reserve the right to act upon the Inspector and Commissary's inquiries to issue licenses for the Ruins' demolition deemed unimportant for the Arts and Erudition. In Our behalf, You will press the Roman People's Law Enforcement Officers, Inspector, and Commissary for Antiquities to secure compliance with Our prescription and guarantee the ancient Construction Sites' restoration, cleanliness, and conservation.
9. In full confirmation of the Constitution granted by Our Predecessor, His Holiness Sixtus IV, in 1474, whose title opens with *Quam Provida;*
   Under the same Monetary, Corporal, and Discretionary penalties, We ban all persons from extracting carved and plain ancient Marbles of all kinds, Inscriptions, Mosaics, Urns, Terracotta, and other ornaments or Monuments of any type that are in the sight of all, hidden, or buried, from all public Churches and annexed Construction Sites;
   The penalties mentioned also apply to Sellers, Buyers, and Associates. Therefore, to make this prohibition completely effective, all the said Churches' Rectors and Administrators, regardless of their grade, dignity, and Privilege, including Reverend Titular Cardinals, Patrons – both Ecclesiastical and Lay – Congregations of Bishops, Regular Clergy, Members of the Council, Rule, and the such like with no exception for Our Reverend Vicar Cardinal are hereby deprived of the right to issue licenses, extract, and transfer said ornaments from Churches and annexed Construction Sites. Henceforth, this power will pertain to You exclusively and be subject to the Inspector for the Fine Arts and Commissary for Antiquities' inspection and report.
10. We command that the same prohibition apply to all Church Paintings, which henceforth may not be removed from their relevant location or alienated. Consequently, their restoration – both *in situ* and elsewhere will be subject to the Inspector for the Fine Arts and Commissary for Antiquities' acknowledgment, consent, and report forwarded to You.
11. To fully enforce Our directives, We command that all Private Owners of Galleries containing Statues and Paintings, Museums of Sacred and Profane Antiquities, collections of either type of artworks; and
    All the persons that do not own Galleries, Museums, or Collections, and are, nonetheless, proprietors of one or several ancient items or precious artworks – especially Statues or Paintings in Rome and its State;
    Must present a detailed account (exact note) of the items owned, listing each and every piece. Said account must be submitted to Our Chamber Secretaries' Records in Rome within a Month. In all the other regions of the State, the documentation must be submitted to the Community Chancellor within two Months of the publication of the here present Edict. In Rome, the Inspector for the Fine arts, the Commissary for Antiquities, or his Assessors contingent on the Inspector's acknowledgment, will perform a scrutiny yearly, or more often if You deem it necessary. In the rest of the State, the review of the items registered by their Owners will fall upon the deputies that You will have appointed for the task. Such appointees will also be entrusted with verifying

whether said items are still in said Owners' possession or have been disposed of in any manner. Failure to present the documentation within the deadlines or submitting incomplete records will result in the confiscation of the items; if the items are under a *fideicommissum*, their monetary value must be paid while the items remain subject to the same restrictions. In the latter case, all the preexisting restrictions persist. Refusing to report the items' disposal accurately and hindering the inspections will lead to the Transgressors being punished as fraudulent exporters.

12. All personnel employed in public Road maintenance, both in Town and Countryside, are banned from wrecking ancient Buildings to obtain Materials and subject to the same penalties inflicted upon Plunderers of public Monuments. Whereas the Laborers employed in widening or deviating Roads will often find Sepulchers, ancient Construction Sites, or Artworks which are prejudicially wrecked, appropriated, or alienated against the Prince's interests; Therefore, We command that all transgressors be punished by the same penalties inflicted upon Plunderers of public Monuments. Notwithstanding, all the Antiquities retrieved will be destined to Our public Museums.
13. All the Masters and Workers who discover removable antiquities while digging foundations, plowing, or performing other Construction Works must immediately report their finds to Your appointed Secretary of the Chamber. In the Provinces, the finds must be registered at the Local Chancellery. The failure to report within ten days of the second notification will result in the items' confiscation and other discretionary penalties that will increase when the omission to report on the findings adds to charges of fraudulent alienation. It falls to You, the Inspector for the Fine Arts, and the Commissary for Antiquities to purchase the items in question at a reasonable price for the public Museums. Therefore, the owner may not avail themselves of the items found before one month of submitting the report. The same report must also be submitted upon finding remains of ancient Houses and Roman Construction sites, albeit with no Antiquities.
14. No person may perform Excavations aimed at recovering Antiquities and hidden Treasures without Your special license, which will guarantee the customary Fiscal rights over a portion of the finds. Once the license has been granted, the Digger and assistant Deputy must inform the Inspector for the Fine Arts and Commissary for Antiquities of the Excavations' starting day. The Inspector and Commissary retain the right to monitor the Excavations in question either directly, through the Assessor for Sculpture, or other Persons appointed by You, in case of Excavations performed far from Rome. Increased vigilance is advised. The Digger must accurately report the items found to Your Secretary of the Chamber in Rome or the Provinces' Community Chancellor. In the absence of such offices, all misdemeanors will be punished depending on the transgression's gravity. All unlicenced Excavations and all transgressions will be punished by the items' confiscation or Five Hundred Ducats if no finds are made.
15. To enforce the present directives and renew the ones issued by Our Predecessors, in all the parts that do not conflict with Our Chirograph's current laws, We command that You and Your Successors have full and exclusive jurisdiction over all the other Tribunals, including the Chambers. Notwithstanding, We wish to encourage the Chiefs of all Tribunals and enterprises, as well as their Ministers and Executives, to cooperate

with Your Tribunal in detecting and countering Contraband and apprehending Transgressors. Furthermore, We advise the greatest care in all that concerns the Fine Arts. In this respect, We command that You act as supreme and independent Magistrate with absolute jurisdiction, vigilance, and authority over Sacred and Profane Antiquities, Fine Arts and their Masters, and artworks in Rome and the Papal State; and
Over Churches, Academies that are not assigned to foreign Countries, and other Societies related to the Arts with no exception. Said powers also prevail over persons of all Dignities – including Cardinals – jurisdictions, and privileges, with no exception for Cardinals, Bishops, Abbots, Titular [priests], and Patrons of Churches. Furthermore, You have the faculty to issue and renew Edicts and take all the measures You might deem useful to foster the Fine Arts and their Masters.

16. We command that You and your Ministers proceed against all the transgressors of these laws either summarily, through investigation, or *ex officio,* even when the items that prompted the Investigation no longer exist. In such cases, We command that the Inspector for the Fine Arts and Commissary for Antiquities punish the Transgressors by the customary penalties and a fine commensurate with his conjectural appraisal. Furthermore, the testimony of only one Witness, along with the Plaintiff's deposition and other supporting facts, will suffice to confirm convictions, except for the appeals, inhibitions, and extrajudicial pleas signed by Us personally.
17. Recommending the fullest and wholehearted implementation of Our determinations, under the current circumstances, and in keeping with Our Treasury's capacity, We renew our commitment to remedy the losses undergone by our public Museums. Therefore, to foster the purchase of new precious items, the Treasury will allot a portion of all its Monuments and proceeds of its fines net of the quota allocated by Law to the Accuser and Executors. Concurrently, We have found it compatible with our Treasury's capabilities to budget ten thousand Pieces for the yearly purchase of assets that will enrich Our Museums' collections. Indeed, these measures are taken with the firm understanding that promoting the Fine Arts will produce Incalculable advantages for both Our Subjects and State. Accordingly, We wish to ensure certainty of punishment for all the Owners and Plunderers that have performed illegal Exports of ancient items; support the masters of the Fine Arts with benefits and honors commensurate with the artists' merits; aid said masters in performing their professions, which contribute to Our City's adornment, its public recognition, and the sustenance of Our Subjects involved in the sector by combining business with pleasure. Therefore, it will be Your particular concern to enforce Our Directives effectively.

To safeguard Our Chirograph – albeit not displayed nor registered at the Chamber and in its Books — against perjury and falsehood in rescripts, procedural defects, unintended flaws in Our decree, or other pretexts albeit juridically valid, Jurisprudential, or prejudicial to third parties;
We hereby prohibit its contestation, revocation, abatement, mitigation *ad viam juris*, and annulment through the *Aperitione oris* or any other legal remedy;
Moreover, each case will be submitted to the rulings, settlements, and interpretations of Our Judges, Tribunals, Collegial Bodies, Congregations, Reverend Cardinals, Legates a Latere, Vicar Legates, Chamberlaines of the Holy Church, Treasurers, Rota, Chamber, and

the such like. Notwithstanding, We suppress the above-mentioned authorities' capacity and jurisdiction to settle and interpret to the contrary.
Henceforth, all the determinations conflicting with Our Chirograph's content and intention at any time and through any authority, either deliberately or out of ignorance, are pre-emptively declared null, void, and invalid. Furthermore, Our Chirograph is intended to bear full and perpetual validity, efficacy, applicability, and strength through Our signature, notwithstanding the degree of Privilege of the Persons, Clergy, and Religious Bodies submitting their requests, applications, and demands for special mentions. Notwithstanding Pius IV's Bull *de Registrandis*, Our Chancellery's regulation *de Jure quaesito non tollendo;* and
All of the Chirographs, Briefs, Ordinances, and Apostolic Constitutions issued by Us or Our Predecessors; and
All of the Notices and Edicts issued, published, and affixed; and
All of the Laws, Statutes, Reforms, Customs, Consuetudes, and any other writing that might contradict Our present Chirograph. Therefore, We Abrogate all of the above-mentioned, invalidating each of their parts, clauses, and registers; and
Through Our Papal Powers, We hereby amend all the substantial and formal flaws and defects that might be present in this Chirograph to grant its fullest and most effective Enforcement.

Issued at Our Apostolic Palace at the Quirinale on October 1st, 1802.
Pius VII Pope of the Popes.

For the fullest effectiveness and enforcement of His Beatitude's beneficent determinations;
To ensure that His Holiness' Chirograph may bring about the conservation and increase of Monuments and Ancient Artworks;
To foster and support the Fine Arts by appointing the Secretary of the Chamber Francesco Gregori in Rome, and the respective Chancelleries and Legal Governors in the Provinces, to the Tasks related to the submission of the accounts and prescribed in said Chirograph;
Hereby, We command that no person may claim ignorance of these Sovereign determinations; and
That the Public be informed of their content through Our Edict, which must be affixed and published in the Capital and Provinces' customary Venues;
Therefore, every Person in the City and State will be held accountable as if they were informed personally.
Furthermore, to guarantee that no Person may ever claim ignorance and that all be informed personally, We command that the present Edict be affixed perpetually by the above-mentioned Secretary of the Chamber in Rome and the Chancelleries of the State. All Chancellors, City Governors, and Towns will take responsibility equally. Consequently, Our Chirograph's determinations must be followed strictly and published together with Our Edict. All transgressors will be punished irreversibly by the penalties mentioned.

Issued at the Apostolic Chamber on October 2nd, 1802.
Pro-Chamberlain Cardinal Giuseppe Doria Pamphilj
Auditor P. Ferrari – General Commissary of the Reverend Apostolic Chamber Giuseppe Pecci

18
Notification

Giuseppe Doria Pamphilj, Cardinal Priest of the Title of Santa Cecilia, Pro-Chamberlain of the Holy Roman Church.
Notwithstanding the previous Edicts issued by Our Predecessors to prohibit all sorts of excavations near this Capital's Walls and preserve them, We nonetheless hear of persistent and harmful digs of Sandstone, Soil, and Clay in proximity to the Walls. Therefore, We refer to the fullest and precise observance of the Edicts mentioned above, particularly the ones dated April 8th, 1717, October 2nd, 1726, September 10th, 1733, and January 5th, 1750.
We hereby ban all Persons of all grades and conditions from excavating – either directly or by proxy – any sort of Sandstone, Soil, Clay, or any other material in proximity of the Walls surrounding Rome. All transgressors will be formally punished by incarceration, 500 golden Ducats of the Chamber, and other Corporal penalties established by our Successors and us depending on the infraction's gravity, the witnesses' reliability, and the investigations' outcome pursuant to the laws.
Furthermore, all Keepers and Supervisors of the Gates, Reviewers, and Inspectors must enforce such prohibitions and guarantee compliance.
In case of transgressions, said Officers will report to the nearest Gate, summon Law Enforcement Officials – who are obliged to comply – and then apprehend and bring the Transgressors to Our Tribunal. Thereupon, the suspects will be judged as specified above. When *in absentia*, the Transgressor's infraction will be investigated thoroughly by all means available to launch a procedure as mentioned above.
Therefore, everyone will be held accountable as if they were personally informed of the present Notification, which will be affixed and published in the customary Venues and Gates of the Capital.

Issued at the Chamber on January 7th, 1803.
Pro-Chamberlain Cardinal Giuseppe Doria Pamphilj
Auditor P. Ferrari – General Commissary of the Reverend Apostolic Chamber Giuseppe Pecci

5

The Grand Duchy of Tuscany

1
Legge contro chi rimovesse o violasse Armi, Inscrittioni o Memorie existenti apparentemente nelli Edifitii così Publici Come Privati

Ottenuta nell'Amplissimo Senato et Consiglio de' XLVIII
il di 30 di Maggio 1571.
Considerando il Serenissimo Gran Duca di Toscana et il Serenissimo Principe Reggente etc.
Quanto ornamento et splendore, così al publico come al privato apportano li Palazzi, Torri, Logge, Casamenti et altri edifitii et muraglie che sono state fabricate, et continuamente si fabricano nella loro dilettissima Città di Fiorenza, suo Contado et Distretto, et che la memoria di quelli che edificano si conserva et perpetua mediante le loro Armi, insegne, Titoli, Inscrittioni affisse, dipinte, scolpite o apposte sopra le Porte, Archi, Finestre, Cantonale o altro luogo publicamente apparente del edifitio o muraglia. Et che, secondo l'uso et inveterata consuetudine della Città (della quale non è memoria alcuna in contrario), non era lecito a chi comperava, o per qual si voglia modo acquistava alcuno edifitio, rimuovere, estinguere o violare le dette Armi et memorie de' construttori o fondatori d'esso.
Et che molti Procuratori, Causidici et Notarii con varie cavillationi et dispute hanno tentato et tentano revocare in dubio et alterare la detta consuetudine, con non piccola ingiuria della dignità et nome de primi patroni et possessori, et di tutte le loro agnationi et Casate: Et volendo con ogni opportuno rimedio prevedere a tali inconvenienti, et chiarire tutti li dubii, et levare l'occasioni delle liti, Loro Altezze insieme con li molto Magnifici et Clarissimi Consiglieri, mosse dalle soprascritte et altre giuste ragioni, per maggiore conservatione della fama et gloria di qualunche ha fatto o farà edifitii in Fiorenza o nelle altre Città, Terre et luoghi del suo felicissimo Dominio, hanno deliberato, previsto, statuito et ordinato.
Che per virtù della presente Legge et Previsione in avvenire nissuna persona di qualsivoglia stato, grado o conditione ardisca o presuma in alcun modo rimuovere, cancellare o in tutto o in parte oscurare, o altrimenti offendere le Armi, Insegne, Imprese, Titoli, Inscrittioni, o altre memorie esistenti sopra le Porte, Finestre, Cantonate, Archi o altri luoghi di fuora apparenti di qual si voglia Palazzo, Casamento, Edifitio o Muraglia così publica come privata, ancorchè per qual si voglia causa havesse acquistato o acquistasse in l'avvenire il dominio o patronato di simile edifitio et muraglia posta tanto nella Città di Fiorenza quanto nel suo Contado et distretto, comprendendo ancora la Città Contado et Montagna di Pistoja et qualunche altra

Città, Terra et luogo parimente privilegiato. Et in oltre per fuggire ogni confusione et dare maggiormente animo che del continuo si edifichi, hanno preveduto.
Che nessuno ardisca o presuma imprimere, o in alcun modo apporre in qualsivoglia luogo di fuora apparente di dette fabbriche et edifitii alcuna sua Arme o altra memoria in compagnia di quella del fondatore et construttore di tal muraglia, quantunche la linea o casata sua fosse mancata et estinta. Dichiarando che dove di fuora non fosse Arme o inscrittione del construttore, il padrone dell'edifitio possa lecitamente mettervi l'Arme sua propria, sotto pena a chi non osserverà, o in qualunche modo trasgredirà di scudi duemila di oro in oro per ciascuna volta, applicata per la metà al Fisco et Camera Ducale, et un quarto alli patroni dell'Arme soprascritte, o alli heredi, o più prossimi parenti del fondatore, et il resto a quel Magistrato, Rettore o Ufficiale che condannerà et riscoterà. Et la cognitione di tali transgressioni quanto alli Magistrati si appartenga et sia de Capitani di Parte et Conservadori di Legge della Città di Fiorenza salva in tra loro la preventione. Et quanto alli Rettori del Contado et Distretto, si aspetti solamente a quelli che hanno l'intera cognitione del criminale. Non obstantibus ecc.

Paolo Vinta

2
All'illmi Signori di Balia

7 Luglio 1597.
Havendo S. Altezza Nostro Signore bisogno di notabili quantità di pietre miste, come Agate, Diaspri, Carcedoni et altre simili dure per far una cappella che vuol fabricare, et sentendo che in questo Stato se ne trovano più cave, vuole e cosi comanda che per publico bando si proibisca a ciascuno l'estrarre fuori delli Stati suoi senza licenzia della medesima in scritto, sotto pena di scudi 25 per carica e della perdita delle bestie che conducessero o trainassero dette pietre. Aggiungendo ancora che a chi troverà nuove cave di pietre di qualità come sopra, denunziandole, se riusciranno a proposito si darà da S. A. buona ricognizione e mancia secondo la qualità di quelle ritrovarà. Cosi dunque le SS. VV. ne faranno distendere e publicare bando nella Città e per lo Stato.
Dio le prosperi.
Alli piaceri delle SS. VV. Illme.

Tommaso Malaspina Governatore

3
Bando

Il Serenissimo Gran Duca di Toscana e per S. Al. S. L'Illmi S. Offiziali di Balia di commissione dell'Illmo et Eccmo Sig.r Marchese Tommaso Malaspina di Villafranca Luogotenente e Governatore generale della Città e Stato di Siena.
Fanno per questo publico bando comandare che havendo S. A. bisogno per fabricare di notabil quantità di pietre mischie dure, come Agate, Diaspri, Calcedoni et altre simili, et sentendo che in questo Stato se ne trovano più cave, per l'avvenire non ardisca alcuno di estrarre fuori delli Stati suoi pietre della qualità suddetta senza licenza della Medesima S. A. in scritto sotto pena di scudi 25 per carica, della perdita delle bestie che conducessero o trainassero dette pietre.
Aggiugniendo ancora che a chi troverà nuove cave di Pietre come sopra, denunziandole se riusciranno a proposito si darà da sua Altezza buona ricognizione e mancia secondo la qualità di quelle che ritrovarà.
Bandito il di 12 di Luglio 1597 per Orazio Lisi

4
Don Ferdinando Gran Duca di Toscana

Essendosi per industria e diligenza di Don Vespasiano del Testa Senese venuto in cognizione di vari luoghi delli Stati nostri di Fiorenza e di Siena mediate et immediate a Noi soggetti dove sono cave di pietre dure preziose da pulimento, come Agate Diaspri et altre simili et di minerali. Et risultando queste sue nuove invenzioni in servizio publico riputazione delli Stati nostri et onor di Iddio poiche Noi et altre pie persone siamo per valercene in ornamenti di Cappelle et Chiese dedicate al culto divino haviamo riputato espediente e necessario il provedere che per l'effetto suddetto tali gioie non solo si ritrovino et cavino dalli luoghi dove si trovano ascosti ma ancora possino haversi in abbondanza secondo che al paese n'è stata libera la natura nè l'estrazione n'impedisca l'uso. Però haviamo eletto et in vertù della presente eleggiamo il prefato Don Vespasiano del Testa come intendente perito, e nuovo inventore delle qualità loro et delli luoghi dove trovar si possino, Commessario a cavarle e farle cavare dalle viscere della terra e luoghi tanto di particolari, come di Università e di privilegiati et esenti di qualsivoglia stato grado preminenza e condizione, e proibire come in vertù delle presenti proibiamo a ciascuno l'estrazione loro per fuora delli Stati nostri, sotto pena della galea a beneplacito, et di scudi cinquanta da applicarsi un quarto all'accusatore publico o segreto un quarto al Giudice esecutore et la metà al fisco nostro. Deputando Giudici di tal pena li Rettori criminari et civili delli luoghi d'onde si cavaranno dette pietre o dove saranno trovati li estrattori. Il Magistrato degli Otto in Firenze et li Capitani di Giustizia di Siena e suo Stato, con che habbia luogo la prevenzione. Comandando Noi a ciascuno di loro in vertù di questa lettera nostra patente che ad ogni istanza del prefato Commissario come sopra deputato faccia nella sua giurisdizione dove si ritrovaranno tali pietre proibire ad ognuno per bando publico il cavarle dalli luoghi dove sono o cavate portarle via senza licenza di lui in scritto sotto le pene suddette. Anzi proveda che li bargelli et esecutori et ogni altro usino diligenza di ritrovare l'inobedienti. Et pagando esso le debite mercedi gli diano e faccino dare ogni aiuto e favore con huomini e bestie per cavare e condurre dette pietre dove egli risolverà. Con rimuovere ogni impedimento che da qualunche persona Collegio et Università, etiam padrone del sito dove sarà la cava, che dare se li tentasse, per quanto ciascuno di essi stima la grazia e teme l'indegnazione nostra. Avvertendoli che circa alla prontezza o renitenza di ciascuno si darà piena fede alla relazione d'esso Commissario per farne quelle dimostrazioni che in simil caso si converranno. In fede di che haviamo fatte fare le presenti fermate di nostra propria mano e sigillate col nostro solito ducal sigillo. Dato in Firenze alli xvij di Maggio 1600.

Il Gran Duca di Toscana
Lorenzo Usimbardi Segretario

5
Bando

Volendo S. Altezza provedere che delli Stati suoi non s'estragghino Pietre che ricavan pulimento, acciò se ne possa havere per ornamenti di Chiese e Cappelle ad honore d'Iddio; et il meno che si può s'abbia a ricorrere a provvederne nelli Stati alieni, ha risoluto et in virtù delle presenti ordina e comanda che il Maestrato degli Otto proibisca per bando pubblico, che delli vicariati di Scarperia, Fiorenzuola, d'alcuna parte del Mugello, di quel di Palazzuolo, della Potesteria di Barga, Commessariato di Volterra, Vicariato di Certaldo et altri luoghi di Montagne dello Stato dove sono si trovano o in avvenire si trovaranno Miniere di Pietre dure di pulimento, come Diaspri, Agate, Calcidonij, Amatisti trasparenti coloriti e simili, non ardisca persona alcuna di qualsivoglia grado stato e condizione, ne ancora per farne d'archibusi, romperle spezzarle con martelli o altro qualsivoglia istrumento per portarle fuora dello Stato sotto pena di scudi 50 et anni dieci di galera. Anzi qualunche persona, tanto pastori bifolci o altri che praticano la campagna, et ogni altro di qualsivoglia grado stato e condizione, ancor padrone del terreno, dove ne sia che n'havrà cognizione o s'abbatterà a trovarle con sperimentarle col facile o in altro modo, debba sotto pena di scudi 25 e due anni di confino a Livorno metterle insieme raccarle o notarle et consegnarle e denunziare incontinenti la Miniera loro al Sindico della Villa e comune del Territorio e tenimento nel quale le troverà. Il qual Sindico sotto la medesima pena sia obbligato a ricevere quelle che gli saranno consegnate e notare e riconoscere la miniera che gli sarà dimostrata e subito rassegnarle al Potestà, Vicario o altro Rettore di Giustizia nel cui territorio saranno trovate. Il qual Rettore deva accettare tanto la consegna delle Pietre che se gli faccia quanto la notizia delle Miniere che se gli dia, con farne scrittura, mandare a riconoscerla e senza dimora darne avviso a Firenze al Ministro della Galleria di S. Altezza sotto pena della privazione dell'Uffizio. E se il Sano o Miniera qual si troverà fosse grande e non portabile possa solamente l'inventore d'esso, o il Sindico o Rettore che anderà a riconoscere provarlo col fucile se fa fuoco e nel resto aspettare che dalla Galleria o altro da deputarsi si mandi a riconoscerlo. Et habbia facoltà di lassar levare li pezzetti piccoli per servizio dell'archibusi a ruota dovendosi come sopra mandare alla Galleria li pezzi saldi e buoni da farne lavoro. Inoltre proibiscesi sotto le suddette pene di scudi 50 e

due anni di confino a Livorno ad ogni persona di qualsivoglia grado stato e condizione il donare vendere contrattare e trasferire di luogo a luogo ancora dentro li Stati di S. A. esistenti, senza licenza in scritto dell'Altezza Sua eccetto che come sopra, le dette pietre greggie. Et similmente a qualunche persona, ministro, Uffiziale et altro di qualsivoglia grado, stato condizione et ministerio l'accettarne da chi glie ne volesse dare, vendere o donare eccetto che come sopra et all'effetto come sopra, sotto la pena suddetta et altre imposte nella legge de presenti.
Il Governatore di Siena parimente faccia bandire e publicare et inviolabilmente osservare con bando di questo medesimo tenore per li Capitani di Massa, Grosseto, Montalcino, Monteamiata, Radicofani, Sovana, et altri dello Stato di Siena.
Dato in Firenze li 4 di Luglio 1602.

Il Gran Duca di Toscana
Lodovico Usimbardi Segretario

6
Deliberazione

24 Ottobre 1602.
Per il Concetto che si ha delle Pitture Buone che non vadino fuori a effetto che la Città non ne perda l'ornamento et li gentil'omini et l'universale ne conservino la reputazione, si considera che il trattare solo delle Buone, o di quelle de' Pittori defunti in generale per la varietà de' Pareri, per le Inventioni et Capricci de' gavillanti et perchè molto più per la poca Cognitione del Bene può essere ne' Ministri di Dogana, in quelli delle Porte della Città et ne Passeggieri, potrebbe seguirne diverse confusioni e disturbi. Però si rappresenta a proposito farne proibitione generale generalissima che per qualsivoglia etc. non se ne possa cavare alcuna della Città né dello Stato respettivamente, sotto pena etc. senza licenza del Luog.te dell'Accademia del Disegno il quale ne harà facultà con la regola et advertenza conveniente. Questa prohibitione piacendo, pare che basti farla per via della Dogana, comandando espressamente, che senza la licenza non se ne sgabelli di alcuna sorte, ne si permetta in alcun modo che se ne cavi di Firenze nè dello Stato, con ordinare alle porte et alli Passeggieri che senza licenza come sopra non ne lascino passare nessuna sotto pena etc. non lasciando però li modi soliti della Dogana.
Doverrà farsi l'ord.ne al Luog.te dell'Accademia che la licenza si faccia senza spesa, sottoscritta da lui et da uno de' principali della professione a sua eletione et sigillata del segno dell'Accademia con il quale si sigilli ancora la pittura licentiata etc.
Concedasi generalmente per tutte le pitture di mano de' pittori che di presente vivono nello Stato di S. A. indifferentemente.
Et ancora si possa concedere per Pitture di Pittori defunti ma con questa limitatione cioè, che per le opere di mano dell'infrascritti nominati non se ne faccia licentia in modo alcuno. Dichiarando che in caso di morte di alcuno de' pittori che di presente vivono in questi Stati, si conceda facultà alla medesima Accademia di potere secondo li suoi Ord.ni dichiarare, se quel tale doverrà o nò essere admesso et descritto nel numero de famosi di già passati et che appresso saranno nominati.

Dovendosi registrare nei libri dell'Accademia insieme con l'ord.ne che ne sarà dato.

1. Michelangelo Buonarroti
2. Raffaello da Urbino
3. Andrea del Sarto
4. Mecherino
5. Il Rosso fiorentino
6. Leonardo da Vinci
7. Il Francia bigio
8. Perino del Vaga
9. Jacopo da Puntormo
10. Titiano
11. Francesco Salviati
12. Agnolo Bronzino
13. Daniello da Volterra
14. Fra Bart.o di S. Marco
15. Fra Bast.o del Piombo
16. Filippo di fra Filippo
17. Antonio Correggio
18. Il Parmigianino

Da levare et aggiugnere a giuditio delli intendenti et volontà etc. etc.
La prohibitione non abbracci li ritratti ne li quadri di paesi ne quadretti da mettere da capo al letto tanto che si fanno in Firenze quanto che fuori etc. non conceda manco il Luogotenente licenza che possino portarsi pur in villa. Non s'impedischino l'opere dei Pittori viventi come sopra.

Fer.
L.o Us.i

7
All'illmi Signori di Balia

Siena, 28 Ottobre 1602.
Di comandamento espresso di S. A. Ser.ma nostro Signore per consideratione messale a benefitio et ornamento publico e privato di questa città le SS. VV. faccino prohibitione e publicatione che nissuna persona o collegio in qualsivoglia modo privilegiato possa cavare di questa città senza licenza in scritto di S. E. Illma alcuna pittura di Pittori morti et celebri, come di Mecharino, del Soddoma, di Raffaello et d'altri di qualche nome e fama o che fossero tenute per tali, ne meno si possino comprare o vendere a effetto di cavarle di Siena e quando di queste tali pitture ne fossero per le Ville o terre non si passino contrattare ne cavar dello Stato come sopra, sotto pena a chi contraverrà della perdita della cosa et del prezzo e di scudi cinquanta et altre afflittive e di confino ad arbitrio di S. E. delle quali pene pecuniarie il quarto sia dell'accusatore segreto o palese et ogn'uno possa essere

accusatore; un quarto del Mag.to o Giudice eseguente dandone la cognit.ne al Capt.no di Giustitia di Siena et a Regolatori, salva la preventione, e per lo Stato a Capitani et Potestà che hanno il criminale et il restante sia del Fisco. Et di così potranno fare estenderne e formarne il Bando al solito ecc. Dio le guardi.
Al piacere di VV. SS. Illme.

Scipione Naldi Auditore
Giov. Batta Marsili Fiscale

8
Bando

Il Serenissimo Gran Duca di Toscana N. S. e per S. Al. Ser.ma gl' Illmi s.ri Uff.li di Balia per commessione dei Molto Illmi et Ecc.mi s.ri Scipione Naldi Auditore e S.r Gio. Batta Marsili Fiscale Deputati al Governo in assenza dell'Illmo et Eccmo Signor Governatore nostro.
A benefizio et ornamento publico e privato di questa Città di Siena fa bandire e comandare d'ordine espresso di S. Al. che niuna persona o collegio in qualsivoglia modo privilegiato possa cavare di questa città senza licenza di S. Ecc.za Illma alcuna Pittura di Pittori morti e celebri come di Mecarino, del Sodoma, di Raffaello o d'altri di qualche nome e fama che fossero tenuti per tali. Nemeno si passino comprare, nè vendere a effetto di cavarle di Siena. E quando di queste tali pitture ne fossero per le ville o terre non si passino contrattare nè cavare dello Stato come sopra. Sotto pena a chi contraverrà della perdita della cosa e del prezzo e di scudi cinquanta et altre afflittive e di confino ad arbitrio di S. Ecc.za Illma. Delle quali pene pecuniarie il quarto sia dell'accusatore segreto o palese (et ogniuno possa essere accusatore) un quarto del Maestrato e Giudice eseguente (Dandone la cognizione al Capitano di Giustizia di Siena et a Regolatori) salva la prevenzione, e per lo Stato a' Capitani e Potestà che hanno il criminale.
Et il restante sia del Fisco.
Dal Palazzo Il di 5 di novembre 1602.

9
Deliberazione

A dì 6 di Novembre 1602.
Per ordine et mandato di S. Alt. Ser.a la Mag.ca Pratica ha commesso alli Maestri della Dogana di Firenze che faccino comandamento a lor Ministri di Dogana, delle Porte di Firenze, Doganieri et passeggieri, che non gabellino e non lascino uscire di Firenze, ne etiam per condurre nelle proprie Ville, ne del resto del dominio, per estrarsi fuori di esso, Pitture di sorte alcuna, senza licentia del Luogotenente di S. Alt. nell'Accademia del Disegno, sottoscritta da Lui, et da uno dei primi di quella professione sigillata col segno della detta Accademia, col sigillare anche col medesimo segno la Pittura acciò non si possa usar fraude, et cavarne una per un altra, sotto pena a detti Ministri, che in contrario facessero, dell'arbitrio di essa Mag.ca Pratica, et questo a fine et effetto,

che la Città di Firenze et il resto del dominio non restino privi delle opere egregie di eccellenti pittori.
Ha similmente comandato S. Alt., che il suo Luogotenente dell'Accademia del Disegno conceda dette licentie in scriptis col parere di uno dei principali della professione, et con la sottoscrizione loro et sigillo dell'Accademia, con far sigillare anca la Pittura, della quale daranno licenza, et tutto si faccia gratis et senza premio alcuno; volendo che generalmente si concedino per tutte le Pitture di mano di Pittori che di presente vivono nelli Stati sudd. indifferentemente.
Et ancora possino concedere dette licentie per le Pitture de' Pittori defunti secondo giudicheranno espediente, havendo riguardo di non le concedere per quelle, che fossero degne di restare nella Città. Ma per le pitture degl'infrascritti non si possa concedere licentia in modo alcuno, ne etiam per condurle in Villa, i nomi dei quali son questi cioè:

1. Michelangelo Buonarroti
2. Raffaello d'Urbino
3. Andrea del Sarto
4. Mecherino
5. Il Rosso Fiorentino
6. Lionardo da Vinci
7. Il Francia Bigio
8. Perin del Vaga
9. Jacopo da Pontormo
10. Tiziano
11. Francesco Salviati
12. Agnolo Bronzino
13. Daniello da Volterra
14. F. Bartolomeo di S. Marco
15. Fra Bastiano del Piombo
16. Filippo di Fra Filippo
17. Antonio Coreggio
18. Il Parmigianino
19. Pietro Perugino

Et che l'Accademia del Disegno abbia facultà di dichiarare secondo i loro Ordini, se alcuno dei pittori viventi, venendo a morte, meritino di essere ammessi nel numero dei Pittori famosi et de soprascritti.
Dichiarando che la detta proibizione non abbracci li ritratti et quadri di paesi, ne quadretti da mettere a capo al letto, sì quelli che si fanno in Firenze che fuori.
Però non mancherà detto Sig.r Luogotenente d'eseguire et far eseguire quanto sopra.

Li Ministri delle Riformag.i de Mand.o

10
Deliberazione

A dì XI di Xbre 1602.
La Mag.ca Pratica ha approvato la deputazione delli 12 pittori principali di questa Città fatta dagli Accademici del Disegno per loro partito legittimamente ottenuto per tutte fave nere, come il Sig.e Luogotenente di detta Accademia ha riferito, sopra il dare le licentie per le pitture da mandarsi fuori della Città di Firenze et suo Dominio, conforme all'ordine ultimamente dato da essa Mag.ca Pratica di commissione di S. Alt. li quali 12 Deputati sono questi cioè:

1. Santi di Tito
2. Jacopo Ligozzi
3. Domenico Passignano
4. Lodovico da Cigoli
5. Alessandro Allori
6. Pietro Sori sanese
7. Gregorio Pagani
8. Lodovico Buti
9. Cosimo Gamberucci
10. Gio. Stradan Fiammingo
11. Jacopo da Empoli
12. Giovanni Bizzelli

Dando facultà a qualsivoglia di essi di sottoscrivere le licentie dell'estrazioni di dette Pitture in compagnia del Sig. Luogotenente di detta Acc.a, in esecuzione del detto primo ordine, dato da essa Mag.ca Pratica et conforme ad esso in tutto et per tutto.

C. Lorenzo Muzii

11
L'accademia del Disegno

Ser.mo Gran Duca,
I Pittori Accademici per l'inserta chiedono temperamento al nuovo ordine che le pitture buone non eschino di qua, e dicono supplicare, così per utile delle gabelle come di se medesimi per che mancando d'esserne loro chieste, tanti forestieri si volgono a Venezia, Milano o Roma donde possono spedirsi senza tante soscrizioni e bolli qui necessari per la Dogana per le porte e pe' passeggieri sendoci molti modi di fraudare anche tal ordine così stretto.
Per informazione posso dirle d'havere inteso in compagnia del P.e Donato dell'Antella detti Artefici, dove sendosi discorso in tal materia senza deviare dal primo ordine e ottimo fine, ma per agevolarne i mezzi, si conchiuse pe' più, che trovandosi la noia maggiore pel gran numero di ritratti nuovi d'huomini Illustri che vanno fuori in Spagna, Francia e fin nell'Indie che di questi il L. I. possa dar licenza che gl'eschino essendo pur bollati con la

fede in carta di man propria del pittore che gl'habbi fatti con punire agramente chi erri in dette fedi, la qual diligenza debba anche bastare a tante copie della Nonziata, e d'altre pitture nuove copiate. Nel resto continuare il rigore incominciato: e quanto a fraudare le vere matrici de' Morti havea io già nell'Accademia proposto il rimedio, che saria questo. Che fuor de' detti ritratti nuovi semplici tutti gli altri quadri, che si vaglino mandare fuori debbano mandarsi alla Residenza dove è stanza da rinchiuderli per quel breve spazio che vi si tenghino e il Mercoledì tornata ordinaria de' Consoli e del L. I. si vegghino per uno de pittori già deputati a darne parere in carta perchè in su quella poss'io soscrivere licenza et essendo alla presenza mia non ci potrà correre fraude di scambiare le copie dalle Matrici, ne velare le buone e pingervi sopra cose nuove a tempera da potersi poi levare con spugna restandovi la prima pittura de' Morti, ma perchè la tornata ordinaria potria non bastare, il detto L. I. habbia obligo di tornarvi il Sabato dopo pranzo con uno dei detti pittori deputati, e soscrivere le pitture, che vi fossero sopragiunte dopo il Mercoledì, e se bene scommodi il detto L. I. che per la soscrizione si va a trovarlo a Casa o dove sia sendoci il ben pubblico non li parrà fatica per trovarsi là il Cancelliere che scrive le polize, et il sigillo da bollare e chi debba avvertirmi della pittura, in brevissimo tempo sarà spedito ognuno, che spesso fin a hora per molti si mette una mezza giornata a finire la pratica di trovarli uno a uno. Non lascierò di aggiungere, che essendo in Pisa, Pistoia, Arezzo et altri luoghi, degne pitture de Morti e delle buone potersi qui per l'Accademia Tribunal Supremo di tutto lo Stato vecchio dare qualch'ordine à Comm.ii e Rettori de luoghi, che consuoni alla mente di V. A. acciò non eschino dello Stato dove sarà facile informarsi da pittori, e da vecchi che habbino affetto all'Arte, e notizia del Disegno haverne una nota in man di chi le si trovino di persone private, che quanto alle ferme in chiese o luoghi pubblici nè di Firenze o altri luoghi si ha havere paura che le si cavino, con che attendendo quant'ella comandi me le inchino. Così Dio la conservi felice.
Firenze 15 Novembre 1603.

Di V. A. S. Umil: Servo
Baccio Valori

Così si faccia Fer.

12
Mandato

A di 11 di Xmbre 1603.
Per ordine et mandato delli Clar.mi SS.ri del Consiglio et Pratica Secreta di S. A. S. et in esecutione d'un benigno Rescritto della prefata Alt. Sereniss.ma de' 30 di Novembre 1603. Li Maestri della Dogana di Fiorenza faccino far comandamento alli Ministri di detta Dogana, Doganieri et Passeggeri dello Stato che non ostante l'ordine dato da d. Magnifica Pratica sotto li 6 di Novembre 1602, o altro pur vero tempo pe conto di non lassar extrar Pitture etc. lassino gabellare, bollare, et passare in l'avvenire tutte le Pitture delle quali appaia la licenza et soscrittione del S. Luogotenente di S. A. nell'Accademia del disegno senz'altro e Comandandone l'osservanza etc.

13
L'accademia del Disegno

Ser.mo Gran Duca,
Essendo stato considerato, alcuni anni sono, in tempo dell'Alt.a Paterna, che del continuo si estraeavano di questa Città et del Dominio Quadri et Pitture d'eccellenti Pittori et che a poco a poco in pregiudizio grave dell'Arte et del nome che havea il felicissimo Stato di V. A. d'avere quantità di quadri et Pitture d'Artefici eccellenti, sotto di 6 Ottobre 1602 per ordine della Mag.ca (Pratica) fu proibito che non si estraesse Quadri et Pitture di xviiij Pittori celebri et nominati, e perciò fu comandato ai Ministri della Dogana che non potessero gabellare di sorte alcuna senza la licenza in scriptis sottoscritta di mano del Luogotenente et d'un Pittore per assicurarsi maggiomente che non ne partissero di quelle del sopradetto numero.
Et perchè detta proibizione non apparisse fatta se non a Ministri della Dogana di Firenze, et sentendo che in Pisa ve ne sono buon numero di diversi famosi et celebri Maestri, quali tuttavia si sente che si estraggono, quando fosse con buona grazia di V. A. a noi parrebbe che fosse a proposito che detto ordine non solo abbracciasse la Città di Firenze, ma Pisa, Pistoia, Arezzo et tutte le altre Città et luoghi dello Stato di Firenze dove fossero simili sorte di quadri de' detti nominati Pittori.
Et perchè in Pisa ve ne sono, secondo che s'intende, buona quantità di Gio. Antonio Sogliani sì come anco ne devono essere in Firenze, et altrove, il quale fu celebre ne suoi tempi et le opere sue sono di molta stima, però parrebbe si potesse aggiungere al numero dei predetti. Et che la medesima proibizione che è nella Dogana di Firenze fosse in tutte le altre di dette Dominio; et rispetto alle soscrizioni dove in Firenze, le polize sono scritte dal Luogotenente et Cancelliere, fuori sieno scritte dal Rettore et dal Cancelliere del Luogo, con deputare respettivamente in detti Luoghi Pittori de' più pratici et idonei che conoschino le mani de' predetti conforme a che si contiene nell'ordine predetto, et per sua maggiore notizia se li manda nota de nomi di detti Pittori, quali sono:

1. Michelangelo Buonarroti
2. Raffaello d'Urbino
3. Andrea del Sarto
4. Mecherino
5. Il Rosso Fiorentino
6. Leonardo da Vinci
7. Il Francia Bigio
8. Perin del Vaga
9. Jacopo da Pontormo
10. Tiziano
11. Francesco Salviati
12. Agnolo Bronzino
13. Daniello da Volterra
14. F. Bartolomeo di S. Marco
15. Fra Bastiano del Piombo

16. Filippo di fra Filippo
17. Antonio Correggio
18. Il Parmigianino
19. Pietro Perugino

Et facendo umilissima reverenza preghiamo dal Sig.r Iddio per la lunghissima et felicissima vita:
Di Firenze della nra solita Residenza li 5 Maggio 1610.
Di V. A. s.ma

Devotissimi Servi
Il Luogot. e Consoli dell'Accad. del Disegno della Città di Firenze

Così si faccia

14
Deputazione Volterrana

Di Firenze 18 Luglio 1744.
Trovando il Consiglio di Reggenza molto giusto e conveniente il provvedere come hanno domandato codesti sigg. Priori nel loro memoriale, perchè in avvenire non passino essere alterati gli antichi riguardevoli monumenti, dei quali è così abbondante il territorio di codesta Città, ha risoluto perciò di formare una speciale Deputazione de' signori Proposto Cav. Guarnacci, Decano Giorgi, Cav. Giuseppe Del Bava e avvocato Cecina.
Questa Deputazione colla saputa di V: S: Illma: farà rinnuovare l'ordine già dato, che non possino intraprendersi nuovi scavi senza la loro licenza in scritto.
Quando stimeranno di accordarla e che il Commissario non abbia motivi in contrario, faranno assistere se vogliono agli scavi senza aggravio dei proprietarj.
Dovranno pigliare una distinta memoria delle antichità ritrovate, e venendo loro richiesta accordar la permissione ancora che siano estratte, se pure il pubblico ai prezzi giusti non stimasse d'arricchire il suo museo.
Soprattutto sarà loro incumbenza di invigilare che non sian commesse delle fraudi in pregiudizio della stima ben grande che hanno acquistato in Toscana e fuori gli studi dei Caratteri Etruschi.
Non s'intende sia per la licenzia di scavare o per le permissioni delle vendite di inferire alcun danno ai proprietari, ma solo che la Deputazione salvando loro il diritto cli patronato e l'interesse, abbia cura che si osservi tutta la dovuta buona fede.
Mancando per rinunzia o per altro motivo alcuno dei presenti deputati, sia pensiero dei tre che resteranno di proporre altri quattro nobili soggetti Volterrani ai sigg. Priori e Collegio acciò sia eletto alla pluralità dei voti quello che sarà reputato il più idoneo e meritevole. Lasciando anche in libertà del sig. Proposto e Priori d'eleggere con un solo partito alla pluralità dei voti, il primo, che sarà posto nella nota della Deputazione.

Finalmente seguendo trasgressioni in materia di scavi, alterazioni cli monumenti o estrazioni devino i signori Deputati darne parte a V. S. Illma, acciò sentita la volontà del Consiglio di Reggenza siano dati ai trasgressori i convenienti gastighi.
E desiderando che questi provvedimenti, e altri che saranno presi occorrendo assicurino il rimedio tanto necessario ai disordini accaduti e che codesto pubblico ne abbia tutta la sodisfazione, mi soscrivo col solito ossequio.

Gaetano Antinori Seg.
Al Sig. Commissario di Volterra

15
Rescritto Imperiale

Sua Maestà Imperiale essendo stata informata del ritrovamento fatto casualmente nel Territorio Sanminiatese, di un ripostiglio di Antiche Monete Romane, vuole che siano riposte nella raccolta delle Medaglie esistenti nella Real Galleria di questa Città tutte quelle monete, che dall'Antiquario Dottore Antonio Cocchi ne saranno state giudicate meritevoli per qualche rara particolarità, o notabile contrasegno in conformità del Rescritto del di 17 Gennaio 1749 e si compiace di accordare all'Inventrice un terzo di quello che essa ha trovato, o il suo valore, e un terzo o suo valore al Padrone del fondo in cui sono state trovate, dedotte le spese, che per tale ritrovamento fossero occorse. Comanda inoltre la C. M. S. che per l'avvenire trovandosi a caso qualche Tesoro, Ripostiglio, o altro antico monumento, l'inventore sia obbligato a denunziarlo, in ricompensa di che gli sarà accordato per sua porzione un terzo delle cose trovate, overo la loro giusta valuta, qualora non possino comodamente dividersi, o sieno monumenti di tal rarità e lavoro che meritino di essere conservati per pubblico adornamento e benefizio, e che chiunque ardisse scavare senza le dovute licenze, o che ritrovando casualmente qualche Ripostiglio, Tesoro, Statue, o altre Antichità non le denunziasse, sia privo della predetta grazia di partecipare delle cose trovate; all'effetto di che resta incaricato l'Auditor Fiscale d'invigilare e di comunicare gli ordini opportuni per l'esecuzione.
Fatto in Firenze li 21 Agosto 1750.

Richecourt Vauthier

16
Editto

Riflettendo il Consiglio di Reggenza quanto sia importante al decoro pubblico, che si conservino tanto nella Città di Firenze, quanto nelle altre Città e Luoghi del Granducato di Toscana le opere illustri e stimabili per la loro antichità e rarità, ed altresì quanto sia pregiudiciale al medesimo la libera estrazione di esse da questi Stati.
Perciò in aumento ed ampliazione delle Leggi del di 6 Novembre 1602 e del dì 31 Dicembre 1603 proibisce ad ogni persona di qualsivoglia stato, grado e condizione, ancorchè occorresse il farsene specialissima menzione, di potere in avvenire estrarre,

o fare estrarre tanto da questa Città di Firenze, quanto dalle altre Città e Luoghi del Granducato per fuori di Stato alcuna sorte di antichi Manoscritti, Iscrizioni, Medaglie, Statue, Urne, Bassirilievi, Dorsi, Teste, Frammenti, Pili, Piedistalli, Quadri e Pitture antiche ed altre opere e cose rare senza la permissione espressa del Consiglio medesimo.
E chiunque sotto qualsivoglia pretesto o quesito colore ardisse di contravvenire o far contravvenire alle proibizioni espresse nel presente Editto, incorra nella pena della perdita della cosa estratta o tentata di estrarsi, e di più sia condannato nel doppio giusto valore della medesima.
La qual pena dovrà applicarsi per un terzo al Fisco per altro terzo all'accusator segreto o palese, e per altro terzo a chi condannerà.
E se i trasgressori non saranno in grado di poter pagare la suddetta pena, in quella vece incorreranno in pena afflittiva ad arbitrio di chi dovrà giudicare.
La cognizione delle dette trasgressioni spetti in Firenze al Magistrato degli Otto, e nelle altre Città a quei Giudici che presiedono al Criminale, i quali potranno procedere contro i trasgressori tanto a querela, quanto ancora ex officio e per inquisizione.
Dato in Reggenza li ventisei Dicembre 1754.

Il Conte di Richecourt
Pier Antonio Guadagni

17
Motu Proprio

Essendo informata S. M. I. delle difficoltà che sono alle volte insorte nella Città di Volterra per causa degli scavi che si fanno in quelle vicinanze ad oggetto di ritrovare i residui di antichità che vi sono in gran copia sepolti, e volendo opportunamente provvedere perché si possa con buon ordine proseguire in tali studiose ricerche:

1. In primo luogo ordina e comanda che sia in libertà di ciascheduno di scavare nel proprio fondo, ovvero nel suolo d'altri con licenza in tal caso del padrone del suolo o del fondo.
2. Che chiunque vorrà scavare tanto nel proprio suolo che nel suolo altrui, debba presentare le sue istanze ai deputati sopra il museo pubblico della Città ed indicare il luogo e il tempo dello scavo da farsi, e giustificare presso i medesimi il consenso del padrone del fondo, e riportare da detti deputati una licenza in scritto che indichi il nome di chi la ha domandata, il luogo dello scavo e il tempo assegnato a scavare. La qual licenza servirà che sia sottoscritta da uno dei predetti deputati e resterà spedita senza veruna spesa.
3. Chiunque vorrà riportare tali licenze non potrà scavare nè in altro tempo nè in altro luogo, e spirato il tempo assegnato, dovrà presentare ai deputati una nota ben distinta delle antichità ritrovate, acciò volendo, passino venderle.
4. E quando voglia vendere tali antichità dovrà dare la preferenza in primo luogo al pubblico di Volterra per arricchire il museo di quella Città, per quel prezzo che sarà fissato da due o tre Periti da concordarsi avanti i deputati, e tal preferenza durerà un mese dal giorno della presentazione di detta Nota, spirato il qual termine il contratto dovrà restar concluso o sciolto, e in mancanza di conclusione s'intenderà sciolto.

5. E spirato detto termine debbono per la detta stima come sopra fissata e durante lo spazio d'un altro mese essere preferiti tutti i Cittadini Volterrani, e in caso di concorrenza fra loro si devenga all'incanto sopra la detta stima, dopo di che sarà permesso al proprietario procurarne l'esito altrove, salva l'osservanza delle Leggi di S: M: sopra l'estrazione fuor di Stato delle cose che potessero venir comprese sotto la disposizione delle dette Leggi. E se il proprietario in tal caso richiederà i deputati di farli un certificato della sua libertà di contrattare, saranno tenuti farglielo gatuitamente.
6. Che chiunque farà lavorare ai predetti scavi senza la detta licenza dei deputati, o farà lavorare fuori del luogo e del tempo nella licenza compreso, o mancherà di notificare le cose ritrovate o le contratterà avanti la notificazione o dopo di essa, in pregiudizio della preferenza accordata alla Città e Cittadini di Volterra, incorrerà nella perdita della roba ritrovata e contrattata senza autorità da applicarsi al museo pubblico di Volterra, e non potrà in avvenire conseguire mai più licenza di escavazione.
7. I deputati predetti non negheranno le predette licenze a verun altro, che nel caso del capitolo precedente di chi ne avesse fatto abuso, avranno bensì l'arbitrio di fare assistere agli scavi ne' luoghi e tempi assegnati a misura del sospetto di occultazione che potessero avere, ed avranno facoltà di commettere agli esecutori che invigilino agli scavi che si facessero senza licenza e fuori dei limiti della licenza, e all'occultazione e asportazione delle cose che si facesse in fraude di quanto sopra vien disposto.

E il Commissario di Volterra provveda come conviene e presti ogni opportuna assistenza per l'esecuzione degli ordini sopra scritti.
Dato in Reggenza 10 Dicembre 1761.

M.e Botta Adorno
Roberto Pandolfini

18
Bando

L' Illmo Sig. Domenico Brichieri Colombi Auditore Fiscale di S. A. R. in esecuzione di Sovrano Rescritto del dì 27 Agosto 1766 ed in aumento della Legge pubblicata li 11 Ottobre 1762, con cui viene ordinato, che trovandosi a caso qualche Tesoro, Ripostiglio o altro antico Monumento l'Inventore sia obbligato a subito denunziarlo a questo R. Fisco o al Tribunale del luogo dove sarà seguito tale ritrovamento, fa pubblicamente notificare come resta proibito ai Ministri della Zecca, orefici, argentieri, a tutti i fonditori, etc. etc. il fondere e distruggere ogni sorta di medaglie, monete, o altre simili anticaglie, senza prima notificarlo al Tribunale del fisco direttamente, o per mezzo del Tribunale del luogo, sotto pena dell'arbitrio rigoroso e della perdita delle cose suddette e loro valuta, da applicarsi metà al Fisco e metà al Delatore o Accusatore palese o segreto.
Ed affinchè i predetti veneratissimi ordini di S. A. R. Nostro Clementissimo Signore siano da tutti indistintamente osservati e non possa alcuno allegarne ignoranza, la presente notificazione che deve aver vigore per tutto il Granducato, compresi ancora i Luoghi privilegiati, dei quali occorresse fare speciale menzione, sarà pubblicata ed affissa ai

luoghi soliti, e dovranno i respettivi Jusdicenti mandare alla Cancelleria del Fisco dentro il termine di due mesi prossimi avvenire, riscontro della seguita pubblicazione; e tutto, etc. Fu pubblicata 17 Ottobre 1766.

Antonio Pescetti
Canc.e Fiscale

19
Pietro Leopoldo per Grazia di Dio Principe Reale d'Ungheria e Boemia, Arciduca d'Austria, Granduca Di Toscana ecc. ecc.

Volendo Noi liberare i nostri amatissimi sudditi dai pregiudizj, ai quali sono stati finquì soggetti per gli Statuti municipali e le Leggi emanate dai nostri RR. Predecessori in materia di Tesori, di Scavi, e di estrazione fuori di Stato di antichi monumenti, e volendo richiamare questi oggetti alla naturale equità, Comandiamo:

1. Che in avvenire sia lecito e permesso a ciascuno, senza alcuna preventiva licenza l'intraprendere scavi, per ritrovare e ritrovati far propri Monumenti dei passati secoli, monete o altre cose preziose antiche, purchè volendolo fare nel suolo altrui o essendovi il pericolo di danneggiare gli Edifizi e Beni contigui, ne abbia il consenso in scritto del Padrone del Fondo o del Confinante, e adempia le condizioni sopra il riparto della roba trovata, o l'indennizzazione, e compisca ogni altro patto con cui il consenso li sarà stato prestato.
2. Chiunque deliberatamente per se o per altri eseguirà tali scavi nell'altrui suolo, senza il consenso del Padrone o del Confinante respettivamente, sarà tenuto per ogni via di ragione a resarcire il danno che avesse cagionato, oltre l'azione dell'ingiuria e del turbato possesso, colla quale potrà pure esser convenuto in giudizio tanto civilmente che criminalmente; E nel primo caso tutto quello che avrà trovato anderà intieramente a profitto del Padrone del fondo, senza che l'inventore possa neppure pretendere il risarcimento delle spese. Se poi tale invenzione fosse seguita a caso, la metà sarà dell'Inventore, e la metà del Padrone del suolo.
3. Quando si trovino Iscrizioni, Statue, Bassorilievi, Urne, Idoletti, Istrumenti di metallo, Medaglie, Gemme intagliate ed altri simili monumenti di antichità, il Direttore della Nostra R. Galleria sull'avviso che ne averà dall'inventore direttamente, o per mezzo del Cancelliere Comunitativo, resta incaricato di prender cognizione di ciò che potrà meritare di essere acquistato per la medesima, e dal Nostro R. Erario sarà pagato il prezzo rigoroso corrispondente alla rarità e bellezza dei monumenti che si acquisteranno.
4. Sarà permesso a chiunque il contrattare, abolita qualunque privativa, e trasportare da un luogo all'altro anco fuori del Granducato qualunque monumento di antichità, salvi gli ordini delle Dogane per il pagamento delle Gabelle nei casi e nei modi che siano dovute.
5. Nascendo dubbio a chi spetti il dare il consenso per gli scavi da farsi nel suolo altrui, o a chi debbono dirsi devolute le cose in esso scavate senza il preventivo consenso che sopra, come pure nel caso di qualche fortuito ritrovamento parimente nell'altrui

suolo, attesi i diversi diritti che sopra un istesso Fondo possono altrui competere, vogliano che si abbia ricorso a quanto dispone in questa materia il *Gius* comune, a cui pure si ricorrerà in qualunque altro caso non espresso nel presente Nostro Editto, e dove venisse direttamente o indirettamente contravvenuto a quanto in questo ci è piaciuto di ordinare.

6. I Giusdicenti conosceranno sommariamente delle istanze che gl'interessati nelle invenzioni facessero per il possibile loro privato respettivo interesse, procurando di togliere al possibile le inutili e animose contestazioni.

Tale è la Nostra Volontà, la quale vogliamo che sia osservata in tutti i luoghi del Nostro Granducato, derogando agli Statuti Municipali ed a tutte le Leggi ed Ordini e Consuetudini veglianti in materia di Tesori e di Scavi di antichità, anco per quello che riguardano la partecipazione al Nostro Regio Fisco, e derogando specialmente al Bando degli 11 Ottobre 1762, agli ordini relativi agli Scavi nel Territorio di Volterra, ed altri che ve ne fossero per qualunque altro Territorio.
Dato li 5 Agosto 1780.

Pietro Leopoldo
V. Alberti – F. Sbratti

20
Rescritto

Resta autorizzato il Direttore della R. Galleria ad accordare le Licenze per l'estrazione di quei Quadri e Pitture, che egli non crederà meritevoli d'acquistarsi per la R. Galleria, dopo aver sentito il parere del Pittor Magni o altri che stimerà conveniente sul merito di tali Quadri e Pitture; E dalla Segreteria di Finanze si partecipino in conformità gli ordini opportuni.
Dato in Firenze li 16 Gennajo 1781.

Pietro Leopoldo
Angiolo Tavanti – D. Schimisveiller

21
Legge sulle Gabelle

30 Agosto 1781.
[...]
8. Comandiamo che all'epoca qui sotto stabilita restin soppresse tutte le Leggi attualmente veglianti, che proibiscono respettivamente l'introduzione, l'estrazione ed il transito per il Nostro Granducato di qualche mercanzia o genere, eccettuate solamente quelle Leggi che riguardano le Nostre Regalie sopra il sale, tabacco e carte da giuoco, e ferma stante la proibizione d'estrarre dal Granducato senza le debite licenze le Pitture antiche, a forma della Legge de' 26 Dicembre 1754 tutt'ora vegliante in questa parte; talchè allorquando comincerà ad avere

effetto la predetta disposizione, qualunque altra mercanzia e genere potrà introdursi, estrarsi e transitare per tutto il nostro Granducato, mediante il pagamento delle Gabelle prescritte nelle respettive Tariffe per l'introduzione, estrazione e transito rispetto al nuovo Territorio riunito, quanto rispetto agli altri Territorj separati che avessero delle Gabelle particolari.

22
Regolamento per le Comunità

27 Marzo 1782.
[...]
Art. 12. Potrà chiunque Possessore di Case, o Palazzi con la licenza del respettivo Giusdicente, ed in Firenze dell'Auditore della Camera delle Comunità da concedersi senza alcuna spesa, rimuovere le Iscrizioni, le Armi gentilizie, e simili monumenti in occasione di resarcirle, o fabbricarle di nuovo, purché le collochi nel sito corrispondente a quello che avevano, o in altra parte dell'Edifizio esposta al Pubblico, ed in caso di demolizione totale della Fabbrica, senza la riedificazione della medesima, a spese del Possessore del fondo demolito si dovranno collocare in qualche fabbrica pubblica, a dichiarazione del Giusdicente o Auditore predetto; all'effetto che non se ne perda la memoria.

23
Dichiarazione della Tariffa Doganale

18 Ottobre 1791.
I quadri e tavole di pitture antiche non potranno estrarsi dal Granducato, in vigore della Legge 26 Dicembre 1754.

1
Law against whoever shall remove or violate Coats of Arms, Inscriptions, or Mementos displayed on Public Buildings and Private Households

As deliberated by the Senate and Council of the Forty-Eight
May 30th, 1571.
Having acknowledged the ornament and splendor that the Palaces, Towers, Lodges, Buildings, Tenements, and Walls of the City, County, and District of Florence express both in public and in private; and
Having considered how the memory of the builders remains through their Coats of Arms, Emblems, Titles, and Inscriptions, either painted, engraved, or affixed;
The Most Serene Grand Duke of Tuscany and the Prince Regent ban all buyers and owners from removing or violating said features from Doors, Arches, Windows, and Braces, or any other fitting, fixture, or portion of the construction visible from the outside, in keeping with the City's most ancient customs.

Many Procurators, Advocates, and Notaries have attempted to revoke or alter such tradition to the detriment of the original owners, their heirs, or House. Therefore, their Highnesses and the Distinguished Councilors have decreed as follows, for the sake and glory of whoever has erected constructions and buildings within the City of Florence or its Dominions.
In compliance with the present Law, no person of whatever standing, condition, or status shall have the right to remove, obliterate, or hide any Coats of Arms, Emblems, Titles, and Inscriptions, or any other Memento, from all external Doors, Windows, Arches, Braces, or any other fitting, fixture, or portion of the construction visible from the outside. Said prohibition applies to both private and public Palace, Building, Tenement, or Wall within the City of Florence, its County and its District, including the Mountain of Pistoia and any other City and Land endowed with equal privileges.
It is also forbidden to paint, impress, or affix one's Heraldry next to that of the founder or builder of the construction in question, even in the case that the founder's House should be extinct.
Owners who falsely declare the absence of any preexisting fittings and fixtures are to be fined two thousand golden crowns. Half of this sum will be allocated to the Revenue Office and the Ducal Chamber, one-quarter of it is for the patrons, heirs, or next of kin of the Heraldry mentioned above. The remainder shall be allotted to the Magistrates or Officers who have issued the fine.
It is the Party Captains and Law-Enforcement Officers' duty to notify the Magistrates of any potential offense. All County and District Governors are to inform the Magistrates only when the crime should be entirely ascertained.
All things to the contrary notwithstanding, etc.

Paolo Vinta

2
To the most Illustrious Lords of Balia

July 7th, 1597.
Needing significant amounts of ore such as Agate, Jasper, Chalcedony, and other similar gemstones for the construction of a chapel; and
Having been informed of the presence of several such quarries in this State;
Our Lord His Highness orders that the extraction rights to the quarries beyond His States be restricted to those in possession of a valid license.
All shipment of unlicensed cargo will be punished by a fine of 25 crowns and the pack animals' confiscation.
Whoever reports to the authorities on the discovery of any prospective quarries shall be awarded a special mention and a prize proportional to the value of the quarry in question.
Thus Your Lordships, may God bless you, shall inform the City and spread the proclamation.
To the pleasure of Your Most Illustrious Lordships.

Governor Tommaso Malaspina

3
Notice

On behalf of the Most Serene Grand Duke of Tuscany, and under the commission of the Most Illustrious and Most Excellent Marquise Tommaso Malaspina of Villafranca, Lieutenant and Governor-General of the City of Siena, the Most Illustrious Officials of Balia proclaim as follows.
Needing significant amounts of ore such as Agate, Jasper, Chalcedony, and other similar gemstones; and having been informed of the presence of several such quarries in this State; His Highness decrees that the extraction rights to the quarries beyond His States be restricted to those in possession of a ducal license.
All shipment of unlicensed cargo will be punished by a fine of 25 crowns and the pack animals' confiscation.
Whoever reports to the authorities on the discovery of any quarries of the kinds mentioned above shall receive a special mention and a prize proportional to the value of the quarry in question.
Notified on July 12th, 1597, by Orazio Lisi

4
Don Ferdinand Grand Duke of Tuscany

Having been diligently informed by Don Vespasiano del Testa the Sienese of the existence of several quarries of Agate, Jasper, and other kinds of raw gemstone and minerals in the States of Florence and Siena; and
Aware that these discoveries shall not only benefit the reputation of our States but bring glory to the Lord as well since they are to be relied upon for the adornment of consecrated Chapels and Churches;
We have deemed it necessary to order as follows.
The location and mining of the above-mentioned ore shall be authorised as long as the minerals are abundant and their extraction is convenient and safe from damage.
On account of his expertise, Don Vespasiano del Testa is hereby appointed Superintendent to the mining extraction and assessment of the quality of the ore in question. His jurisdiction shall also extend to particular grounds such as Universities and estate subject to privilege and exemption of any status, grade, preeminence, and condition.
All export beyond our States is forbidden and punishable by a sentence to the galleys and a fine of fifty crowns. One-quarter of this sum is to be allocated to the accuser, either public or secret as they may be; another quarter is for the judge who issued the injunction. The remainder shall be allotted to our Revenue Office.
The criminal and civil Provosts from the jurisdictions where the quarries are located are to act as Prosecuting Judges. The Magistrates of the Eight in Florence and the Captains of Justice in Siena and its State will ensure patrol and prevention.
All unlicensed export and shipment are to be banned pursuant to said Superintendent's requests and authorisations. The superintendents shall notify such interdiction of each of the jurisdictions involved.

Furthermore, the aforementioned magistrates shall also ensure that all Captains of Justice and law-enforcement officers be thorough in imposing penalties and facilitating licensed extraction and shipment when approved. Full assistance is to be provided to those who should require additional workforce and pack animals upon payment of a fee. Magistrates must also overcome any possible resistance from those persons, Colleges, Universities, and estate owners that should contravene our orders, loyal as they may be to Us. All should be warned that their compliance, or the lack of it, will be reported by the Superintendent in full detail, upon which reports We shall act as We deem most befitting.
We herewith sign this measure and impress it with our ducal seal.
Issued in Florence on May 17th, 1600.

The Grand Duke of Tuscany
Secretary Lorenzo Usimbardi

5
Notice

In order to prevent any further mining extraction of raw gemstones for the adornment of Churches and Chapels and to limit its purchase from any alien State, His Highness orders as follows.
The Magistracy of the Eight shall hereby notify this ban in the Vicariates of Scarpiera, Fiorenzuola, Palazzuolo, Certaldo, and part of Mugello, the Commissariat of Volterra, the Commune of Barga, and any other mountainous region in the State where there are or might be quarries of raw gemstone such as Jasper, Agate, Chalcedony, coloured transparent Amethyst and suchlike.
All persons, regardless of their standing, status, or condition, are interdicted from chipping, breaking, or mining said stones using hammers or tools of any sort, including arquebuses. The exportation beyond the State's borders is also forbidden under pain of fifty crowns and ten years on the galleys.
Furthermore, those countryfolk and estate owners who should chance upon a vein or come to know about it either by word of mouth or by testing it on a flintlock are to proceed as follows, regardless of their standing, status, and condition.
Under pain of twenty-five crowns and a two-year banishment in Livorno, the persons mentioned above must immediately collect the stones and deliver them to the Mayor of the Villa and Commune of the Territory where the discovery has taken place. Under the same pain, the Mayor will subsequently take the quarry's bearings, take custody of the stones and deliver them to the Chief Magistrates, Deputy Chiefs, or Provosts of Justice of the area in question. It will then be the Provost's duty to inform His Highness' Minister of the Gallery on pain of losing his Office.
In cases where the Stones were too big for shipment, the Mayor or Provost shall go to the site in person to test them on a flintlock and wait for a deputy from the Gallery. Only in such cases will they be allowed to collect the samples deemed suitable for construction and fit to be sent to the Gallery.

Without His Highness' written license, all donations, sale, or shipment, either within His State or to other States, are punishable by 50 crowns and a two-year banishment to Livorno, regardless of the offender's standing, status, and condition, and with the exception of the samples mentioned above.
The same applies to all those persons, ministers, or Officers of any standing, status, condition, and rank who should donate or sell the Stones for any reason other than those mentioned above, under the same pain previously mentioned.
The Governor of Siena shall enforce the same ban and notify it to the Captains of Massa, Grosseto, Montalcino, Monteamiata, Radicofani, Sovana, and others of the State of Siena.
Issued in Florence on July 4th, 1602.

The Great Duke of Tuscany
Secretary Ludovico Usimbardi

6
Deliberation

October 24th, 1602.
The Concept of what makes a Good Painting, and which ones should not be exported, is one that might lead to great confusion and disturbance. Such is the case not only because of the wide variety of Opinions, Fantasies, and Whims of those who engage in such subtle discussions but also because of the Ignorance of what is Good on the part of many Ministers of Customs and City Gates, and Travelers.
For these very reasons, and much to the benefit of the City's adornment, gentlemen, and universal reputation, it is of the utmost importance to ensure that the Good Paintings, or those by the departed Painters, remain within our borders.
Consequently, their export outside the City and State is forbidden and punishable, etc. in the absence of a license issued by the Deputy of the Academy of Drawing.
Such restriction is to be rigorously enforced at the Customs Offices so that in no case whatsoever shall Travelers be allowed to export said Paintings outside Florence and its State without authorisation.
Submitting the request for a license will be free of charge. It must be signed by the Academy' Deputy together with another expert Painter of His choosing and sealed with the Academy's stamp, which will then be used to seal the painting itself, etc.
The above equally applies to all the Paintings by Painters who currently reside in His Highness's State, as well as to those of the departed, with the exception of the ones listed below, which shall by no means ever be granted a license.
In the event of death, the Academy reserves the right to include, register, and rank said living painters in the list of those who must for no reason be exported.

1. Michelangelo Buonarroti
2. Raphael from Urbino[105]

105 Raffaello da Urbino (1483-1520). Variations: Raffaello Sanzio, Raphaele Urbinas.

3. Andrea del Sarto
4. Beccafumi[106]
5. Rosso Fiorentino[107]
6. Leonardo da Vinci
7. Francia Bigio[108]
8. Perino del Vaga
9. Jacopo da Pontormo
10. Titian
11. Francesco Salviati
12. Agnolo Bronzino
13. Daniele da Volterra
14. Fra Bartolomeo di San Marco[109]
15. Fra Bastiano del Piombo
16. Filippo di Fra Filippo[110]
17. Antonio Correggio
18. Parmigianino[111]

To be added or removed at the discretion of the members of the board, etc.
Said restriction does not apply to those portraits and landscapes created in Florence and elsewhere that are often hung at the head of the bed, etc.
The transfer of paintings to country Villas is equally forbidden, with the exception of the works by any living Painters as decreed above.

Ferdinand
Ludovico Usimbardi

7
To the most Illustrious Lords of Balia

Siena, October 28th, 1602.
At the express command of His Highness our Most Serene Lordship and to the benefit of the city's public and private adornment, Your Lordships shall impose the following restrictions to all those persons and colleges not issued with a license by His Most Illustrious Excellency.
The purchase and sale of paintings by renowned departed Painters such as Beccafumi, Sodoma,[112] Raphael, and others of any fame, are forbidden to all persons and colleges,

---

106 Domenico di Jacopo di Pace (1486-1551). Variation: Domenico Beccafumi.
107 Giovan Battista di Jacopo di Gasparre (1494-1540).
108 Francesco Francia (1447 or 1449-1517).
109 Baccio della Porta (1472-1517).
110 Filippo Lippi (1406-1469).
111 Girolamo Francesco Maria Mazzola (1503-1540).
112 Govanni Antonio Bazzi (1477-1549).

regardless of their privilege. Said paintings' export is equally prohibited beyond the borders of Siena and its State whenever such works are kept in villas or the countryside. Any offenders shall be punished by the confiscation of the item and its payment, a fine of fifty crowns, and banishment, at His Excellency's discretion. One-quarter of the fine is to be allocated to the accuser, either public or secret, as they may be; another quarter is for the Magistrate or Judge that has informed the Captain of Justice of Siena and the Chief Magistrates who hold the offender in custody. The remainder is to be allotted to the Revenue Office.
The Notice shall henceforth be drafted and spread under the customary procedure, etc.
May God look upon you with favor.
To the pleasure of Your Most Illustrious Lordships.

Auditor Scipione Nardi
Tax Officer Giovanni Battista Marsili

8
Notice

On behalf of Our Lordship, the Most Serene Grand Duke of Tuscany and on the commission of the Illustrious and Excellent Lords Scipione Nardi, Auditor, and Giovanni Battista Marsili, Tax Officer, the Most Illustrious Officers of Balia decree as follows.
To the benefit of the public and private adornment of the city of Siena, all persons and colleges of any privilege who have not been issued with a license by His Excellency are banned from exporting Paintings of renowned departed Painters such as Beccafumi, Sodoma, Raphael, and others of any fame. Sale and purchase for the same purpose are equally prohibited. The restriction also applies to the Paintings kept in the countryside and its villas.
All offenders shall be punished by the confiscation of the item and the sale's payment, a fine of fifty crowns, and banishment, at His Excellency's discretion. One-quarter of the fine is to be allocated to the accuser, either public or secret as they may be; another quarter is for the Magistrate or Judge that has informed the Captain of Justice of Siena and the Chief Magistrates who hold the offender in custody unless the crime has been prevented. The remainder is to be allotted to the Revenue Office.
From the Palace, November 5th, 1602.

9
Deliberation

November 6th, 1602
On the mandate of His Serene Highness, the Magistracy has ordered the Masters of Customs of Florence to instruct their Ministries of Customs, Ministries of the Gates of Florence, Customs Officers, and travelers as follows.

Said Officials shall not allow nor tax the export of Paintings from Florence towards the countryside or any destination in the absence of a license issued by His Highness' Deputy at the Academy of Drawing. The license is to be signed by Him and another expert Painter and sealed with the Academy's stamp, which shall then be used to seal the individual Painting.
The Ministers who should fail to comply or are found guilty of fraud are liable to punishment at the Magistracy's discretion in order for Florence and its dominions not to lose its works of art and excellent painters.
His Highness has also decreed that his Deputy at the Academy of Drawing should issue said license free of charge, in writing, and with an attached assessment report prepared by an expert Painter. The authorisation shall then be signed by both and sealed with the Academy's stamp, which will be subsequently used to seal the Painting itself.
The licensing of Paintings by Painters currently living in the States mentioned above may be issued in all cases.
However, special care is advised for the Paintings by the departed. Under no circumstances should licenses be issued for Paintings deemed worthy of remaining in the City. As for the Painters listed below, said restrictions extend to transfer to the countryside as well.

1. Michelangelo Buonarroti
2. Raphael from Urbino
3. Andrea del Sarto
4. Beccafumi
5. Rosso Fiorentino
6. Leonardo da Vinci
7. Francia Bigio
8. Perino del Vaga
9. Jacopo da Pontormo
10. Titian
11. Francesco Salviati
12. Agnolo Bronzino
13. Daniele da Volterra
14. Fra Bartolomeo di San Marco
15. Fra Bastiano del Piombo
16. Filippo di Fra Filippo
17. Antonio Correggio
18. Parmigianino
19. Pietro Perugino

In the event of death, the Academy reserves the right to include any said painters in the list of those who must for no reason be exported.
Said restriction does not apply to those portraits and landscapes created in Florence and elsewhere that often are hung at the head of the bed, etc.
To be enforced by the Deputy.

The Ministers of the Reform of Mandate

10
Deliberation

December 11th, 1602.
The Magistracy has approved the selection of the City's 12 principal painters drafted by the Academy of Drawing.
As reported by the Academy's Deputy, the Academy has unanimously voted black beans concerning the appointment of the experts who are to inspect, assess, and approve the licensing of the Paintings in Florence and its Dominions, in conformity with the order issued by His Highness' Magistracy.
The list of the selected reads as follows:

1. Santi di Tito
2. Jacopo Ligozzi
3. Domenico Passignano
4. Ludovico da Cigoli
5. Alessandro Allori
6. Pietro Sori Senese
7. Gregorio Pagani
8. Ludovico Buti
9. Cosimo Gamberucci
10. Jan Van der Straet (Fleming)
11. Jacopo da Empoli
12. Giovanni Bizzelli

The above are hereby authorised to endorse the transfer of any of said Paintings under license of the Deputy of said Academy and in conformity with the Magistracy's instructions.

C. Lorenzo Muzio

11
The Academy of Drawing

Most Serene Grand Duke,
The Painters of the Academy plea and beg that you soften the new decree that prohibits the export of the good paintings, in the interests of both themselves and the tax revenues. Currently, many foreigners are turning to Venice, Milan, and Rome, where the export requires far less paperwork at the Gates and Customs Offices, and the risks of becoming victims of forgery are way fewer.
For your information, I will tell you about a discussion that Painter Donato dell'Antella and I once happened to take part in. On that occasion, while thinking about how to meet your wishes best, the Academy's Artists reported that the law is actively hindering the transfer

of new portraits that belong to gentlemen who are about to move to places such as Spain, France, or the Indies.

Most of those present suggested that perhaps in such cases, the Illustrious Deputy might be more lenient in granting a license and yet comply with your instructions by attaching an additional statement of authorship signed by the Painter himself. Of course, any false declarations would be punished with the same diligence that should also apply to the many copies of the Annunziata and other newly made reproductions.

As for the remainder, we could still maintain the same rigor with which we started, tackling all forgery of the Dead with the measures I had previously proposed at the Academy. Aside from the newly made ones, all the paintings to be transferred should be kept under lock in Residence rooms until the Wednesday sitting of the Council is convened. This course of action would allow the Consuls, the Illustrious Deputy, and the painter in charge of the assessment to draft an appraisal upon which I could then base my license without running the risk of having the Original replaced with a forged copy. Furthermore, we would also prevent that type of fraud where unlicensed paintings are covered up with a phony tempera drawing that is subsequently brushed off with a sponge.

However, since the ordinary sitting might not be enough, we could instruct the Illustrious Deputy and the assessing painters to return on Saturday after lunch to countersign the paintings delivered after Wednesday. Because this might, to some extent, inconvenience the Illustrious Deputy, we could consider calling on him at his Home. Otherwise, we could first summon the Chancellor that writes the licenses and provides the seals and stamps, together with the assessing deputy. The entire procedure could then be handled in a short time once the Deputy has arrived – shorter indeed than the half-day currently needed to reach them one by one.

I also wish to add that many of the good paintings, as well as those by the Departed, may be currently found in other towns such as Pisa, Pistoia, and Arezzo. Therefore, the Academy should instruct the Supreme Tribunal of the olden State to order that the local Superintendents and Provosts prohibit the paintings' export in conformity with Your Highness' desires.

I am sure it would be simple to have painters and connoisseurs provide and list the Drawings' whereabouts and whether they belong to private owners or are kept in churches or public venues in Florence and elsewhere.

Looking forward to receiving your orders, I defer to your commands. May God preserve your joy.

Florence, November 15th, 1603.

Your Most Serene Highness' Humble Servant
Baccio Valori

So be it, Ferdinand

12
Mandate

December 11th, 1603.
On the mandate of the Distinguished Lords of the Council and His Serene Highness' Secret Practice, and for the implementation of a benign Decree of His Most Serene Highness dated November 30th, 1603, the Masters of Customs of Florence shall order as follows.
Notwithstanding the order regarding the restrictions on the export and transfer of Paintings, etc., issued by the Magnificent Practice on November 6th, 1602 and other dates; The Ministers of said Customs Office, their Officers, and Travelers of the State are now to tax, stamp, and allow the transit of all the Paintings with attached the license and signature of His Highness' Deputy at the Academy of Drawing.
No further documentation is required, in compliance, etc.

13
The Academy of Drawing

Most Serene Grand Duke,
Back in the days of Your Highness's Father, many valuable Paintings by excellent Painters would often be exported outside our City and Dominions indiscriminately, much to the detriment of the City's Arts and Your Highness' State's good fame. Consequently, it was to preserve such an exceptional reputation that, on October 6th, 1602, the Magistracy prohibited the transfer of all the Paintings created by a selection of our nineteen most renowned Artists. Accordingly, the order was issued that the Ministers of Customs should restrict all taxation to the Works licensed by the Deputy and countersigned by a Painter.
However, We now happen to hear that a haphazard export of Paintings is taking place in the City of Pisa, where many other acclaimed Maestros reside and work.
Therefore, We would advise that your Highness extend the ban to Pisa, Pistoia, Arezzo, and any other City or location where similar trade might be occurring at present.
Moreover, since We hear that a number of the Works by Giovanni Antonio Sogliani, whose Paintings can be found in Florence as well, are currently kept in Pisa and elsewhere, Your Highness might like to include the Artist in the list of the Nineteen, considering how well-known and esteemed he was, back in his days.
The prohibition that has so far applied to Florence would thus be extended to the other Dominions. The overseeing Deputy and prominent Painters' approval and licensing would also be carried out by the other Cities' Provosts and Councilors, with the aid of those local Painters who are well acquainted with the style of the Nineteen, whose list is attached below.

1. Michelangelo Buonarroti
2. Raphael from Urbino
3. Andrea del Sarto
4. Beccafumi
5. Rosso Fiorentino

6. Leonardo da Vinci
7. Francia Bigio
8. Perino del Vaga
9. Jacopo da Pontormo
10. Titian
11. Francesco Salviati
12. Agnolo Bronzino
13. Daniele da Volterra
14. Fra Bartolomeo di S. Marco
15. Fra Bastiano del Piombo
16. Filippo di fra Filippo
17. Antonio Correggio
18. Parmigianino
19. Pietro Perugino

We hereby defer to Your Highness' judgment. May the Lord grant you a long and prosperous life
Florence, from our Residence, May 5th, 1610.

Your Serene Highness' Most Devout Servants
The Deputy and Consuls of the Academy of Drawing of the City of Florence

So be it

14
Deputation of Volterra

Florence, July 18th, 1744.
Whereas the Council of the Regency has found it just and convenient to act as requested by their lordships the Priors in their memorial, and in order to preserve the City's territory's numerous and outstanding ancient monuments from any future alteration;
The Council appoints their lordships Superintendent Sir Guarnacci, Dean Giorgi, Sir Giuseppe Del Bava, attorney at law of Cecina, as members of a Deputation specially briefed with the task of renewing the ban on all excavations that have not been licensed by the aforementioned and notified to Your Most Illustrious Excellency.
All the excavations granted by the Deputies and Commissary shall be open to the public, provided that the rights of ownership are safeguarded.
Any antiquities found will then be registered on a distinct Memorandum and licensed for sale, upon request and prior to their extraction, unless the public should deem it more convenient to retain possession of the item for its City museum against proper payment.
It is the Deputation's special assignment to prevent any frauds that might prejudice the high reputation that the Studies of the Etruscan Alphabet have gained both in Tuscany and abroad.

No misuse is meant, nor shall it ever come to pass that the site owners' interests will be damaged on account of the Deputation's doings: its only function will be to certify, regulate, and supervise the excavation and sale of said items.
In the event of resignation or inability of one of the current appointees, the remaining three members shall nominate four other Volterran notables. The Priors and College will subsequently scrutinise the latter to elect the most suitable and deserving candidate by majority vote. However, the Superintendent and Priors reserve the right to unilaterally elect the first candidate in the Deputation's memorial by majority vote.
Finally, it will be the Deputies' duty to inform Your Most Illustrious Lordship of any infractions relating to the excavations, the alteration of monuments, or the export of items, and sanction any offenders pursuant to the resolutions of the Council of the Regency.
Looking forward to the successful enforcement of this measure and the ones yet to come in order to contrast the recent disorders, I send You my best regards.

Secretary Gaetano Antinori
To His Lordship, the Commissary of Volterra

15
Imperial Resolution

Upon hearing about the fortuitous discovery of a cache of Ancient Roman Coins in San Miniato's territory, His Imperial Highness wishes as follows.
The coinage which the Antiquarian Doctor Antonio Cocchi will evaluate as exceptionally rare or noteworthy shall be stored within the collection of Ancient Roman Medallions of the City's Royal Gallery, pursuant to the Resolution of January 17th, 1749.
One-third of the find – or its monetary value – is to be allotted to its Discoverer; another third – or its monetary value – is for the owner of the estate on which they have been unearthed, net of excavation expenses.
His Highness further commands that, in the event of future findings, the discoverer be obliged by law to report the Treasure, Cache, or any other ancient monument and rewarded with the one-third either of the find itself or its monetary value.
However, the claimant will receive due compensation if the find cannot be apportioned or is especially worthy of being retained and displayed for the public adornment and benefit.
Remuneration is renounced in the event of unlicensed findings or fortuitous discoveries of Caches, Treasures, Statues, or other Antiquities that have gone unreported.
The Tax Hearings Officer will hereby oversee and enforce His Highness' commands.
Issued in Florence on August 21st, 1750.

Richecourt Vauthier

16
Edict

Whereas the Council of the Regency has reflected on how important it is, for the public decor, that the City of Florence and the other Cities and Locations of the Grand Duchy of Tuscany retain the outstanding works that are so remarkably antique and rare; and
Acknowledging that a free export of said works would significantly prejudice its State;
The Council extends and enhances the Laws regulating the export of artworks issued on November 6th, 1602, and December 31st, 1603.
All persons, regardless of their standing, status, or condition where relevant, are banned from exporting works of art outside the City of Florence and the other Cities and Locations of its Grand Duchy, both directly and by proxy. Henceforth, the restriction will apply to ancient Manuscripts, Inscriptions, Medallions, Statues, Vases, Bas-reliefs, Busts, Heads, Fragments, Pillars, Pedestals, Paintings, Ancient Pictures, and any other craft or rarity that the Council has not approved.
In disregard of their pretext or political patronage, all violations are punishable by the confiscation of the artefact and a fine of twice the value of the piece in question.
One-third of the fine is to be allocated to the Revenue Office, one-third is for the accuser, either public or secret as they may be, and one-third shall be allotted to the magistrate holding office.
Furthermore, the failure to pay the fine will result in a punitive sentence to be established by the incumbent magistrate.
In Florence, said office is to be held by the Magistrate of the Eight; in all other Cities, it lays in the Criminal Court Judges' capacity to proceed either upon complaint, *ex officio*, or following an investigation.
Issued at the Regency on December 26th, 1754.

Count Richecourt
Pier Antonio Guadagni

17
Motu Proprio

Whereas His Imperial Majesty has been informed of the difficulties arisen in Volterra on account of its excavations; and
Wishing to ensure that the researches be adequately run;
His Imperial Majesty commands as follows.

1. All are free to dig in their estate at will; the excavation on property or estate belonging to other parties is contingent on the owner's agreement.
2. All excavation, either on one's own or another party's land, is conditioned on the approval by the City Museum deputies. The application for a permit must include the excavation's duration, its location, and the other party's signed agreement where relevant. Subsequently, said deputies will attach a license bearing the applicant's

name, the duration, and the location. The license is to be signed by one of the deputies and is free of charge.

3. Once issued, the license is restricted to the indicated time and location. Upon expiration of the license, the applicant must produce a clear report on their finds if they wish to sell them.
4. In the event of the sale of said antiquities, Volterra's city museum retains its precedence over all other prospective buyers. The item's price will be established by two or three Appraisers appointed by the deputies. The museum's right of priority expires within one month from the Report's submission. At the end of the term, the contract will be considered terminated or no longer binding if the termination has not occurred.
5. Upon expiration of the above-mentioned term, a month-long priority must then be given to the Citizens of Volterra. In the event of multiple bidders, the guide price at the subsequent auction must be the one previously established by said Appraisers. At the end of the one-month term, the owner will be allowed to turn to other offerors pursuant to His Majesty's Laws regarding the export of such goods outside the State. The owner is entitled to a certificate stating their right of free sale. The certificate will be issued free of charge by the deputies.
6. Circumventing the regulations on the issuance of a license, or not respecting the license's duration and location; omitting to report either a portion or the entirety of any prospective finds; neglecting the rights of priority granted to the City and Citizens of Volterra will result in the confiscation of the finds or assets for sale and a perpetual ban from performing further excavations. The finds or assets will be assigned to the City Museum.
7. All applicants have the right to be issued a license, except those mentioned in the previous article. Further, said deputies will have the discretion to assign fraud supervisors to any excavations suspected of illegitimacy or concealment. The period of probation will extend proportionately with the level of suspicion. The assigned supervisors will also have the authority to enforce the measures established in the previous article and ensure that no excavation be carried out without due license, in infringement of said terms, or under suspicion of concealment and fraudulent extraction.

Hereby, the Commissary of Volterra must implement the aforementioned orders and act accordingly.
Issued by the Regency on December 10th, 1761.

Marquise Botta Adorno
Roberto Pandolfini

18
Notice

For the implementation of the Royal Resolution of August 27th, 1766;
In order to extend the Law issued on October 11th, 1762, regarding the obligation to produce a report for the Royal Revenue Office or local Tribunal, upon discovery of any Treasures, Caches, or ancient Monuments;
The Most Illustrious Sir Domenico Brichieri Colombi – Tax Auditor of His Royal Highness – confirms and notifies that;
All those Ministers of the Mint, goldsmiths, silversmiths, founders, etc., who smelt medallions, coinage, or similar antiquities of any kind without notifying the Tribunal of the Revenue or their Local Tribunal beforehand, will be punished by the confiscation of said items and their value. Half the antiquity's monetary worth will be allotted to the Revenue Office, while the other half is for the Informer or Accuser, public or secret as they may be.
To better enforce His Royal Highness and Most Merciful Lord's orders and ensure that no one should claim ignorance of the law, this Notice will apply to the whole of the Grand Duchy, including any Privileged Locations that should need special mention. Therefore, it will be affixed in all of the usual venues. Furthermore, it is the Local Magistrates' duty to apprise the Chancellery of the Revenue Office within two months after the publication of the present Notice.
Issued on October 17th, 1766.

Antonio Pescetti
Chancellor of the Revenue Office

19
Peter Leopold Royal Prince of Hungary and Bohemia, Archduke of Austria, Grand Duke of Tuscany, by the Grace of God etc.

Whereas We wish to free our beloved subjects of the limitations imposed on them by the Municipal Statutes and Laws enacted by our Royal Predecessors with regard to Treasures, Excavations, and exports of ancient monuments beyond the State's borders; and
Whereas We wish to restore such matters to their natural balance;
We, therefore, command that:

1. Henceforth, all excavations aimed at the discovery and possession of ancient Monuments, coinage, and other similar antiquities, will take place free of license, on condition that – if the digs take place on another party's estate, and there is a danger of damage to the adjacent Edifices and Assets – the Owner of the Estate or Neighbor provide written consent. Furthermore, the discoverer must abide by the finds' conditions of apportionment, indemnity, and any other clause contained in said agreement.
2. Whoever carries out excavations without the consent of the Owner or Neighbor – either on their account or in someone's behalf – must compensate for the prospective damage, the offense, and the trespassing and is liable to both civil and criminal action.

In the former case, the finds will be entirely devolved to the Owner of the estate. The offender is not entitled to any form of compensation. In the event of contingent findings, the value must be shared between the two parties – the Finder and the Owner of the estate – equally.

3. Upon discovery of Inscriptions, Statues, Bas-reliefs, Vases, Idols, Metal Tools, Medallions, carved Gems, and other similar antiquities, the Director of Our Royal Gallery has been instructed to select any items deemed worth purchasing. Therefore, the Discoverers or Community Chancellors will inform the Director of the prospective finds so that Our Royal Revenue Office may offer a price strictly proportional to the artefact's rarity and beauty.
4. In abrogation of the preexisting legal restraints, all bargains, sales, and exports of antiquities within and beyond the Grand Duchy are hereby free from restrictions, pursuant to the Customs Office's regulations on Taxes and Duties.
5. The relevant dispositions in the Common Legislation (*Ius Commune*) must be referred to in the event of disputes on the assignment of the excavation rights on third-party property. The same applies in case of doubts on the allotment of fortuitous finds or finds that occurred without the Owner's permission, as mentioned above, and pursuant to the Discoverers' rights on the other party's Estate. The common legislation must also appertain to all of the cases not mentioned in Our Decree, whenever Our orders are directly or indirectly violated.
6. The Magistrates must grant both parties that are acting in their private interest a brief hearing in order to avoid any disorders during litigation.

Such is Our Will for the whole of Our Grand Duchy, notwithstanding the Municipal Statutes, Laws, Orders, and Customs in force in the field of Treasures and Excavations of antiquities, as well as the regulations regarding Our Royal Revenue Office; in derogation from the Notice of October 11th, 1762, on the Excavations within the Territory of Volterra, as well as any other Notice regarding any other Territory.
Issued on August 5th, 1780.

Peter Leopold
V. Alberti – F. Sbratti

20
Resolution

The Director of the Royal Gallery is hereby authorised to issue Export Licenses for all of those Paintings and Pictures deemed unworthy of purchase by the Royal Gallery, after consulting the Great Painters or other pertinent experts on the value of said Paintings and Pictures. The Secretariat of the Revenue Office will, therefore, act pursuant to His orders.
Issued in Florence on January 16th, 1781.

Peter Leopold
Angiolo Tavanti – D. Schimisveiller

21
Law on the Customs Duties

August 30th, 1781.

[...]

8. Henceforth, We command that all the current laws that prohibit the introduction, export, and transit through Our Grand Duchy of goods of all kinds are revoked.

The laws concerning Our Donations of salt, tobacco, and playing cards, along with the ban on the unlicensed export of ancient Paintings, will withstand, pursuant to the Law of December 26th, 1754, which is currently in force.

Hereby, all kinds of merchandise are movable in the whole of our Grand Duchy, upon payment of the Duties prescribed in the list of Tariffs on the introduction, export, and transit of goods both through the new united Territory, and the separate Territories that uphold special Duties.

22
Community Regulations

March 27th, 1782.

[...]

Art. 12. Under license of the competent Magistrate, or, in Florence, the Auditor of the Community Chamber, and free of charge;

All the Owners of Houses and Palaces are hereby authorised to remove the Inscriptions, Coats of Arms, and similar monuments, on condition that they either restore or reconstruct them at their previous site or on other grounds visible to the Public within the original Premises.

In the event of the demolition of said Premises and the absence of a replacement, the Owner must transfer the craft, at their own expense, to another Public Edifice, notifying the Magistrate or Auditor, so as to not lose its memory.

23
Declaration of the Customs Duty

October 18th, 1791.

In force of the law issued on December 26th, 1754, no paintings and ancient panels may be exported outside the Grand Duchy.

6

The Kingdom of Denmark

1
Til Bisperne udi Danmark og Norge Antiqviteter anrørendes

Vi Christian IV etc. bede Eder og ville at I eders mueligste Flid anvender, allevegne udi Eders Stigt, at opsøge og antegne alleslags Antiqviteter og Documenter efter medfølgende Fortegnelses Indhold, og at I saadanne med Flid lader optegne og engang inden Paaske førstkommendes udi vort Cancellie lader indlevere.
IIafn. 11 Aug. 1622.

1. Skal forfares i Capitelets Archiver hvad for *documenta historica manuscripta* der udi ere, og hid fremskikkes i Cancelliet.
2. Hos alle lærde Mænd i deres Stifter særdeles Geistlige, saa og hos Kirkerne ingen undertagen, hvad *documenta antiqua historica* de haver, og mod Reversal (dennem som det tilhører at tilskikkes) hid forskikkes.
3. Skal alle Runebogstaver skrevne eller i Steen, heele eller Stykker, eller Træ udhugne, eller paa Metalbelter, og saadanne opsøges, og med Antegnelser hvor de ere at finde, og en rigtig nøiagtig Afskrift af dennem hid forskikkes, og kan Lineamenta med Kride paa Stenene bedst drages og siden aftegnes, og Provsterne og Præsterne forelægges med al Flid strax derom at forfare, og endelig Beskeden til Bisperne fremskikke, som strax skal det udi Cancelliet indskikke.
4. Alle Fortegnelser paa hvis *relationibus* i hver Sogn berettes de *locorum antiquitate vel origine, de prœliis, incolis,* om Steenhobe og deres formeente Aarsager og Betydninger, og alt hvis til *Chorographiam* kan tiene.
5. Alle *Calendaria runica* paa Træe og ellers.
6. Alt hvis Cleresiet særdeles *de antiquitatibus, modo numerandi runico, stellarum nominibus, antiquis ritibus*, og alt hvis som kan tiene til vores danske *historias* at enodere *og antiquitates gentis nostrœ at deducere*. Item *de moneta, ponderibus & mensuris antiquis tam liquidorum quam aridorum*; item *pannorum, viarum*. Hvilket alt for bemeldte til Paaske hid i Cancelliet skulde leveres.

Til Bisperne i Sielland, Skaane, Fyen, Ribe, Aarhuus, Viborg, Vendelboe, Opslo, Stavanger, Bergen, Throndhiem.

1

To the Bishops of Denmark and Norway regarding the Antiquities

We, Christian IV etc. ask You and would like You to use your utmost Diligence, everywhere [in line] with Your Level, in seeking out and recording all kinds of Antiquities and Documents according to the Contents of the accompanying List; and [We require] that You diligently have them submitted to and verified by our Chancellor sometimes before Easter.

Copenhagen. Aug. 11th, 1622.

1. It shall be examined, in the Archives of the Chapter, which *handwritten historical documents* are kept there; and forward them here through the Chancellery.
2. All the learned Men in their Institutions, particularly Clergymen, as well as the Churches not recognised, [shall examine] which *ancient historical documents* they have; [these], together with their Reverse [the rear part] (the one to which they belong to) shall be sent [here].
3. All Rune Letters written in Stone, both whole and in Pieces, or carved on Wood, or metal Belts, and such like, shall be searched for; a really accurate Transcript, together with Notes on where they were found, shall be sent here. Outlines with Chalk of the Stones can [be made] and then drawn up. The Provosts and Priests shall be acknowledged immediately with all Diligence [about the pieces that are] about to perish. Finally, forward the Message to the Bishops [so that they can] submit it immediately to the Chancellery.
4. All Inventories whose *descriptions* in each Parish report *about the country's ancientness or origin, the battles, the inhabitants,* and about Stone Houses and their presumed Causes and Meanings, and everything about their *Chorography,* [shall be reported].
5. All *runic Calendars* on Wood and other [materials].
6. All the Clerics [shall note] in particular *antiquities, the runic methods of counting,* the *names of the stars, the ancient rites,* and everything that can serve our Danish *history and determine the antiquities of our nation.* [This includes] *coins, weights and measures both liquid and dry;* also *cloths, roads.* All of which is to be delivered and reported here in the Chancellery before Easter.

To the Bishops of Zealand, Scania, Funen, Ribe, Aarhus, Viborg, Vandel, Oslo, Stavanger, Bergen, Trondheim.

7

The Kingdom of Sweden

1
Kongl: Mayst:tz Placat och Påbudh Om Gamble Monumenter och Antiquiteter

Wij Carl,
medh Gudz Nådhe, Sweriges, Göthes och Wendes Konung och Arf-Förste, StoorFörste til Finland, Hertigh vthi Skåen, Estland, Ljffland, Carelen, Bremen, Vehrden, Stetin-Pommern, Cassuben och Wenden, Förste til Rügen, Herre öfwer Ingermanland och Wissmar;
Så och Pfaltz-Grefwe widh Rhein i Beyern, til Gülich, Clewe och Bergen, Hertigh, etc.
Göre witterligit, allthenstund Wij medh stoort Misshag förnimme, huruledes icke allenast the vhrgambla Antiquiteter qwarlefwor och efterdömen, som alt ifrån Hedendomen, vthaff framfarne Sweriges och Götha Konungars, sampt andre theras Förnämlige Mäns och Vndersåthares Manlige Bedriffter, som för thetta öfwer heele Wårt Rijke, deels vthi stoore Borger, Skantzar och Steenkumbel, deels vthi Stoder och andre Stenar medh Runaskrifter ingraffne, deels vthi theras Griffter och Ättebacker vthi temmelig myckenheet bestådt hafwa, medh sådan wårdlöössheet och olofligit Sielffzwåld handteras, at the dageligen mehr och mehr förderfwade och vthödde blifwa;
Vthan och the Monumenter som både aff Konungar, Drottningar och Förstar, sampt andre Förnähme aff Ridderskapet och Clerkeriedt vthi Wåre Christne Kyrckior til theras Heder och åminnelse, hafwe warit lämbnade, alldeles förödas, och aff androm försåtheligen intagas och åwerkas, hwilket såmyckit mehra står til at ogilla och affwäria, som sådane Monumenter böre skattas ibland the ting, hwilke så aff sig sielff som för insticktelsen skull, från all wahnrycht och ohelgelse frij och försäkrade, jemwäl til Wåra Förfäders och heele Wårt Rijkes odödelige Beröm merckeligen ländande äre.
Ty hafwe Wij aff then serdeeles nijt Wij til föllie aff Wåre Förfäder Sweriges Konungar öfwer alt sådant billigt böre draga, så wäl til at offentligen betyga thet missnöye Wij til een slijk oreda, som ofwanbemelt är, fattat hafwe, såsom och at här efter beskydda och handhafwa alle sådanne ting för wijdare olofligh handtering, för gott och nödwendigt ansett at biuda och befalla alle Wåre trogne Vndersåtare som thetta i någon måtto angå kan, eftersom Wij här medh och i krafft aff thetta Wårt allmenne Placat them biude och befalle, först, at ingen ehoo han är, skal effter thenne dagh, understå sigh på någrehanda sätt at nederbryta eller föröda the Borger, Huus, Fästen, Skantzar eller Steenkumbel, som ännu på een eller annan Orth kunna wara tilfinnandes, ehuru ringa ock thess Aflefwor

wara måge, icke heller i någon måtto förspilla the Stoder eller Steenar, som medh någon Runaskrifft kunne wara ritade, vthan them alldeeles orubbade på sine rätte forne ställen blifwa låta, tillijka medh alle stoore hoopburne Jordhögar och Ättebakker, ther månge Konungar och andre Förnähme, sine Grafwar och Hwijlorum stadgat hafwe, efftersom Wij alle sådane gamble Monumenter, som vppå någon Wår och Cronones Jord, egen eller skatte, antingen then Oss än tilhörer, eller för thetta tilhördt hafwer, och nu på något sätt affhänd är, belägne finnes, ifrån all sielfwilliande åwerckan, icke annars än woro the Wår enskylte Egendom, alldeles frijkalle, och vthi Wår Konungzlige Hägn och Beskydd anamma låte;

Förseendes Oss i thet öfrige til Wåre trogne Vndersåtare aff Ridderskapet och Adelen, at om några sådane Antiquiteter på någon theras vhrminnes egne Frelsejord belägne wore, the icke thessmindre wille om thess Conservation draga then Försorg, som thenne Wår nådige Intention, Saksens wichtigheet, och theras egen Heder kan wara lijkmätigt.

Sedan biude Wij och, at ingen Högh eller Lågh, Andelig eller Werldzlig, aff hwadh Stånd eller wilkor then och wara må, skal wara loff eller tillåteligit at röfwa eller råna the Konungzlige, Förstlige eller andre Förnehme Persohners Griffter, som ännu antingen vthi the ödelagde eller än stående Kyrckior och Closter kunne quarre finnas, mycket mindre them til sine egne Grafwar at förbyta, eller på något sätt tilfoga theras gamble och rätte ågander (åga = äga) ther widh något Meen eller Intrång;

Effter som Wij ther hoos wele at alle Kyrkior och Clöster sampt theras Tygh, Redskap, Prydnat på Wägger och Fönster, Målningar eller hwariehanda innandöme, som något tänckwärdigt kunne innehålla, tillijka medh alle the dödas och afflidnas Grafwar och Graffstellen in vthi Kyrkior eller vthe på Kyrkiogårdarne, then Wårdnat, Frijd och Säkerheet bewijsas må, som medh theras Christelige Instichtelser, Bruuk och Öffning enligit är, så at sluteligen alla the Ting, the wari sigh så ringa som the för någons ögon synas kunna, som lijkwäl til Stadfästelse eller Åminnelse aff någon Historisk Bedrifft, Person, Orth eller Slächt lända kan, måge granneligen tagas i acht och skiötzel, och icke gifwas någrom tilstånd thet ringeste ther aff at spilla eller förderfwa;

Och ther någon skulle vnderstå sigh her emoot i någon måtto at giöra och Wår Befalning öfwerträda, wele Wij at then samme icke allenast therföre, som för all annor Wår Budz Föracht och olaglig åwerckan, plichta, vthan och Wår höga Onåde vndergifwin wara skal; Skulle och något Missbruuk, Oreda eller Åwerkan aff någrom tilförende föröfwat wara emoot något aff the Ting som i thetta Wårt Placat ihugkomne finnes, tå befalle Wij alfwarligen, at alt sådant behörligen och vthan någons anseende rättas, och vthi förrige tilstånd sättias må.

Hwarföre Wij och i synnerheet befalle icke allenast Wår ÖffwerStåthållare i Stockholm, General-Gouverneurer, Gouverneurer, Landzhöffdingar, Ståthållare, Borgmästare och Rådh i Städerne, Befalningz- Lähns- Fierdingz- och Sexmän å Landet, at the öfwer thetta Wårt Placat noga och alfwarligen hand hålla; Vthan och Erchiebiskopen, Biskoperne, Superintendenterne, Prowesterne och Kyrkioherderne öfwer hele Wårt Rijke, at the hwar å sin Orth thet allmenneligen förkunna, och jemwäl wackta på the Ting som i theras Stiffter, Contracter och Församblingar finnes, och aff ofwanberörde Art bestå, til hwilken ände Wij och befalle alle i Gemeen som om slijke saker någon Kunskap hafwa, eller och til äfwentyrs några gamble Skriffter, Böcker, Breff, Mynt eller Insegel kunne hafwa om händer, at the sådant hoos sine Kyrkioherder eller och Wåre Befalningzmän angifwa, på

thet Wij igenom them ther om kungiorde, måge wijdare om thess Communication beställa låta.
Här alle i gemeen, och hwar och een i synnerheet som wederbör, hafwe sigh hörsamligen at effterrätta. Til yttermehra wisso hafwe Wij thetta medh Wårt KongL Secret och Wår högstährade Elskelige käre FruModers, sampt the andre Wåre och Wårt Rijkes respective Förmyndares och Regerings Vnderskrifft, bekräffta låtit.

Datum Stockholm then 28. Novembris Anno 1666.
Hedewig Eleonora
(Locus Sigilli)
Sewedh Bååt, i R. Drotzetens ställe
Gustaff Baner, i R. Marskens ställe
Gustaf Otto Steenbock, S. R. Ammiral
Magnus Gabriel de la Gardie, S. R. Cansler
Gustavus Soop, i R. Skattemestarens ställe

1
His Royal Majesty's Placat and Decree regarding Old Monuments and Antiquities

We Charles,
by the grace of God, King and Principal Heir of Sweden, King of the Goths and the Wends, Grand Duke of Finland, Duke of Scania, Estonia, Livonia, Karelia, Bremen, Vehrden, Stettin-Pomerania, Kashubia, Wenden, Duke of Rugen, Lord of Ingria and Wismar,
And also Palatinate Count of the Rhine in Bavaria, of Gülich, Clewe, and Bergen, Duke, etc.
We hereby make publicly known [the following instruction].
It is with great discontent that We experience how the Antiquities, Remains and Monuments of Time immemorial, which [were formed] during heathen Times by the deceased Kings of Sweden and Gothia, as well as other eminent Men and Subjects, after their significant Achievements throughout Our Realm; some [of these are] Castles, Strongholds and Cairns, some other [of these] are Monuments and Stones with runic Inscriptions, some other [of these] are great quantities of Tombs and Burial Sites. They are treated altogether with such Recklessness and unlawful Self-indulgence [by some individuals], so that day by day they succumb to wreckage and destruction.
Also, as the Monuments which have been left by Kings, Queens and Princes, and other Eminent Nobles and Clergymen in our Christian Churches for their Honor and Memory, are destroyed, occupied and damaged by other [individuals], [in ways] that must be condemned and averted; and as these Monuments should be treasured as objects which, for themselves and in Virtue of their Creation, must be saved from desecration and disrepute to the immortal Glory of our Ancestors and our entire Realm.
For these Reasons, in view of the particular Zeal that Our Ancestors Kings of Sweden have dutifully exerted, and to openly confirm Our discontent for the above-mentioned disorders, henceforth We have determined to protect and manage [these monuments]

against unlawful Behaviors. Thus, We instruct Our faithful Subjects regarding the good and necessary [conducts of practice], according to this Our public Placat. First, from today onwards no one – whomever they may be – shall tear apart or destroy in any manner Castles, Houses, Fortresses, Strongholds or Cairns, which still stand in any place or just one place, regardless of how small these Remains are; nor should anyone in any way ravage Standing Stones or Stones with runic inscriptions; instead, they should leave them unscathed in their former proper places altogether; the same applies to all the vast Mounds of Earth and Burial Sites, where many Kings and other worthy People have established their Tombs and resting Places, as well as any other old Monuments placed on Our Land or the Land pertaining to the Crown, may this be Our Property or taxable Property, regardless of whether it is now Our property or was it so in the past and now being surrendered. All these [items] are protected against willful Injury as if it were Our private Property, thus under Our Royal Custody and Trust.

Regarding Our faithful Subjects of the House of Nobility, if such Antiquities are located in their Tenured Lands from Time immemorial, We compel them to care for their Conservation, accomplishing Our Intention and this Important Matter, as their Honor would require.

Furthermore, We declare that no-one, of High or Low Status, may he be Cleric or Secular, pertaining to any Rank or Class, is permitted to plunder or rob tombs of Royals, Princes or other Nobles, which may be found in ruined or still standing Churches or Monasteries; neither is he allowed to use them for his personal interest, or in any way which would cause Damage or Infringement to the old rightful Proprietors.

As it is Our will that all the Churches and Monasteries, including their Inventories, Accoutrements, Decorations on Walls and Windows, Paintings or any other Kind of mindfully created interior, as well as Tombs and Burials inside Churches or outside their Churchyards, shall be ensured Care, Peace, and Safety according to the related Christian Customs, Practices and Exercises; We [hereby command that] all these Items, no matter how small they are, serving as Evidence and Remembrance of any Historic Deed, Person, Place or Family, shall be carefully respected and cared for; no permit should be granted to waste or destroy even the smallest Part thereof.

And if anyone attempts to disregard or contravene Our Commandment, it is Our will that he should suffer like anyone else who disregards Our other Decrees and should also be subjected to Our High Disgrace.

Should there be any Abuse, Disorder, or Damage carried out to any of the Objects mentioned in this Placat, We command earnestly that such Act be corrected and restituted to its former Condition.

For this reason, We command that not only Our General State Holders in Stockholm, General Governors, Governors, Provincial Governors, Land Owners, Mayors and Councils in the Cities, Province and Town Constables in the Countryside shall watch over this Placat's complete and careful [application], but also the Archbishop, Bishops, Superintendents, Provosts and Vicars in Our Realm, shall – in their Position – publically proclaim and watch over the abovementioned typologies of Objects placed in their Dioceses, Deaneries, and Parishes; to this end We also order that every Person who may be aware of such Things or may possess old Scriptures, Books, Letters, Coins or Seals, shall report to his Vicars or Our Constables, so that We may be able to be in touch through them.

Every Person in general, and everyone in particular, shall dutifully oblige. Furthermore, We confirm this with Our Royal Seal and the signatures of Our Highly Honored and Beloved Mother and other Members of Our Regency Board.

Given in Stockholm, November 28th, 1666.
Hedewig Eleonora
(Locus Sigilli)
Seved Bååt – Royal Justice
Gustav Banér – Royal Marshall
Gustaf Otto Stenbock – State Royal Admiral
Magnus Gabriel de la Gardie – State Royal Chancellor
Gustav Soop – Royal Treasurer

8

The Kingdom of Portugal

1
Alvarà de Lei

Ord. Liv. 5. Tit. 12. Par. 5.
Alvará, em que se declarou, que incorresse nas mesmas penas dos que fabricão moeda falsa a pessoa, que desfizesse edificio, estatua, marmore, lamina, ou chapa, em que estiverem esculpidas algumas figuras, ou tiverem letreiros antigos, ou desfizer moeda, ou medalha antiga.
1721.

EU El Rei faço saber aos que este Alvará de Lei virem, que, por me representarem o Director e Censores da Academia Real da Historia Portugueza, Ecclesiastica e Secular, que procurando examinar por si, e pelos Academicos, os Monumentos antigos, que havia, e se podião descobrir no Reino, dos tempos, em que nelle dominárão os Phenices, Gregos, Penos, Romanos, Godos e Arabios, se achava que muitos, que pudérão existir nos edificios, estatuas, mármores, cippos, laminas, chapas, medalhas, moedas e outros artefactos, por incúria e ignorancia do vulgo se tinhão consumido, perdendo-se por este modo um meio mui proprio e adequado, para verificar muitas noticias da veneravel antiguidade, assi Sagrada, como Politica;
e que seria mui conveniente á luz da verdade e conhecimento dos Seculos passados, que, no que restava de semelhantes memorias, e nas que o tempo descobrisse, se evitasse este damno, em que póde ser muito interessada a gloria da Nação Portugueza, não só nas materias concernentes á Historia Secular, mas ainda á Sagrada, que são o instituto, a que se dirige a dita Academia:
E desejando eu contribuir com o meu Real poder, para impedir um prejuizo tão sensivei e tão damnoso á reputação e gloria da antiga Lusitania, cujo Dominio e Soberania foi Deos servido dar-me:
Hei por bem, que daqui em diante nenhuma pessoa, de qualquer estado, qualidade e condição que seja, desfaça, ou destrua em todo, nem em parte, qualquer edificio, que mostre ser daquellcs tempos, ainda que em parte esteja arruinado;
e da mesma sorte ás estatuas, mármores e cippos, em que estiverem esculpidas algumas figuras, ou tiverem letreiros Phenices, Gregos, Romanos, Gothicos e Arabicos;
ou laminas, ou chapas de qualquer metal, que contiverem os ditos letreiros, ou caracteres;

como outrosi medalhas, ou moedas, que mostrarem ser daquelles tempos, nem dos inferiores até o reinado do Senhor Rei D. Sebastião;
nem encubrão, ou occultem alguma das sobreditas cousas:
e encarrego ás Camaras das Cidades e Villas deste Reino tenhão muito particular cuidado em conservar e guardar todas as antiguidades sobreditas, e dessemelhante qualidade, que houver ao presente, ou ao diante se descobrirem nos limites do seu destricto;
e logo que se achar, ou descubrir alguma de novo, darão conta ao Secretario da dita Academia Real, para elle a communicar ao Director, Censores e mais Academicos:
e o dito Director e Censores com a noticia, que se lhes participar, poderáõ dar providencia, que lhes parecer necessaria, para que melhor se conserve o dito monumento assi descoberto;
se o que assi se achar e descobrir novamente, forem laminas de metal, chapas, ou medalhas, que tiverem figuras, ou caracteres, ou outrosi moedas de ouro, prata, cobre, ou dequalquer outro metal, as poderáõ mandar comprar o Director e Censores do procedido da consignação, que fui servido dar para as despesas da dita Academia;
e as pessoas de qualidade, que contravierem esta minha disposição, desfazendo os edificios daquelles Séculos, estatuas, mármores e cippos;
ou fundindo laminas, chapas, medalhas, e moedas sobreditas;
ou tambem deteriorand-oas em fórma, que se não possão conhecer as figuras e caracteres;
ou finalmente encubrindo-as e occultando-as, alem de incorrerem no meu desagrado, experimentarão tambem a demonstração, que o caso pedir, e merecer a sua desattenção, negligencia, ou malicia;
e as pessoas de inferior condição incorrerão nas penas impostas pela Ordenação do *Liv.* 5. *Tit. 12. Par. 5.* aos que fundem moeda;
e porque os que acharem algumas laminas, chapas, medalhas e moedas antigas, as quereráõ vender e reduzir a moeda corrente, as Camarás serão obrigadas a compralas e pagalas promptamente pelo seu justo valor, e as remetteráõ logo ao Secretario da Academia, que fazendo-as presentes ao Director e Censores, se mandará satisfazer ás Camaras o seu custo;
e para que em tudo se cumpra este Alvará, como nelle mando, ordeno ao Regedor da Casa da Supplicação, Governador da Relação e Casa do Porto, e aos Desembargadores das ditas Casas, Corregedores desta Cidades, e aos mais Corregedores, Ouvidores, Provedores, Juizes, Justiças, Officiaes e pessoas de meus Reinos e Senhorios, que o cumprão e guardem, e fação inteiramente cumprir e guardàr, como nelle se contem.
E para que venha á noticia de todos, mando ao Doutor Joseph Galvão de Lacerda, do meu Conselho e Chanceller mor dos ditos meus Reinos, faça publicar este meu Alvará na Chancellaria, e anviar logo Cartas com o traslado delle, sob meu Sello e seu signal, a todas as Camaras das Cidades e Villas do Reino, sem exepção alguma, e ainda ás das Terias dos Donatarios, e aos Corregedores, Ouvidores das Comarcas, e aos dos mesmos Donatarios, em que os Corregedores não entrão por Correição, aos quaes mando, que logo o publiquem e fação publicar em todos *òs Lugares das suas Comarcas;*
e se registará nos livros do Desembargo do Paço, Casa da Supplicação, e do Porto, aonde semelhantes se costumão registar;
e este proprio se lançará na Torre do Tombo.

Braz de Oliveira o fez em Lisboa Occidental a 20 de Agosto de 1721.
Manoel Galvão de Castel-Branco o fez escrever.
REI.

1
Law Permit

Ord. Liv. 5. Tit. 12. Par. 5.
Permit in which it is declared that the person who dismantle any building, statue, marble, metal sheet, or plate on which are carved figures, or has old signs, or melt coins, or old medals, shall incur in the same penalties inflicted to those who manufacture counterfeit currency.
1721.

I, The King, make it known to those who came to this Charter that, according to what the Director and the Censors of the Royal Academy of Portuguese, Ecclesiastic and Secular History communicated to me, they have been seeking to examine for themselves and the Academics, the ancient Monuments that are and could be discovered in the Kingdom; [these monuments] are from the times in which Phoenicians, Greeks, Carthaginians, Romans, Goths, and Arabs dominated; as [the director and the censors] considered that many statues, blocks of marble, milestones, metal sheets, plates, medals, coins, and other artefacts that existed in buildings have been consumed or destroyed due to the carelessness and ignorance of common people, causing the loss of excellent and adequate means to verify several accounts of their venerable antiquity, both Sacred and Political;
and as it would be very convenient for the sake of truth and knowledge of the past Centuries that, for what is left of such memories and those which might be discovered with time, this damage is avoided; since [these memories] are of the greatest interest for the glory of the Portuguese Nation, in the matters concerning not only Secular but also Sacred History, which constitute the foundations on which the said Academy focuses:
And as I wish to contribute with my Royal power to prevent such a considerable and damning harm to the reputation and glory of the ancient Lusitania, whose Dominion and Sovereignty God entrusted me:
From now on, it would be good that no person, of any state, quality, and condition whatsoever, dismantle or destroy in whole or in part any building, which proves to be of those times, even if it is partly ruined;
and similarly statues, marbles, and milestones, in which figures are carved, or presenting Phoenicians, Greeks, Romans, Gothic, and Arabic inscriptions;
and plates, or sheets of any metal, which contain said inscriptions, or characters;
as well as medals, or coins, which prove to be from those times, or from those inferior [ages] until the reign of the Lord King Sebastian;
any of the above-mentioned things shall neither be covered nor hidden:
furthermore, I order that the Chambers of this Kingdom's Cities and Villas shall take particular care to preserve and keep all the above-mentioned antiquities, and any other

of similar quality, which may exist at present, or in the future, if they are found within the limits of their district;
and as soon as they found, or discover any new one, they shall report it to the Secretary of the said Royal Academy, for him to inform the Director, the Censors, and the other Academics:
the said Director and the Censors, with the information they have, will be able to take any action which seems necessary to them so that said discovered monument would be preserved at its best;
in the case that metal sheets, plates, or medals with figures, or characters, or other coins of gold, silver, copper, or any other metal, are discovered, the Director and the Censors will be entitled to buy them, following the procedures of the consignment, which I was able to give for the expenses of the said Academy;
and the people of quality, who infringe this disposition, by ruining the buildings of those Centuries, as well as statues, marbles, and milestones;
or by melting the above-mentioned sheets, plates, medals, and coins;
or even by altering their forms, in a way that one cannot recognise their figures and characters;
or finally by covering them up and hiding them, not only will incur my displeasure, but will also experience its consequences, as the case requires, deserving also your [the king's high functionary] inattention, negligence, or malice;
the persons of inferior status will incur the penalties imposed by the Ordinance of Liv. 5. Title 12. Par. 5. concerning those who forge money;
and since those who find some old sheets, plates, medals, and coins want to sell them and transform them into money, the Chambers will be obliged to buy these [items] and pay them promptly at their fair value; the objects shall be forwarded immediately to the Secretary of the Academy, who will present them to the Director and the Censors, so that the cost can be reimbursed to the Chambers;
and with the intention to fulfil this Permit completely, as I command, I order to the Governor of the House of Supplication, the Governor of Relation and the House of Porto, and the Judges of the said Houses, the Internal Affairs of these Cities, and the other Internal Affairs, as well as the Ombudsmen, Providers, Judges, Magistrates, Officials and persons of my Kingdom, including the Landlords, to fulfil and keep it entirely, following what is contained in it.
And in order for the Academy to receive this news, I entrust Doctor Joseph Galvão de Lacerda, my Councilor and Chancellor of the said Kingdom, to publish this License in the Chancellery, and send its Copy immediately, under my Seal and your [the king's high functionary] seal, to all the Chambers of the Kingdom's Cities and Villas, without any exception, even those of the Lands in the Colonies, and the Magistrates, Auditors of the Districts, as well as those in the same Colonies, where the Magistrates do not enter through the Office, to whom I order to publish it in all the Places of their Districts;
and it will be registered in the books of the Court Disembarkation, the House of Supplication, and the Port, where similar ones are usually registered;
and this copy will also be deposited in the [archive of] Torre do Tombo.

Braz de Oliveira did so in Lisbon Occidental on August 20th, 1721.
Manoel Galvão de Castel-Branco made him write.
THE KING.

9

The Province of Drenthe

1
Resolutie van Drost en Gedeputeerden van Drenthe van 21 Juil 1734. Ordre tegen het wegvoeren van Veltstenen

Drost en Gedeputeerde Staten der Landschap Drenthe:
Erenfeste, vrome, wyze, voorzienige en discrete bijzonder goede vrunden!
Wij zenden U. L. hiernevens een ordre tegens het onbehoorlyk wegvoeren van veltstenen, vrındelijk begerende en amptshalven ardonnerende, dat dezelve voorts ter eerster gelegenheit gepubliceert worde.
Waartoe ons verlatende, bevelen U. L. In Gods heijlige protectie.
Uit Assen, den 21 Julij 1734
[was geparapheert] C. B. J. Schwartz vt
Ter ordonnantie,
[Get.] S. Nysingh
Aan de respective Scholtessen in het Landschap.

Alzo wij in gewisse ervaringe zijn gekomen, dat op veele plaatsen in deze Landschap, in het verkopen en weg-voeren van Velt-Stenen, merkelijke excessen worden begaan, niet alleen door de Markgenoten selfs, maar ook door de meijeren en andere gedisqúalificeerde ingesetenen; met te verkopen en doen removeren van Mark-Stenen, voordestenen en andere Scheijdstenen, ja selfs ook van de so genaamde Hunebedden, die allenthalven als waardige monumenten en van Oúds beroemde gedenk-teikenen behoorden geconserveert te worden; So is 't dat Wij mits dezen wel ernstlijk interdiceren en verbieden aan alle en een jegelijk, om enige Scheijd-Stenen, mitsgaders de Stenen van de So genaamde Húnebedden te mogen verkopen, removeren of vervoeren, bij de poene van hondert goltgúldens t'elken reijse te verbeúren, boven de waardije van de verkofte of weggevoerde Stenen.
Wordende de Scholtessen gerecommandeert en gelast tegens de voorsr: mesúses te vigileren, en ook de ingesetenen deser Landschap geordonneert, de contraventeúrs op de Goor-Spraken aan te brengen, bij de poenen en breúken op het verswijgen gestatúeert. En sal dese Onse ordre stand grijpen en strictelijk worden geexecuteert, ter tijd daar over nader, ofte anders bij de Heeren Ridderschap en Eijgenerfden, of bij ons sal sijn gedisponeert.
Actúm Assen, den 21. Julij 1734.

[was geparapheert:] B. J. Schwartz
Ter ordonnantie,
[Get.] S. Nijsingh

2
Resolutie van Drost en Gedeputeerden van Drenthe van 27 Mei 1790

[reissue]

1
Resolution of the Bailiff and the Representatives of Drenthe of 21st July, 1734. Order against the removal of the land Stones

The Drost and the Provincial Representatives of the Province of Drenthe.
Honorable, pious, wise, providential and discreet, and excellent friends!
Herewith We send You an order against the improper removal of fallen stones, kindly desiring and at the same time decreeing that this shall be published at the first opportunity. Therefore, I leave You, recommending You to be in God's divine protection.
From Assen, 21st July, 1734.
C. B. J. Schwartz
By ordinance,
S. Nysingh
To the respective municipalities in the Province.

As we have come to know with certainty that in several places in this Province the sale and removal of Field Stones are perpetrated with incredible excesses, not only by the Commoners in general but also by the Tenants and other disqualified inhabitants; [they carry out] the sale and allow the removal of Stones from common, cultivable and other [kinds of] Lands Stones to mark boundaries, including the so-called Hunebeds, which should rather be preserved as venerable monuments and longstanding memorials everywhere. For these reasons, We require that these [abuses] shall be seriously interdicted and forbidden to each and every one of you, and [no one shall be] allowed to sell, remove or transport any of the aforementioned Boulders, and also the so-called Hunebeds; the fine [for the transgressors is] of one hundred gold guilders for each violation, on top of the value of the sold or removed Stones.
The Sheriffs are recommended and instructed the following: to invigilate over the misuses; and also the inhabitants of the Province are commanded: to denounce the offenders to the Grand Juries, incurring [themselves] a fine and penalty for covering up [the crime]. Moreover, Our order will be effective and strictly executed, and further [recommendations will be] decreed later on by either the Lords Nobles and Commoners or by us.
Given in Assen, on 21st July, 1734.
C. B. J. Schwartz, chairman

By ordinance,
S. Nysingh, secretary

2
Resolution of the Bailiff and the Representatives of Drenthe of 27th May, 1790

[reissue]

10

The Duchy of Milan

1
Maria Theresia
Dei Gratia Regina Hungariae Bohemiae etc. Archidux Austriae etc.
Dux Mediolani etc.

Milano, 13 Aprile 1745.
Giorgio Cristiano del Sacro Romano Impero Principe di Lobkovitz, Duca di Sagano etc. Cavaliere dell'Insigne Ordine del Toson d'Oro, Consigliere Intimo attuale di Stato di Sua M.tà, Generale Maresciallo di Campo, Colonnello d'un Reggimento di Corazzieri, Comandante Generale delle Truppe della M.tà Sua in Italia, Gov.e e Cap.no Generale per Interim della Lombardia Austriaca.
Avendoci rappresentato gl'ascritti nell'Accademia della Pittura, Scultura, ed Architettura sotto l'Invocazione dell'Evangelista S. Luca, che vedendo risultare in vilipendio di dette professioni la toleranza d'alcuni abusi insensibilmente introdotti in questa Metropoli, e Stato, anche in poco decoro della Religione, e desiderando di andare al riparo per togliere que' mali, che col diferirne la provvidenza si potrebbero fare maggiori con grave pregiudizio non meno della Gioventù studiosa, che delle medesime, hanno con la facoltà concessali non solo dalla gloriosa memoria dell'Augustissimo Imperatore Carlo Sesto con due suoi Reali dispacci de' 15 Agosto 1716, e 29 Luglio 1733, ma eziandio con altro de' 7 Marzo 1744 della Maestà della Regina nostra Clementissima Sovrana, che Dio Guardi, previa l'approvazione del Senato, stabiliti alcuni Ordini e Statuti, e supplicatoci di dare le dovute disposizioni, affinché abbiano d'essere con particolar editto fatti palesi a tutti per la puntuale osservanza sotto le pene in essi espresse in caso d'innobbedienza, d'applicarsi per un terzo alla Regia Camera, e per gli altri due in servizio della Chiesa dell'Accademia, e Studj pubblici.
Siamo venuti in determinare, per manifestare quanto ci stà a cuore di promuovere i vantaggi di questi buoni e fedeli sudditi, sentito anche il parere del Regio Fisco, che si pubblichi la presente.
In virtù della quale facciamo noti a tutti li Ordini e Statuti stabiliti dagl'ascritti nella suddetta Accademia, che sono del seguente tenore.
Primieramente che niun Pittore forastiere quale non sia di grido possa far opere pubbliche in Milano ne in alcun luogo di questo Stato senza prima essere stato esaminato, riconosciuto, ed approvato dall'Accademia per virtuoso, sotto le pene arbitrarie ad essa

Accademia, e parimenti, che niun altra persona di qualsivoglia sorte, stato e condizione ne sotto qualsisia pretesto tanto Pittori, Indoratori, Falegnami, Pattari, Barbieri, e qualunque altr'arte, che possa aprire, e tener bottega ardisca dopo la pubblicazione di questi far negozio di Quadri in pubblico, ne in privato senza averne espressa licenza in scritto dalla stessa Accademia sotto pena della perdita d'essi Quadri, e di scudi venticinque d'applicarsi per la terza parte alla R.a Camera, e per le altre due alla Chiesa dell'Accademia, ed alla stessa Accademia.

Inoltre, che nissuno di detti rivenditori possa pigliare lavori sopra di se per far dipingere ad altri, e principalmente Quadri d'Altare per Chiese, e Luoghi pubblici, quando non sieno riconosciuti dall'Accademia per buoni operatori sotto pena del valore dell'opera, e dell'opera stessa da disporsene con la partecipazione dell'Ill.mo Sig.r Protettore.

Che detti Rivenditori non possano tenere in pubblica Bottega, nè in privato Immagini dipinte o scolpite non fatte col dovuto decoro contro i Commandamenti del Sacro Concilio di Trento, ne altra cosa contro la Sacra Scrittura o lascive, sotto pena della perdita d' essi Quadri, o Sculture da disporsi come sopra.

Che le Immagini Sacre, come pure quelle de' Sommi Pontefici, o de' Principi non si possano tenere per terra esposte alle ingiurie del fango, e de' cani, e trovandosi talimente per la prima volta si ammoniranno i Padroni di detti Quadri, per la seconda si porteranno via detti Quadri, e per la terza, oltre la perdita de medesimi, pagheranno dieci Scudi di pena da esigersi ed applicarsi come sopra.

Di più si proibisce a Facchini, Ciurmaglie, e ad altra sorta di gente il portar Quadri pubblicamente nelle mani scoperti ne altrimenti per farne pubblica mercanzia nelle Piazze e strade della Città, come se fosse cosa vile, e meccanica, siccome tanto ad essi, quanto ai rivenditori l'introdurre Quadri forastieri in Milano per farne mercanzia sotto la pena della perdita d'essi Quadri, e di Scudi venticinque d'applicarsi come sopra per ciascuna volta, quando essi Quadri non siano dapprima riconosciuti, e marcati col sugello dell'Accademia per oviare alle frodi, che per l'avvenire, come pel passato è successo, potessero succedere a pubblico pregiudizio.

E perché sono nati di tempo in tempo moltissimi litigi a causa delle stime de Quadri e Sculture non fatte da Periti dell'arte; laonde per evitare que' disordini, che succedono alla giornata, con evidente danno del pubblico, si proibisce assolutamente alli Pattari, Falegnami, rivenditori e ad altre persone, che si spacciano intendenti lo stimare giudizialmente le opere di Pittura, Disegni, o Sculture, e come se fatte non fossero, e di niun valore in caso che se ne ingerissero, che perciò li Giudici di questa Città e Stato dovranno per l'avvenire valersi nelle Cause contenziose, divisioni, Minorità etc. per stimatori idonei delle cose spettanti alla professione di Pittura, Scultura, ed Architettura solamente degli Accademici del disegno come sopra per tale effetto deputati, o collegiati riguardo agl'Architetti, dichiarando, che sia osservato inviolabilmente tale Statuto ed ordine, e che niuno, che non sia Accademico come sopra deputato, o che non sia altro Accademico da ambedue le parti espressamente concordato, possa giudizialmente stimare le opere spettanti alle suddette professioni sotto la pena di Scudi cinquanta per ciascuna volta da esigersi ed applicarsi come sopra oltre l'invalidità della stima.

Ed acciochè le opere buone, che sono meritevoli di vivere sempre non siano distrutte, si ordina, e proibisce a qualsivoglia Pittore, Scultore, ed Architetto, e ad altri professori, o non professori, tanto Accademici, quanto non Accademici, che non ardiscano disfare, o ritocare pitture, o sculture antiche, e moderne pubbliche senza prima d'essere dall'Accademia visitate, sotto pena di Scudi venticinque, comprendendo nelle medesime proibizioni e pene, li scalpellini, scavatori, calcinati, o siano Maestri di muro, Imbiancatori ed altri trasgressori del presente ordine, li quali s'intendino tenuti alla pena di sopra come se fosse stata loro personalmente intimata.

Si proibisce espressamente a ciascuno Maestro di Pittura il tenere alle loro Scuole non più di due scolari ad aprendere l'arte, e ciò per togliere que' disordini, e quelle defformità sì obrobriose alla virtù, che la rendano vile; mentre si vede perdersi da molti la loro fresca età in questo studio senza profitto alcuno, defraudando la speranza de' poveri parenti, che poscia, dalla necessità costretti, si scorge da tanti scuolari cambiare l'esercizio di virtù sì nobile in altri vilissimi in disdoro, e vilipendio di essa; laonde in avvenire il rimedio sarà, che dovranno tali scuolari essere dapprima riconosciuti dall'Accademia, e ritrovatigli idonei circa li buoni costumi, ed in comoda, o almeno in mezzana fortuna, per potersi mantenere ne studi per tutto quel tempo, che dalla medesima Accademia sarà stimato convenirsi, si concederà loro licenza di potersi esercitare in sì bell'arte, ed in caso d'innobedienza saranno li Maestri multati secondo parerà convenirsi all'arbitrio della stessa Accademia colla partecipazione dell'Illustrissimo Sig.r Protettore.

Qualsisia professore di quelle arti, che sono dipendenti dal dissegno, come Miniatore, Ricamatore, Indoratore, Pittore di targhe, fogliami, e chiariscuri, Scultore in legno, e Intagliatore in rame, non potrà, ne dovrà esercitare la sua arte con vendere ed aprire Bottega, se prima non sarà esaminato, ed approvato dell'Accademia; al qual effetto saranno deputati due Esaminatori della medesima arte per intendere dell'abilità, e sufficienza di chi farà instanza per esercitare simili esercizi, e ciò ad effetto, che si debbano prestare al pubblico opere se non ottime, almeno sufficienti riguardo al comune beneficio.

E perchè si è veduto, e tuttavia si vede dall'esperienza, che stante la mala qualità de' colori, e delle imprimiture che si vendono da colorari nascere grandissimo pregiudizio al pubblico, perché le pitture in brieve perdono la loro vivacità, e diventano molto diverse da quel di prima; perciò saranno soggette le Botteghe d'essi colorati alla visita delle loro tele, e colori, che si usano per dipingere dalli delegati a tal fine dall'Accademia; e dovranno essere soggetti agli Ordini, e pesi stabiliti dalla medesima.

Qualsivoglia Professore tanto di pittura, scultura, ed altro, dipendente dal dissegno, non ardirà intromettersi ne por mano nelle opere da altri incominciate, che ancor vivono, senza la licenza del medesimo Autore, sotto pena di Scudi venticinque per ciascuna volta da esigersi, ed applicarsi come sopra, oltre il dover risarcire il danno a chi prima ne diede principio, lo che sarà liquidato dall'Accademia, e suoi delegati. Che se poi l'opera cominciata restasse impedita per mero capriccio, o interesse dell'Autore, e che negasse ad altri il consenso di perfezionarla, in tal caso basterà al sostituto aver licenza dal Principe dell'Accademia per non incorrere in alcuna pena.

Di più ancora se alcuno de' suddetti professori tanto Accademici, che Aggregati, ed altri subentrerà in qualche lavoro, già patteggiato da altro professore per meno prezzo, non potendo poi con esso condurre l'opera a perfezione in disonore della professione e danno del prossimo, pagherà venticinque scudi di pena da esigersi, ed applicarsi come sopra, non essendo il dovere di mendicare i lavori, e strapazzare le opere in danno di chi le ha ordinate.

Ed essendo ancora troppo di pregiudizio al pubblico, che ogni innesperto muratore voglia fare da Capo Mastro con prendere assonti di regolare fabbriche, ed anche di loro invenzione così sproporzionata al buon ordine dell'Architettura benché sieno cose de' privati, del che ne succede, che non intendendo li dissegni gli vengono dati dagli Architetti, vogliono poi aggiungere in quelli, o sminuire gli ornamenti, e proporzioni con grave studio dissegnate dall'Autore, li quali posti in opera sono tacciati da chi li vede con sommo disdoro dell'Architetto, che ne diede un ben pesato dissegno, e non sapendo questi poi anche la maniera di porli in opera, si sono più volte osservati cadere a terra nel terminarli con sommo pregiudizio di chi li fa erigere, a' quali hanno fatto credere essere sufficienti, e non avendo questa sorta di gente il modo di poterli rifare a loro spese, sono obbligati li Padroni di nuovamente soccombere alla spesa di una mala proporzionata fabbrica.
Perciò stabilisce l'Accademia, che niuno possa adimandarsi Capo Mastro se non sarà esaminato ed approvato da due Architetti Accademici, li quali prenderanno ancora due Capi Mastri di già approvati per esaminarli sopra ciò che s'appartiene per la pratica loro, e conosciuti sufficienti ad esercire la loro carica saranno tenuti stare al risarcimento di tutti li mancamenti anche de' loro subalterni nelle fabriche ed opere, che da medemi si faranno.
E volendo noi, che gli accennati Statuti ed Ordini sieno irremissibilmente adempiti, ed osservati, dichiariamo che li trasgressori de' medesimi, oltre le pene espresse in detti Statuti, ed Ordini, incorreranno altresì in altre maggiori ad arbitrio nostro.
Ed affinché non possi da alcuno allegarsi ignoranza, ordiniamo che la presente sia pubblicata in tutte le Città e luoghi di questo Stato.

Il Principe Lobkovitz

1
Maria Theresa
By the Grace of God Queen of Hungary, Bohemia etc. Archduchess of Austria etc. Duchess of Milan etc.

Milan, April 13th, 1745.
Georg Christian of the Holy Roman Empire, Prince of Lobkowicz, Duke of Sagan, etc., distinguished Knight of the Order of the Golden Fleece, Personal State Counselor of Her Highness, Field Marshal General, Colonel of a Cuirassiers Regiment, General Commander of Her Highness' Troops in Italy, interim General Governor and Captain of Austrian Lombardy.
Whereas the members of the Academy of Painting, Sculpture, and Architecture have informed us, under Saint Luke Evangelist's prayer, that their professions and Religion itself are being ruthlessly abused and besmirched in this Metropolis and State; and
Whereas We wish to address those troubles whose deferral might cause even more significant problems for the studying Youth and the Arts;
Whereas the members of the Academy, pursuant to the Capacities conferred by the glorious Augustus Charles VI in the dispatches dated August 15th, 1716, and July 29th, 1733,

and by our Gracious Queen – God bless Her – on March 7th, 1744, have established, upon the Senate's approval, several Orders and Statutes; and

Whereas the members of the Academy have pled that We take appropriate measures and decree relevant sanctions that will be notified to the public and allotted into one-third for the Royal Chamber and two-thirds for the Church of the Academy and the Public Studies.

Therefore, in the interest of our loyal subjects, in keeping with the Royal Revenue Office's judgment, and pursuant to the Orders and Statutes established by the Academy, We decree as follows:

First, no foreign Painter of little notoriety will have the right to undertake any public projects in Milan unless they are examined, recognised, and approved as highly proficient by the Academy, under its self-established pains. Likewise, no Painter, Gilder, Carpenter, Second-hand Dealer, Barber, or any other professional who can set up shop, will have the right to deal in Paintings without a license drafted by the Academy. The ban applies to all transactions – either public or private – regardless of wealth, state, and condition. All offenders will be punished by the confiscation of the Paintings and a twenty-five crown fine. The sum will be allotted into one-third for the Royal Chamber and two-thirds for the Academy and its Church.

Furthermore, none of the professionals mentioned will have the right to take orders or commission Paintings, such as Altarpieces for Churches and Public Venues, without the Academy's recognition of their reliability as intermediaries. All transgressions will be punished by a fine equal to the artwork's value and the confiscation of the artwork itself, which will be conducted under the Illustrious Sir Protector's supervision.

Said retailers do not have the right to retain Figures – either painted or sculpted, both in public Shops and in private – which are improper, averse to the Holy Council of Trent's Commandments, lascivious, or contrary to the Sacred Scriptures. All transgressions will be punished by the confiscation of the Paintings or Sculptures, as is mentioned above.

No Sacred Images, nor the Portraits of the Supreme Pontiffs and Princes, may be kept on the floor exposed to mud and dogs. Upon their first transgression, the Owners of said Paintings will, therefore, receive a reprimand. The second infraction will then be punished by the Paintings' seizure, whereas the third will result in the confiscation and an additional fine of ten Crowns, to be exacted and processed as mentioned above.

Moreover, all Porters, Crews, and the like are banned from carrying unveiled Paintings by hand in public and selling them in the City's Squares and Streets as if they were nothing but trivial merchandise or mechanical crafts. All the intermediaries and retailers introducing and trading foreign Paintings in Milan will be punished by the confiscation of the Paintings and twenty-five Crowns to be exacted each time, as mentioned above. The legitimate trade is limited to Paintings recognised and imprinted with the Academy's seal to avoid the types of fraud that have already taken place and might occur again in the future.

Since the estimate of Paintings and Sculptures performed by amateur art Appraisers has often led to heated quarrels, and to avoid the disorders that have so far taken place daily, much to the detriment of the public, We decree as follows:

All the Second-hand Dealers, Carpenters, retailers, and the like who profess to be art appraisers officially appointed to estimate Paintings, Drawings, or Sculptures, and should designedly underestimate the value of a work that is about to be imported, are banned from performing all kinds of assessment. The City and State's Judges must henceforth avail themselves of the Academics of Drawing or Scholars of Architecture, as mentioned above, appointed specifically to the evaluation of Paintings, Sculptures, and Architecture, when dealing with litigations, inheritance settlements, unfitness to plead, etc.

Furthermore, the Judges must ensure compliance with this Statute and order and guarantee that the judicial estimate of the artworks in question is carried out by the Academics mentioned above, respectively, and agreed upon by both parties. All transgressions will be punished by a fine of fifty Crowns, to be exacted and processed each time as mentioned above, and the illegitimate estimate's invalidation.

To preserve the good artworks, which deserve to last over time and escape destruction, all Painters, Sculptors, and Architects – regardless of their being professors, Academics, or neither – are banned from retouching or remodeling paintings, ancient sculptures, and modern public artworks that the Academy has not appraised. All transgressors will be punished by a fine of twenty-five Crowns, including stonemasons, diggers, plasterers, Bricklayers, or house Painters and other offenders who are equally liable for the pains mentioned above as if they were given notice personally.

All Master Painters are expressly forbidden to have more than two pupils at their Schools, to avoid the disorders and sheer ugliness that may vilify the Arts' virtues. Many disciples waste their youth and disappoint their relatives' expectations, eventually turning to practices that smear Art's good virtue. Consequently, the pupils will have to be recognised by the Academy as moral persons with sufficient means to provide for themselves during their studies. The duration of their apprenticeship will be set conveniently by the Academy, which will issue a traineeship license in the arts. All transgressions will be punished by a fine imposed on the Masters and established by the Academy, in conjunction with the Illustrious Sir Protector.

All the art professors involved in drawing, such as Miniaturists, Embroiderers, Gilders, Panel, leafage, and chiaroscuro painters, Wood Carvers, and Copper Carvers, are banned from practicing their profession and setting up Shop unless they have been previously examined and approved by the Academy. To that effect, two Examiners of the profession in question will be appointed to appraise each candidate's skillfulness and suitability. The necessary requirement will have to be the creation of artworks that are either excellent or at least good enough for the public's benefit.

Since the low quality of the colours and priming sold by several colourists have already damaged the community's prestige, and because they have often altered many artworks or compromised their vividness, all the canvases and colours created in the colourists' Workshops will be scrutinised thoroughly. The Academy, pursuant to its Orders and criteria, will be in charge of the entire process.

All the Professors involved in painting, sculpture, and the other activities related to the arts of drawing are banned from altering any artworks begun by other living artists unless they have a license by the Creator. All transgressions will be punished by a fine of twenty-five Crowns to be exacted and applied, as mentioned above. Furthermore, the offender must compensate the original Creator under the supervision of the Academy and its delegates. Any prospective substitute will have to apply for a license by the Prince of the Academy if the Creator should leave their work unfinished – either intentionally or at whim – and deny consent to its further development.

Moreover, by replacing the original Creator of an artwork, the professors mentioned above – regardless of their being Academics, Associates, or else – become liable of a fine of twenty-five crowns if they fail to deliver a work honorable for their professional category and beneficial to the community. The penalty will be exacted and applied as mentioned above, pursuant to the prohibition to appropriate and alter artwork to the commissioning party's detriment.

Furthermore, our community is often damaged by the disproportionate stonework of inexperienced builders who, claiming to be Master Masons, take on commissions for private construction sites and erect buildings that contrast with Architecture's principles and harmony. Not understanding the Architects' designs, they often happen to add unnecessary parts or downplay the role of ornaments and proportions so that the Authors' original blueprints are eventually realised to ruin the Architects' good name in the eyes of the beholders. Moreover, the poor rendition of the Architects' well-pondered designs may sometimes lead to collapses, as has been the case on many occasions, to the detriment of the Owners and commissioners. The builders' knavery and inability to finance a second construction ultimately results in the Owners having to fund the entire project anew.

Therefore, the Academy decrees that no one may claim the title of Master Mason unless they have been examined in their sphere of competence and approved by two of the Academy's Architects, who will perform the assessment with the aid of two authorised Master Masons. All the newly appointed Master Masons are liable for compensating for any shortcomings caused by either themselves or their subordinates.

To guarantee the fulfilment and compliance with the Statutes and Orders, We decree that all offenders will be punished by both the penalties mentioned in said Statutes and Orders and other stricter measures of Our choice.

We also order that the here present decree be posted in all the State's Cities and venues so that no one may lawfully claim ignorance.

Prince Lobkowicz

11

The Kingdom of Spain

1
M. 4 de Agosto de 1752
Al Ecc.mo S.or Marq.s de la Ensenada

Ecc.mo S.or,
El Proyecto adjunto es el que se ha discurrido mas adequado para la essecuciòn del reconocimiento de las antiguedades de España. Si su Mag.d se dignase aprobarle serà el mas â proposíto para este Viaje el Academico numerario Velazquez Caballero del Abito de Santiago. Su edad, que no llega â treinta años, su estado libre, su robustez suma, y sobre todo su acreditada intelígencia en estos asuntos, le proporcionan de manera que dificilmente se podra encontrar otro de iguales circunstancias: scrivase V. E. prevenirme en todo lo que me resta que hacer interim que ruego â [...].

2
Proyecto,
De la instruccion, que havrà de darse al Academico, â quien S. Mag.d cometiese el viage de España

Si fuese del agrado del Rey, que se averiguen las antiguedades de España, y se recojan sus monumentos mas importantes, la persona, â quien S. Mag.d fiare esta Comision, deberà practicarla, arreglandose en todo â las instrucciones siguientes.
Viajarà todas las Provincias del continente de la España, empesando por Estremadura, y siguiendo despues subcesivamente por la Andalucias, Reyno de Murcia, Valencia, Calataluña, Aragon, Navarra, Viscaya y sus Provincias, las dos Castillas, Asturia, Leon y Galicia.
Se dirigirà en derechura â las Capitales de las Provincias; donde procurarà informarse de todo el territorio; y adquirir todas las noticias, que juigare ser conducentes para desempeñar su comision: y desde aqui harà sus viajes â los pueblos immediatos.
En los pueblos grandes, ó en aquellos donde haia de practicar en publico alguna diligencia concerniente â su comision, se presentarà antes â las Justicias, participandoles la orden que lleba de S. Mag.d.

Harà todas las observaciones, que sean conducentes para averiguar las antiguedades de España, y la antigua Geographia de esta Provincia.

Registrarà las ruinas de los mas famosos pueblos de la antiguedad; y las reliquias de sus mas sumptuosos edificios; como los Theatros, Amphitheatros, Circos, Naumachias, Aqueductos, Puentes, Arcos de Tropheos, Templos, Thermas, y sepulcros. Los medirà, dibujarà, y explicarà.

Estas dimensiones las harà por el pie de hierro, que le havrà d'entregar el Director de la Academia; en cuis poder deberà quedarse otro igual al que llevase.

Podrà hacer algunas ligeras excavaciones, quando estas fuesen convenientes para el desempeño de su comision; pero si estas debieren ser mas largas, costosas, ó en perjuicio de alguno, no las practicarà sin representarlo antes â S. Mag.d por medio del Director de la Academia, y obtener su real permiso.

Copiarà todas las inscriptiones antiguas, assi de letras desconocidas, como Latinas, Gothicas, Arabes, y Hebreas; y formarà de todas ellas una Collecion.

Recogerà las Estatuas antiguas, baxos relieves, Camafeos, piedras gravadas, y medallas, y las demas reliquias comprobadas de la antiguedad, comprandolas de las personas, que voluntariamente se determinen â venderlas.

Siempre que el precio de estas cosas sea algo exesivo, no pasarà â acer la compra de ellas, sin participarlo â S. Mag.d del prop.o modo, por medio del Director de la Academia, y obtener su real beneplacito.

Cuidarà de que todas estas alhajas se conduscan â donde S. Mag.d mandare: y entre tanto deberà hacer, que las Estatuas, baxos relieves, y demas monumentos, cuia conduccion no sea tan facil, se coloquen en parages seguros, y si puedes ser, en las Casas del Ayuntamiento de los pueblos; encargando â las Justicias su conservacion, hasta tanto que S. Mag.d disponga de ellas.

Emviarà una quenta justificada de todo lo que expendiese en estas excavaciones, y compras.

Procurarà ver los Gabinetes de algunas personas particulares, y observarà en ellos todo quanto pueda conducir â ilustrar, y averiguar las antiguead de España.

Tendrà una correspondencia seguida con el Director de la Academia, â quien participarà el curso de su viaje; para siempre que S. Mag.d guste informarse de todo, ó quiera mandarle algo de nuevo, sepa el lugar de su destino.

Ademas de estos avisos subcesivos, irà formando un Diario, puntual de todo su viaje, con expresion de las cosa, que en el la haian ocurrido, i los descubrimientos, i observaciones, que hubiere hecho.

Segun fuese concluiendo el viage de cada una de las Provincias en particular, darà quenta à S. Mag.d de todo lo que en ella haia observado, los descubrimientos, que hubiese hecho acerca de la Geographia antigua, los monumentos de la antiguedad, que hubiese descubierto, y todo lo demas que fuese del asumpto de su Comision.

Todo esto, y lo demas, que haia de representar â S. Mag.d lo participarà â su Ministro Secretario del Despacho Universal por medio del Director de la Academia.

Llebarà consigo un dibujante habil, que execute con exactitud los dibujos, y diseños de los monumentos, que descubriese en el discurso de su Viage.

Se le darà un Real Despacho para todas las Justicias, â fin de que por su parte concurraran â los designios de S. Mag.d y de ningun modo le impidan el cumplimiento de su Comision.

Tambien se le darà un Pasaporte, para que assi â el, como â sus Criados se les dì el aloxamiento, y Bagages necesarios, del mismo modo que se practica con los militares.
Para ayuda de costa del gasto suyo, de sus Criados, y dibujante, se le daràn cinquenta doblones cada mes por el tiempo de su Comision.
Tambien se le daran las cantidades necesarias para los gastos de las excavaciones, y compras, de lo qual havrà de dar una quenta exacta.

3
[Licencia para Velázquez]

D. Zenon de Somodevilla, Marq.s de la Ensenada, Caballero de la insigne Orden del Toyson d'Oro, y de la R.l. O.rd. General, Comendador de Piedrabuena, y de Peña del Martor en la de Calatrava, Cavallero Gran Cruz de la Religion de S. Juan, del Consejo del Estado de S. M., Secretario de Estado, y del Despacho Universal de Guerra, Marina, Indias, y Hazienda, Superintendente General della, y con Honores de Lugar – teniente General del Almirantargo, General de España, i de las Indias:
Por quanto D. Luis Velazquez, de la Academia R.l de la Historia, se halla nombrado para ir â averiguar, y reconocer las Antiguedades de España, recorriendo â este fin las Provincias de la Peninsula; manda el Rey â los Capitanes, y Comandantes Generales de ellas, â los Intendentes, Governadores, Corregidores, Justicias, i demas Personas â quienes toque, y se presentare este Despacho, faciliten al expresado D. Luis Velazquez todo el favor, auxilio, y asistencia que pidiese, y necesitase para el desempeño de su Comision, sin ponerle, ni permitir se le ponga el menor impedimiento, ni dilacion, y que hagan franquear, y poner de manifiesto los Archivos, y Protocolos publicos, que indicase para sacar de ellos las noticias, que le pareciere, y copias simples, ó autorisadas de los Documentos, y demas papeles que tuviesen conexion directa ó indirecta con su encargo; pues assi conviene al servicio de S. Mag.d .

Dado en S. Lorenzo el Real â 2 de Noviembre del 1752.
El Marques de la Ensenada

4
[Commission à Velázquez]

Conformandose el Rey con lo propuesto por la Real Academiade la Historia en papieles de V. S. del 6 de Junio y 4 de Agostode este año, viene en que D.n Luiz Velazquez haga el viage de España para averiguar y reconocer las antiguedades de ella, practicando en este encargo lo que se prescribe en la adjunta Instruccion, y lo que ademàs tuviere la Academia por conveniente advertirle para su mejor desempeño.
Por el tiempo que se mantuviese en esta Commission desde el dia que por aviso de U.es conestare aver partido para ella, ha resuelto S. M. Se le assita por la Thesoreria General con cinquenta doblones al mes, de que costearà su viaje, y el del dibujante, que llevarà consigo; y ha mandado que en quenta de esta assignacion se le anticipan dos messadas,

y tambien otros cien doblones para los gastos de las escavaciones, y compras, que se le encargan en la Instruccion, y para continuarlas, se le irà soccorriendo del mismo modo segun las noticias, que fuere U.es comunicando.
Participalo â U.es de orden de S. M. para que haciendolo presente en la Academia, se de' por esta y U.es cumplimiento â ello en la parte que les toca.
Dio es g.e â U.es m.es a.es como deseo.

En Lorenzo el Real 2 de Noviembre de 1752.
Marq.es de la Ensenada

5
Instruccion, que hade Observar D.n Luis Velázquez de la Real Academia de la Historia, en el viage â que està destinado para averiguar y reconozer las antiguedades de España

1. Decorrerà en su viage todas las Provincias de el continente de España, empezando por Extremadura, y continuando por las Andalucias, Reyno de Murcia, Valencia, Calathaluña, Aragon, Navarra, Guypuzcoa, Vizcaya, Alaba, Quatro Villas de la Costa, Asturias, Galicia, Leon, y las dos Castillas; cuia escala no alterarà sin expresa superior orden.
2. En cada Provincia pasarà primeramente a la Capital, endonde ve informarà de lo que haya digno de observacion en aquel parage, y recogidas estas noticias y las que en èl pueda adquirir de el resto de la Provincia, se transfirirà â los demas Lugares en que espere descubrir algo de importancia.
3. En los Pueblo grandes, y en âquellos donde haya de practicar alguna diligencia concerniente a su Comision se presentarà antes a las Justicias con la orden que llevarà de S. M. para que le auxilien y presten toda la asistencia que pidiere, franqueandole los Archivos, y Registros Publicos para que saque de ellos las noticias que hubiese menester, certificadas, y autorizadas en devida forma.
4. Harà en cada Provincia las observaciones, y diligencias que sean conducentes al descubrimiento de las antiguedades de ella, y de la antigua Geographia del Pais, con especificacion de los districtos, Pueblos, Rios, Terrenos en que se dieron Batallas, ò succedieron cossas memorables, y otras semejantes circunstancias.
5. Registrarà las Ruinas de los mas famosos Pueblos de la antiguedad, y las Reliquias de sus mas sumptuosos edificios, como los Theatros, Amphitheatros, Circos, Naumachias, Aqueductos, Puentes, Arcos de Tropheos, Templos, Thermas, y Sepulcros, los medirà, dibujarà, y explicarà.
6. Harà estas dimenciones por el pie de Hierro que le avra de entregar el Director de la Academia, en cuis poder quedarà otro igual al que llevase.
7. Podrà hazer algunas ligeras excavaciones si fuese necesario para el desempeño de su Comision; pero si estas deviesen ser mas largas, costosas, ó en perjuicio de alguno, no las practicarà sin representarlo antes â S. M. por medio del Director de la Academia, para obtenerse su Real permiso.

8. Copiarà todas las inscripciones antiguas, asi de letras desconocidas, como Latinas, Gothicas, Arabes, y Hebreas, y formarà de todas ellas una Collecion.
9. Recogerà las Estatuas antiguas, Baxos reliebes, Camafeos, piedras grabadas, Medallas, y las demas reliquias comprovadas de la antiguedad, comprandolas de las personas que voluntariamente se determinen â venderlas; como su coste no sea excesibo, pues pasando de una cantidad moderada, esperarà la Real aprobazion antes de efectuar la compra.
10. Cuidarà de que todas estas Alhajas se conduscan âdonde S. M. mandase, y entretanto harà que las Estatuas, baxos relieves, y demas Monumentos cuia conduccion no sea tan facil, se coloquen en parages seguros, y si puedes ser, en Casas del Ayuntam.to de los Pueblos, encargando â las Justicias su conservacion hasta tanto que S. M. disponga de ellas.
11. Llevarà quenta muy exacta y justificada de todo lo que expendiese en estas excavaciones, y compras y la remitisa con Cargo y Data del dinero que se le fuese librando para estos gastos.
12. Procurarà veer los Gavinetes de algunas personas particulares, y observarà en ellos todo quanto pueda conducir â ilustrar, y averiguar las antiguead de España.
13. Tendrà una correspondencia seguida con el Director de la Academia âquien participarà el curso de su viaje, y lo que fuese praticando en èl para que lo ponga en noticia de S. M. y si hubiese que prebenirle, se sepa â donde se le han de dirigir las ordenes.
14. Ademas de estos avisos succesivos, ira formando un Diario puntual de todo su viaje, con expresion de lo que en èl le haya succedidos, y las observaciones, y descubrimientos que hubiese hecho.
15. Segun fuese concluyendo el reconocimiento de cada una de las Provincias en particular, darà quenta de todo lo observado en ella, y averiguaciones hechas en punto de la Geographia antigua, monumentos de la antiguedad, y todo lo demas que fuere del assumpto de su Comision.
16. Llevara con sigo un Dibujante habil que execute con exactitud los Dibujos, y diseños de los monumentos que descubriesse en el discursode su viage.
17. Esperase, que en èl procederà con el acierto que prometen los buenos informes, que se han dado al Rey de su persona, talentos, aplicacion, y juicio, dejando satisfechos todos los respectos que deven impeler su honor, y estimazion al desempeño de su encargo de esta confianza.

San Lorenzo el Real, 2 de Noviembre 1752.
El Marques de la Ensenada

6
Real Cedula de S. M. Y Señores Del Consejo, por la qual se aprueba y manda observar la Instruccion formada por la Real Academia de la Historia sobre el modo de recoger y conservar los monumentos antiguos descubiertos ó que se descubran en el Reyno

Año 1803, Madrid en la Imprenta Real.

Don Cárlos por la Gracia de Dios, Rey de Castilla, de Leon, de Aragon, de las Dos Sicilias, de Jerusalen, de Navarra, de Granada, de Toledo, de Valencia, de Galicia, de Mallorca, de Menorca, de Sevilla, de Cerdeña, de Córdoba, de Córcega, de Murcia, de Jaen, de los Algarbes, de Algecira, de Gibraltar, de las Islas de Canaria, de las Indias Orientales y Occidentales, Islas y Tierra-firme del mar Océano; Archiduque de Austria; Duque de Borgoña, de Brabante y de Milan; Conde de Abspurg, de Flándes, Tirol y Barcelona; Señor de Vizcaya y de Molina &c.

A los del mi Consejo, Presidentes, Regentes y Oidores de mis Audiencias y Chancillerías, Alcaldes, Alguaciles de mi Casa y Corte, y á todos los Corregidores, Asistente, Intendentes, Gobernadores, Alcaldes mayores y ordinarios, y otros qualesquiera Jueces y Justicias de estos mis Reynos, así de Realengo, como de Señorío, Abadengo y Ordenes, y á todas las demas personas de qualquier grado, estado ó condicion que sean, á quienes lo contenido en esta mi Cédula toque, ó tocar pueda en qualquier manera:

SABED, que á conseqüencia de lo que tuve á bien encargar á mi Real Academia de la Historia con el deseo de hallar algun medio que pusiese á cubierto las antigüedades que se descubren en la Península de la ignorancia que suele destruirlas, con daño de los conocimientos históricos y de las artes, á cuyos progresos contribuyen en gran manera, me propuso por medio de mi primer Secretario de Estado un plan razonado de las diligencias y medidas que juzgaba poderse adoptar para el reconocimiento y conservacion de los monumentos antiguos que en gran número tiene el tiempo sepultados en España. Por este plan, que me digné aprobar, se confiere á la citada Academia la inspeccion general de las antigüedades que se descubran en todo el Reyno. Y siendo forzoso, para que pueda exercerla, que todas las personas que tienen conocido influxo, autoridad y jurisdiccion, Prelados, Cabildos y Corregidores la den aviso de todos los hallazgos de antigüedades que lleguen á su noticia, y la presten auxilio en todo quanto penda de sus facultades; con este fin manifesté al mi Consejo en treinta de Enero del año próximo ser mi voluntad circulase órdenes á los mismos Prelados, Cabildos y Corregidores del Reyno para que así lo cumpliesen, contribuyendo con su zelo á que no se pierdan unos monumentos en cuya conservacion interesa la instruccion pública, y aun el honor de la Nacion. Publicada en el mi Consejo esta mi resolucion, pidió y se le pasó de mi órden el referido plan; y en su vista, y de lo expuesto por mis Fiscales, en consulta de veinte y seis de Marzo del mismo año próximo me hizo presente sería muy oportuno, para la mas completa verificacion de los fines insinuados, el que se formase desde luego, y se le remitiese á efecto de reconocerla, la instruccion que segun el citado plan habia de imprimir y publicar la Academia, y se extendiese de todo una mi Real Cédula, para ocurrir de este modo á las dificultades ó inconvenientes que pudiese haber en la execucion de algunos de sus capítulos, especialmente los que tratasen de instrumentos de archivos particulares, ó de monumentos y memorias que tambien lo fuesen. Habiéndome conformado con el dictámen del mi Consejo, se previno de mi órden á la Academia formase, como lo hizo, la Instruccion que indicó, y es la siguiente.

Instruccion formada de órden de S. M. por la Real Academia de la Historia sobre el modo de recoger y conservar los monumentos antiguos descubiertos ó que se descubran en el Reyno.

1. Por monumentos antiguos se deben entender las estatuas, bustos y baxos relieves, de quales quiera materias que sean, templos, sepulcros, teatros, anfiteatros, circos, naumachias, palestras, baños, calzadas, caminos, aqüeductos, lápidas ó inscripciones, mosaycos, monedas de qualquiera clase, camafeos: trozos de arquitectura, colunas miliarias; instrumentos músicos, como sistros, liras, crótalos; sagrados, como preferículos, símpulos, lituos, cuchillos sacrificatorios, segures, aspersorios, vasos, trípodes: armas de todas especies, como arcos, flechas, glandes, carcaxes, escudos: civiles, como balanzas, y sus pesas, romanas, reloxes solares ó maquinales, armilas, collares, coronas, anillos, sellos: toda suerte de utensilios, instrumentos de artes liberales y mecánicas; y finalmente qualesquiera cosas, aun desconocidas, reputadas por antiguas, ya sean Púnicas, Romanas, Cristianas, ya Godas, Arabes y de la baxa edad.
2. De todos estos monumentos serán dueños los que los hallasen en sus heredades y casas, ó los descubran á su costa y por su índustria Los que se hallaren en territorio público ó realengo (de que es dueño S. M.) cuidarán de recogerlos y guardar los los Magistrados y Justicias de los distritos. Puestos en custodia, los descubridores, poseedores y Justicias respectivamente darán parte y noticia circunstanciada de todo á la Real Academia de la Historia por medio de su Secretario, á fin, de que esta tome el correspondiente conocimiento, y determine su adquisicion por medio de compra, gratificacion, ó segun se conviniese con el dueño.
3. Cooperarán á todo lo dicho en quanto se de su parte (como personas ilustradas) los M. RR. Arzobispos, RR. Obispos, Abades, Cabildos y demas superiores Eclesiásticos, así como los Magistrados seculares, indagando y adquiriendo, noticias de los hallazgos, y poniéndolos en la de la Academia, segun y para los fines enunciados en el artículo 2°.
4. Los descubridores tendrán el mayor cuidado, de notar puntualmente el parage de los hallazgos, para que por este medio pueda la Academia conjeturar ó resolver á qué Pueblo, Colonia ó Municipio pudiéron pertenecer; expresando con exáctitud á quantas leguas, millas ó pasos esten de Ciudad, Villa, Lugar, rio, monte ó valle conocido, y hácia qué region celeste de ellos, esto es, si al Levante, Norte, Sur ó Poniente.
5. Si en algunas Ciudades ó Pueblos hay antigüedades de las indicadas en el artículo 1°, halladas en otro tiempo, y que aun existan en parages en que puedan aniquilarse por descuido, ó por injuria del tiempo, sus dueños ó las Justicias darán noticia del mismo modo que se ha dicho, para que la Academia la tenga de ellas, y vea las ventajas que puede sacar nuestra Historia secular ó eclesiástica.
6. La Academia quedará agradecida á los buenos patriotas que coadyuven á la ilustracion de la patria por el medio de buscar, cónservar y comunicarla los monumentos antiguos arriba nombrados; sin que por eso dexe de satisfacer á los poseedores de las cosas halladas el tanto en que se convinieren, quedando la conduccion de ellas á cargo de la Academia.
7. Generalmente las Justicias de todos los Pueblos cuidarán de que nadie destruya ni maltrate los monumentos descubiertos ó que se descubrieren, puesto que tanto interesan al honor, antigüedad y nombre de los Pueblos mismos; tomando las

providencias convenientes para que así se verifique. Lo mismo practicarán en los edificios antiguos que hoy existen en algunos Pueblos y despoblados, sin permitir que se derriben, ni toquen sus materiales para ningun fin; antes bien cuidarán de que se conserven: y en el caso de amenazar próxima ruina, lo pondrán en noticia de la Academia por medio de su Secretario, á efecto de que esta tome las providencias necesarias para su conservacion.

Esta Instruccion la dirigí al mi Consejo, á fin de que exáminándola sirviese para los efectos que me habia propuesto; y habiéndolo executado, con presencia de lo expuesto por mis tres Fiscales, se acordó expedir esta mi Cédula. Por la qual os mando á todos y cada uno de vos en vuestros respectivos lugares, distritos y juris dicciones veais la Instruccion inserta, guardeis y cumplais lo dispuesto en ella, y lo hagais guardar, cumplir y executar, sin permitir su con travencion en manera alguna. Y encargo á los M. RR. Arzobispos, RR. Obispos, y á los Cabildos de las Iglesias Metropolitanas y Catedrales, sus Visitadores ó Vicarios, y á los que lo sean Capitulares en Sede vacante, á los Cabildos de las Iglesias Colegiatas, Capillas Reales, Abades y demas Ordinarios Eclesiásticos que exerzan jurisdiccion, y á los Superiores ó Prelados de las Ordenes Regulares, y de las Militares, Párrocos y demas personas Eclesiásticas, hagan observar lo dispuesto en esta mi Cédula, sin consentir con ningun pretexto su contravencion; contribuyendo con su ilustrado zelo, como conviene al honor de la Nacion, y al adelantamiento de la instruccion pública, á que por la expresada mi Real Academia se consigan los fines á que se dirige esta mi Cédula, prestándola con el mismo objeto todos los auxilios que pendan de su autoridad y respectivas facultades: que así es mi voluntad; y que al traslado impreso de esta mi Cédula, firmado de D. Bartolomé Muñoz de Torres, mi Secretario, Escribano de Cámara mas antiguo y de Gobierno del mi Consejo, se le dé la misma fe y crédito que á su original.

Dada en Madrid á seis de Julio de mil ochocientos y tres.
YO EL REY.
Yo Don Juan Ignacio deAyestaran, Secretario del Rey nuestro Señor, lo hice escribir por su mandado
Don Joseph Eusta quio Moreno
Don Bernardo Riega
Don Domingo Fernandez de Campománes
Don Sebastian de Torres
Don Andres Lasauca
Registrada, Don Joseph Alegre
Teniente de Canciller mayor, Don Joseph Alegre
Es copia de su original, de que certifico.

1
August 4th, 1752
To the Most Excellent Lord Marquis de la Ensenada

Most Excellent Lord,
The attached Project is the one that has been considered suitable to carry out the recognition of the antiquities in Spain. If His Majesty consents to approve it, the regular academic Velázquez Knight of the Order of Santiago will be the most fitting [person to carry out] this Travel. His age, which is less than thirty years old, his free status, his overall robustness, and above all his accredited intelligence in these matters endow him with such [qualities] that it is hardly possible to find another [candidate] with the same circumstances. May Your Excellence write me; I beg you to warn me about everything that remains for me to do [...].

2
Project,
Concerning the instruction to the Academic that His Majesty will entrust [to carry out] the travel in Spain

Suppose the King allowed [the plan] to discover the antiquities in Spain and collect the most important monuments. In that case the person His Majesty will appoint to this Commission should follow these instructions faithfully.
He will travel throughout all the Provinces of the mainland of Spain, starting from Estremadura and subsequently continuing with Andalusia, Reign of Murcia, Valencia, Catalonia, Aragon, Navarra, Biscay, and its Provinces, the two Castile, Asturias, Leon, and Galicia.
He will go directly to the Capitals of the Provinces; there he will try to find out [information] on the entire territory and acquire news that he will evaluate beneficial to achieve his commission, and from there he will execute his trips to the towns nearby.
In the large towns, or in those where it is good to be cautious in public regarding this commission, he will present himself before the Justice with the order of His Majesty.
He will accomplish all the examinations conducive to discovering the antiquities of Spain and the ancient Geography of each Province.
He will look for the ruins of the most famous ancient towns and the relics of its most magnificent buildings, such as Theaters, Amphitheaters, Circuses, Naumachias, Aqueducts, Bridges, Arches of Trophies, Temples, Thermal Baths, and tombs. He will measure, draw up, and explain them.
These measurements will be done using the iron foot, which he will receive from the Director of the Academy; the latter will keep another identical [tool].
He can carry out some minor excavations if these are convenient to accomplish the commission. However, if these are longer, more expensive, or detrimental to someone, he can only undertake them after presenting an instance to His Majesty through the Director of the Academy and obtaining his royal permission.

He will copy all the ancient inscriptions, as well as the unknown characters, such as Latin, Gothic, Arab, and Hebrew; and he will form a Collection of all of these [reproductions].
He will collect the ancient Statues, bas-reliefs, Cameos, engraved stones, medals, and other verified relics from antiquity, by buying them from the people who voluntarily decide to sell them.
If the price of these items is excessive, he will not purchase them without first informing [the King] through the Director of the Academy and obtaining his royal approval.
He will take care that all these treasures are transferred where His Majesty requires; and in the meantime, he will make sure that the Statues, bas-reliefs, and the other monuments whose relocation is not so easy, are stored in safe places, possibly in the Houses of the Town Hall; the local Judges shall take responsibility of their conservation until His Majesty disposes of them.
He will transmit the evidence of expenditure related to all the costs that would occur in these excavations and purchases.
He will try to visit the Cabinets of specific people, to analyse anything that can lead to illustrate and discover the antiquity of Spain.
He will keep an ongoing correspondence with the Director of the Academy, informing him about the progression of his trip; in the case that His Majesty wants to ascertain anything or send him something, he would know where to locate him.
In addition to these successive notices, he will draft an accurate Diary on the entire travel, recording the events that have occurred, the discoveries, and any of his personal observations.
When the journey in each of the specific Provinces concludes, he will update His Majesty regarding what he has observed, the discoveries on the ancient Geography, the newly detected monuments of antiquity, and anything else that might concern his Commission. These and the other [reports] that are to submit to His Majesty will first pass through his Minister Secretary of the Universal Office and the Director of the Academy.
He will bring with him a skilled draftsman, who shall execute accurate drawings and designs of the monument that will be discovered during the Travel.
He will be given a Royal Dispatch to present to all the Judges so that they can support for what they can the plans of His Majesty, and in no way prevent him from achieving his Commission.
He will also be given a Passport, so that he and his Servants are provided with accommodation and necessary Baggage, in the same way as it is practiced with soldiers.
To sustain his expenses, as well as those of his Servants and his draftsman, he will be assigned fifty doubloons each month for the time of his Commission.
He will also be reimbursed for the costs incurred for the necessary excavations and purchases, of which he will compile a detailed report.

3
[Passport for Velázquez]

Lord Zenon de Somodevilla, Marquis de la Ensenada, Knight of the distinguished Order of the Golden Fleece, and the Real Order General, Commander of Piedrabuena, and Peña del Martor in Calatrava, Knight of the Gran Cruz of the Religion of Saint John, the Council of the State of His Majesty, Secretary of the State and the Universal Office of War, Navy, Indies, and General Superintendent of the Treasury, with the Honors of Place – General Lieutenant of the Admiralty, General of Spain and the Indies:
Since Don Luis Velázquez, from the Real Academy of History, is appointed to find out and recognise the Antiquities of Spain, he is traveling for this purpose in the Provinces of the Peninsula; The King commands to the Captains, and their General Commanders, Mayors, Governors, Intendants, Judges, and the other Persons that might be concerned who will be presented this Dispatch, to provide the said Don Luis Velázquez with all courtesy, support, and assistance that he might request and need for the accomplishment of his Commission, without impede him, or allowing others to impede him; they shall authorise and open [for him] the Archives and public Protocols, which are suitable to find any news he might need, [allowing him to make] transcriptions or authorised copies of the Documents, and any other paper which has a direct or indirect connection with this order; this to fulfil the service of His Majesty.

Given in S. Lorenzo el Real in November 2nd, 1752.
The Marquis de la Ensenada

4
[Appointment of Velázquez]

As the King has approved what the Royal Academy of History proposed in Your papers of June 6th and August 4th of this year, Don Luiz Velázquez will undertake the trip in Spain to find out and identify its antiquities; he will follow in this assignment what prescribed in the attached Instruction, and also what the Academy might consider convenient to recommended for its best performance.
For the time that he is engaged in this Commission until the day that, after our notice, he terminates it, His Majesty will assist him thought the General Treasury with fifty doubloons per month; he will [use this sum] to cover the expenses for the trip and the draftsman; and He has ordered that he will be given two monthly installments in advance, together with a further hundred doubloons for the expenses of the excavations and the purchases, as indicated in the Instruction; to continue with these, he will be assisted in the same way, according to the news that he will forward.
We communicate You this order of His Majesty, so that the Academy and Yourself comply in the parts which involve you.
Might God be generous with you as you wish.

Lorenzo el Real, November 2nd, 1752.
Marquis de la Ensenada

5

Instruction, to be observed by Don Luis Velázquez of the Royal Academy of History, on the travel aimed at discovering and recognising the antiquities of Spain

1. In his journey he will traverse all the Provinces of mainland Spain, starting from Extremadura, and continuing with Andalusia, Reign of Murcia, Valencia, Catalonia, Aragon, Navarra, Guipúzcoa, Vizcaya, Álava, the four Villas in the Coast, Asturias, Galicia, Leon, and the two Castile; their order will not be altered without an express order.
2. In each Province, he will first go to the Capital, where he will gather information on what is worthy of observation; after collecting this news and those that can be acquired across the Province, he will move to the next Place where he expects to discover something important.
3. In the large towns, and in those where it is best to be cautious concerning this Commission, he will present himself before the Justice with the order that His Majesty will provide him; this will allow him to receive all the needed assistance and gain access to the Archives and Public Registries, to get the required news certified and duly authorised.
4. In each Province, he will accomplish the investigations and procedures conducive to discovering the antiquities and the ancient Geography of the Country, identifying the districts, Towns, Rivers, and Lands where the Battles took place or other memorable events occurred, and further similar occurrences.
5. He will register the Ruins of the most famous ancient Villages and the Relics of their most magnificent buildings, such as Theaters, Amphitheaters, Circuses, Naumachias, Aqueducts, Bridges, Trophies, Arches, Temples, Thermal Baths, and Tombs; he will measure, draw up, and explain them.
6. These measurements will be obtained by using the Iron foot, which he will be given by the Director of the Academy; the latter will have another identical [tool].
7. He may carry out some minor excavations if these are helpful to accomplish the Commission. However, suppose these are longer, more expensive, or detrimental to someone, in that case he will not undertake them without first presenting an instance to His Majesty through the Director of the Academy and obtaining his Royal permission.
8. He will copy all the ancient inscriptions, including those with unknown characters, such as Latin, Gothic, Arab, and Hebrew; he will form a Collection with all these [reproductions].
9. He will collect the ancient Statues, Bas-reliefs, Cameos, engraved stones, Medals, as well as other verified relics from antiquity, by buying them from the people who voluntarily decide to sell them if their cost is not too high. If their cost is [more than] moderate, he will wait for the Royal approval before finalising the purchase.
10. He will ensure that all these Treasures are transferred where His Majesty requires. In the meantime, he will make sure that the Statues, bas-reliefs, and the other Monuments whose transportation is not so easy, are stored in safe places, possibly in the Town Hall Houses; the local Judges are entrusted with their conservation until His Majesty disposes of them.

11. He will record accurate evidence of expenditure of all the costs of these excavations and purchases, and he will send it together with the Cargo and Date so that the money of these expenses can be reimbursed to him.
12. He will try to see the Cabinets of some particular people, to detect anything that can lead to illustrate and discover the antiquity of Spain.
13. He will keep an ongoing correspondence with the Director of the Academy, informing him about the trip's progression and what has happened so that His Majesty can be informed too; if he wishes to send him anything, he would know where to direct the orders.
14. In addition to these successive notices, he will draft an accurate Diary on the entire travel, recording the events, discoveries, and any other personal observation.
15. When the investigations in each of the specific Provinces conclude, he will present an account of what he has observed, the discoveries on the ancient Geography, the monuments of antiquity, and anything else that might fall under the assumptions of this Commission.
16. He will be accompanied by a skilled Draftsman, who shall execute with exactitude the Drawings and designs of the monuments discovered during the travel.
17. Hopefully, he will proceed successfully, and meet the good recommendations that the King has received regarding his talents, application, and judgment, satisfying all the respects that imply his honor and esteem, to accomplish this commission with trust.

San Lorenzo el Real, November 2nd, 1752.
The Marquis de la Ensenada

6
Royal Charter of his Majesty and the Lords of the Council, to approve and impose the Instruction formed by the Royal Academy of History, concerning the methods to collect and conserve the ancient monuments that were or will be discovered in the Reign

Year 1803. Madrid, Royal Printing House.
Don Carlos, by the grace of God, King of Castile, Leon, Aragon, the Two Sicilies, Jerusalem, Navarra, Granada, Toledo, Valencia, Galicia, Majorca, Minorca, Seville, Sardinia, Cordoba, Corsica, Murcia, Jaen, Algarve, Algeciras, Gibraltar, the Canary Islands, Oriental and Occidental India, the Islands and the Solid ground of the Ocean sea; Archduke of Austria; Duke of Bourgogne, Brabant and Milan; Count of Habsburg, Flanders, Tyrol and Barcelona; Lord of Biscay and Molina and Co.
To the people of my Council, the Presidents, Regents, and Auditors of my Audiences and Speeches, the Mayors and Clerks of my House and Court, and all the Chief Magistrates, Assistants, Superintendents, Governors, Main and Ordinary Judges, and any other Judge and Authority of this Reign, including those of the Manor houses, Abbeys and Orders, and all the other persons of any rank, status or condition, to whom the content of this Charter may concern in any way: Everyone MUST BE INFORMED that after entrusting the Royal Academy of History to find a solution to protect the Antiquities that are discovered in the Peninsula, against the ignorance of those who destroy them, causing detriment to the knowledge of history and the arts, [the Royal Academy] through my Prime Minister has elaborated a reasoned plan concerning the

procedures and the ways to be adopted to control and preserve the ancient monuments that are copiously buried in Spain. According to this plan, which I have approved, it is conferred to the mentioned Academy the general control on the antiquities discovered in the entire Reign. For its application, it is prescribed that all the people that have a recognised influence, authority and jurisdiction, Prelates, Councils of Canons, Chief Magistrates, shall give notice about the discoveries of antiquities of which they are aware, providing to their safeguards according to their faculties; with this goal in mind, I manifested to my Council my willingness to publish, by January 30th of next year, an order to the Prelates, Councils of Canons, and Chief Magistrates of the Reign, to impose them [these rules], so that they would contribute with their zeal to not to lose any monument whose conservation concerns public instruction, and the honor of the Nation. After my Council published this resolution, the order passed [to the Academy]; and according [to the Academy], as exposed by my Prosecutors in the consultation of March 26th, it would be proper, for the most thorough accomplishment of the proposed goals, to form [...] an instruction that, following the mentioned plan, will be printed and published by the Academy itself, as well as compile a Royal Charter, to resolve the difficulties or the inconveniences that could arise during the implementation of some of the Instruction's chapters, in particular those related to the instruments of specific archives, monuments, or memories. After confirming the procedures with my Council, we ordered the Academy to form the Instruction, which follows below.

Instruction formed after the order of his Majesty by the Academy of History on how to collect and preserve the ancient monuments that were or will be discovered in the Reign.

1. Ancient monuments are intended as statues, busts, bas-reliefs of any material, temples, sepulchers, theatres, amphitheaters, circuses, naumachiae, arenas, thermal baths, avenues, roads, aqueducts, gravestones or inscriptions, mosaics, coins of any class, cameos; pieces of architecture, milestones; musical instruments, such as sistrums, liras, castanets; sacred objects such as praefericulum, sìmpulum, lituus, knives for sacrifices, axes, aspersoriums, vases, tripods; weapons of any species, such as bows, arrows, lead bullets, shells, shields; civil [objects], such as weighing scales and their weights, roman scales, sundials or mechanical clocks, bracelets, collars, crowns, rings, seals; any kind of utensil, instrument of both liberal and mechanical arts; and finally any other thing, that is also still unknown, considered ancient, also Punic, Roman, Christian, and even Goths, Arabic, or Medieval [items].
2. All these monuments are to be considered property of those who discover them in their lands or houses or find them at their expense and work. Regarding the [monuments] found in a public or royal territory (His Majesty's property), it will be the responsibility of the Magistrates and the district's Authorities to collect and preserve them. Once [the monument] is under protection, the finder, owner or Authority will give detailed notice to the Royal Academy of History through its Secretary, so that [the Academy] can adopt the proper [solution], determining whether [the object] should be acquired, through purchase or reward, or obtained convening [a method] with the owner.
3. Everyone will cooperate to [the application of] these [rules] according to their function (as illustrious persons), Archbishops, Bishops, Abbots, Canons and also superior

Ecclesiastics, as well as Secular Magistrates, by investigating and acquiring information related to the discoveries, and by transferring them to the Academy, following the prescriptions of article 2.

4. The discoverers have the primary responsibility to take punctual note of the location of the finding so that the Academy can make a hypothesis and resolve [questions related to] the People, Colony or Town to which they might belong; they must take detailed note about how many leagues, miles, or steps there are from the renowned closer City, Village, Site, river, mount or valley, and about the cardinal directions, that is Levant, North, South or West.
5. If in any City or Town there are Antiquities as indicated in article 1, which were found in the past and still exist in the site, and which are in danger of being destroyed for carelessness or the injury of time, their owner or the Authority shall give notice as prescribed above, so that the Academy can take care of them, bringing advantages to our History, both secular and ecclesiastic.
6. The Academy will be grateful to the good patriots that contribute to the distinction of the homeland through the [activities] of searching, conserving, and recording the ancient monuments mentioned above; for this reason, [the Academy] will satisfy the owners of the findings as it is convenient, taking charge of the management [of the findings].
7. Generally, the Authorities of all the Towns have to make sure that no one would destroy or mistreat the monuments that are or will be discovered, since these are connected to the honor, antiquity, and reputation of the Town itself; they shall take all the solutions apt to make this happen. The same resolution applies to ancient buildings that exist both in some Towns and desert areas, to avoid that the materials [belonging to them] are either destroyed or removed; [the authorities] will make sure that these are conserved; and in the case that they are close to the ruination, they will send a notice to the Academy through its Secretary, so that it can undertake all the solutions necessary to its conservation.

I sent this Instruction to my Council, so that it could revise [and adjust it] to the effects that I had in mind; and after accomplishing this duty, in the presence of my three Fiscals, [the Council] agreed to submit me this Charter. With this intention, now I send to each of you and your respective places, districts, and jurisdictions the attached Instruction, asking you to observe and accomplish its prescriptions and make others observe, accomplish and execute them without allowing any sort of contravention. I entrust the Revered Archbishops, Bishops, Canons of the Metropolitan Church and Cathedral, its visitors' Vicars, and the Capitols with vacant sit, Canons of Collegiate Churches, Royal Chapels, Abbots and other Regular Ecclesiastics that practice jurisdiction, and Superiors or Prelates of the Regular Orders, and Military Orders, Parish Priests and other Ecclesiastic people, to observe the dispositions of my Charter, without consenting contraventions under any excuse; [this by] contributing with their illustrious zeal, as is convenient to the honor of the Nation, and the advancement of the public instruction, so that the mentioned Real Academy can accomplish the goals described in this Charter, using all the means, authority and respective faculties: this is my will; the [legal] copy of this Charter is undersigned by Don Bartolomé Muñoz de Torres, my Secretary, oldest Notary of the Chamber and the Rulers of my Council, who gives credit to the original copy.

Madrid, July 6th, 1803.
ME, THE KING.
Me, Don Juan Ignacio Ayestaran, Secretary of the King our Lord, put it into words under his mandate
Don Joseph Eustaquio Moreno
Don Bernardo Riega
Don Domingo Fernandez de Campomànes
Don Sebastian de Torres
Don Andres Lasauca
Registered, Don Joseph Alegre
Lieutenant of major Chancellor, Don Joseph Alegre
This is a certified copy of the original document.

12

The Kingdom of Naples

1
Bando da Parte di Sua Maestà, e del suo Tribunale della Regia Camera della Summaria.
Prammatica LVII

La Maestà del Re Nostro Signore si è degnata rimettere a questo Tribunale un suo Sovrano Dispaccio, spedito per Segreteria di Stato, d'Azienda, Guerra, Marina, e Commercio, in data 24 Luglio del corrente anno del tenor seguente, cioè:

Le Provincie, onde questo Regno di Napoli è composto, essendo nei tempi antichi abitate da' Greci, e da' Romani, che allettati dalla fertilità, ed amenità del suolo, e dell'aria ne fecero le loro maggiori delizie; hanno in ogni tempo somministrato in grandissima copia de' rari monumenti d'antichità agli uomini di quella studiosi, di statue, di tavole, di medaglie, di vasi, e d'istrumenti o per sacrificj, o per sepolcri, o per altri usi della vita, o di marmi, o di terra, o di metalli. Ma perchè niuna cura e diligenza è stata per l'addietro usata in raccoglierli, e custodirli, tutto ciò che di più pregevole è stato dissotterrato, s'è dal Regno estratto, onde il medesimo ne è ora assai povero, dove altri Stranieri de' lontani Paesi se ne sono arricchiti, e ne fanno i loro maggiori ornamenti, grandissimi profitti traendone, e per intelligenza dell'antichità, e per rischiaramento dell'Istoria, e della Cronologia, e per perfezione di molte Arti. Il Re Nostro Signore tutto ciò nella sua mente con rammarico rivolgendo, e considerando, che negli Stati più culti dell'Europa l'estrazione di sì fatte reliquie d'antichità, senza espressa licenza de' Sovrani è stata vietata, e la loro proibizione osservata esattamente; ha deliberato a si fatto male si ponghi una volta rimedio, acciò questo Regno non vada sempre più impoverendosi di ciò che abbonda, per farsene abbondanti l'altre Provincie di Europa, che ne sono povere da loro stesse. A questo effetto mi ha comandato, che in suo Real Nome ordini, come fo, al Tribunale della Regia Camera, che publichi Bando, che in ogni futuro tempo dovrà valere, così in questa Città, come per le Provincie, che nessuna persona di qualunque stato, grado, e condizione che sia, ardisca da ora in avanti estrarre, o fare estrarre o per mare, o per terra, dalle Provincie del Regno per Paesi esteri, qualunque monumento antico, cioè di statue, o grandi o piccole che sieno, di tavole, in cui caratteri sieno incisi, di medaglie, di vasi, d'istrumenti, ed ogni altra cosa antica, o sia di terra, o di marmo, o d'oro, o d'argento, o di bronzo, o d'ogni altro metallo, senza che preceda l'espressa licenza di S. M.; e ciò sotto la pena della perdita della roba che s'estrae, e di anni tre di galera per gl'Ignobili, e d'anni tre di relegazione per li Nobili,

e sotto la medesima proibizione d'estrazione, e pene, siano comprese le pitture antiche, o in tele, o in tavole, o di legno, o di rame, o d'argento, o tagliate da muri. Comanda altresì la M. S., che intorno alla maniera di procedere contra i Contravvegnenti, pruova del delitto, e quando il medesimo s'intenda consumato, dovranno avere luogo le precedenti Leggi, colle quali l'estrazione è stata proibita, dichiarando in oltre che si avrà per consumato il delitto per mare, non solo quando le robe suddette si troveranno già imbarcate, ma anche allorchè si saranno ritrovate vicino le marine, i luoghi d'imbarco, in atto che si trasportano per imbarcarsi; E per terra, allorchè l'Estraente sarà ritrovato vicino i confini, o avrà voltate le spalle alle Regie Casse, in cammini, ed in circostanze tali, per cui verisimilmente si debba credere che le robe erano per estraersi dal Regno. Ma come non intende S. M. che all'in tutto, e generalmente l'estrazione suddetta sia proibita, ma solo di quello che, o per eccellenza di lavoro, ed artificio, o per altra rarità merita esser tenuto in pregio; a quest'effetto comanda, che la Camera destini persona, o persone dotate non solo di bastante perizia in si fatte cose, ma anche d'integrità, e rettitudine, affinchè se taluno desiderasse licenza per l'estrazione d'alcune delle suddette reliquie d'antichità, o di pitture, possa farle riconoscere dalla Persona a ciò deputata; e quando ella giudichi non contenere pregio tale, onde meritino esser tenute care, e non dannoso estrarre, faccia certificato di potersene l'estrazione permettere, affinchè quello producendosi in questa Segreteria di Stato, d'Azienda, Guerra, Marina, e Commercio, se ne possa dalla M. S. concedere la licenza, senza della quale qualunque estrazione come criminosa sarà punita. Partecipo tutto ciò a V. S. Illustrissima per intelligenza della Regia Camera, affinchè la medesima ne faccia subito pubblicare il Bando corrispondente, ed invigili poi per l'esatta osservanza del medesimo, procedendo contro de' Tragressori all'esecuzione delle pene.
Napoli li 24 Luglio 1755.

El Marques de Squillaci

Quale preinserto Biglietto lettosi dall'infrascritto Signor Marchese D. Vincenzo Natoli Spettabile Consultore del Regno di Sicilia, Presidente Decano di detta Regia Camera, e Commissario, fu il medesimo rimesso all'Illustre Marchese Signor D. Carlo Mauri, Avvocato Fiscale del Regal Patrimonio, da chi in vista del medesimo preinserto Biglietto si fece la seguente istanza del tenore videlicet – Die 28 mensis Julii 1755. Fiscus instat exequi Regale Rescriptum, et emanati Bannum cum insertione ejusdem, salvis etc.

E prepostosi il tutto in questa medesima Regia Camera dal riferito Illustre Marchese Spettabile Consultore Signor D. Vincenzo Natoli Presidente Decano, e Commissario, ne fu dalla medesima a sua relazione con Decreto del suddetto dì 28 Luglio ordinato, di eseguirsi detti Regali ordini giusta l'istanza del Regio Fisco, e farsi Consulta a S. M. per la destinazione delle persone, a tenore dell'appuntamento d'essa Regia Camera, nel quale si stabilì rappresentarsi a S. M., che in esecuzione di questo Sovrano Dispaccio, stimava questo Tribunale, che per la ricognizione delle medaglie, statue, tavole, dove sieno incisi caratteri, vasi, istrumenti, e qualunque altro monumento di antichità, o sia di terra, o di marmo, o d'oro, o d'argento, o di bronzo, o di qualunque altro metallo, si destinasse il Reverendo D. Alessio Simmaco Mazzocchi Canonico della Cattedrale di questa Città, uomo dotato non solamente di somma perizia in sì fatte cose, ma anche di una gran probità,

ed onoratezza: Per la ricognizione poi delle Pitture antiche, o sieno in tele, o in tavole, o di legno, o di rame, o d'argento, o tagliate da muri, si destinasse il Magnifico D. Giuseppe Bonito Pittore di S. M., uomo perito assai in questa materia, ed altresì intero e probo, affinchè qualora la Maestà del Re Nostro Signore, si degnava approvare la destinazione di tali persone, s'avesse potuto poi da questa Regia Camera procedere all'emanazione del Bando, ed al di più che si conviene per esecuzione de' suddetti cennati Sovrani Ordini.
E fattasi da questa predetta Regia Camera la divisata Consulta alla prefata Maestà, si è degnata altresì, con Dispaccio spedito per detta Segreteria in data de' 27 Agosto corrente anno, approvare la destinazione proposta da questo Tribunale del suddetto Reverendo Canonico D. Alessio Simmaco Mazzocchi, e del suddetto Magnifico D. Giuseppe Bonito Pittore di Sua Maestà, ciascuno per riconoscere rispettivamente i generi di roba distinti nel citato appuntamento di questa Regia Camera, con che però la ricognizione delle statue debbasi incaricare, ed appoggiare al Magnifico D. Giuseppe Canart Statuario di S. M. uomo assai meritevole, così per la probità, come per l'espertezza grande in simili materie; e nell'istesso tempo si è benignata S. M. nuovamente incaricare a questa Regia Camera la pubblicazione del corrispondente Bando, a tenore dell'espressato Sovrano Dispaccio de' 24 Luglio di questo corrente anno.
Per tanto, affinchè questa Regal Determinazione di S. M. venga a notizia di tutti, nè si possa allegar causa d'ignoranza, col presente Bando da pubblicarsi nei luoghi soliti di questa Capitale, e Regno, s'ordina e comanda, che niuna Persona di qualunque grado, o condizione si sia, da oggi in avanti, dopo la pubblicazione del presente, ardisca di estrarre da qualsivoglia luogo di questa predetta Capitale, e Regno, ciascuno dei generi di sopra enunciati, senza espressa licenza di S. M., sotto la pena della perdita della roba, e di anni tre di galea per gl'Ignobili, e di relegazione per li Nobili, a rispetto di tutti gli enunciati generi de' monumenti d'antichità espressati in detto Regal Dispaccio.
Publicetis et referatis. Datum Neap. ex Regia Camera Summariae die 25 mensis Septembris 1755.

Balthaxar Citus M. C. L.
Vincentius Natoli – Natalis De Amato Mag. Ad.
Carolus Pagano Act.
Pubblicata a di 16 Ottobre 1755.

2
Bando da arte di Sua Maesta', e del suo Tribunale della Regia Camera della Summaria.
Prammatica LVIII

La Maestà del Re N. S. si è degnata rimettere a questo Tribunale un suo Sovrano Dispaccio, spedito per la Segreteria di Stato, di Azienda, Guerra, Commercio, e Marina, in data de' 24 Luglio del corrente anno, qual è del tenor seguente videlicet.
Con varie leggi in diversi tempi pubblicate, è stata proibita da questo Regno l'estrazione dell'oro, e dell'argento, cosi lavorato, come in verghe, o in massa, senza espressa licenza del Governo. Ultimamente la Maestà del Re N. S. ha voluto, che senza sua licenza fosse

anche proibita l'estrazione di tutte le Reliquie d'antichità, o di statue, o di medaglie, o d'istrumenti, o di vasi, o di tavole, in cui caratteri sieno incisi, o di pietra, o di terra, o di oro, o di argento, o di bronzo, o di altro metallo, ed anche di pitture antiche in tele, e tavole, di legno, di rame, o di argento, o tagliate da muri. Confermando la Maestà Sua la suddetta proibizione sotto le pene già dichiarate, e stabilite, Ordina ancora, che non si possano dal Regno estrarre, senza licenza della Regia Camera, pietre lavorate, e marmi di miniere del Regno; e che coloro, che ardissero contravvenire a questa proibizione, o estraendole, o facendole per altri estrarre, incorranno alla pena, e della perdita della roba, e di un anno di galea se Ignobili, e di un anno di relegazione, se Nobili. Dichiara altresì la Maestà Sua, che nel caso che taluno ottenesse espressa licenza per l'estrazione, non si possa, sotto le pene stabilite, la medesima eseguire, se non pagandosi prima un conveniente diritto di tratta, che si stabilisce nella maniera seguente. Per le pietre il tre per cento, secondo la stima, che dovrà farsene dalla Persona perita, che sarà destinata a questo effetto dal Tribunale della Camera. Per l'antichità, e pitture antiche, il sei per cento, anche secondo la stima da farsene dalle Persone perite, da destinarsi similmente dalla stessa Regia Camera. Per l'argento lavorato, o in verga, o in massa, carlini quindici ad oncia. Partecipo tutto ciò di Real ordine a V. S. Illustrissima per intelligenza del Tribunale della Regia Camera, ed affinchè la medesima ne faccia pubblicar Bando, da valere in ogni futuro tempo, cosi in questa città, come nelle Provincie del Regno, ed invigili all'osservanza, procedendo all'esecuzione delle pene contro i trasgressori.
Palazzo li 24 Luglio 1755 – El Marques de Squillaci.

Signor Marchese Cito – Die 28 mensis Julii 1755. Domino Natoli - Citus M. C. L.

Quale preinserto Biglietto lettosi dall'infrascritto Illustre Signor Marchese D. Vincenzo Natoli Spettabile Consultore del Regno di Sicilia, Presidente Decano di detta Real Camera, e Commissario, fu quello rimesso all'Illustre Marchese, Signor D. Carlo Mauri Avvocato Fiscale del Real Patrimonio, da chi in vista del medesimo si fece la seguente istanza del tenor videlicet. Die 28 Julii 1755. Fiscus instat emanati banna cum insertione Regalis ordinis; salvis etc.
E propostosi il tutto in questa medesima Regia Camera dal riferito Illustre Marchese Spettabile Consultore Signor D. Vincenzo Natoli Presidente Decano Commissario, ne fu dalla stessa a sua relazione sotto il suddetto di 28 Luglio ordinato decreto, di eseguirsi detto Real ordine, giusta l'Istanza del Regio Fisco, e farsi Consulta a S. M. per la destinazione delle Persone, a tenore dell'appuntamento di essa Regia Camera; col quale si stabilì rappresentarsi a S. M., che in esecuzione di questo Sovrano Dispaccio stimava il Tribunale, che per la ricognizione, e stima delle medaglie, statue, tavole, ove sieno incisi caratteri, vasi, istrumenti, e qualunque altro monumento d'antichità, o sia di terra, o sia di marmo, o d'oro, o di argento, o di bronzo, o di qualunque altro metallo, si destinasse il Rev. D. Alessio Simmaco Mazzocchi Canonico della Cattedrale di questa Città, uomo dotato non solamente di somma perizia in si fatte cose, ma anche di una gran probità, ed onoratezza: Per la ricognizione poi, e stima delle pitture antiche, o sieno in tela, o in tavole, o di legno, o di rame, o d'argento, o tagliate da' muri, si destinasse il Magnifico D. Giuseppe Bonito Pittore di S. M., uomo perito assai in questa materia, ed altresì intero, e probo: E finalmente per la ricognizione, e stima de' marmi, e pietre lavorate, delle miniere di questo Regno, si destinasse il Magnifico D. Giuseppe Canart Ingegnere, e Statuario di S. M.,

uomo meritevole per la probità, ed espertezza di simili materie, affinchè qualora la Maestà del Re N. S. degnata si fosse di approvare la destinazione di tali persone, si fosse potuto poi da questa predetta Regia Camera procedere all'emanazione del Bando, ed al di più, che conveniva per esecuzione del cennato Sovrano Ordine. E fattasi da questa predetta Regia Camera la divisata Consulta alla prefata Maestà, si è degnata altresì per detta Segreteria, inviare il seguente altro Dispaccio del tenor videlicet.

«El Re se hà dignado aprobar la destinacion, que la Camera ha propuesto en Consulta de 19 del corriente, de D. Alexo Simmaco Mazzocchi Canonigo de la Cathedral de esta Ciudad; D. Joseph Bonito Pintor de Camera de S. M., y D. Joseph Carnat sù Estatuario, para reconocer, y opinar Medallas, Estatuas, y toda suerte de antiquidad, de Pintura, Escoltura, y Arquitectura; corno tambien Marmoles, y Piedras labradas de las Minas de este Reyno, antes de acordarse el Real Permiso para extracion, con que però se ne encargue al mencionado Canart el reconocimiento de Estatuas; y en sù conseguencia me manda decir a V. S., que con la Camera haga publicar el correspondiente Bando de prohibicion, à tenor de lo resuelto por S. M. en 24 de Julio proximo passado; Dios guarde à V. S. muchos anos corno desseo.
Palacio à 27 de Agosto de 1755.
El Marques de Squillaci – Senor Marques Cito».

Per tanto, affinchè questa Real Determinazione di S. M. venga a notizia di tutti, nè si possa allegare causa d'ignoranza, col presente Bando da pubblicarsi ne' luoghi soliti di questa Capitale, e Regno; si ordina, e comanda, che niuna persona di qualunque grado, o condizione si sia, da oggi in avanti, dopo la pubblicazione del presente, ardisca di estrarre da qualsivoglia luogo di questa predetta Capitale, e Regno, Reliquie di antichità, come sono statue, medaglie, istrumenti, vasi, tavole di quali si sieno caratteri, sieno incise, o di pietra, o di terra, o di oro, o di argento, o di bronzo, o di qualunque metallo; pitture antiche in tele, tavole di legno, rame, o in argento, o tagliate da' muri, senza espressa licenza di S. M., sotto la pena della perdita della roba, e di tre anni di galea per gl'Ignobili, e di relegazione per li Nobili, siccome fu già dichiarato, e stabilito con altro Bando emanato, in vigore di altro Dispaccio, per gli espressati generi d'antichità; E parimente, che nessuno ardisca estrarre da qualunque luogo di questa Capitale, e Regno, pietre lavorate, e marmi delle miniere di questo Regno, oro, ed argento, cosi lavorato, come in verghe, o in massa, sotto pena della perdita della roba, e di un anno di galea per gl'ignobili, e di relegazione a' Nobili; Ed ottenendo la divisata licenza, debba sotto le pene stabilite, pagare i diritti prescritti, e contenuti nel preinserto Real Dispaccio, a tenore della ricognizione, e stima che se ne faranno da' prenominati rispettivi periti destinati per detti generi, che occorreranno estraersi.
Pub. et Ref. etc. Datum Neapoli ex Regia Camera Summariae.
Die 25 mensis Septemb. 1755.

Balthaxar Citus M. C. L.
Vincentius Natoli – Natalis De Amato Mag. Act.
Carolus Pagano Act.
Pubblicata a dì 16 Ottobre 1755.

3
Bando da parte di Sua Maestà, e del suo Tribunale della Regia Camera della Summaria.
Prammatica LIX

Fin dal di 16 Ottobre dell'anno 1755 in esecuzione di Real ordine di Sua Maestà Cattolica (Dio guardi), allora felicemente Regnante in questi Regni, fu nelle dovute forme pubblicato Bando del tenore seguente videlicet.

La Maestà del Re nostro Signor si è degnata rimettere a questo Tribunale suo Sovrano Dispaccio etc. (come nel n. prec.).

Al presente si è compiaciuto S. M. (Dio guardi) rimettere a questo suddetto Tribunale della Regia Camera altro suo venerato Dispaccio, spedito per la Segreteria di Stato della Casa Reale, ed affari Esteri in data del dì 2 del corrente mese di Agosto, qual è del tenor seguente: «Vuole il Re, che cotesta Camera disponga la rinnovazione del Bando pubblicato a' 16 Ottobre 1755, relativo all'estrazioni delle antichità da questa fedelissima Città, e Regno, con pubblicarsi anche per le strade degli Orefici, e comprendersi altresì i Mezzani, che s'intrigano in simili negozi, e sotto le pene contenute nel Bando; alle quali per li Forestieri si aggiunga lo sfratto dal Regno; con ordinarsi di più alle Dogane, e Sbarre de' confini del Regno, d'impedire l'estrazione fuora del medesimo, con invigilare all'esito della roba, anche per l'esazione de' diritti stabiliti, e contenuti nell'altro Bando sotto l'istesso dì, ed anno, in caso che la estrazione siegua con Real permesso. Lo partecipo di Real ordine a V. S. per l'adempimento. Palazzo 2 Agosto 1766. Bernardo Tanucci.

Signor Marchese Cavalcanti. Die 10 Augusti 1766. Exequatur, et Registretur».

Per tanto affinchè così l'espressato Bando pubblicato a' 16 Ottobre 1755, come la riferita altra nuova Reale Determinazione contenuta nel soprascritto Dispaccio de' 2 Agosto corrente mese ed anno, sieno da tutti esattamente adempiuti, ed eseguiti, giusta la di loro serie, contenenza, e tenore, nè si possa da chicchessia allegare causa d'ignoranza, si ordina, e comanda col presente Bando, da pubblicarsi nei luoghi soliti di questa Capitale, e Regno, ed anche per le strade degli Orefici, che con effetto nessuna persona, di qualunque grado, e condizione si sia, niuno affatto eccettuato, ardisca di estrarre, o di fare estrarre da qualsivoglia luogo di questa Capitale, e Regno, reliquie d'antichità, come sono statue, medaglie, istrumenti, vasi, e nè anche tavole incise di quali si vogliano caratteri, o che sieno le sopraddette reliquie di antichità di pietra, o di terra, o di oro, o di argento, o di bronzo, o di qualunque metallo; E che parimente nessuno ardisca di estrarre, o fare estrarre da qualunque luogo di questa Capitale, e Regno, pitture antiche in tele, tavole di legno, rame, oro, od argento, o tagliate da' muri, senza l'espressa licenza di S. M., sotto la pena della perdita della roba, e di tre anni di galea per gl'Ignobili, e di tre anni di relegazione per li Nobili, a tenore del soprainserto Bando pubblicato a' 16 Ottobre 1755. E parimente si ordina, e comanda, che nessuna persona di qualsivoglia grado, e condizione, ardisca di estrarre, o far estrarre da qualunque luogo di questa Capitale, e Regno, pietre lavorate, e marmi delle miniere di questo Regno, oro, ed argento, così lavorato, come in verga, o in massa, sotto la pena della perdita della roba, di un anno di galea per gl'ignobili, e di relegazione per li Nobili, e qualora poi taluno per l'espressate estrazioni otterrà la licenza Reale, debba sotto le stesse stabilite pene pagare i diritti prescritti nel sopradetto Bando

pubblicato a' 16 Ottobre 1755, a tenore della ricognizione, e stima che da' sopra riferiti Periti destinati si farà de' generi, che occorrerà di estraersi. Di più si ordina, e comanda, che alle sopraccitate rispettive stabilite pene debbano in caso di contravvenzione soggiacere, non solamente coloro, che estrarranno, o faranno estrarre da qualunque luogo di questa Capitale, e Regno i sopraddescritti generi vietati, senza l'espressa Reale licenza, e senza pagare i dovuti stabiliti diritti, ma altresì debbono soggiacere alle stesse pene anche i Mezzani, che s'intrigano in simili negozi; E qualora i contravvegnenti fossero forestieri, in tal caso oltra le suddette pene, debba aggiungersi contra di essi anche lo sfratto da questo Regno. E finalmente si ordina, e comanda agli Officiali delle Regie Dogane, e Sbarre de' confini di questo Regno, che invigilino con tutta la maggiore attenzione nelle robe, che si estraggono per fuora, affinchè così s'impedisca l'estrazione de' soprannominati generi senza l'espressa licenza del Re nostro Signore, e qualora vi fosse il Real permesso, in tal caso poi si esigano i rispettivi diritti stabiliti, e contenuti nel soprainserto Bando pubblicato a' 16 Ottobre 1755 – Publicetis, et referatis.
Datum Neapoli ex Regia Camera Summariae die 14 mensis Augusti 1766.

Angelus Cavalcanti M. C. L.
Dominicus Cardillo, Laurentius Paternò, Petrus Maria Savisetti, Caesar Coppola, Dominicus Figliola, Joannes Celentano, Joannes Ferrari, Januarius De Ferdinando, Ferdinandus Genise, Bernardinus Bolza, Nicolaus De Crescentio, Petrus Lignola.
Vidit P. R. C. – Joseph Caravita Realis Patr. Fisci Patronus
Vidit P. R. C. – Thomas Varano Realis Patrim. Fisci Patronus
Cons. Thomas Abbamonte – Secr. Per S. M. Regiae Camerae

Pubblicata a dì 9 Settembre 1766.

4
Bando da parte di Sua Maestà, e del suo Tribunale della Regia Camera della Summaria.
Prammatica LX

Fin dal dì 25 Settembre dell'anno 1755, d'ordine della Maestà del Re Cattolico, che allora felicemente regnava in questo Regno, fu emanato Bando del tenor seguente cioè:
Carolus Dei gratia Rex utriusque Siciliae, Hierusalem, lnfans Hispaniarum, Dux Parmae, Placentiae, Castri, et Magnus Princeps Hereditarius Hetruriae.
Bando da parte della prefata Maestà, e del suo Tribunale della Regia Camera della Summaria.
La Maestà del Re N. S. si è degnata rimettere a questo Tribunale un suo Sovrano Dispaccio etc. (come nel n. 2).
Ma poichè non ostante il cennato Bando fin dal detto tempo emanato, e pubblicato nelle dovute forme, pure si è preinteso, che da taluni sotto pretesto d'ignoranza siasi contravvenuto a quanto nel medesimo fu prescritto, ed ordinato. Perciò la Maestà del Re Nostro Signore (Dio guardi) si è degnata rimetterci un Dispaccio spedito per Segreteria di Stato, Casa Reale, ed Affari Esteri, in data degli 11 Marzo corrente anno 1769, il quale è del tenor che segue cioè:

«Aviendose enterado el Rey per papel de V.S. de' 8 del corriente de las escusas aduzidas por el Conte Gaetani de la venta de quadros antiquos a Forasteres, de ignorar la ley de no extraherse ni Pintura, ni Escultura antiqua sin expresso Real Permiso de S. M., ha resuelto S. M. y manda que V. S. haga publicar, y fixar en todas las partes de esta Capitai donde convenga un Edicto, en que se prohiba absolutamente a todos, y qualesquiera persona la extracion del Reyno, de toda suerte de Pinturas, Estatuas, y otras alhajas antiquas sin la circunstancia de aver implorado antes, obtenido el Real Permiso de S. M. vajo las penas à los Controventores de la confiscation de la cosa y del duplo. Dios etc.
Caserta 11 Marzo 1769 Bernardo Tanucci – Senor Marques Cavalcanti».

Per tanto affinchè una tale Sovrana Determinazione venga a notizia di tutti, nè si possa più allegare causa d'ignoranza, col presente Bando da pubblicarsi ne' luoghi soliti di questa Città, si ordina, e comanda, che senza pregiudizio delle pene incorse da coloro, che hanno finora contravvenuto all'accennato Bando, da ora in poi niuna persona di qualunque grado, o condizione si sia, ardisca di estrarre da qualsivoglia luogo di questa predetta Capitale, e Regno, Reliquie di antichità, come sono statue, medaglie, istrumenti, vasi, tavole di quali si vogliano caratteri, sieno incise, o di pietra, o di terra, o di oro, o di argento, o di bronzo, o di qualunque metallo, pitture antiche in tele, tavole di legno, rame, o in argento, o tagliato da' muri, o qualunque altra specie di galanterie antiche, senza espressa licenza di S. M.; e ciò sotto le pene contenute tanto nel soprainserto Bando de' 25 Settembre 1755, quanto nel citato ultimo inserito Reale Dispaccio degli 11 Marzo corrente anno 1769. E parimente si ordina, che nessuno ardisca estrarre da qualunque luogo di questa Capitale, e Regno, pietre lavorate, e marmi delle miniere di questo Regno, oro ed argento, così lavorato, come in verghe, o in masse, senza l'espressa Sovrana licenza, sotto le sopraddette pene contenute nel soprainserto Bando, ed ultimo Reale Dispaccio; ed ottenendo poi taluno la divisata licenza, debba sotto le stesse suddette pene pagare i diritti stabiliti, e prescritti nell'inserto Bando de' 25 Settembre 1755, a tenore della ricognizione, e stima, che se ne dovrà fare da' Periti destinati per la ricognizione di detti generi estraendi, nella maniera prescritta in detto Bando de' 25 Settembre 1755, etc.
Pub. et Ref. etc. – Datum Neapoli ex Regia Camera die 17 mensis Martii 1769.

D. Angelus Cavalcanti M. C. L.
D. Dominicus Cardillo, D. Januarius De Ferdinando, D. Joannes D'alessandro, D. Caesar Coppola, D. Joannes Celentano, D. Andreas Ruoti, D. Laurentius Paternò, D. Petrus Maria Sanvinsenti, D. Ferdinandus Genise, D. Dominicus Figliola, D. Petrus Lignola, D. Joannes Bruno.
Vidit P. R. C. D. Joannes Ferraro, Regal. Patr. Fisci Patronus
Vidit P. R. C. D. Joseph Caravita, Regal. Patr. Fisci Patronus
Cons. U. J. D. D. Thomas Abbamonte a Secr. per S. M. In Regia Camera
Joseph Corracchioli Act.

Pubblicata a dì 4 Aprile 1769.

5

Bando che nel Real nome, e di R. ordine si promulga dall'Ill. Cav. Don Gio. Franc. Paternò Castello dei Principi Biscari, Reg. Custode delle Antichità delle Valli Demone e Noto

Stando a cuore di S. M. (D. G.) la conservazione delle Antichità, che si ritrovano nella Città di Catania, con suo R. Dispaccio de' 7 Febbraro 1802, per via della Real Segreteria dell'Ecclesiastico, Annona, ed alla Polizia è venuta in prescrivere la formazione del presente Editto, in forza del quale si proibisce di fare Scavi, o piantar fondamenta di Fabbriche, senza il precedente permesso del Cav.re Don Gio. Francesco Paternò Castello di Catania, Regio Custode delle Antichità delle Valli Demone e Noto, senza alcun pagamento per tale permesso. E ciò sotto la pena di Onze 20, e di un anno di carcere tanto a' Proprietari degli Edifici, quanto agli Architetti in ogni controvenzione, secondo è stato prescritto da S. E. Ema Signor Presidente del Regno con dispaccio dei 22 Settembre 1802, comunicato per via della Regale Segreteria di Stato, e Guerra, a detto Cavaliere di Paternò Castello Regio Custode.

In Catania oggi che corrono li ... Ottobre 1802.

1

Notice from His Majesty and the Royal Court of Audit. Pragmatic Sanction LVII

On behalf of His Majesty the King, the Secretariat of the State, Enterprise, War, Navy, and Commerce has notified this Court of the following Royal Directive on July 24th of the current year.

In the olden times, the Provinces of the Kingdom of Naples were inhabited by Greeks and Romans drawn here by the fertile soil and pleasant air. Through the centuries, these peoples left our scholars a remarkable number of rare antiquities such as monuments, statues, tablets, medallions, vases, sacrificial and funerary utensils, and daily tools for carving marble, plowing the land, and forging metals.

However, our carelessness eventually led to the reckless export of the Kingdom's finest discoveries towards Foreign Countries that are long-sighted enough to treat them as their greatest ornamentations and make a massive profit out of them, also in terms of Historical Understanding, insight into the ancient past, and Artistic Refinement.

With all this in mind, and regretfully considering how the most cultivated European States have long since enforced strict bans on the unlicensed export of antiquities;

His Lordship the King decrees that action be taken to prevent any further impoverishment of our prosperous Kingdom in favor of other European Countries with little or no heritage. For this purpose, He has commanded that I, on His Behalf, order the Royal Chamber's Tribunal to publish the following Notice.

Henceforth, the permission to export antiquities such as statues — both small and big – tablets bearing inscriptions, medallions, vases, tools, and any other ancient item made of

clay, marble, gold, silver, bronze – or any other metal – is restricted to the persons issued with His Majesty's license.
The ban applies to all the City and Provinces' subjects – regardless of their status, grade, and social condition. Furthermore, it refers, without distinction, to shipments made by land and sea, both within the Kingdom and to other Countries.
All offenses will be punished by the confiscation of the goods. The Commoners will serve three years on the galleys, whereas the Noblemen will be sentenced to three years of confinement.
Said prohibitions and penalties also extend to the unlicensed export of ancient paintings – canvases, panels in wood, copper, and silver, frescoes cut from walls.
Moreover, His Majesty commands that crime detection, prosecution of the Offenders, and collection of evidence be carried out pursuant to the existing Laws on export control. The detection of offenses by sea applies not only to cargo that is shipped or in the process of being embarked but also to goods found in the vicinity of marinas and docks. Conversely, the detection of offenses by land is valid when the Exporter is located near the state's borders, unprovided with a permit from the Royal Treasury, or found on paths and in circumstances deemed suspicious.
However, His Majesty does not intend to prohibit all exports indistinctly: the ban is exclusively aimed at protecting those works of rarity, inventiveness, and excellence, which deserve the highest esteem.
For this purpose, He commands that the Court appoint one or more experienced appraisers – who can also be relied upon for their integrity and rectitude – to assess future applications for the export of antiquities and paintings. Accordingly, the relics recommended for a permit will be those that the appraiser deems of lesser value in that their export would not do any harm.
The Secretariat of the State, Enterprise, War, Navy, and Commerce must, hereby, produce the related certification in order for His Majesty to issue the license required by law. All unlawful exports will be sanctioned.
I herewith inform Your Most Illustrious Lordship so that You may direct the Royal Court to issue a relevant Notice, oversee its enforcement, and prosecute any Offenders pursuant to the existing penalties.
Naples, July 24th, 1755.

The Marquis of Squillace

The attached Order was notified to the Court by Marquis Sir Don Vincenzo Natoli – Esteemed Consultant of the Kingdom of Sicily, Presiding Dean of said Royal Court, and Commissary – and subsequently forwarded to the Illustrious Marquis, Sir Don Carlo Mauri – Tax Advocate of the Royal Treasure – by those who drafted the following motion; On July 28th, 1755, the Treasury pledged to enact the Royal Decree and issue a public Notice pursuantly, without prejudice etc.

On the same date, this Royal Court – in keeping with what the Esteemed Consultant, Presiding Dean, and Commissary, Sir Don Vincenzo Natoli reported – decreed that the

Royal Orders be enforced pursuant to the Royal Treasury's motion and offered His Majesty a Consultation on the appointment of a team of appraisers.
Consequently, the Royal Court suggested the designation of Reverend Don Alessio Simmaco Mazzocchi – Canon of this City's Cathedral – for the evaluation of medallions, statues, panels bearing inscriptions, vases, tools, and any other ancient relic made of clay, marble, gold, silver, bronze, or any other metal. The Reverend is, in fact, a decent and honorable man, as well as an expert in his field.
In regard to the evaluation of the ancient Paintings – canvases, panels in wood, copper, or silver, and frescoes cut from walls– the Royal Court advised appointing His Majesty's Painter, the Magnificent Don Giuseppe Bonito, as he is a gentleman of complete integrity who is very knowledgeable in this field.
Upon His Majesty's approval – and pursuant to the Dispatch forwarded by said Secretariat on August 27th of the current year – the Royal Court will publish a Notice and oversee the enforcement of said Royal Orders. Following the Consultation, said Reverend Canon Don Alessio Simmaco Mazzocchi, and said Magnificent Don Giuseppe Bonito – Painter of His Majesty – have been appointed appraisers in their respective fields of expertise.
However, the evaluation of statues will hereby fall upon the Magnificent Don Giuseppe Canart – Sculptor of His Majesty – who is a man of honesty and great experience in this field.
Hereupon, His Majesty has again instructed this Court to issue a Notice, pursuant to the Royal Dispatch dated July 24th of the current year, to make this Royal Decree known to all and ensure that no person will claim their ignorance of the law. Therefore, the Notice will be posted in all of the usual locations of the Capital and Kingdom.
Hereby, the export of the aforementioned items outside the Capital and Kingdom is restricted to Persons with a license issued by His Majesty, regardless of grade and social condition.
All offenses will be punished by the confiscation of the antiquities listed in said Royal Decree. The Commoners will serve three years on the galleys, whereas the Noblemen will be sentenced to confinement.
To be published and proclaimed. Issued in Naples by the Royal Court of Audit on September 25th, 1755.

Deputy Consulting Magistrate Baldassarre Cito
Consulting Magistrate Vincenzo Natoli, of Amato
Treasurer Carlo Pagano
Published on October 16th, 1755.

2
Notice from His Majesty and the Royal Court of Audit. Pragmatic Sanction LVIII

On behalf of His Majesty the King, the Secretariat of the State, Enterprise, War, Navy, and Commerce has notified this Court of the following Royal Directive on July 24th of the current year.

In this Kingdom, several laws from different ages have restricted the export of gold and silver – either embossed, as ingots, or nuggets – exclusively to the persons issued with a Government license.
His Majesty the King had recently ordered to further restrict all export of ancient Relics, statues, medallions, tools, vases, tablets bearing inscriptions – made of either stone, clay, gold, silver, bronze, or any other metal – to persons licensed by the Court. Said restriction also applies to ancient paintings on canvas, panels in wood, copper, silver, and frescoes cut from walls.
Hereby, His Majesty upholds said prohibitions – under the pains notified and established previously – and orders that the export of carved gems and marble from the quarries of the Kingdom be restricted to the persons issued with a Royal Court license.
All offenders – either direct or by proxy – will be punished by the confiscation of the goods. The Commoners will serve one year on the galleys and the Noblemen one year of confinement.
Furthermore, His Majesty declares that, under the pains established by law, all licensed exports be subject to the following customs duties, to be calculated on the value estimated by the expert Appraisers appointed by the court: three percent on stone and six percent on antiquities and ancient paintings. Both types of revenue will be allocated to the Royal Court of Audit.
The customs duties imposed on embossed silver, silver ingots, and nuggets will amount to fifteen Neapolitan Carlini an ounce.
I hereby notify Your Most Illustrious Lordship and the Royal Court of Audit so that it may publish a Notice applicable henceforth to the City and Provinces of the Kingdom. The Court will also enforce the law and its penalties pursuantly.
Issued at the Palace on July 24th, 1755 – The Marquis of Squillace.

To His Lordship Natoli, Deputy Consulting Magistrate Sir Marquis Cito – July 28th, 1755.

The attached Order was notified to the Court by Marquis Sir Don Vincenzo Natoli – Esteemed Consultant of the Kingdom of Sicily, Presiding Dean of said Royal Court, and Commissary – and, subsequently, forwarded to the Illustrious Marquis, Sir Don Carlo Mauri – Tax Advocate of the Royal Treasure – by those who drafted the following motion. On July 28th, 1755, the Treasury pledged to publish the Notices and attached Royal Orders, without prejudice etc.
On the same date, this Royal Court – in keeping with what the Esteemed Consultant, Presiding Dean, and Commissary, Sir Don Vincenzo Natoli reported – decreed that the Royal Orders be enforced pursuant to the Royal Treasury's motion and offered His Majesty a Consultation on the appointment of a team of Appraisers.
Consequently, the Royal Court suggested the designation of Reverend Don Alessio Simmaco Mazzocchi – Canon of this City's Cathedral – for the evaluation and estimate of medallions, statues, panels bearing inscriptions, vases, and tools, and any other ancient relic made of clay, marble, gold, silver, bronze, or any other metal. The Reverend is, in fact, a decent and honorable man and an expert in his field.
In regard to the evaluation and estimate of the ancient Paintings – canvases, panels in wood, copper, or silver, and frescoes cut from walls – the Royal Court advised appointing

His Majesty's Painter, the Magnificent Don Giuseppe Bonito, as he is a gentleman of complete integrity who is very knowledgeable in this field.
Finally, the evaluation of marbles and carved stones from the state's quarries will fall upon the Magnificent Don Giuseppe Canart – Engineer and Sculptor of His Majesty – who is a man of honesty and vast experience in this field.
Upon His Majesty's approval, the Royal Court will publish, as planned, a Notice and oversee the enforcement of said Royal Orders. Therefore, said Secretariat will also forward the following Dispatch pursuantly.

«After the Consultation of October 19th, the King ratifies the Court's appointment of Don Alessio Simmaco Mazzocchi – Canon of the City's Cathedral, Don Giuseppe Bonito – Painter of His Majesty's Court, and Don Giuseppe Canart – Sculptor, as appraisers and assessors of Medallions, Statues, and any type of antiquity, Painting, Sculpture, and Structure. The appointed appraisers will also evaluate all the Marble and Carved Stones extracted from the Kingdom's quarries prior to a Royal License issuance. Hereby, Canart is specifically assigned to the appraisal of Statues.
Furthermore, the King wishes that You and the Court publish a Notice of prohibition pursuant to His Majesty's resolution dated July 24th. May God grant you many long years of prosperity.
Issued at the Palace on August 27th, 1755.
The Marquis of Squillace – Sir Marquis Cito».

Therefore, to make this Royal Decree known to all and ensure that no person will claim ignorance of the law, the Notice will be posted in the Capital and Kingdom's usual locations. Henceforth, the export outside the Capital and Kingdom of ancient Relics is restricted to the persons issued with a license from His Majesty, regardless of grade and social condition. Said Relics include statues, medallions, tools, vases, tablets bearing inscriptions or carvings – either made of stone, clay, gold, silver, bronze, or any other metal – ancient paintings on canvas, or panels made of wood, copper, silver, or frescoes cut from walls.
All offenses will be punished by the confiscation of the antiquities listed. The Commoners will serve three years on the galleys, whereas the Noblemen will be sentenced to confinement, as stated in the previous Notice and Dispatch.
Further restrictions apply to the export from any location within this Capital and Kingdom of carved stone and marble mined in the Kingdom's quarries, and gold or silver either embossed, as ingots, or nuggets.
All offenses will be punished by the confiscation of the goods. The Commoners will serve one year on the galleys, whereas the Noblemen will be sentenced to confinement.
Upon the issuance of a license of export, and under the aforementioned pains, the holder must pay the duties stated in the attached Royal Dispatch pursuant to the appraisal and assessment carried out by said experts on the listed goods in question.
To be published and proclaimed etc. Issued in Naples by the Royal Court of Audit on September 25th, 1755.

Deputy Consulting Magistrate Baldassarre Cito
Consulting Magistrate Vincenzo Natoli, of Amato

Treasurer Carlo Pagano
Published on October 16th, 1755.

3
Notice from His Majesty and the Royal Court of Audit. Pragmatic Sanction LIX

The following Notice has been duly posted ever since October 16th, 1755, pursuant to the Royal Order of His Catholic Majesty – God bless – who at the time reigned graciously over our Kingdom.
His Majesty – God bless – hereby notifies the Court of both the precedent and the current Royal Dispatches forwarded by the Royal Secretariat of the Royal House and Foreign Affairs on August 2nd of the current year.
«The King commands that the Court renew the Notice published on October 16th, 1755, regarding the export of relics from this loyal City and Kingdom. He also orders that it be posted in the districts of the Jewelers and Intermediaries involved in this business, under the pains contained in the Notice combined with deportation in the case of Foreigners.
Furthermore, the Customs and Border Offices of the Kingdom must prevent the illegal export of antiquities, monitor the transit of goods, and collect the duties set on licensed cargo by the previous Notice.
I hereby inform You Lordship and prompt you to enforce this Royal Order. The Palace, August 2nd, 1766. Bernardo Tanucci.
Sir Marquis Cavalcanti. August 10th, 1766. Enforced and Registered».

Therefore, the following measure is authorised pursuant to the Notice published on October 16th, 1755, and the Royal Decree in the Dispatch of August 2nd of the current year, in compliance with their content and tenor, so that they be enforced precisely, and no one may claim their ignorance.
The present Notice must be posted in the Capital and Kingdom's usual locations, as well as in the districts of the Jewelers.
Henceforth, all persons without exception, regardless of their grade and social condition, are banned from exporting outside this Capital and Kingdom – both directly and by proxy – relics such as statues, medallions, tools, vases, and tablets bearing any kind of script, made of either stone, clay, gold, silver, bronze, or any other metal.
Furthermore, the export – both direct and by proxy – outside this Capital and Kingdom of ancient paintings on canvases and panels in wood, copper, and silver, or frescoes cut from walls, is restricted to the persons licensed by His Majesty. All offenders will be punished by the confiscation of the goods. The Commoners will serve three years on the galleys and the Noblemen one year of confinement, pursuant to the Notice published on October 16th, 1755.
Moreover, all persons without exception, regardless of their grade and social condition, are banned from exporting outside this Capital and Kingdom – both directly and by proxy – carved stones and marble from this Kingdom's quarries. Said restriction also applies to gold and silver, either embossed, as ingots, or nuggets. All offenders will be punished by

the confiscation of the goods. The Commoners will serve one year on the galleys and the Noblemen one year of confinement.

Conversely, upon the issuance of a Royal license of export, the holder must pay the duties mentioned in the Notice published on October 16th, 1755, pursuant to the aforementioned Experts' appraisal and assessment on the listed goods in question.

All the respective penalties mentioned above refer to offenders exporting the items listed outside the Capital and Kingdom either directly or by proxy and to the holders of licenses who do not pay the established duties. The same penalties are applicable to any Intermediaries involved, while in the case of foreigners, deportation outside the Kingdom will also be enforced.

Finally, the Royal Customs and Border Offices' Officers must monitor the transit of all goods attentively to prevent the unlicensed export of the items mentioned above. In the case of holders of Royal Permits, the Officers must collect the duties mentioned in the attached Notice published on October 16th, 1755.

To be published and proclaimed. Issued in Naples by the Royal Court of Audit on August 14th, 1766.

Deputy Consulting Magistrate Angelo Cavalcanti,

Domenico Cardillo, Lorenzo Paternò, Pietro Maria Savisetti, Cesare Coppola, Domenico Figliola, Giovanni Celentano, Giovanni Ferrari, Gennaro di Ferdinando, Ferdinando Genise, Bernardino Bolza, Nicola de Crescenzo, Pietro Lignola.

Notified to Giuseppe Caravita – Patron of the Royal Court, Patron of the Royal Treasury

Notified to Tommaso Varano – Patron of the Royal Court, Patron of the Royal Treasury

Sealed by Tommaso Abbamonte – Secretary of His Majesty's Royal Court

Published on September 9th, 1766.

4
Notice from His Majesty and the Royal Court of Audit. Pragmatic Sanction LX

The following Notice was issued on September 25th, 1755, by order of His Catholic Majesty the King, who at the time reigned graciously over our Kingdom.

Charles, King by God's grace of the Two Sicilies and Jerusalem, Infante of Spain, Duke of Parma, Piacenza, and Castro, Great Hereditary Prince of Tuscany. Notice issued by His Majesty and his Royal Court of Audit.

Our Lordship, His Majesty, has forwarded his Royal Dispatch this Court etc. (as in number 2).

Despite the issuance and due publication of said Notice, there have been reports of offenders claiming ignorance of its directives. Consequently, on behalf of His Majesty – God bless – the Royal Secretariat of State, Royal House, and Foreign Affairs forwarded the following Dispatch on March 11th, 1769.

«Having been informed by Your letter, dated the 8th of the current month, of the excuses put forward by Count Gaetani on the sale of ancient paintings to some Foreigners;
And acknowledging that the Count claims his ignorance of the ban imposed on the unlicensed export of ancient Paintings and Sculptures;
Therefore, His Majesty orders that You publish a Notice in all of the Kingdom's venues, forbidding all persons from exporting all types of Paintings, Statues, and other ancient relics, without a license issued by His Majesty himself. All offenders will be punished by the confiscation of the goods and a fine of twice the items' value. May God etc.
Issued in Caserta on March 11th, 1769. Bernardo Tanucci – Sir Marquis Cavalcanti».

Accordingly, to make this Royal Decree known to all and ensure that no person will claim their ignorance of the law, the present Notice will be posted in the City's usual locations and enforced without prejudicing the penalties already imposed on its violators.
Henceforth, the export outside the Capital and Kingdom of Relics such as statues, medallions, tools, vases, and tablets bearing any kind of script, made of either stone, clay, gold, silver, bronze, or any other metal; and
The export of ancient paintings on canvas or panels made of wood, copper, silver, or frescoes cut from walls, or any other ancient artefact;
Are restricted to the persons issued with a license by His Majesty, regardless of grade or social condition, under the pains stated both in the attached Notice of September 25th, 1755 and in the Royal Dispatch of March 11th, 1769.
Moreover, the export outside the Capital and Kingdom of carved stones, marble from the Kingdom's quarries, and gold or silver either embossed, as ingots, or nuggets, is restricted to the persons issued with a license by His Majesty, under the pains stated in the aforementioned Notice and Royal Dispatch.
Upon the issuance of said license, and under the aforementioned pains, the holder must pay the duties stated in the attached Notice of September 25th, 1755, pursuant to the appraisal and assessment carried out by the appointed Experts on the listed goods in question, as indicated in said Notice of September 25th, 1755 etc.
To be published and proclaimed. Issued in Naples by the Royal Court of Audit on March 17th, 1769.

Deputy Consulting Magistrate Don Angelo Cavalcanti.
Don Domenico Cardillo, Don Gennaro di Ferdinando, Don Giovanni D'Alessandro, Don Cesare Coppola, Don Giovanni Celentano, Don Sir Andrea Ruoti, Don Lorenzo Paternò, Don Pietro Maria Sanvincenti, Don Ferdinando Genise, Don Domenico Figliola, Don Pietro Lignola, Don Giovanni Bruno.
Notified to Don Giovanni Ferraro – Patron of the Royal Court, Patron of the Royal Treasury
Notified to Don Giuseppe Caravita – Patron of the Royal Court, Patron of the Royal Treasury
Sealed by Don Tommaso Abbamonte – Secretary of His Majesty's Royal Court
Treasurer Giuseppe Corracchioli

Published on April 4th, 1769.

5

Notice promulgated on behalf of the King by the most Illustrious Cavalier Don Giovanni Francesco Paternò Castello of the Biscari Princes, Royal Warden of the Antiquities in the Valleys of Demone and Noto

Having at heart the safeguard of the Antiquities located in the City of Catania, on February 7th, 1802, Don Giovanni, on behalf of His Majesty, issued a Royal Dispatch for the Royal Secretariat of Ecclesiastical Affairs, Supplies, and the Police, which led to the preparation of the here present Notice.

Hereby, it is forbidden to start Excavations or dig foundations for construction sites without the prior permission of Cavalier Don Giovanni Francesco Paternò Castello from Catania – Royal Warden of the Antiquities in the Valleys of Demone and Noto. The issuance of the permit is free of charge.

All offenses will be punished by a fine of 20 ounces and one year's imprisonment, both for the Owners of the Premises and the Architects, as prescribed by the President of the Kingdom, His Excellency, in the dispatch forwarded to said Royal Warden, Cavalier di Paternò Castello, by the Royal Secretariat of State and War on September 22nd, 1802.

Catania, October 1802.

13

The Republic of Venice

1
Eccelso Consiglio dei X

Venezia, 20 Aprile 1773.
Vanno l'uno all'altro succedendo a merito delli studj, e delle zelanti sollecitudini degl'Inquisitori di Stato quei vantaggi che sono promossi nello scoprimento delli disordini dall'applicazione de rimedj.
Presenti all'osservazioni loro quelli che derivati sono dall'irregolarità con che vengono custoditi li quadri più insigni opere di celebri autori esistenti nelle chiese, scuole, monasteri ed altri luoghi della città e dell'isole circonvicine, prestano questi ben degno argomento alla comunicata ora letta, che con distinta considerazione si accoglie e si aggradisce; Nella quale viene ad evidenza dimostrata la necessità d'un pronto e valido provvedimento, che assicuri la preservazione e manutenzione d'un così raro e pregevole ornamento della Dominante, che attrae l'amirazione de Forestieri. Coglier volendosi però dalli maturi consigli loro frutto corrispondente all'importanza degli oggetti, mentre si approva che formato si sia l'indicato catalogo in cui a luogo per luogo stanno descritti li quadri medesimi, trova questo Consiglio di stabilire che in quel modo e con quei mezzi che saranno creduti opportuni debbano esser consegnati alli respettivi superiori, parrochi, guardiani e direttori, coll'obbligo a medesimi della risponsibilità, proibendo loro di farne sotto qualsiasi titolo cambiamento, alienazione e vendita, ed aggiungendo quel più che per il buon ordine e disciplina della materia convenisse.
E perché vi si accoppiano quelle più vigorose determinazioni che da mano autorevole procedono, e che si comprendono necessarie, onde assicurarne l'esecuzione, restando raccomandato all'impegno degl'Inquisitori di Stato l'affare, sarà merito loro il disponere gl'ordini conferenti e destinarvi una qualche ispezione di approvato conoscitore con quelle commissioni che occorressero e con quelle disposizioni insieme che vagliano a vieppiù animarlo all'adempimento de' propri doveri etc.
½ - | -12-0-3-.

Excelsi Consilii Xm Secretarius
Joannes Zon

2
Inquisitori di Stato

Venezia, 31 Luglio 1773.

Conoscendo la maturità del Consiglio X importante e necessario il togliere quella scandalosa facilità con cui furono arbitrariamente asportati e venduti anche a stranieri compratori delli migliori e più insigni quadri esistenti nelle Chiese, Scole e Monasteri della Dominante e dell'isole circonvicine, nell'atto di prescrivere con il decreto 20 aprile decorso varie salutari providenze al suespresso oggetto tendenti, trovò di rimettere agl'Inquisitori di Stato l'affare, raccomandando al zelo loro il disponete quelle maggiori avvertenze e cautele che vieppiù assicurassero la preservazione di un tanto raro e pregevole ornamento alla Città. E siccome fu in essa deliberazione stabilita la massima di destinare un generale Ispettore, il quale dovesse aver cura dell'esecuzione, così le prime applicazioni del Tribunale rivolte furono a rinvenire persona, che fornita delle qualità necessarie, atta fosse a ben servire in tale incombenza. Gettato però l'occhio sopra Antonio Zanetti noto per la probità sua, e per la perizia e cognizione che possiede nel disegno, di cui ha date prove anche nel libro da lui composto della Veneziana Pittura, cadde sopra di esso la scelta colle seguenti commissioni. Formato avendo egli in obbedienza al comando ingiontogli un catalogo di tutti quei quadri che sono opera di celebri e rinomati autori, e tratta dal medesimo una nota a luogo per luogo di dette pitture, sta a carico dell'Ispettore il farne la consegna alli respettivi Superiori, Parrochi, Direttori e Guardiani delle Chiese, Scole e Monasteri, non compresi quelli che sono di juspatronato di Sua Ser.tà e delli NN. UU. Procuratori di S. Marco, con debito tanto agli attuali che alli successori di custodirli, conservarli e di rendersi risponsabili di qualunque asporto o mancanza succedesse, dovendo essi rilasciare all'Ispettore corrispondente ricevuta ed obbligazione giusta la formula esistente presso il Tribunale, che a questo fine si è fatta stampare.[113] Indi resi da lui consapevoli li detti Parrochi, Direttori e Superiori della publica volontà che loro risolutamente inibisce qualsiasi vendita o asporto dei quadri consegnati, sarà debito dell'Ispettore il riconoscere di tempo in tempo se l'esecuzione corrispondi in ogni parte e dovere, o se per avventura fosse tentata o introdotta novità alcuna o disposizione contraria alla mente publica; osservar pure dovendo se per la situazione ove sta posto il quadro o per trascuraggine di chi è risponsabile della custodia, o per altra causa attrovasse alcuno di essi nel pericolo di guastarsi e perire. Doverà esso semprecchè occorresse o di accomodare alcun quadro o di ristaurare il luogo ove è collocato, rilevarne il bisogno e riferirlo al Tribunale

113 Nota dei Quadri esistenti nella Chiesa... consegnati... in ordine al Decreto dell'Eccelso Consiglio dei X. 20 Aprile 1773, con obbligo di responsabilità; proibendosi sotto severe pene ogni trasporto, cambiamento, alienazione o vendita di essi Quadri con qual si sia titolo. Si eccettuano i casi di fabbrica o di ristauro; dovendosi allora ottenerne una espressa licenza di trasporto, in quei modi che saranno prescritti.
E la presente Nota dovrà essere partecipata da... ai Guardiani, Gastaldi o Priori di Scuole ed Arti della Chiesa medesima, se ve ne fossero, o ad altre persone che potessero aver titoli sopra qualcuno dei Quadri descritti, che s'intenderanno perciò tutti soggetti agli obblighi di responsabilità e d'altro, come sopra, respettivamente ai Quadri di loro giurisdizione per gli effetti comandati nel sovraccitato Decreto.
E per sua cauzione... averà da essi Guardiani, Gastaldi ed altri un attestato in forma della partecipazione seguita, nei modi più chiari e sicuri.
Dovrà in oltre questa Nota riporsi nei Registri... e riportarsi in quelli delle Scuole e Fraternite, a lume e norma comune di chi succederà nelle Cariche, o con altro qual si sia titolo di sopraintendenza, per la successiva responsabilità ed esecuzione degli obblighi sovraccennati, in tutti i tempi a venire.

per averne il permesso, dietro il quale sarà cura sua che ciò sia fatto nel miglior modo sopraintendendo all'operazione ed avvertendo che sia questa appoggiata a persona capace di ben eseguirla. Dello stesso modo e colla medesima avvertenza e metodo, averà l'Ispettore a dirigersi ed estendere le sue osservazioni anche rispetto a quelle pitture che esistono nelle Chiese e Monasteri dell'isole circonvicine presentando il catalogo loro, e facendone colla stessa risponsabilità a' Superiori la consegna. E perché sommamente importa l'avere di tempo in tempo esatte informazioni dell'esecuzione e degl'effetti, doverà esso Ispettore rassegnare a SS. EE. ogni semestre esatta relazione delle osservazioni che averà praticate, e degli abusi e disordini che scoprisse, suggerendo secondo li casi quell'ulteriori provvedimenti che convenissero, ed adempiendo quelle commissioni che in seguito le fossero dal Tribunale aggiunte per la migliore e buona direzione di questo affare, anche rispetto alla Terraferma.
Ciò disposto volendo poi l'equità del Consiglio X che retribuito adeguatamente sia il servizio di detto Ispettore affine anche di vieppiù animarlo all'esatto adempimento di sue incombenze, sono venute SS. EE. in deliberazione di stabilire ed assegnare al medesimo ducati effettivi centovinti all'anno, la metà de' quali averà ad essergli corrisposta nel mese di marzo, e l'altra in settembre, al momento che verrà da lui presentata la commessagli relazione. Non lasciandosi infine senza riflesso il merito che egli si conciliò nell'aver somministrati lumi e notizie[114] le quali han dato argomento a così provvide ed utili deliberazioni, dirette a troncare il progresso agl'enunciati disordini, trovò di giustizia il Tribunale l'accordare al medesimo per una volta tanto ducati cento effettivi in ben dovuta retribuzione all'opera sua, et alli studj con indefessa fatica lodevolmente prestati. Di che ordinarono SS. EE. che sia fatta nota a lume de successori.

---

114 *Osservazioni intorno alla custodia delle pitture pubbliche delle Città della Terra-ferma.*

1 Quasi tutte le Città della Terra-ferma hanno un libro che descrive attentamente le pitture pubbliche di esse Città; cosicchè facile sarebbe ad ognuno il formare un esatto Catalogo delle più degne.

2 Di più alcuna fra esse ha le Vite dei Pittori suoi stampate con le opere loro; e ora si sta preparando dal Conte Giacomo Carrara la pubblicazione delle Vite de' Pittori di Bergamo e del territorio.

3 In ognuna delle Città medesime vi sono, fra Nobili spezialmente, dilettanti ed intelligenti di pittura, che si potrebbero nominare, molto informati delle opere migliori che sono appresso di loro. Conservano essi vivissime le idee d'onore nel possedere quadri di famosi autori. Un testimonio è l'applauso universale che accompagnò la restituzione del quadro di Paolo Veronese alla Chiesa di Treviso. I stranieri trovano assai difficil anzi impossibil cosa l'acquistare quadri di quelle gallerie, non che de pubblici luoghi.

4 Un comando sopra la custodia delle pitture pubbliche si ascriverebbe a grande onore non che a carico ed esigerebbe tutto il geniale impegno, oltre la dovuta ubbidienza a pubblici voleri.

5 Intimata che fosse a quelle Città e ai Deputati di esse con una circolare la volontà pubblica espressa negli emanati Decreti e comunicati ad essi i metodi prescritti in questa Dominante, si potrebbe lasciar loro la libertà di spiegarsi, se in tutto esso metodo potesse ad essi convenire, per i diversi modi delle loro costituzioni, rassegnando sempre ogni alterazione all'approvazione sovrana. Le relazioni che può avere ogni metodo possono essere diverse, secondo i modi dei rispettivi paesi. Basta che ugualmente tutto si accordi nel fine, e nella osservanza esatta de pubblici comandamenti.

6 Tutte le novità, alterazioni e proggetti di alienazioni, precisamente proibite da sovraccennati Decreti, dovrebbero con la maggior sollecitudine essere riferite al Tribunale. Questo si potrebbe fare col mezzo del pubblico Inspettore eletto per la Dominante col quale si comunicassero e queste e ogni altra vertenza occorrente in questa materia; per dover essere da lui presentata a SS. EE. e riceverne le precise deliberazioni.

7 Per l'urgente bisogno del braccio del Principe, che mai occorresse si potrebbe assegnare il ricorso ai Pubblici Rappresentanti, riserbando sempre il seguito d'ogni caso alle disposizioni del Supremo Tribunale ecc. ecc.

Flaminio Corner Inquisitor
Piero Barbarigo Inquisitor
Zuanne Minotto Inquisitor

3
[Nomina di un nuovo Ispettore]

Venezia, 27 Novembre 1778.
Mancato di vita ne' giorni scorsi Antonio Zanetti in cui si univano probità esperienza e molta cognizione nel disegno e pittura come dall'annot. 31 Luglio 1773 rimase colla morte sua vacante il posto al quale era stato prescielto d'Ispettore sopra li Quadri delli più insigni e rinomati Pittori esistenti nelle Chiese, Scuole Conventi e Monasteri della Dominante e delle Isole circonvicine. Quanto però fu provida ed utile l'instituzione di questa carica in vista all'importantissimi contemplati oggetti tanto necessaria rendendosi la sostituzione al defunto Zanetti di persona egualmente idonea e capace a ben sostenerla si sono SS. EE. dopo prese le più accurate informazioni sopra il degno e riputato Professore Gio. Battista Mengardi fornito di ottime qualità e di tutte quelle condizioni che erano a desiderarsi destinandolo a quelle incombenze che venivano dal Zanetti esercitate. Fatto a lui tenere il catalogo formato da esso suo Precessore in cui sono descritti a luogo per luogo tutti li

---

Notizie ed osservazioni intorno alla pubblica tutela che si vuole assumere de' quadri pubblici della Città ed isole circonvicine.
La copia e la qualità delle pubbliche pitture di questa Città è forse la più rara e preziosa suppellettile che l'adorna; e che invita fra le altre singolarità ad ammirarla i stranieri dei paesi più colti.
Conviene soffrire con pace che il tempo ne sminuisca l'intera bellezza. È questa la legge delle umane cose. Ma non è da tolerarsi che si lascino esse pitture interamente perire: è quello ch'è più detestabile che vengano asportate, alienate e vendute a forestieri come segui in questi ultimi tempi.
Testimonj ne sono tre palle d'altare, e le portelle dell'organo della Chiesa di S. Giacomo di Murano, opere sublimi di Paolo Veronese, vendute al Ministro d'Inghilterra per pochi zecchini.
Una palla unica pittura di Girolamo Bassano figliuolo di Giacomo il vecchio ch'era nella Chiesa di S. Gio. Novo, venduta all'istesso Ministro con altri quadri.
Le portelle dell'organo ch'erano nella Parrocchiale di S. Nicolò pitture di Carletto figliuolo di Paolo Veronese, la maggior parte ritoccate dalla mano dell'istesso Paolo vendute al fu Residente Anglico Murray con altri quadri di qualche merito. Oltre queste altre opere famose che si vedeano in altri pubblici luoghi alienate furono senza riguardo veruno.
Che la pubblica autorità ne avesse cura per il passato, si ha qualche testimonio di fatto. S'imperli ne' principii di questo secolo la vendita già conclusa del famoso quadro dell'arca di Noè, dipinto da Giacomo Bassano, ch'è in Santa Maria Maggiore; e posto fu in essa il S. Marco di rilievo dorato per ordine pubblico.
La tradizione conserva memorie di simili atti pubblici, che tuttavia non si trovano scritti ne registri.
Alla custodia e conservazione delle pitture de' Palazzi pubblici di S. Marco e di Rialto si è provveduto con più Decreti dell'Ecc.mo Senato.
Restano le pitture delle Chiese Scuole e Oratori, che sono in pericolo di perire o di essere vendute, non essendovi autorità pubblica suprema che lo impedisca o ispezione che invigili.
Sarebbe da desiderarsi e da comandarsi che fosse fatto un esatto Catalogo o Inventario di tutte le pitture esistenti nei sopradetti luoghi degne singolarmente della pubblica tutela a norma del quale restasse impedito ogni esporto, o vendita arbitraria e per i restauri necessarii che potessero occorrere si dovesse impetrare le licenze, previa l'inspezione e la relazione di approvato conoscitore.
Emanato Decreto di questo Eccelso Consiglio in simil materia, è da credersi che ne seguissero altri simili provvedimenti per le pitture di que' pubblici luoghi che dipendono da particolari giurisdizioni, cioè delle Chiese Ducali, delle Scuole grandi e di quelle Chiese e Conventi che dipendono dall'Ecc.me Procuratie.

Quadri che sono opera di celebri autori e tratta dal medesimo la nota di detti Quadri che furono allora consegnati alli respettivi Superiori Parocchi Guardiani eccettuate le Chiese e Conventi che sono di juspatronato di Sua Serenità o de' NN. UU. Procuratori di S. Marco. Portandosi immediatamente a visitare tutti li Quadri descritti farà un esatto confronto per assicurarsi se tutti presentemente esistono senza la minima mancanza e renderà conto nella prima relazione, che doverà da qui a sei mesi presentare, se l'esistenza tanto per qualità che per numero sia a dovere. Confermerà ad essi Parocchi Superiori e Guardiani il debito di conservarli e custodirli per dover d'ogni arbitrio disordine e difetto render conto: al predetto fine sono stati loro consegnati giusta le rispettive ricevute ed obbligazioni presentate invigilando esso Ispettore per scoprire se tentato fosse o succedesse alcun asporto alienazione ovvero omissione per riferirlo al Tribunale per il dovuto compenso, sarà obbligo di detto Ispettore il tenersi attento per conoscere se tutti li Quadri suddetti sieno ben tenuti e custoditi o se alcuno ve ne fosse o per trascuraggine di chi incombe o per accidentale motivo in pericolo di guastarsi nel qual caso riferendolo indicherà se fosse necessario un qualche ristauro e provvedimento e quale, per dover avutone dal Tribunale il permesso scegliere e destinare persona capace per tal lavoro che occorresse, il quale farà egli eseguire a perfezione e senza pregiudizio alcuno di quella opera. E perché importa avere esatta informazione dell'esecuzione doverà perciò l'Ispettore rassegnare a SS. EE. di sei in sei mesi in sua relazione le osservazioni che averà fatte, li disordini che scoprisse e il bisogno che vi fosse, suggerendo secondo l'esiggenze quelle providenze che credesse d'aggiugnere, e prestandosi a tuttociò che dal Tribunale le fosse nel proposito comandato anche rispetto alla Terra Ferma. Averà egli per tali sue incombenze lo stesso assegnamento che aveva il Zanetti di ducati 120 centoventi valuta corrente all'anno da esiggerli ogni semestre posticipati all'occasione che presenterà l'indicata sua relazione. Il che resta annotato a lume de' successori e per la sua esecuzione.

Gerolamo Zustinian Inquisitor
Giulio Correr Inquisitor
Girolamo Diedo Inquisitor

4
[Nomina di un nuovo Ispettore]

Venezia, 23 Aprile 1796.
Cessato avendo di vivere recentemente Gio. Battista Mengardi, rimase vacante l'inspezione sopra li Quadri delli Pittori più insigni esistenti nelle Chiese, Scuole, Conventi e Monasteri della Dominante ed Isole circonvicine, alla quale fu destinato, come nella annotazione 27 Novembre 1778.
Continuando però a reputarsi provida ed utile questa instituzione, e volendosi provedervi di persona idonea, e capace, dopo prese le più accurate notizie sopra li talenti, l'esperienza, e la probità di Francesco Maggiotto Pittore Accademico, il Tribunale ha deliberato di destinarlo a quelle incombenze che il defonto Mengardi ha esercitate.
Fatte a lui tenere il Catalogo formato dal fu benemerito Antonio Zanetti, e tratta avendo egli da quello, e dalle Carte posteriori che gli si fecero parimenti consegnare, la nota di

tutti i Quadri, che furono allora consegnati alli respettivi Superiori, Parrochi, Guardiani, eccettuate le Chiese, e Conventi che sono di Juspatronato di Sua Serenità, o di NN. UU. Procuratori di San Marco.
Portandosi immediatamente a visitare tutti li Quadri descritti, farà un esatto confronto per assicurarsi, se tutti presentemente esistono, senza mancanze, e renderà conto nella prima relazione che doverà da qui a sei mesi presentare, se l'esistenza, tanto per qualità, che per numero, sia a dovere.
Confermerà ad essi Parrochi, Superiori, e Guardiani, il debito di conservarli, e custodirli, per dover d'ogni arbitrio, disordine, e difetto, render conto, al qual fine sono stati loro consegnati giusta le respettive ricevute, ed obbligazioni presentate, invigilando esso Inspettore, per scoprire, se tentato fosse, o succedesse alcun asporto, alienazione, ovvero ammissione, per riferirlo al Tribunale per il dovuto compenso.
Sarà obbligo di detto Inspettore il tenersi attento per conoscere, se tutti li Quadri sudetti sieno ben tenuti e custoditi, e se alcuno ve ne fosse o per trascuraggine di chi incombe, o per accidentale motivo, in pericolo di guastarsi, nel qual caso, riferendolo, indicherà se fosse necessario un qualche ristauro e provedimento, e quale; per dovere (avutone dal Tribunale il permesso) scegliere, e destinare persona capace per tal lavoro che occorresse, il quale egli farà eseguire a perfezione, e senza recar alcun pregiudizio a quell'opera.
E perché importa avere esatta informazione dell'esecuzione, doverà perciò l'Inspettore rassegnare a SS. EE. di sei in sei mesi in sua relazione, le osservazioni che averà fatte, li disordini che scoprisse, ed il bisogno che vi fosse, suggerendo, secondo l'esigenze, quelle providenze che credesse d'aggiungnere, e prestandosi a tutto ciò che dal Tribunale le fosse nel proposito comandato, anche rispetto alla Terra Ferma. Averà egli per tali sue incombenze lo stesso assegnamento che aveva il Mengardi di Ducati centoventi Valuta Corrente all'anno, da esigersi ogni semestre posticipati, all'occasione che presenterà la prima, e le successive sue relazioni.
E ciò resta annotato a lume de' successori, e per la sua esecuzione.

Zuanne Zusto Inquisitor di Stato
Giacomo Boldù Inquisitor di Stato
Francesco Lippomano Inquisitor di Stato

5
Eccelso Consiglio dei X

Venezia, 23 Luglio 1791.
Per l'ora letta comunicata, che con distinta considerazione si accoglie, risultano ben chiari e dimostrati a questo Consiglio gli utili esercizi di cura e di vigilanza, che gli Inquisitori di Stato in mezzo alle più gravi ed importanti applicazioni non intermettono di prestare, per patrio zelo e decoro, anche all'argomento delle insigni Pitture di rinomati Professori, che adornano le Chiese, Monasteri, ed altri pubblici Luoghi della Dominante al loro Tribunal raccomandato colle Deliberazioni 20 Aprile 1773 all'essenzial oggetto di preservarle da rei trafughi, ed arbitrarie alienazioni ad esteri compratori. Degnamente impegnando le loro sollecitudini li conosciuti perniciosi effetti cagionati dalle ingiurie del tempo, a quali soggiacciono alcune delle più celebri di quest'opere, ed il prossimo pericolo, in cui sono esposte d'irreparabile perdita, qualor non vi

si presti un pronto rimedio, si rimarcano le zelanti insinuazioni praticate, affine d'impedirne il minacciato inconveniente verso dei particolari proprietari, e dei Direttori delle Comunità che le possedono, per condurli ad intraprenderne a loro spese gli opportuni ristauri, non riuscite però, fuorchè presso d'alcune poche, attesa la riconosciuta povertà, ed impotenza della maggior parte delle medesime. Penetrato però questo Consiglio dall'esposto abbandono, e pubblico danno, e dall'equivalente deperimento, non contemplato dalle surriferite deliberazioni, al quale ogni giorno più si accostano gli unici, e preziosi Quadri descritti nelle accompagnate Note, i quali fra il numero degli altri molti pregiudicati di minor merito, esigono li presidi della pubblica tutela e provvidenza; e riflettendo alla cura che ne hanno l'estere Nazioni, le quali ammirando simili preziose opere ne fanno a caro prezzo raccolta, e gelosa custodia in pubbliche Galerie a maggior splendore, e ornamento delle Capitali, reputa opportuno di far pervenire alla cognizione dei Savi del Collegio i lumi e note surriferite, ricercandoli a devenire col Senato a quelle deliberazioni che sul proposito saranno riputate dalla loro prudenza.
-|-15-1-0

Excelsi Consilii Decum Secretarius
Ioseph Gradenico

1
The Excellent Council of the Ten

Venice, April 20th, 1773.
The thorough inquiries and zealous dedication shown by our State Inquisitors have so far yielded many consecutive successes in the detection and resolution of deficiencies.
One primary object of their investigation was the peculiar manner in which the most illustrious painters' works are kept in churches, schools, monasteries, and other locations within the city and its nearby isles. Therefore, the resolution of such irregularities will base its course on our State Inquisitors' well-founded insight, which We welcome dearly.
Their reports have highlighted the need for swift and incisive action to preserve and upkeep the Domineering's most unique ornaments, which many Foreigners admire so intensely. Therefore, wishing to make the most of their advice on such valuable artworks, We approve the compilation of a catalog which will describe the paintings kept in each place. To this end, the Council will establish, extend, and strengthen at will the means to entrust the respective superiors, parish priests, keepers, and directors with said paintings, under the prohibition to alter, alienate, or sell them. To ensure the effectiveness of these necessary measures, in conjunction with other robust dispositions that come from a source of authority, the supervising State Inquisitors will appoint an expert who, in case of need, will be commissioned to carry out inspections, provide support, etc.
½-|-12-0-3-.

The Excellent Council of the Ten
The Secretary Giovanni Zon

2
State Inquisitors

Venice, July 31st, 1773.

The members of the Council of the Ten are famously well aware of the importance of preventing the removal and arbitrary sale of our finest and most famous paintings, which have also been purchased by foreigners. The relocation of the artworks has been shamefully easy, affecting the Domineering and nearby isles' Churches, Schools, and Monasteries far too often to be acceptable.

Consequently, the Council's decree dated April 20th prescribed several measures to address the issue under the supervision of our State Inquisitors, recommending their most particular caution and attention to ensure that the City's rarest ornaments be adequately safeguarded.

Furthermore, the deliberation led to the appointment of a general Inspector to oversee its implementation, and to this end, the Tribunal intervened to find the most suitable candidate. After learning of Antonio Zanetti and his acclaimed probity, expertise, and knowledge of drawing demonstrated in his book on Venetian Painting, the Tribunal finally nominated and assigned him to the following duties.

The Inspector must compile a catalog of paintings by famous and renowned artists, noting the locations where they are kept, and deliver the paintings in question, together with a copy of each note, to all the respective Superiors, Parish Priests, Directors, and Keepers of Churches, Schools, and Monasteries, to the exclusion of the ones under the patronage of His Serenity and Our Humble Procurators of Saint Mark's. The custody, upkeep, and supervision of these paintings, to ensure that they are not transferred or altered, falls within the responsibilities of said Superiors, Parish Priests, Directors, and Keepers of Churches, Schools, Monasteries, and their successors. Consequently, they will issue the Inspector with a receipt and a preprinted obligation pursuant to the procedures established by the Tribunal.[115] Moreover, the Inspector must inform said Parish Priests, Directors, and Superiors of the public determination that prohibits the sale or removal of the paintings with which they are entrusted, monitoring their performance from time to time so that no changes are made to the set procedure and provisions to the detriment of the public's welfare. The Inspector must also ascertain whether the paintings are placed in a suitable position, adequately tended, and kept safe from damage and destruction.

---

115 Note of the Paintings present in the church... delivered... pursuant to the Decree of the Excellent Council of the Ten, April 20th, 1773, under mandatory responsibility; the transportation, alteration, alienation, or sale of said Paintings is forbidden notwithstanding and severely sanctionable. An exception is made for construction sites or restoration, in which case the applicants will need a license of transportation as prescribed.
This Note must be forwarded by... to the Keepers, Stewards, or Priors of the Church's Schools and Crafts, where present. In the absence of these professionals, said mandatory responsibility and conditions will fall upon anyone who has authority over any listed Paintings within their jurisdiction, as described in the Decree mentioned above.
As a precautionary measure, said Keepers, Stewards, and the others, will issue... with a certificate clearly stating their participation.
Furthermore, this Note will be filed in the... Registers. A copy of this document will be kept in the Schools and Fraternities in question so that the Offices' successors and superintendents of any kind may be informed of the responsibilities, procedures, and obligations mentioned above.

If required, he must notify the Tribunal of the need for any relocation or restoration of paintings and the locations where they are kept, await for permission, and superintend the procedure so that it is carried out correctly and run by someone capable.
Similarly, the Inspector will warn, monitor, and report about the paintings kept in Churches and Monasteries on the nearby islands, leaving his catalog in the Superiors' custody. Given the importance of periodically receiving accurate information regarding their conduct and activities, the Inspector must present Their Excellencies with a semi-annual report on his observations, the infractions and disorders detected, and his suggestions on how to address each case appropriately, pursuant to the Tribunal's indications. The said procedure also applies to the Mainland.
Moreover, the Council of the Ten wishes to stimulate the Inspector's motivation in the performance of his duties by paying an adequate salary. Consequently, Their Excellencies have decreed that he should be offered one-hundred and twenty ducats a year net, half in March and half in September when he presents his reports. Furthermore, in recognition of his merits in providing the information and clarifications[116] that led to the resolution of the disorders mentioned above, the Tribunal has found it fair to award him a lump-sum payment of one-hundred ducats net.
Finally, Their Excellencies order that such tireless work, study, and commendable labor be notified to the memory of all our successors.

Inquisitor Flaminio Corner
Inquisitor Piero Barbarigo
Inquisitor Giovanni Minotto

---

116 *Observations on the custody of public paintings in the Cities of the Mainland.*

1 Nearly all the Cities of the Mainland are in possession of a book with an accurate description of their every single public painting, which would make it easy to draft a detailed list of the most outstanding items.

2 Several Cities had the Lives of their Painters put on print alongside their works; Count Giacomo Carrara is currently about to publish the Lives of the Painters of Bergamo and its Territory.

3 All of these Cities have amateur critics and connoisseurs, especially among the Nobility, who are well informed on the best works in their area and are worthy of an appointment. They also take special pride in that their Cities own paintings by famous artists, as proven by the acclaim generated by the restitution of Paolo Veronese's painting to the Church of Treviso. Foreigners find it difficult or impossible to purchase paintings kept in such galleries and other public venues.

4 Being given authority over the public paintings' custody would represent the highest honor, requiring considerable effort, commitment, and abidance to the public's will.

5 Once the Cities and their Deputies have been notified of the public's will expressed in the Decrees that have been issued and informed on the methods prescribed by the Domineering, they could be granted the liberty to choose a suitable course of action in keeping with their respective constitutions, provided they submit any proposed changes to the sovereign's approval. Of course, the methods adopted by each City may vary depending on the country's customs, as long as the general spirit and object of the public decrees remain unchanged.

6 All the changes, alterations, and planned alienations must be notified to the Tribunal at the earliest opportunity. To this end, the public Inspector nominated by the Domineering might be of use, acting as a liaison in cases of controversy, informing Their Excellencies, and taking precise orders from them.

7 When the Prince's swifter ruling was needed, We could resort to our Public Representatives, assign each case's follow-up to the Supreme Tribunal, etc.

3
[Appointment of a new Inspector]

Venice, November 27th, 1778.
After Antonio Zanetti's demise and the loss of his probity, experience, and knowledge of drawing and painting, as noted on July 31st, 1773, his post as Inspector of our most illustrious and renowned Painters' artworks in Churches, Schools, Convents, and Monasteries of the Domineering and its near Isles became vacant.
Indeed, this position has been providential for said paintings' preservation to such an extent that the late Zanetti must be replaced as soon as possible. Therefore, wishing to appoint an equally suitable and competent substitute, Their Excellencies have collected detailed information on the highly reputed Giovanni Battista Mengardi. The Professor has proven to be endowed with all of the skills needed to succeed Zanetti in performing his duties.
Consequently, the Professor will be entrusted with his Predecessor's catalog, which contains the location, description, and annotations of all the Paintings by famous authors assigned to Superior Parish Keepers, with the exception of the Churches and Convents under the patronage of His Serenity and Our Humble Procurators of Saint Mark's. Furthermore, he will immediately inspect all of the listed Paintings personally, verify their condition, and draft a preliminary report, to be presented within the next

---

News and observations on the proposal for the tutelage of public paintings in the City and nearby isles.
The large number and quality of this City's public paintings is perhaps its rarest and most precious adornment, for which reason the foreigners from the most cultivated countries visit and admire it.
Of course, one must resign to the fact that time takes its toll over the City's beauty, as is natural with all human things. Nevertheless, abandoning our paintings to their fate entirely or allowing their indiscriminate transfer, alienation, or sale to foreigners – as has been the case lately – is not something We will tolerate anymore.
Among the artworks so foolishly squandered there are: a few sublime works of Paolo Veronese such as three altarpieces and the panel doors to the organ in the Church of San Giacomo of Murano, which were sold to the Minister of England for only a few sequins; an altarpiece by Girolamo Bassano, son of Jacopo the Elder, in the Church of San Giovanni Nuovo, sold to the same Minister together with other paintings; the panel doors to the organ in the Parish of San Nicolò, painted by Paolo Veronese's son Carletto (Carlo Veronese) and in most cases retouched by Paolo himself, which were sold to the late English Resident Murray, together with other paintings of some merit. These and several other artworks kept in public venues were thus alienated carelessly.
However, things have not always been the way they are currently, and there was a time when the public authorities did take good care of our heritage. One such instance was when, at the beginning of the century, the concluded sale of Jacopo Bassano's famous *The Animals Entering Noah's Ark*, kept in Santa Maria Maggiore, was revoked; by public decree, the painting was eventually impressed with Saint Mark's golden emblem.
According to tradition, many other public intervention cases like this have nevertheless been omitted from the registers.
Our Excellent Senate has issued several Decrees for the custody and conservation of the paintings in the public Palaces of Saint Mark's and Rialto.
Nevertheless, the paintings kept in Churches, Schools, and Oratories are still in danger of destruction or sale because of the absence of supreme authorities for prevention and inspectors for surveillance.
Therefore, it would be advisable to commission an accurate Catalog or Inventory of all the paintings kept in the locations mentioned above to guarantee tutelage against their export and arbitrary sale or restoration in case of need. In the latter case, the necessary licenses' issuance will be preceded by an approved expert's inspection and report.
Following this Excellent Council's Decree, We suggest issuing other similar rulings for paintings kept in locations that depend on particular jurisdictions, namely Ducal Churches, Scuole Grandi, and Churches or Convents that depend on the Excellent Procurators.

six months, stating whether said artworks correspond to the number and quality of the items cataloged. They will then renew the Superior Parish Priests and Keepers' liability in case of willful misconduct or want of any kind: to this end, they have been entrusted with the paintings pursuant to the receipts and affidavits issued under the Inspector's supervision. To ensure that no attempts are made at removing or alienating the items – in which case he must inform the Tribunal to receive due compensation – the Inspector will remain vigilant and guarantee the Paintings' upkeep and custody. Damage or danger due to the keepers' neglect or accidental reasons must be reported indicating any restoration measures needed. The Tribunal will then grant permission to appoint the most suitable professionals for the works required to maintain the paintings' integrity and conservation. Given the importance of accurate information regarding the state of the restoration works, the Inspector must also present Their Excellencies with a semi-annual report on his observations, any possible misconducts, and the future need for intervention, and he will comply with all of the Tribunal's orders regarding the Mainland.
Finally, as compensation for his service, he will receive the same salary as Zanetti of 120 ducats a year, to be paid every six months upon presentation of his semi-annual report. To be noted for the benefit of his successors and its execution.

Inquisitor Gerolamo Giustinian
Inquisitor Giulio Correr
Inquisitor Girolamo Diedo

4
[Appointment of a new Inspector]

Venice, April 23rd, 1796.
As Giovanni Battista Mengardi has recently passed away, the post as inspector of our illustrious Painters' Paintings in Churches, Schools, Convents, and Monasteries of the Domineering and its near isles, to which he had been appointed on November 27th, 1778, has been left vacant.
Whereas this office is still regarded as providential and useful, and because We wish to recruit someone capable and suited to the task, the Tribunal collected accurate information on the Academic Painter Francesco Maggiotto's talents, experience, and probity, finally decreeing that he should succeed to the late Mengardi in the duties he performed.
Therefore, Maggiotto will be responsible for the Catalog compiled by the estimable Antonio Zanetti and the successive Files that list all the Paintings committed to Superiors, Parish Priests, and Keepers, with the exception of the Churches and Convents under the patronage of His Serenity or Our Humble Procurators of Saint Mark's.
Furthermore, he will immediately inspect all of the listed Paintings personally, verify their condition, and draft a preliminary report, to be presented within the next six months, stating whether said artworks correspond to the number and quality of the items cataloged. He will then renew the Parish Priests, Superior, and Keepers' responsibility to preserve and care for these paintings, as they are liable for the arbitrariness, misconducts, and damage that may occur, pursuant to the respective receipts issued. The Inspector will

also remain vigilant and notify the Tribunal of any illegal transportation, alienation, and omission, to conveniently take action.
Moreover, the Inspector must ensure that the paintings are well kept and tended, indicating any restoration and provisions needed in case of damage or danger caused by the keepers' neglect or occurred accidentally. Consequently, the Tribunal will grant permission to choose and appoint the most suitable professionals for the works required. The person selected must work to the best of their capabilities without compromising the paintings in question.
Given the importance of accurate information regarding the state of the restoration works, the Inspector must also present Their Excellencies with a semi-annual report on his observations, any possible misconduct, and the future need for intervention. They will also comply with all of the Tribunal's orders regarding the Mainland.
Finally, as compensation for his service, he will receive the same salary as Mengardi of One Hundred Twenty Ducats a year, at the current value, to be paid deferred every six months upon presentation of each of his semi-annual reports. To be noted for the benefit of his successors and its execution.

State Inquisitor Giovanni Giusto
State Inquisitor Giacomo Boldù
State Inquisitor Francesco Lippomano

5
The Excellent Council of the Ten

Venice, July 23rd, 1791.
Herewith, in acknowledgment of the notification that has now been disclosed, the Council recognises the valuable care and vigilance implemented by our State Inquisitors who, out of zeal and decorum, and amidst the most considerable difficulties, have defended the Paintings created by our illustrious Professors.
These artworks, which adorn our Churches, Monasteries, and other public Venues in the Domineering, have been secured against theft and arbitrary alienation to foreign purchasers under the Decree notified to the Tribunal on April 20th, 1773.
Whereas the lethal effects caused by the ravages of time are always close at hand, and the danger of irreparable loss threatens the most famous artworks constantly, the individual proprietors and Community Directors have been pressured into restoring and upkeeping the paintings in their possession at their own expense. However, in most cases preventing these threats was not possible due to financial inadequacy and insufficient authority.
Therefore, this Council will intercede to avert all the risks of negligence, public detriment, and deterioration that are not covered by previous decrees and whose tackling is becoming increasingly urgent.
Furthermore, the care devoted to the unique and precious Paintings listed in the attached Notes, which require public tutelage and maintenance more than all the other items of lesser quality, must equal the effort of the foreign Nations that invest considerable sums in

collecting, cherishing, and safeguarding the artworks in Galleries that adorn and beautify their Capitals.
Consequently, the Council considers it advisable to notify the College's Elders of the deliberations and proposals mentioned above, inviting them to issue any decree they might deem fitting, in conjunction with the Senate.
-|-15-1-0

The Secretary of the Excellent Council of the Ten
Giuseppe Gradenico

14

The Margraviate of Ansbach-Bayreuth

1
Landesväterliches Ausschreiben, 1780

Wir haben bereits in einem gedruckten Ausschreiben vom 4 Julius 1771 gnädigst befohlen, daß in Unsern fürstlichen Landen auf die Erhaltung der Monumente mit mehrerem Fleiß, als vormals geschehen werden sollen.
Nachdem aber diese Unsere gnädigste Verordnung zu Unsern billigen Mißfallen nicht überall mit gehöriger Aufmerksamkeit beobachtet worden ist; also finden wir Uns vermüßiget, weitere ernstliche Vorkehrungen deßhalb zu treffen, und befahlen demnach gnädigst, daß erstlich in Ansehung der Kirchen und Kapellen, dann anderer öffentlicher geistlichen und Schulgebäude, sowohl bey Reparir- als gänzlicher Einreißung derselben, sorgfältigst darauf werden solle, daß keinem Monument, se sey von Metall, Stein oder Holz, und bestehe in Grab- oder anderen Steinen, wie auch hölzernen Tafeln, worauf Wappen oder Inschriften gegraben, gehauen oder gemahlt sind, kein Schade durch einige Zerschlagung, Abhauung, Durchlöcherung, Übertünchung, oder sonst auf andere Art zugeführt werde.
Sollte auch allenfalls die Nothdurft erfordern, daß dergleichen Monumente, zumal bey Einreissung ganzer Gebäude, von ihrer Stelle verruckt oder abgenommen werden müssen, so ist solches mit möglichster Behutsamkeit zu bewerkstelligen, und sind alsdann die Monumente einstweilen zu verwahren, bis sie entweder bey Aufrichtung des neuen, oder nach geschehener Reparatur des alten Gebäudes wieder an ihrem vorigen oder sonst schicklichen Ort aufgerichtet, befestiget und ein gemauert werden können.
Besonders ist auch bey Verwertung neuer Kirchenstühle, oder bey Veränderung der alten, ein fleißiges Augenmerk von sämtlichen Geistlichen auf die Erhaltung der Monumente zu richten, indem es schon öfters geschehen ist, daß hiebey ein oder anders derselben Schaden genommen hat.
Sollte sich auch bey Einreissung dergleichen alter geistlichen Gebäude in dem Grundstein, in dem Altar, in dem Thurmknopf, oder in andern Orten etwas an Reliquien eines Heiligen, an Münzen, an Schriften u. d. g. vorfinden, so ist eine Specifikation hierüber zu fertigen, und solche mit den vorgefundenen Antiquitäten mittelst Berichts an Unsere Regierung einzusenden.

Trüge es sich auch zu, daß irgend ein Monument, weil es vielleicht an einem dumpfigten und feuchten Ort befindlich, oder der Witterung zu sehr ausgesetzt ist, wie auch durch das Alterthum an der Schrift, Mahlerey, oder sonsten Schaden nehmen wollte, so daß vielleicht in kurzer Zeit nicht mehr davon zu erkennen oder zu lesen seyn dürfte, so ist deshalb an gedachte Unsre Regierung von den Geistlichen gleichfalls ein Anzeige zu erstatten, damit allenfalls noch bey Zeiten eine Abzeichnung davon genommen, und solche in Unserm geheimen Archiv zu Plassenburg zum Andenken verwahret werden könne.
Sollten aber an manchen Orten on Liebhabern des Alterthums und der vaterländischen Geschichte dergleichen Abzeichnungen oder Abschriften von den Monumenten genommen worden seyn, oder künftig noch gemacht werden, so wird es Uns zum gnädigsten Wohlgefallen gereichen, wenn solche an ermeldtes geheimes Archiv zu Plassenburg zur gleichfalsigen Abzeichnung oder Abschriftnehmung communiciret werden wollen.
Was zweytens öffentliche weltliche Gebäude, als Schlösser, Amt- und Rathäuser etc. betrifft, so ist sich durchgehends nach vorstehender Verordnung, wie bey geistlichen Gebäuden zu richten, und sollen Unsre sämtliche Beamte sowohl, als Burgermeistere und Rath in Städten und auf dem Land eifrigst auf die Erhaltung der Monumente beflissen seyn, auch in allen Fällen, wo eines derselben Schaden leiden oder gar verlohren gehen könnte, möglichste Achtsamkeit gebrauchen, und sehalb ihre Berichte zu rechter Zeit erstatten, welches sonderlich bey Abbrechung der hie und da noch zu sehenden Ueberbleibsel von alten Schlössern und Gemäuern, es mögen Monumente an Wappen und Inschriften daran befindlich seyn oder nicht, zu beobachten ist, damit dergleichen *Rudera*, ehe sie durch ihre totale Destruktion, und darauf erfolgende Verödigung der Nachwelt gänzlich aus den Augen kommen, vorher abgezeichnet, Protokolle über deren Lage und Beschaffenheit verführet, und sodann durch die Aufbehaltung in Unserm oftgedachten geheimen Archiv zu Plassenburg der Vergessenheit entrissen werden mögen.
Zu noch unbezweifelter Befolgung diese Unserer gnädigsten Verordnung gebieten Wir zugleich allen Schreinern, Schlossern, Maurern und Zimmerleuten Unsers Obergebürgischen Fürstenthums ernstlich, daß sich keiner derselben bey zu erwarten habender schweren Strafe unterstehen solle, einem Monument, es sey von Holz oder Stein, auf welchen ein Wappen oder eine Schrift zu sehen ist, irgend einen Schaden zuzufügen, sondern in allen Fällen mit möglichster Behutsamkeit damit u verfahren, und keine Hand anzulegen, bevor sie nicht in Ansehung geistlicher Gebäude bey dem Superintendent oder Pfarrer, in Ansehung der weltlichen Gebäude aber bey der Obrigkeit jedes Orts die Anzeige davon gemacht haben.
Damit auch keiner derselben jemals eine Entschuldigung vorbringen könne, so soll von dieser Verordnung ein Exemplar in jede Zunftlade obbesagter Handwerker geleget, und an ihren gewöhnlichen Jahrtägen öffentlich verlesen werden, worüber Unsere Beamte, welche das Zunftrichteramt zustehet, mit allem Ernst zu sehen haben.
Gleichwie Wir übrigens nichts zweifeln, daß Unsere sämtliche Beamte, auch Jagd- und Forstofficialen auf die Erhaltung derjenigen Steine, Kreuze, Bäume, Marter- und anderer Säulen, welche unsere Landesgränzen bezeichnen, folglich in diesem Bezug auch als öffentliche Monumente zu betrachten sind, ohnehin alle mögliche Sorgfalt nach ihren obhabenden Pflichten verwenden werden; als versehen Wir Uns gnädigst, daß so ein als das andere aufs genaueste befolget, und dieser Unserer so nötig als nützlichen Verordnung überall gebührend nachgelebt werde.

Hieran geschiehet Unser gnädigster Befehl.
Datum Bayreuth, den 10 April 1780.
Alexander, Markgraf zu Bayreuth

1

Appeal from the Sovereigns of the Nation, 1780

In a printed Letter of July 4th, 1771, We have already graciously ordered that, in Our Royal Lands, the Preservation of the Monuments should be more diligent than before.
However, since Our most gracious Decree, to Our Displeasure, has not been observed everywhere with due Attention, We find ourselves obliged to take further severe Precautions in this regard. Therefore, We graciously instruct that Care should be taken towards any Monument, first concerning Churches and Chapels, then other public spiritual and school Buildings, both when they are Repaired and entirely in Ruin. No Monument, made of Metal, Stone, or Wood, and consisting of Gravestones or other Stones, as well as wooden Panels on which Coats of Arms or Inscriptions are dug, hewn or painted, should be harmed by means of Smashing, Cutting, Perforating, Whitewashing or anything else produced in another Way.
If it is Necessary to move or remove such Monuments from their Place, especially when entire Buildings are torn down, this should be done with the greatest possible Care. These Monuments are to be temporarily kept until they are either reestablished within a new Building or Repairs are made to the old Building; they can be erected, fixed, and walled up in their previous or otherwise appropriate Place.
In particular, when new Pews are used, or the old ones are changed, all Clergymen should pay diligent Attention to preserving the Monuments, as it has often happened that one or the other of them has been damaged.
Should such old spiritual Buildings be torn down in [the areas of] the foundation Stone, the Altar, the Tower Button, or other Places, and something related to the Relics of a Saint, Coins, Writings, etc. is found, a Description is to be made; the Descriptions concerning the discovered Antiquities are to be sent to Our Government by means of a Report.
It could also happen that a Monument, perhaps because it is in a humid and damp Place, or it is too exposed to the Weather conditions, suffers from Damages to the Inscriptions, Paintings, or other Items, so that within a short Time it would be no longer recognisable or comprehensible; then, the Clergy must send a Report to Our Government, so that at least a Copy of it can be taken in due Time, to be kept in our secret Archive in Plassenburg as a Memory.
However, if in some Places the Lovers of Antiquity and patriotic History have taken such Copies or Models of the Monuments, or if these will be made in the Future, it will be Our most gracious Pleasure if such Copies are sent to the secret Archive in Plassenburg so that they can be registered or reproduced.
With regard to the second [group of monuments, that is] secular public Buildings, such as Castles, Office and Town Halls, etc., the above Ordinance is to be observed throughout, as in the case of the religious Buildings. All Officials, such as Mayors and Councilors in Cities

and the Countryside, should be most Zealous and Diligent in preserving the Monuments; in the case that one of them suffers from Damage or is lost, they should exercise the greatest possible Care, and make the Reports in a suitable Time, especially when Fractures in the Monument's Remains are visible here and there. Old Castles and Walls, whether or not there are Coats of Arms and Inscriptions, should be monitored, so that such Remains are recorded in advance, before they become utterly unavailable to Posterity due to their total Destruction and subsequent Desolation. Records should note their Location and Nature and then be kept in Our secret Archive at Plassenburg to save [these monuments] from oblivion.

For the certain observance of Our most gracious Ordinance, We seriously command that all Woodworkers, Locksmiths, Bricklayers, and Carpenters, under the infliction of severe Punishments, shall not cause damage to any Monument, either made of Wood or Stone, or on which one Coat of Arms or Inscription is visible; rather, they should in all Cases use the greatest possible Care, and not lay Hands on it, neither concerning spiritual Buildings, nor about secular Buildings, before having reported it to the Superintendent, or Pastor, or Authority of each Place.

A Copy of this Ordinance shall be placed in every Letterbox of the above-mentioned Craftsmen's Guild so that none of them can ever make an Excuse and read out publicly on their usual Days; Our Officials, who are entitled to the Guild judge's Office, have to oversee this with all Seriousness.

Similarly, We do not doubt that all our Officials, including the Seekers and First Officials, are concerned with the preservation of those Stones, Crosses, Trees, Pillars of Torture, and other Pillars that mark our National Borders; it will be their Duty to take all possible Care, as these [items] are to be regarded as public Monuments too. We graciously take Care that one and the other [prescriptions] will be followed precisely and that this necessary and useful Ordinance will be duly followed up everywhere.

Our most gracious Command is hereby given.

Date Bayreuth, April 10th, 1780.

Alexander, Margrave of Bayreuth

15

The Landgraviate of Hesse-Kassel

1
Verordnung Landgraf Friedrichs II. von Hessen-Kassel vom 22. Dezember 1780 zur Erhaltung der im Lande befindlichen Monumente und Altertümer

Verordnung, die im Lande befindlichen Monumente und Altertümer betreffend.
Von Gottes Gnaden.
Wir Friedrich, Landgraf zu Hessen, Fürst zu Hersfeld, Graf zu Catzenelnbogen, Dietz, Ziegenhayn, Nidda, Schaumburg und Hanau etc. etc. Ritter des Königl. GroßBrittannischen Ordens vom blauen Hosenbande, wie auch des Königl. Preussischen Ordens vom schwarzen Adler, etc. etc.

Fügen hierdurch zu wissen: Nachdem Uns daran gelegen ist, daß die in Unseren Landen befindliche Monumente und sonstige Alterthümer möglichst erhalten werden; So haben Wir gnädigst gutgefunden, in dieser Absicht folgendes zu verordnen.

1. Wann an Kirchen, Kapellen, Schul- und andern geistlischen Gebäuden, desgleichen an Amts-Rathhäusern, Schlössern, und sonstigen offentlichen Gebäuden eine Reparation nöthig ist; So soll hierbey sorgfältigst darauf gesehen werden, daß kein Monument, es sey von Metall, Stein oder Holz, und bestehe in Grab- oder andern Steinen, oder hölzernen Tafeln, worauf Wappen oder Innschriften gegraben, gehauen, oder gemahlt sind, durch Zerschlagung, Abhauung, Durchlöcherung, Uebertünchung, oder sonst auf irgend eine Art Schaden leide.
2. Würde aber die Nothdurft erfordern, daß dergleichen Monumente, zumal bey Einreissung ganzer Gebäude, von ihrer Stelle verrückt, oder abgenommen werden müssen; So ist solches mit möglichster Behutsamkeit zu bewerkstelligen, und sind alsdann die Monumente einstweilen wohl zu verwahren, bis sie entweder bey Aufrichtung des neuen, oder nach geschehener Reparatur des alten Gebäudes wieder an ihren vorigen, oder einen sonst schicklichen Ort gebracht, und befestiget werden können. Besonders ist auch bey Verfertigung der Kirchenstühle, oder bey Verändrung der der alten, von sämmtlichen Geistlichen ein fleißiges Augenmerk dahin zu richten, daß keine Monumente zerrüttet und verletzt werden.

3. Wann ferner bey Einreissung dergleichen alten Gebäude auf den Grundsteinen, im Altar, Thurmknopf, oder andern Orten, Münzen, Schriften, oder sonstige Monumente sich vorfinden; So soll hiervon eine Specification aufgestellt, und an die Regierung berichtlich eingeschickt werden.
4. Wir gebieten zugleich allen Schreinern, Schlossern, Maurern und Zimmerleuten ernstlich, daß keiner bey Vermeidung schwerer Strafe sich unterstehen soll, einem Monument, es sey von Holz oder Stein, auf welchem ein Wappen oder eine Schrift zu sehen ist, Schaden zuzufügen, sondern in allen Fällen mit möglichster Behutsamkeit damit zu verfahren, und keine Hand daran zu legen, wenn nicht zuvor in Ansehung der geistlichen Gebäude bey dem Prediger, in Ansehung der weltlichen Gebäude aber bey der Obrigkeit des Orts Anzeige davon geschehen ist.
5. Trüge es sich zu, daß irgend ein Monument, weil es an einem dumpfigten und feuchten Orte befindlich, oder der Witterung zu stark ausgesetzt wäre, oder auch durch das Alterthum an der Schrift, Mahlerey, und sonst Schaden litte; So soll darüber an die Regierung Bericht erstattet, und allenfalls noch zeitig eine Abzeichnung davon gemacht werden.
6. Wann jemand Münzen, und sonstige Alterthümer findet; So soll er solches dem nächsten Beamten anzeigen, und, in soferne des gefundene annehmlich ist, nicht nur die Vergütung des innern Werths, sondern auch nach Befinden ein mehrers gewärtigen, bey denen aber, die das Gefundene verheimlichen, soll solches confiscirt werden, und derjenige, der es angeben wird, den dritten Theil des Werths bekommen.
7. Wann den Goldschmidten und Gold- und Silber-Fabricanten ohne Ausnahme Medaillen zu Händen kommen; So sollen sie selbige nicht einschmelzen, sondern vorher der Obrigkeit davon Anzeige thun.
8. Uebrigens befehlen Wir Unseren sämmtlichen Land-Räthen, Inspectoren, Metropolitans, Predigern, Beamten und *Commissariis locorum* hierdurch grädigst, mit aller Aufmerksamkeit dahin zu sehen, daß dieser Unsrer Verordnung in allen Stücken gehörig nachgelebet werde.

Urkundlich Unsrer eigenhändigen Unterschrift und beyge druckten Fürstl.
Secret-Insiegels.
Cassel, den 22ten December 1780.
Friedrich L. z. Hessen
Vt. Wittorf

1
Ordinance of Landgrave Frederick II of Hesse-Kassel of December 22nd, 1780, for the preservation of the Monuments and Antiquities within the State

Ordinance concerning the Monuments and Antiquities in the Country.
By the Grace of God.

We Friedrich, Landgrave of Hesse, Prince of Herzfeld, Count of Katzenelnbogen, Dietz, Ziegenhain, Nidda, Schaumburg and Hanau etc. etc., Knight of the King, Great Brittan Order of the Blue Garter, as well as the Royal Prussian Order of the Black Eagle, etc. etc.

This is to be known: Since We believe it is important that the Monuments and the other Antiquities located in Our Lands be preserved to the greatest possible Extent; We have graciously established to enact the following Intentions.

1. In the case that Repairs are necessary on Churches, Chapels, Schools, and other spiritual Buildings, as well as official Town Halls, Castles, and other public Buildings; Subsequently, Care should be taken to ensure that no Monument, made of Metal, Stone, or Wood, and consisting of Gravestones or other Stones, as well as wooden Tablets on which Coats of Arms or Inscriptions are dug, carved or painted, shall be damaged by smashing or Cutting down, Perforating, Whitewashing, or any other kind of Harm.
2. In the case that is Necessary to move or remove such Monuments from their Place, especially when entire Buildings are torn down; Subsequently, this is to be done with the greatest possible Care: the Monuments are to be temporarily kept until they can be either brought back to their previous Place if the new Building is erected, or the old Building has been repaired, or they can be brought to another suitable Place and fortified. Particularly when the Pews are made, or when the old ones are changed, all the Clergy must pay careful Attention to ensure that no Monument will be broken or injured.
3. Furthermore, in the Case that such old Buildings are demolished on [the areas of] the Foundation Stones, the Altar, the Tower Button, or other Places, and Coins, Writings, or other Monuments are found; A Description of these [items] is to be drawn up and sent to the Government in a Report.
4. At the same Time, we seriously command all Woodworkers, Locksmiths, Bricklayers, and Carpenters that, in order to avoid severe Punishments, they shall not cause Damage to any Monument, either made of Wood or Stone, or on which a Coat of Arms or Inscription is visible; all of them shall deal with it with the greatest possible Care, and not lay Hands on it unless this has been reported in advance to the Pastor with regards to the spiritual Buildings, and the local Authorities with regards to the secular Buildings.
5. It might occur that a Monument, because it is in a damp and humid Place, or it is too exposed to the Weather conditions, or because of its Antiquity, suffers from Damages to its Inscriptions, Paintings, and other Things; a Report shall be submitted to the Government on this, and if necessary, its Drawing made in due time.
6. When someone finds Coins and other Antiquities; Subsequently, he should report this to the closest Official, and, provided that what he found it satisfactory, expect not only the Reimbursement of its intrinsic Value but also more, depending on the Cases; but those who conceal their Findings will lose all these Items after confiscation; those who declare it will get the third Part of its Value.
7. When Goldsmiths and Gold and Silver Fabricants, without exception, find Medals; Subsequently, they should not melt these down but report the Findings to the Authorities in due time.

8. Incidentally, We hereby order our Regional Councilors, Inspectors, Metropolitans, Preachers, Officials, and Local Commissaries to enforce all due Attention to ensure that all Parts of Our Ordinance are adequately followed up.

Documented by Our handwritten Signature and printed with the Prince.
Secret Island.
Kassel, December 22nd, 1780.
Friedrich L. z. Hesse
Vt. Wittorf

16

The Prussian States

1
Allgemeine Landrechts für die Preußischen Staaten, 1794

[...]

33. Soweit die Erhaltung einer Sache auf die Erhaltung und Beförderung des gemeinen Wohls erheblichen Einfluß hat, soweit ist der Staat deren Zerstörung oder Vernichtung zu entersagen berechtig.
34. Soweit die Benutzung einer Sache zucr Erhaltung des gemeinen Wohls erforderlich ist, kann der Staat die Benutzung befehlen und die Unterlassung derselben durch Strafgesetze ahnden.
35. Statuen und Denkmäler, die auf öffentlichen Plätzen errichtet werden, darf niemand, wer er auch sei, beschädigen oder ohne obrigkeitliche Erlaubnis wegnehmen oder einreißen.
36. Noch weniger dürfen, ohne dergleichen Erlaubnis, Gebäude in den Städten, die an Straßen oder öffentliche Plätze stoßen, zerstört oder vernichtet werden.
37. Dergleichen Gebäude muß der Eigentümer, soweit es zur Erhaltung der Substanz und Verhütung alles Schadens und Nachteils für das Publikum notwendig ist, in baulichen Stande unterhalten.
38. Vernachlässigt er diese Pflicht dergestalt, daß der Einsturz des ganzen Gebäudes oder eine Gefahr für das Publikum zu besorgen ist, so muß die Obrigkeit ihn zur Veranstaltung der notwendigen billigen Frist, allenfalls durch Zwangsmittel anhalten.

[...]

71. In allen Fällen, wo sich findet, daß ein ohne vorhergegangene Anzeige unternommener Bau schädlich oder gefährlich für das Publikum sei, oder zur groben Verunstaltungen einer Straße der eines Platzes gereicht, muß derselbe nach den Anweisungen der Obrigkeit geändert werden.
72. Die Straßen und öffentlichen Plätze dürfen nicht verengt, verunreinigt oder sonst verunstaltet werden.

1
General Land Law for the Prussian States, 1794

[...]

33. Insofar as the Preservation of an Object has considerable Influence on the Perpetuation and the Promotion of the common Benefit, the State is entitled to authorise its Destruction or Annihilation.
34. As far as the Use of an Item is Necessary to preserve the common Benefit, the State can order its Use and penalise the Failure to do so by penal Law.
35. Statues and Monuments erected in public Places must not be damaged by anyone, whoever they are, or taken away or torn down without official Permission.
36. Even less may city Buildings that meet Streets or public Spaces be destroyed or annihilated without such Permission.
37. The Owner must maintain such Buildings in good structural Conditions, insofar as it is necessary to maintain their Nature and prevent any Damage and Disadvantage for the Public.
38. If he neglects this Duty in such a Way that the Collapse of the entire Building or any danger to the Public is feared, the Authorities must impose the necessary reasonable Deadline, if necessary, by means of Coercion.

[...]

71. If it is found that a Construction undertaken without prior Notice is harmful or dangerous to the Public or is about to disfigure a Street or a Square grossly, [its project] must be improved according to the Authorities' Instructions.
72. The Streets and public Spaces must not be narrowed, polluted, or vandalised.

Appendix: Chronology of Laws and Provisions

- 1425, 31 March (Papal States) – Pope Martin V, *Etsi in Cunctarum orbis Provinciarum*
- 1462, 28 April (Papal States) – Pope Pius II, *Cum Almam Nostram Urbem*
- 1474, 7 April (Papal States) – Pope Sixtus IV, *Cum Provida Sanctorum Patrum decrete*
- 1515, 26 September (Papal States) – Pope Leo X, appointment of a Prefect for the Marbles of Rome
- 1534, 28 November (Papal States) – Pope Paul III, appointment of a Commissary of Antiquities
- 1556, 20 December (Papal States) – Julius III, *Motu Proprio* (not translated)
- 1562, 11 July (Papal States) – Pope Pius IV, *Motu Proprio* (not translated)
- 1571, 30 May (Grand Duchy of Tuscany) – Duke Cosimo I de' Medici, *Legge contro chi rimovesse o violasse Armi, Inscrittioni o Memorie*
- 1580, July (Papal States) – Conservators of the City, *De officio Conservatorum* (reissue)
- 1597, 7 and 12 July (Grand Duchy of Tuscany) – Duke Ferdinand I de' Medici, provisions on gemstones and quarries
- 1600, 17 May (Grand Duchy of Tuscany) – Duke Ferdinand I de' Medici, measures on quarries and gemstones of Florence and Siena
- 1602, 4 July (Grand Duchy of Tuscany) – Duke Ferdinand I de' Medici, *Bando* to extend the measures on quarries and gemstones to the minor towns

- 1602, 24 October (Grand Duchy of Tuscany) – Duke Ferdinand I de' Medici, *Deliberazione* on the paintings of Florence

- 1602, 28 October and 5 November (Grand Duchy of Tuscany) – Duke Ferdinand I de' Medici, provisions on the paintings of Siena

- 1602, 6 November (Grand Duchy of Tuscany) – Duke Ferdinand I de' Medici, extension of the *Deliberazione* on the paintings of Florence to the custom houses

- 1602, 11 December (Grand Duchy of Tuscany) – Duke Ferdinand I de' Medici, *Deliberazione* on the licences to export paintings

- 1603, 15 November (Grand Duchy of Tuscany) – Duke Ferdinand I de' Medici, extension of the *Deliberazione* to Pisa, Pistoia, and Arezzo

- 1603, 11 December (Grand Duchy of Tuscany) – Duke Ferdinand I de' Medici, *Mandato* on the export of paintings

- 1610, 5 May (Grand Duchy of Tuscany) – Duke Cosimo II de' Medici, reissue and extension of the *Deliberazione* on the paintings of Florence

- 1622, 11 August (Kingdom of Denmark) – King Christian IV, *Til Bisperne udi Danmark og Norge Antiqviteter anrørendes*

- 1624, 5 October (Papal States) – Pope Urban VIII, *Editto Aldobrandini: Prohibitione sopra l'estrattione di Statue di marmo o di metallo, Figure, Antichità e simili*

- 1630, no date (Kingdom of Sweden) – King Gustav II Adolf, appointment of a State Antiquarian

- 1646, 29 January (Papal States) – Pope Innocent X, *Editto Sforza: Editto sopra l'estrattioni, e cave di Statue, Figure, Intagli, Medaglie. Inscrittioni di marmo, di mischio, metallo. Oro, Argento, Gioie, e cose simili antiche e moderne*

- 1666, 28 November (Kingdom of Sweden) – Regency, *Placat och Påbudh Om Gamble Monumenter och Antiquiteter*

- 1666, 18 December (Kingdom of Sweden) – Regency, protocol with the *Placat* instructions and extracts (not translated)

- 1686, 5 February (Papal States) – Pope Innocent XI, *Editto Altieri: Prohibitione sopra l'estrattione di Statue di marmo o metallo, Figure, Antichità e simili*

- 1686, 5 July (Kingdom of Sweden) – King Carl XI, *Placat II* (not translated)

- 1701, 18 July (Papal States) – Pope Clement XI, first *Editto Spinola: Prohibitione sopra l'estrattione di Statue di marmo, o metallo, Figure, Antichità e simili*

- 1704, 30 September (Papal States) – Pope Clement XI, second *Editto Spinola: Editto sopra le Pitture, Stucchi, Mosaici, et altre Antichità, che si trovano nelle cave, Inscrizioni antiche, Scritture, e Libri manoscritti*[117]

- 1717, 3 April (Papal States) – Pope Clement XI, fourth *Editto Spinola: Prohibizione sopra l'estrazione di Statue di marmo, o metallo, Figure, Antichità e simili*

- 1721, 20 August (Kingdom of Portugal) – King John V (João V), *Alvarà de Lei*

- 1726, 21 October (Papal States) – Pope Benedict XIII, *Editto Albani: Editto sopra li scalpellini, segatori di marmi, cavatori et altri*

- 1733, 10 September (Papal States) – Pope Clement XII, *Editto Albani: Prohibizione dell'estrazione delle Statue di marmo, o metallo, Pitture, Antichità e simili*

- 1734, 21 July (Drenthe in the Netherlands) – Provincial Bailiff and Representatives, *Resolutie van Drost en Gedeputeerden van Drenthe*

- 1744, 18 July (Grand Duchy of Tuscany) – local governors under Emperor Francis I of Habsburg-Lorraine (François I), provisions for the site of Volterra

- 1745, 13 April (Duchy of Milan, under Austria) – Empress Maria Theresa, provisions on public paintings and sculptures

- 1750, 5 January (Papal States) – Pope Benedict XIV, *Editto Valenti Gonzaga: Proibizione della estrazione delle Statue di marmo, o metallo, Pitture, Antichità e Simili*

- 1750, 21 August (Grand Duchy of Tuscany) – Emperor Francis I of Habsburg-Lorraine (François I), *Rescritto Imperiale* on the site of San Miniato

- 1752, 2 November (Kingdom of Spain) – Academy of History, *Instrucción de Viaje*

- 1753, 14 July (Kingdom of Spain) – King Ferdinand VI of Bourbon (Fernando VI), *Real Decreto* to approve the *Instrucción de Viaje*

- 1754, 26 December (Grand Duchy of Tuscany) – local governors under Emperor Francis I of Habsburg-Lorraine (François I), *Editto* on the exports of artefacts

117 The third *Editto Spinola*, issued under Pope Clement XI on 14 May 1712, is not included in this volume, as it was dedicated to documents and books: this is a specific category of heritage that would require different analysis.

- 1755, 24 July (Kingdom of Naples) – King Carlos III of Bourbon, royal announcement for the *Prammaticae*

- 1755, 16 October (Kingdom of Naples) – King Carlos III of Bourbon, *Prammatica LVII* and *Prammatica LVIII*

- 1761, 10 December (Grand Duchy of Tuscany) – Emperor Francis I of Habsburg-Lorraine (François I), *Motu Proprio* on the site of Volterra

- 1766, 9 September (Kingdom of Naples) – King Ferdinand IV of Bourbon, *Prammatica LIX*

- 1766, 17 October (Grand Duchy of Tuscany) – Duke Peter Leopold of Lorraine, *Bando* on the discovery of new antiquities

- 1769, 4 April (Kingdom of Naples) – King Ferdinand IV of Bourbon, *Prammatica LX*

- 1773, 20 April (Republic of Venice) – Council of Ten, approval of the catalogue of paintings

- 1773, 31 July (Republic of Venice) – State Inquisitors, appointment of an Inspector of Public Paintings

- 1778, 27 November (Republic of Venice) – State Inquisitors, appointment of a new Inspector of Public Paintings

- 1780, 10 April (Margraviate of Ansbach-Bayreuth) – Margrave Christian Friederich Karl Alexander, *Landesväterliches Ausschreiben*

- 1780, 5 August (Grand Duchy of Tuscany) – Duke Peter Leopold of Lorraine, liberalisation of excavations and exports

- 1780, 22 December (Landgraviate of Hesse-Kassel) – Landgrave Friedrich II, *Verordnung, die im Lande befindlichen Monumente und Altertümer betreffend*

- 1781, 16 January (Grand Duchy of Tuscany) – Duke Peter Leopold of Lorraine, *Rescritto* to sell paintings

- 1781, 30 August (Grand Duchy of Tuscany) – Duke Peter Leopold of Lorraine, *Legge* on the custom duties to export paintings

- 1782, 27 March (Grand Duchy of Tuscany) – Duke Peter Leopold of Lorraine, *Regolamento per le Comunità* on inscriptions and coat of arms

- 1790, 27 May (Drenthe in the Netherlands) – Provincial Bailiff and Representatives, *Resolutie van Drost en Gedeputeerden van Drenthe* (reissue)

- 1791, 23 July (Republic of Venice) – Council of Ten, resolution to restore public paintings

- 1791, 18 October (Grand Duchy of Tuscany) – Duke Ferdinand III of Lorraine, ban to export paintings (reissue)

- 1794, 5 February (Prussian States) – Friederich Wilhelm II, *Allgemeine Landrechts für die Preußischen Staaten*

- 1796, 23 April (Republic of Venice) – State Inquisitors, appointment of a new Inspector of Public Paintings

- 1801, 21 August (Papal States) – Pope Pius VII, *Editto* to abrogate the old licences of excavation

- 1802, 22 September (Kingdom of Naples) – Don Giovanni Francesco Paternò, *Bando* for the valleys of Demone and Noto

- 1802, 1 and 2 October (Papal States) – Pope Pius VII, *Editto Doria Pamphilj*

- 1803, 7 January (Papal States) – Pope Pius VI, *Notificazione* on the excavations on the city walls

- 1803, 6 June (Kingdom of Spain) – King Carlos IV of Bourbon, *Real Cédula: Instrucciòn sobre el modo de recoger y conservar los monumentos antiguos, que se descubran en el Reyno, baxo la inspecciòn de la Real Academia de la Historia*

Bibliography

Adlercreutz, T. (2017). The Royal Placat of 1666. Briefly about background and further Importance, in: Alatalu, R. et al. (eds). *Historical Perspective on Heritage Legislation. Balance between Laws and Values.* Tallin: Icomos, 6-15.

Almagro Gorbea, M. and Maier Allende, J. (2003). La Real Academia de la Historia y la Arqueología española en el Siglo XVIII, in: Beltran Fortes, J. et al. (eds). *Illuminismo e Ilustraciòn. Le antichità e il loro protagonisti in Spagna e in Italia nel XVIII secolo.* Roma: l'Erma di Bretschneider, 1-27.

Arvidsson, B. (2018). Biskop Peder Winstrups diktverk 'Den Danske Hornblæser': politisk allegori och kristen emblematik. *Stiftshistorisk småskrift – Lunds stift* 10, 1-56.

Bakker, J. A. (1979). Protection, Acquisition, Restoration, and Maintenance of the Dutch Hunebeds since 1734: an active and often exemplary policy in Drenthe (I), in: Es, W. A. van et al. (eds). *Berichten van de Rijksdienst voor het Oudheidkundig Bodemonderzoek* 29. Amersfoort: Rob, 143-183.

Bakker, J. A. (2010). *Megalithic Research in the Netherlands (1547-1911). From 'Giants Beds' and 'Pillar of Hercules' to accurate investigations.* Leiden: Sidestone Press.

Bakker, J. A. (2011). Paalwormen, dijken, hunebedden en onze eerste monumentenwet, in: Van der Velde, H. M. and Jaspers, N. L. (eds). *Van graven in de prehistorie en dingen die voorbijgaan. Studies aangeboden aan Eric Lohof bij zijn pensionering in de archeologie.* Leiden: Sidestone Press, 281-324.

Baldacci, V. (2000). *Le riforme di Pietro Leopoldo e la nascita della Toscana moderna.* Firenze: Regione Toscana.

Bédat, C., and Lafuente Ferrari, E. (1989). *La Real Academia de Bellas Artes de San Fernando (1744-1808). Contribución al estudio de las influencias estilísticas y de la mentalidad artística en la España del siglo XVIII.* Madrid: Fundación Universitaria Española.

Collecção da Legislação Antiga e Moderna do Reino de Portugal (1819). Parte II. Coimbra: Real Imprensa da Universidade, 415-418.

Collijn, I. (1933) (ed.). *Katalog der Ornamenttischsammlung des Magnus Gabriel De la Gardie in der Kgl. Bibliothek zu Stockholm.* Stockholm: Almiquist & Wiksells.

Condemi, S. (1987). *Dal 'Decoro et Utile' alle 'Antiche Memorie'. La tutela dei beni artistici e storici negli Antichi Stati Italiani.* Bologna: Nuova Alfa.

Conti, A. (1988). *Storia del restauro e della conservazione delle opere d'arte.* Milano: Electa.

Cucina, C. (2005). Le rune al tempo di Cristina, fra Goticismo e bibliofilia, in: Poli, D. (ed.). *Cristina di Svezia e la cultura delle Accademie*. Conference proceedings (Macerata and Fermo, May 2003). Roma: Calamo, 153-170.

Curzi, V. (2004). *Bene culturale e pubblica utilità. Politiche di tutela a Roma tra Ancien Régime e Restaurazione*. Roma: Minerva.

D'Alconzo, P. (1999). *L'anello del Re. Tutela del patrimonio storico-artistico nel Regno di Napoli, 1734-1824*. Firenze: Edifir.

D'Alconzo, P. (2011). Guardando Roma da una prospettiva decentrata: spunti di riflessione su norma e prassi della tutela del patrimonio storico-artistico nella seconda metà del XVIII secolo, tra il Regno di Napoli e la Spagna, in: Meyer, S. A. and Rolfi Ožvald, S. (eds). *Il Laboratorio del Settecento. Legislazione, tutela, pubblico e mercato nella seconda metà del XVIII secolo*. Firenze: LibroCo., 16-22.

D'Alconzo, P. (2022). A comparative reading to move beyond a historiographic paradigm: the approach to the protection of the artistic and archaeological heritage in the kingdoms of Naples and Spain in the first half of the 18th century, in: Mannoni, C. (ed.). *Arte, Legge, Restauro. L'Europa e le prime prassi per la protezione del patrimonio*. Venezia: Ca' Foscari ed.

Emiliani, A. (1974). *Una politica dei beni culturali*. Torino: Einaudi.

Emiliani, A. (1978). *Leggi, bandi, provvedimenti per la tutela dei beni artistici e culturali negli Antichi Stati Italiani: 1571-1860*. Bologna: Alfa.

Gabardón de la Banda, J. F. (2017). La tutela del patrimonio monumental en la España de Carlos III. *Anuario Jurídico y Económico Escurialense* L, 557-578.

Galanakis, Y. (2022). How (not) to protect the past? Heritage protection efforts & power struggles in early modern Greece, in: Mannoni, C. (ed.). *Arte, Legge, Restauro. L'Europa e le prime prassi per la protezione del patrimonio*. Venezia: Ca' Foscari ed.

García Sánchez, J. (2008). La Real Academia de San Fernando y la Arqueología. *Academia. Boletín de la Academia de Bellas Artes de San Fernando* 106/107, 9-48.

Grice, G. (2015). *Cabinet of curiosities: Collecting and understanding the wonders of the natural world*. New York: Workman Publishing.

Hafstein, T. V. (2003). Bodies of Knowledge. Ole Worm & Collecting in Late Renaissance Scandinavia. *Ethnologia Europaea* 33/1, 5-20.

Huse, N. (1984). *Denkmalpflege. Deutsche Texte aus 3 Jahrhunderten*. München: Beck.

Jensen, O. W. (2006). *Fornlämningsbegreppets historia. En expose över 400 år*. Stockholm: Riksantikvarieämbetet.

Johannesson, K. (1991). *The Renaissance of the Goths in sixteenth-century Sweden. Johannes and Olaus Magnus as Politicians and Historians*. Berkley: University of California Press.

Klindt-Jensen, O. (1975). *A History of Scandinavian Archaeology*. London: Thames & Hudson.

Kroll, F. L. (2006). *Geschichte Hessen*. München: Beck.

Le Bras, G. (1976). *La Chiesa del diritto. Introduzione allo studio delle istituzioni ecclesiastiche*. Bologna: il Mulino.

Levenson, J. (1993). *The Age of the Baroque in Portugal*. New Haven: Yale University Press.

Levi, D. (2008). The administration of Historical Heritage. The Italian case, in: Fisch, S. (ed.). *National approaches to the governance of Historical Heritage over time. A comparative report.* Amsterdam: Ios, 103-126.

López-Trujillo, M. A. (2006). *Patrimonio. La lucha por los bienes culturales Españoles, 1500-1939.* Gijòn: Trea.

Maiden, M. (1995). *A linguistic history of Italian.* London: Longman.

Maier Allende, J. (2002). *Comisión de Antigüedades de la Real Academia de la Historia. Documentación general, catálogo e índices.* Madrid: Real Academia de la Historia.

Maier Allende, J. (2003). II Centenario de la Real Cédula de 1803. La Real Academia de la Historia y el inicio de la legislación sobre el Patrimonio Arqueológico y Monumental en España. *Boletín de la Real Academia de la Historia* 200/3, 439-473.

Maier Allende, J. (2012). La Corona y la institucionalización de la Arqueología en España, in: Almagro Gorbea, M. and Maier Allende, J. (eds). *De Pompeya al Nuevo Mundo. La Corona española y la arqueología en el siglo XVIII.* Madrid: Real Academia de la Historia, 333-360.

Mannoni, C. (2021a). Tutela del patrimonio in età barocca. Tra Svezia e Stato Pontificio, il 'Placat' per la protezione delle antichità scandinave. *Il Capitale Culturale. Studies on the Value of Cultural Heritage* 23, 309-331.

Mannoni, C. (2021b). Protecting antiquities in early modern Rome: the papal edicts as paradigms for the heritage safeguard in Europe. *ORE Open Research Europe – European Commission* 1/48, 1-12.

Mannoni, C. (2022a). *Artistic canons and legal protection. Developing policies to preserve, administer and trade artworks in nineteenth-century Rome and Athens.* Frankfurt: Max-Planck Institute for Legal History and Legal Theory.

Mannoni, C. (2022b) (ed.). *Arte, Legge, Restauro. L'Europa e le prime prassi per la protezione del patrimonio.* Venezia: Ca' Foscari ed.

Mora, G. (1998). *Historia de mármol. La arqueología clásica española en el siglo XVIII.* Madrid: Polifemo.

Navarrete Martínez, E. (1999). *La Academia de Bellas Artes de San Fernando y la pintura en la primera mitad del siglo XIX.* Madrid: Fundación Universitaria Española.

Nizza da Silva, M. B. (2009). *Reis de Portugal: D. João V.* Lisbon: Temas & Debate.

Padoa Schioppa, A. (2016). *Storia del diritto in Europa. Dal medioevo all'età contemporanea.* Bologna: il Mulino.

Piva, C. (2007). *Restituire l'antichità. Il laboratorio di restauro della scultura antica del Museo Pio Clementino.* Roma: Quasar.

Piva, C. (2014). Anton Maria Zanetti e la tradizione della tutela delle opere d'arte a Venezia: dalla critica d'arte all'attività sul campo, in: Piva, C. (ed.). *Il restauro come atto critico. Venezia e il suo territorio.* Venezia: Ca' Foscari ed., 83-114.

Price, N. S., Talley, M. K. and Melucco Vaccaro, A. (1996). *Historical and Philosophical Issues in the Conservation of Cultural Heritage.* Los Angeles: The Getty Conservation Institute.

Real Cédula de S. M. y Señores del Consejo (1803). Madrid: Imprenta Real.

Rodriguez Villa, A. (1878). *Don Cenon de Somodevilla, Marqués de la Ensenada. Ensayo biográfico.* Madrid: M. Murrillo.

Rossi Pinelli, O. (1978-1979). Carlo Fea e il Chirografo del 1802. Cronaca, giudiziaria e non, delle prime battaglie per la tutela delle Belle Arti. *Ricerche di Storia dell'Arte* 8, 27-41.

Rossi Pinelli, O. (1986). Chirurgia della memoria: scultura antica e restauri storici, in: Settis, S. (ed.). *Memoria dell'antico nell'arte italiana*, vol. 3. Torino: Einaudi, 181-250.

Rossi Pinelli, O. (2014) (ed.). *La storia delle storie dell'arte.* Torino: Einaudi.

Ridley, R. (1992). To protect the Monuments: The Papal Antiquarian (1534-1870). *Xenia Antiqua* 1, 118-154.

Salas Álvarez, J. (2010). El *Viaje de España* del Marqués de Valdeflores. Un intento fallido de catalogación de los monumentos y antigüedades de España. *Spal. Revista de Prehistoria y Arqueología* 19, 9-34.

Schnapp, A. (1993). *La conquista del Passato. Alle origini dell'archeologia.* Milano: Leonardo [original edition: *La conquête du passé. Aux origines de l'archéologie.* Paris: Carré].

Schück, H. (1932). *Kgl. Vitterhets Historie och Antikvitets Akademien. Dess Förhistoria och Historia*, vol. 1. Stockholm: Antikvitetskollegiet.

Settis, S. (2020). *Modernità di Raffaello. Dalla lettera Leone X alla Costituzione Italiana.* Roma: Ministero per i beni e le attività culturali e per il turismo, Scuderie del Quirinale.

Speroni, M. (1988). *La tutela dei beni culturali negli Stati Italiani preunitari.* Milano: Giuffrè.

Stein, P. (1999). *Roman Law in European History.* Cambridge: Cambridge University Press.

Tomassetti, L. (1857-1872) (ed.). *Bullarum diplomatum et privilegiorum sanctorum romanorum pontificum*, 23 vols. Augusta Taurinorum: Franco, Fory, Dalmazzo.

Toscano, M. (2007). Giuseppe Canart da scultore a restauratore (1738-1790). Un percorso biografico e professionale, in: Poso, R. (ed.). *Riconoscere un Patrimonio. Storia e Critica dell'attività di conservazione del patrimonio storico-artistico in Italia Meridionale (1750-1950).* Galatina: Congedo ed., 43-75.

Tuneld, J. (1934). *Prästrelationerna från Skåne och Blekinge av år 1624.* Lund: Gleerup.

Tuneld, J. (1960). *Prästrelationerna från Skåne och Blekinge av år 1667 och 1690.* Lund: Gleerup.

Ullgren P. (2015). *En makalös historia. Magnus Gabriel De la Gardies uppgång och fall.* Stockholm: Norstedts.

Valsecchi, C. (2022). 'Quanto ornamento e splendore'. Gli Stati italiani e la tutela del patrimonio storico e artistico in età moderna, in: Mannoni, C. (ed.). *Arte, Legge, Restauro. L'Europa e le prime prassi per la protezione del patrimonio.* Venezia: Ca' Foscari ed.

Valsecchi, C. and Carcereri De' Prati, C. (2009). Tutelare il patrimonio culturale in Italia. Uno sguardo storico. *Rivista giuridica di urbanistica* 4, 504-578.

Wescher, P. (1988). *I furti d'arte. Napoleone e la nascita del Louvre.* Torino: Einaudi.

Wolf, A. (1884). *Allgemeine Deutsche Biographie*, vol. 19. Leipzig: Duncker & Humblot.